PEARSON CUSTOM SOCIOLOGY

Formerly published as Intersections, Crossroads & Inequalities

EDITORS

KATHLEEN A. TIEMANN
University of North Dakota
Introduction to Sociology, Social Problems & Issues, Inequalities & Diversity

RALPH B. MCNEAL, JR.
University of Connecticut
Introduction to Sociology

BETSY LUCAL
Indiana University South Bend
Inequalities & Diversity

MORTEN G. ENDER
United States Military Academy, West Point
Inequalities & Diversity

COMPILED BY:

Mt.Hood Community College
Introductory Sociology

PEARSON

Senior Vice President, Editorial: Patrick F. Boles
Editor: Ana Díaz-Caneja
Development Editor: Abbey Lewis
Editorial Assistant: Hannah Coker
Operations Manager: Eric M. Kenney
Production Manager: Jennifer Berry
Rights Manager: Michael E. Mushlitz
Art Director: Renée Sartell
Cover Designer: Renée Sartell

Cover Art: "Figures," courtesy of Eugenie Lewalski Berg; "Abstract Crowd," courtesy of Diana Ong/Superstock; "R&B Figures," courtesy of Diana Ong/Superstock; "Bramante's Staircase," courtesy of Veer/Photodisc Photography; "Hand Prints," courtesy of Veer/Photodisc Photography; "People Running-Falling," courtesy of Veer/Campbell Laird; "Sunbathers on Beach," courtesy of Veer/Scott Barrow; "Parada Gay, Florianapolis_25 (colorful balloons being set free)," courtesy of Paul Mansfield Photography/Getty Images; "Family Tree, Relatives," courtesy of Kudryashka/ iStockphoto.com.

Printed in the United States of America.

V3NL

Please visit our website at *www.pearsonlearningsolutions.com*

Attention bookstores: For permission to return any unsold stock, contact us at *pe-uscustomreturns@pearson.com*.

Pearson Learning Solutions, 501 Boylston Street, Suite 900, Boston, MA 02116
A Pearson Education Company
www.pearsoned.com

ISBN 10: 1-256-20183-9
ISBN 13: 978-1-256-20183-0

Contents

SOCIOLOGY

SOCIOLOGY

Like you,

I know people who drink, people who do drugs, and bosses who have tantrums and treat their subordinates like dirt. They all have good jobs. Were they to become homeless, some of them would surely also become "alcoholics," "addicts," or "mentally ill." Similarly, if some of the homeless women who are now so labeled were to be magically transported to a more usual and acceptable setting, some of them—not all, of course—would shed their labels and take their places with the rest of us somewhere on the spectrum of normality.

There are many homeless people in America and that is a shame. Shame on you, shame on me, shame on America. Shame because it is the result of choices we have made, shame because it does not have to be. . . . Homeless people are homeless because they do not have a place to live.

The connection between homelessness and poverty points to major system failures at the lower and sometimes middle level of our wage-labor hierarchy. The major failure is the inability of the system, even in the best of times, to provide jobs for all who are able and willing to work. Every day, millions of would-be workers are told that our society has nothing for them to do, that they are not needed, that they and their dependents are surplus.

Another major system failure, equally destructive, is the fact that a growing number of men and women—individuals and heads of families—are workers but remain poor. . . . These workers file papers, mop floors, clean the tables, or guard whatever needs guarding. At the end of the day, they say "OK, I've done what you asked me to do. What am I worth?" And our society answers, through the employer, "Not much. Not even enough to live on."[1]

An Introduction *to the* Foundations of Sociology

The homeless are often viewed as nameless, faceless, voiceless people loitering on street corners and huddled under bridges. It's easy for us to turn a blind eye to the problem if we don't feel a personal connection to the man panhandling on the sidewalk or the woman seeking warmth beneath a flimsy cardboard box.

In *Tell Them Who I Am: The Lives of Homeless Women*, professor and sociologist Elliot Liebow gives a voice to the homeless women he encounters. The homeless are no longer anonymous people on the street corner; they now have names and faces. Nobody chooses to be homeless, Liebow writes, but sometimes circumstances turn against him or her. Homelessness can happen anywhere, even on a college campus, as I found out one semester: I learned that one of my students often stayed in the library until closing time. She didn't have a place to live, so she read in the library until closing and then walked to a local store to sleep in the clothing aisles. She was pregnant, and her parents had kicked her out of the house. Of course, none of this was planned; it simply happened. And I was left, like Liebow, to wonder why a country as developed as the United States has allowed homelessness to become a "normal" part of its culture.

Liebow's book is a blueprint of what sociology is all about. He gathers information, explains his findings, and then thinks about the bigger picture. He questions social policies and draws his own conclusions. A sociologist like Liebow does not try to pinpoint one specific cause of homelessness in the United States. Instead, he tackles the issue from all angles.

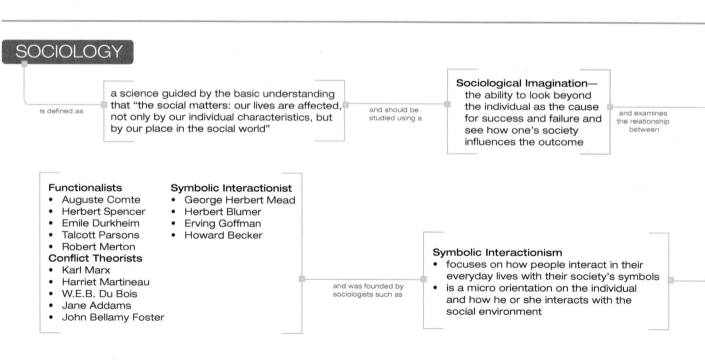

SOCIOLOGY

is defined as a science guided by the basic understanding that "the social matters: our lives are affected, not only by our individual characteristics, but by our place in the social world"

and should be studied using a

Sociological Imagination— the ability to look beyond the individual as the cause for success and failure and see how one's society influences the outcome

and examines the relationship between

Functionalists
- Auguste Comte
- Herbert Spencer
- Emile Durkheim
- Talcott Parsons
- Robert Merton

Conflict Theorists
- Karl Marx
- Harriet Martineau
- W.E.B. Du Bois
- Jane Addams
- John Bellamy Foster

Symbolic Interactionist
- George Herbert Mead
- Herbert Blumer
- Erving Goffman
- Howard Becker

and was founded by sociologists such as

Symbolic Interactionism
- focuses on how people interact in their everyday lives with their society's symbols
- is a micro orientation on the individual and how he or she interacts with the social environment

get the topic: WHAT IS SOCIOLOGY?

Sociology Defined

How do you define sociology? You might say that it's the study of society, the study of how people live, or the study of people's interactions with one another. This is all true, but these answers only scratch the surface. According to the American Sociological Association, **sociology** is a science guided by the basic understanding that "the social matters: our lives are affected, not only by our individual characteristics but by our place in

> **SOCIOLOGY** is a science guided by the basic understanding that "the social matters: our lives are affected, not only by our individual characteristics but by our place in the social world."

the social world."[2] Like any science, sociologists seek to understand the facts of a situation while keeping an open mind about what they are studying. In addition to this, we strive to keep our personal opinions at bay.

MAKE CONNECTIONS

Using Video Games to Study Sociology

Have you ever wanted to control someone else's actions? Leave it to video games to allow you to act out such a fantasy. One of the most popular is *The Sims*, a strategic computer game that simulates real life. You decide when your character sleeps, eats, and even bathes. More recently, the game *Façade* has sprung forth a similar idea. While *The*

Sims and *Façade* play up the entertainment factor, they also provide a lesson in sociology.

Players of *The Sims* and *Façade* manipulate characters in a virtual world to see the effects certain behaviors have on the characters' lives. Your characters become depressed when they have little interaction with others, just like in real life.

The Sims and *Façade* allow you to study the effect people's actions have on themselves and others. The best part is that in the simulated world, the consequences are not real, so

you don't have to be afraid to test how extreme behaviors affect your characters.

>>> **ACTIVITY** Think about a real-world theory you'd like to use *The Sims* or *Façade* to test. How would you use the game to test the theory? What do you think the outcome of your study will be? Write a few paragraphs describing your proposed sociological study. If you have access to either of these video games, go ahead and test your theory!

Developing a Sociological Imagination

One of my students recently lost her job at a nearby automotive factory. She attended classes during the day and worked at a convenience store at night. Being a single mother of two, she had no one to watch her kids while she was at work. Without supervision, her children were falling behind in school, hanging out on street corners, and getting into trouble. Like many single parents, she had no other options and no idea what else to do.

When we think of kids in trouble, many of us probably blame the parents. But, in this situation, does the blame rest solely on her shoulders? Famous American sociologist C. Wright Mills (1916–1962) would say no. Mills asserted that people must understand how outside forces contribute

Individual Choice vs. Social Forces
- **Solidarity**—the level of connectedness a person feels to others in the environment
- **Social Control**—the social mechanisms that regulate a person's actions

and is studied using one of three theoretical paradigms

Functionalism
- views society as a system of interrelated parts
- is a macro orientation because it studies how social structures affect how a society works

and

and

Conflict Theory
- studies issues such as race, gender, social class, criminal justice, and international relations
- is a macro orientation because it studies how the struggle for resources holds society together

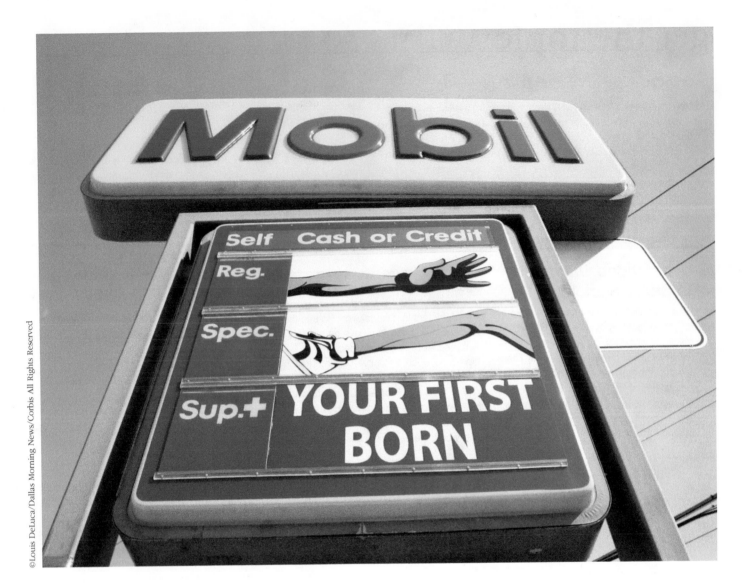

to someone's situation. In other words, Mills wanted us to develop a **sociological imagination**—the ability to look beyond the individual as the cause for success and failure and see how one's society influences the outcome.[3]

Developing a sociological imagination helps you understand your place in a complex world. We must grasp both the history and the biography of a situation to generate this imagination. Mills argued that most of us see social issues through biography; that is, our personal point of view.[4] This **micro**, or small-scale, reference focuses our attention on the individual. We must also understand how history and social structure affect the individual. By including this **macro**, or large-scale, point of view in our imagining of the social world, we can understand it more clearly. These factors influence both our individual choices and our interpretation of events. So, using the sociological imagination gives us more than an individualistic interpretation of the world.[5]

Let's consider my student's situation this time using our sociological imaginations. Is outsourcing labor to blame for her situation? When U.S. companies close because of cheaper overseas labor, workers in the United States suffer. Ultimately, the goal of most businesses is to make the biggest profit possible, so owners can't resist the lure of hiring cheap labor. With gas and food prices skyrocketing,

> **When working-class parents struggle to put food on the table, some might blame their predicament on a lack of education or motivation.** People using a sociological imagination, however, might attribute other forces, such as rising gas prices, to the parents' predicament.

many businesses must adjust their budgets accordingly and find less expensive ways of doing things. Some people win and others lose, as in my student's case. If my student had not lost her job, would her children still be in trouble? Probably not. She reported that when working her old job, she was home every day when they got home from school. Now, she rarely sees them. What's clear is that when thinking sociologically about an issue, simple answers rarely explain the complexities of human situations.

Emile Durkheim's Theory on Suicide

There are often several biographical, social, and historical causes for every event—from homelessness to unemployment to suicide. Using a socio-logical imagination means that we consider the impact on the individual from these points of view. Ever wonder why someone would commit suicide? Suicide is perhaps the most personal type of death, and yet in the 1897 book *Suicide*, sociologist Emile Durkheim (1858–1917) pro-posed that two social forces, solidarity and social control, influence the chance of a person taking his or her own life.[6] **Solidarity** refers to the level of connectedness a person feels to others in the environment, and **social control** refers to the social mechanisms that regulate a person's actions.[7] These two social forces are independent factors that help predict the type of suicide someone might commit.

When people lack solidarity, **egoistic suicides** occur. People who commit these suicides have few social connections, feel isolated and alone, and are more likely to fall into despair. Of course, this doesn't mean that all "loners" are suicidal. It only shows that having low levels of solidarity increases the odds for egoistic suicides.

Solidarity levels also influence the likelihood of **altruistic suicides**. These suicides result when the level of solidarity is exceptionally high. Because the individual is deeply connected to a group, he or she views the best interests of the group as superior to all other interests. This par-ticular analysis might explain the rationale behind *kamikaze* pilots and suicide bombers.

SOCIOLOGICAL IMAGINATION is the ability to look beyond the individual as the cause for success and failure and see how one's society influences the outcome.

MICRO means small-scale.

MACRO means large-scale.

SOLIDARITY refers to the level of connectedness and integration a person feels to others in the environment.

SOCIAL CONTROL refers to the social mechanisms that regulate a person's actions.

EGOISTIC SUICIDES are suicides that result from a lack of solidarity, occurring among those who have few social connections, feel isolated and alone, and are more likely to fall into despair.

ALTRUISTIC SUICIDES are suicides that occur when the level of solidarity is exceptionally high and when the individual views the group's interest as superior to all other interests.

∨
∨
∨ **Durkheim identified four different types of suicide—egoistic, altruistic, fatalistic, and anomic**—illustrated in the graphic below.[8]

DURKHEIM'S FOUR TYPES OF SUICIDE

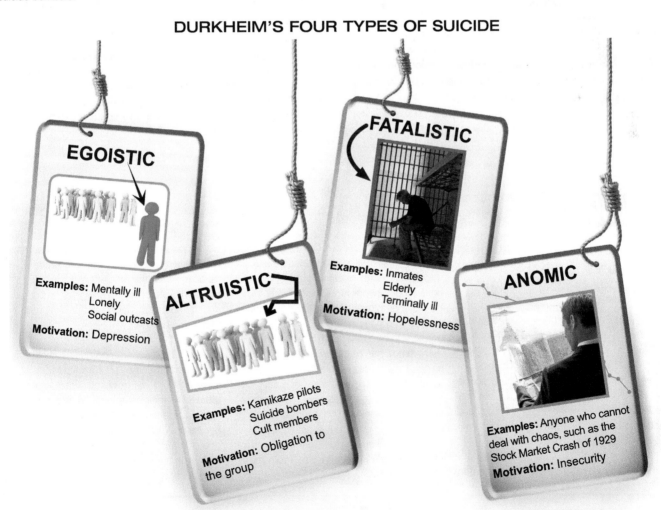

EGOISTIC
Examples: Mentally ill
Lonely
Social outcasts
Motivation: Depression

ALTRUISTIC
Examples: Kamikaze pilots
Suicide bombers
Cult members
Motivation: Obligation to the group

FATALISTIC
Examples: Inmates
Elderly
Terminally ill
Motivation: Hopelessness

ANOMIC
Examples: Anyone who cannot deal with chaos, such as the Stock Market Crash of 1929
Motivation: Insecurity

FATALISTIC SUICIDES are suicides that result from too much social control.

ANOMIC SUICIDES are suicides that occur as a result of rapid change, usually economic.

PARADIGM refers to a theoretical framework through which scientists study the world.

FUNCTIONALISM is a theoretical framework that defines society as a system of interrelated parts.

CONFLICT THEORY is a theoretical framework that views society as an unequal system that brings about conflict and change.

SYMBOLIC INTERACTIONISM is a theoretical framework that focuses on how people interact with others in their everyday lives.

INDIVIDUAL CHOICE AND SOCIAL FORCES

You've probably guessed by now that social factors often influence our personal choices. They provide a context in which we make decisions. Again, consider the act of suicide. Most of my students suggest that this is totally an individual choice, and in fact it is. However, certain trends arise in the data on suicides that indicate people who are at higher risk of taking their own lives.

Time of year, profession, and age all predict the likelihood of suicide. According to the Centers for Disease Control and Prevention:

- Suicide rates in the United States are lowest in winter and highest in spring. During the winter holidays, most people are surrounded by friends and family. However, in the spring this socialization may end. The lack of integration might increase the odds of an egoistic suicide.

- Police officers have a high risk of suicide. Perhaps this is because they work long hours and are exposed to violent and graphic scenes. Add to this fact that they have easy access to guns, and you can see some structural characteristics that may lead them to fatalistic thinking and suicide.

- Generally, the rate of suicide increases with age. Furthermore, men are more likely to commit suicide than women. Men over the age of 65 have the highest rates of suicide in the United States. This may also be due to fatalism, because when people age, they may have more illnesses and/or physical limitations that increase the risk of suicide.[11]

Unlike altruistic suicides, **fatalistic suicides** are related to the level of one's social control. This type of suicide happens when a person feels that his or her future is bleak and there is no way for the situation to improve. Individuals who live in hopeless environments—such as prisons and long-term health-care facilities—are more likely to commit fatalistic suicide.

During times of social unrest, **anomic suicides** increase. Anomie refers to social instability caused by economic and social turmoil. Durkheim predicted that modernization and industrialization would bring an increase in anomic suicides because people must adjust to their new situations, and these adjustments result in a change of societal rules and norms. As a result, many of the social institutions that had once regulated society, such as religion, lose their power.[9] In times of change, certain individuals will decide that living through the chaos is more than they can handle, so they will take their own lives.

Although Durkheim's theory is more than a century old, it's still an important way to consider the tension between social forces and individual choice.

Suicide might be seen as an individual decision, but there are many social factors that seem to influence suicide rates. We cannot use these factors to specifically predict who will and will not kill themselves, but we can understand that one's environment influences the rate of suicide in a society. Other factors such as one's family makeup and the relative size of a group of people born during the same time period also play a role.[10]

It is important for you to note that these factors do not cause individuals to commit suicide per se; however, they do indicate groups who are at a higher risk of killing themselves. When sociologists examine an issue, such as suicide, homelessness, or any other social event, they use their sociological imagination to help consider how social factors influence an individual's choice. How do sociologists use the sociological imagination to study the larger world? Let's examine three important theoretical perspectives and the sociologists who helped develop them.

THINK SOCIOLOGICALLY

Homelessness—Individual Choice vs. Social Factors

Have you ever heard someone argue that people choose to be homeless? You might have even made the argument yourself. In *Tell Them Who I Am: The Lives of Homeless Women*, Liebow says, "it is, perhaps, all too easy to fall into homelessness, but being there is not easy at all."[12] When many people are living paycheck to paycheck, it's not hard to imagine someone waking up one day and finding that they don't have enough money to pay a mortgage or buy groceries.

Liebow finds that most homeless women are actually working-class women who have fallen on hard times. Once these women "fall into homelessness," they find it tough to climb out of that dark hole. Finding work is especially difficult because employers shy away from hiring people who have no home. Even if a homeless woman actually finds a job, many times her wages will not be enough to pay for a house, especially when she must spend a good part of her salary on transportation to get to work. The rest of her money is likely to be spent on food for her family and other necessities. As a result, her children grow up in an environment with little privacy and few role models for success.

Although Liebow does not suggest that homelessness is impossible to overcome, he does argue that society is doing little to help. With the cards seemingly stacked against homeless people, what choice do they *really* have?

>>> **ACTIVITY** Visit a homeless shelter in your community. Talk to the people there and find out how social factors contributed to their situations. How did they arrive at the shelter? What were their lives like before? Write a paragraph describing one of the people you met, analyzing the factors that led to that person's homelessness.

think sociologically: WHAT ARE THE CHARACTERISTICS OF THE THREE MAJOR SOCIOLOGICAL PARADIGMS?

Before I ever knew anything about sociology, I had a worldview. Being born in the United States to a religious, working-class family, my parents' teachings shaped my point of view. Had I been born in China, Chad, or Chile, I would likely think differently about the world. How do you view the world? What personal beliefs or ideas do you value most? It might be difficult to respond to these questions, but I bet you have some pretty definitive answers. When sociologists take in the world, they do it through a **paradigm**—a theoretical framework through which scientists study the world.

In the United States, most sociologists view the world through three major paradigms—functionalism, conflict theory, and symbolic interactionism. **Functionalism** is a theoretical framework that defines society as a system of interrelated parts. This paradigm is a macro approach to sociological study because it focuses on larger social structures rather than individuals. When you think about functionalism, it may be helpful to think about the human body. The body has built-in mechanisms that help it maintain a normal body temperature. This is your body's way of trying to maintain its optimal functioning. If you are stranded outside in freezing temperatures, you will start shivering in an attempt to regulate your body temperature. Society is similar in many ways. When something happens to throw a social system off-kilter, certain forces step in to help balance things out again.

Conflict theory is a theoretical framework that views society as being in a constant struggle over scarce resources. This constant struggle inevitably results in an unequal system. Similar to functionalism, conflict theory is also a macro approach, as this theory is concerned with various interested groups battling for power. Inequality of wealth and power in society is often the focus of modern conflict theory. For example, conflict theorists might examine how the chasm between the rich and the poor affects people's opportunities in our society. It's no surprise that children who come from privileged backgrounds can afford to receive the best educations, participate in organized sports, and take music lessons. However, children from poorer families may not get these same opportunities, and this lack of opportunity puts them at a disadvantage.

Symbolic interactionism is a theoretical framework that focuses on how individual interactions between people influence them and how these interactions can impact society. Symbolic interactionism is primarily a micro approach to sociology because it is concerned with the individual's role in creating society. The use of "symbols," such as words, gestures, body language, and facial expressions, influence how people communicate. Our actions communicate meaning. For example, if you're having a "bad day," what does that mean? One student once told me he had a "bad day" every time it rained. If that is the case, could such a definition of reality influence how you behave toward others on your job or in the classroom? How might his "bad day" influence the "days" of others? Interactionists constantly seek to understand how small interactions influence the larger society.

Corey Holms/Getty Images; ©Rick Wilking/Reuters/Landov

>>> In 2010, home foreclosures became a "sign of the times." The stress of tough economic times can push some people, who probably would not have ever thought of suicide, to take that step. **Can you see Durkheim's point about anomic suicide in such cases?**

SOCIAL LAWS are statements of fact that are unchanging under given conditions and can be used as ground rules for any kind of society.

SOCIAL STATICS are the existing structural elements of society.

SOCIAL DYNAMICS are the changes in the existing structural elements of society.

As you can see, sociologists often approach their study of society from either a macro or micro perspective. In sociology, the macro approach is most commonly used, as it examines larger social groups and institutions and their effects on society. This is part of what separates sociology from psychology, as psychology operates on a micro level by studying the workings of the human mind. Although some sociological studies focus on the individual, the primary concern is the effect that these individuals have on the rest of society and the influence that society has on the individual. Each sociological paradigm can combine aspects of macro and micro approaches, and yet they all seek to understand the process by which people influence society and society affects them.

Sociologists from each paradigm often analyze similar issues, such as why homelessness exists or how children learn about the social world. However, the questions they ask as they analyze these issues differ. The chart below illustrates how functionalists, conflict theorists, and symbolic interactionists approach learning about society.

Sociologists use these questions to help them build theories about the world. So, is one school of thought better than the others? Not necessarily. In fact, the worldviews of most sociologists are rather eclectic or diverse. They may use each paradigm to illuminate different issues or use all three to look comprehensively at a single issue. If you consider Liebow's work, for example, you'll see that he uses bits and pieces of each paradigm to understand homelessness. Liebow finds that a society's structures create homelessness (functionalism), and people with wealth and power control those structures and are generally abusive to the poorest of the poor (conflict theory). Those who experience homelessness often create in themselves self-fulfilling prophecies that help them remain mired in their plight

(symbolic interactionism). Liebow uses each of these ideas to create a complete view of why homelessness exists in our society.

Emerging Paradigms

New sociology students may think that these are the only three paradigms in sociology. Although these are the core paradigms in sociology and essential for you to understand, social thinkers have gone beyond these three. Let's look at a few emerging paradigms often used in sociology. We'll revisit some of these in chapters where they best apply.

FEMINIST THEORY

Feminist theory is a gendered and interdisciplinary approach that seeks to answer how the social world is ordered around gender. In short, how do women fit into a social world that has been traditionally controlled by men? Feminists often ask, "Why is the social world the way that it is?" and "Can the social world be changed to make it a place for all people?" How do race, ethnicity, social class, and age all interact with gender to determine the outcomes for individuals?

Feminist theories can fall into one of three types. *Gender inequality theories* focus on how women's experiences of the social world are different from those of men. Often, this focuses on sexist patterns that limit women's opportunities for work, education, and other social needs. *Gender oppression theories* suggest that men oppress women by keeping and maintaining power over them through purposeful discrimination. *Structural oppression theories* suggest that women's oppression is rooted in capitalism and patriarchies that keep women on the margins of the social world. The oppressive nature of the social world is rooted in the structures of patriarchy and capitalism, which ultimately leads to the oppression of women.[13]

EXCHANGE THEORY

Exchange theorists suggest our social experiences consist of a series of rewards and costs. People inherently seek to maximize their rewards and minimize their costs, thus leading to their choice of social action.[14] Often,

COMPARING THE THEORETICAL PARADIGMS

	Functionalism	Conflict Theory	Symbolic Interactionism
Level of Analysis	Macro	Macro	Micro
Core Questions	• What keeps society functioning smoothly? • What are the parts of society and how do they relate? • What are the intended and unintended outcomes of an event?	• How are wealth and power distributed in society? • How do people with wealth and power keep them? • Are there groups that get ahead in this society and why? • How are society's resources and opportunities divided?	• How do people co-create the society? • How does social interaction influence, create, and sustain human relationships? • Do people change behavior from one setting to another, and if so, why?

>>> Moths with colors that stand out in their environment are beautiful, but such colors may not function well as a survival mode. **Similarly, societies that cannot adapt may not survive.**

Harry Taylor ©Dorling Kindersley, Courtesy of the Natural History Museum, London

exchange theory appeals to thinkers on a micro level, such as why you may select the particular mate you choose. If a girl is dating a boy but becomes exasperated with his manners when they are dining out, she may choose to break up with him because she perceives the costs of staying in the relationship as higher than the rewards. Of course, exchange theory also has a macro point of view. Is it really in the best interests of any country to export all of their manufacturing jobs simply because the countries to which they send those jobs can provide cheaper labor? In calculating the value of the exchange, one must consider not only the short-term rewards (immediate profits), but also the potential long-term consequences (economic collapse when transportation of goods gets interrupted).

ENVIRONMENTAL THEORY

This is perhaps the most recent emerging paradigm. This perspective seeks to blend social thought and ecological principles to discover how environmental attitudes have changed, as well as how environmental policies and justice influence society. Environmental social thinkers often seek to understand how societies adjust to ecological changes. How many people can actually live in a specific area? This idea is known as the carrying capacity of an area. Often, we believe that human beings are an exception to the ecological limits of carrying capacity. Environmental theory suggests this is not necessarily true. For environmental sociology, human beings are merely one more type of organism sharing the ecological space with animals. Dealing with the reality of limits becomes an important component of the social world. How do societies adapt, and if they fail to adapt, will they continue to survive? These questions and more are at the core of environmental social thought.

The Functionalist's Worldview

Although philosophers have always tackled the issues surrounding how people and society fit together, it was not until French philosopher Auguste Comte (1798–1857) coined the term *sociology* that the discipline got its name.[15] The oldest sociological paradigm, functionalism owes much to Comte, who is considered the father of sociology.

Comte felt that sociology should strive to discover **social laws**—statements of fact that are unchanging under given conditions and can be used as ground rules for any study of society. In order to discover these laws, Comte proposed that we study **social statics**, or the existing struc-

tural elements of society, and **social dynamics**, or the change in those elements. He believed that by discovering the interplay between structures and dynamics we could develop social laws that would help improve society. To date, we have no social laws, but some sociologists are still trying to develop them. Although few people follow Comte's theories today, his basic ideas are the groundwork on which functionalism is based.

As we've discussed, functionalism is a theoretical framework that defines society as a system of interrelated parts. These parts work in concert with one another to satisfy the needs of society as a whole. According to functionalists, society is relatively stable, which means that things occur in society for a specific function and those functions help maintain stability.

Social institutions such as the family, economy, educational system, and political system are critical for society to function properly. Understanding how these and other social institutions work in a society is of great interest to functionalists. Since these parts are interrelated, each has an impact on the others. Remember my student who lost her job? The economic system influenced the family system, which may, if her children continue to get into trouble, interact with the criminal justice system. Performing functional analysis can be layered and quite complex.

Functionalism suggests that a society's values and norms provide the foundation for the rules and laws that it creates. These norms regulate the relationships between social institutions. Therefore, general agreement on these norms must occur for a society to achieve balance.

All of the social structures, from the minor day-to-day interactions with friends to the complex cultural traditions and customs, work together to keep society running. Functionalists, however, have differing views about how these structures cooperate with one another. Some compare society to a living, breathing organism; others analyze the expected and unexpected outcomes of a social event, while still others wonder what exactly it is that holds a society together. Although it's the oldest theoretical approach, functionalism remains an important way to consider society. On the next few pages, we'll investigate some early functionalists and you can see who these ideas come from. Early theorists like Herbert Spencer and Emile Durkheim contributed to the growth and development of the functionalist perspective.

HERBERT SPENCER

Herbert Spencer (1820–1903) was a British intellectual whose ideas furthered the development of functionalism. Spencer's study of sociology was informed by Charles Darwin's theory of natural selection. Darwin argued that natural selection—a process resulting in the evolution of organisms best adapted to the environment—makes evolution occur. Spencer viewed society as a biological organism, and as such, it can evolve, thrive, or die. For him, some societies are "more fit" than others because they adapt better to changes in the environment. From Spencer, you can see a type of thinking often called **"social Darwinism"**—a notion that suggests strong societies survive and weak ones become extinct.[16]

Spencer's idea informs a social theory that, in essence, evaluates the superiority or inferiority of a society based on its ability to be strong and survive. For example, in a recent class discussion about homelessness, one of my students stated, "Homeless people can't follow the rules that everyone else does; their homelessness is their own fault." Do you see Spencer's ideas in her comments? How do her words reflect the idea of social Darwinism? On the macro level, do you think some societies are superior to others? Would you suggest that the United States reached its success due to its own merit? If so, you think a bit like a social Darwinist.

EMILE DURKHEIM

Like Spencer, French intellectual Emile Durkheim (1858–1917) also viewed society as an organism. You should recognize Durkheim's name from our discussion of suicide earlier in the chapter. Durkheim was one of the first true sociologists, in that he used data to test theories. His work provides the basis for much of functionalist thought.

Durkheim's work suggested that solidarity is a vital component that holds society together. Solidarity integrates, or holds society together, because people see themselves as unified. He points out that the type of society influences the type of solidarity. Durkheim divided solidarity into two different types, mechanical and organic. **Mechanical solidarity** refers to the state of community bonding in traditional societies in which people share beliefs and values and perform common activities. It's this bond that works to keep society running smoothly.[17]

As societies become more complex, their type of solidarity changes from mechanical to organic. **Organic solidarity** occurs when people live in a society with a diverse division of labor. Division of labor refers to the many different jobs we have today. This forces people to depend on one another for survival. Ask yourself, when was the last time you ate something you either grew or killed yourself? For most of us, the answer is never. Food is essential for survival, and yet most of us require a complex division of labor to feed ourselves. Truckers, grocers, and farmers all

must do their parts so we can eat.[18] This organic connection ensures that we get the things we need and holds society together. Beliefs remain important in a modern society, but what binds people together is their organic solidarity.[19]

Durkheim's ideas about solidarity are just the tip of the iceberg, though. A number of American thinkers drew inspiration from Durkheim and expanded his ideas into what is known as functionalist thought.

Functionalism in the United States

After Albion Small created the first department of sociology in 1892 at the University of Chicago, a new academic discipline began to emerge across the United States.[20] This budding science provided social thinkers a place to study the workings of society. One of these thinkers was Talcott Parsons.

TALCOTT PARSONS

Functionalist Talcott Parsons (1902–1979) was a giant in the field of sociology in the United States. Parsons was interested in creating grand theories that attempted to explain every aspect of the human experience and how social systems interconnect. For Parsons, society was much like a bicycle wheel, made up of independent yet interdependent parts. When properly balanced, each independent spoke connected to the hub keeps the wheel spinning. But if just one spoke breaks on your wheel, the entire wheel will eventually fall out of balance. Similarly, society is an interrelated system, and if one part fails to work, the whole system suffers.[21]

Parsons also commented on the inertia of social systems, meaning that they tend to remain at rest, if they are at rest, or stay in motion, if already in motion. For example, when you go bowling, you must take a bowling ball and use your own force to make it roll down the alley. Once the ball starts rolling, it tends to keep rolling until the pins and the end of the alley stop it. Although the friction from the floor may slow it down, some other force must stop it. Parsons pointed out that the social world acts the same way. Thus, in order to change a society, some great force must impact the system or it will remain unchanged. This is because societies naturally will find a balance. Thus, change is unlikely and often disruptive. Of course, once the process of change starts, the

<<< **Amish farm communities** in Pennsylvania **have mechanical solidarity because everyone lives in much the same way, does the same things, and shares the same values.**

system will continue on that path until some counterreaction occurs due to social inertia.[22]

ROBERT MERTON

Functionalist Robert K. Merton (1910–2003), a contemporary of Parsons, sought to create a middle-range theory that could bridge the gap between grand theories and the study of individual parts of society. He did this by breaking society into parts and studying them individually to better understand the whole.[23] This idea is widely accepted in sociology today, as most sociologists have an area of expertise, be it race, gender, crime, inequality, population, or a host of other issues. It is possible to spend a career pursuing knowledge in one of these areas, seeking to create theories of the middle range that describe these issues and how they influence society. Merton's work also shows how sociologists are rarely "pure" theorists in any area.

One of Merton's greatest theoretical contributions to functionalism was his understanding that social realities have both intended and unintended **functions**—social factors that affect people in a society. Merton identified two types: **manifest functions**, or factors that lead to an expected consequence or outcome, and **latent functions**, or factors that lead to an unforeseen or unexpected consequence. Merton suggested that when looking at

SOCIAL DARWINISM is a notion that suggests strong societies survive and weak ones become extinct.

MECHANICAL SOLIDARITY refers to the state of community bonding in traditional societies in which people share beliefs and values and perform common activities.

ORGANIC SOLIDARITY occurs when people live in a society with a diverse division of labor.

FUNCTIONS are social factors that affect people in a society.

MANIFEST FUNCTIONS are functions that lead to an expected consequence or outcome.

LATENT FUNCTIONS are functions that lead to unforeseen or unexpected consequences.

any social event, sociologists should ask the question, "For whom is this functional?" By doing this, we'll do a complete analysis because we'll consider both manifest and latent functions. For example, one could argue that the manifest function of outsourcing jobs is to improve a company's profits while providing cheaper goods to consumers. However, the latent function of such a system creates tension for families whose jobs are lost, and who then might lose their homes. For Merton, one cannot complete a functional analysis without considering both manifest and latent functions.[24]

THE FUNCTIONALISTS—AT A GLANCE

CRITICISMS OF FUNCTIONALISM

In the mid-20th century, functionalism was the dominant theoretical approach. However, its dominance has waned in more recent years. Critics of functionalism sometimes claim that this paradigm does not take into account the influences of wealth and power on the formation of society. From a purely functionalist point of view, all social structures

exist because they meet some need. For example, years ago in the town in which I live, downtown area stores had hitching posts in front of them. Now they're gone because no one rides a horse for transportation anymore. If and when cars become obsolete, society will find some other way to deal with transportation issues. However, in the meantime, cars serve an essential function for society.

BOURGEOISIE refers to members of the capitalist class.

PROLETARIAT refers to members of the poor working class.

FALSE CONSCIOUSNESS is a person's lack of understanding of his or her position in society.

CLASS CONSCIOUSNESS is an understanding of one's position in the class system.

Functionalists are accused of supporting the status quo, even when it may be harmful to do so. Consider the invention of the automobile. Certainly it has made society more mobile and provides freedom of movement for millions. And yet, if we fail to consider the latent consequences of this invention, we do not fully understand it. Thus, supporting the car means supporting the air pollution, acres of parking lots, and potential accidents that come with it.

Functionalists suggest that societies will naturally find a balance point on their own. If change occurs, it will do so slowly, and this is actually in the best interest of society. However, if you think about certain social problems, such as homelessness, is this something that should be addressed slowly or quickly? Although it is easy to point out that certain individual traits may lead some to live in shelters, is it really good for anyone to have people sleeping on the streets? The lack of affordable housing in society remains a problem. Although Liebow argues that the United States does not have enough cheap housing or high-paying work for all of its citizens, he points out that a lack of a decent wage drives much of the poverty that results in homelessness. In this way, he criticizes the functional argument that the balance point is fair. Thus, is the United States really a "land of opportunity" for everyone?

As you consider homelessness or other societal issues, ask yourself for whom is the system functional? Whom does the system benefit? Functionalists might argue that society works for the greatest number of people. Change will arise when problems become "big enough." However, critics would argue that this belief results in many minorities being ignored. Who speaks for the homeless? What choice did my student have about globalization and the loss of her job? The functionalist perspective often fails to recognize how inequalities in social class, race, and gender perpetuate imbalance in our society.

The conflict theory paradigm arose as a response to some of functionalism's weaknesses. Conflict theorists want to analyze how these social inequalities affect society as a whole.

The Conflict Theorist's Worldview

Remember, conflict theory is a theoretical framework that views society in a struggle for scarce resources. So, what is scarce? Two main concerns for conflict theorists are economic wealth and power. Such theorists acknowledge that we live in an unequal society. Why? It could be because there is not enough "stuff" to go around, or it could be because those with the "stuff" don't want to let go of it. In either case, conflict theory suggests that we're all struggling for more "stuff," whether that "stuff" is power in a marriage or wealth in the world.

Conflict theorists, like functional ones, tend to focus on macro issues, viewing how society's structures contribute to the conflict. Modern conflict theorists often look at the inequality of a capitalist economic system. Such a system breeds inequality, as it rewards some at the expense of others. Once you have power, you want to keep it. For this reason, the wealthy elites are more likely to create advantages for themselves, even if their actions put others at a disadvantage.

In general, the essence of conflict theory suggests that a pyramid structure of power and wealth exists in society. The elite at the top of the pyramid determine the rules for those below them. Under such a system, laws, institutions, and traditions support their authority. When Liebow discusses the lack of adequate wages and the shame we all deserve because we permit homelessness to exist, he is in essence suggesting that those of us who are not homeless are, in part, responsible for those who are because we allow the system to ignore these people.

Many theorists who use the conflict paradigm might examine macro conflicts between different groups of society, different countries, or different social classes. The study of inequality in sociology always involves a consideration of conflict theory. Therefore, the paradigm applies to social class, race, gender, marriage, religion, population, environment, and a host of other social phenomena. If you believe that discrimination, ageism, sexism, racism, and classism occur in society because some people have the power to promote their desires over others', then you think like a conflict theorist.

Modern feminist theory, or the study of how gender affects the experiences and opportunities of men and women, often takes a conflict-oriented point of view. Women throughout the world are often still subordinate to men. In some countries, this might mean women cannot choose their own husbands or procure jobs of their choosing, while in this country it can be illustrated by opportunities afforded to women. You'd be hard-pressed to find women CEOs in the biggest companies. Of the top 500 companies in the United States, women lead fewer than 15.[25] Feminists often suggest this occurs because men want to maintain their positions of power in society and strive to keep women out. Do you see the conflict perspective here?

A student once pointed out that women often find themselves at the short end of the "financial stick" and powerful people take advantage of the poor. When I labeled her views as Marxist, she immediately took offense and denied my claim. However, it was evident to me that her views originated from the thoughts of Karl Marx, a founder of conflict theory.

KARL MARX

Karl Marx (1818–1883) was a German theorist, social activist, and writer who analyzed the effects of capitalism—an economic system in which private individuals own businesses and control the economy. Believing that capitalism corrupted human nature, Marx hoped for a utopia in which equality reigned. At his core, Marx was not that different from Comte because he wished to understand society to improve it for all.

Marx suggested that in a capitalist system, the **bourgeoisie**, or members of the capitalist class, own most of the wealth because they control the businesses. Since increasing profit is their first goal, owners pay workers as little as possible. Liebow, too, notices this when he encounters homeless women who actually have some form of employment, but don't make enough money to afford housing. Employers generally pay these women as little as possible, and the women have no way to fight the system.

Marx called the workers in a capitalist system the **proletariat**, the poor working class of society. They do all the work and the owners reap all the benefits. The proletariat lives in an unending cycle in which they work for low pay and then use those wages to survive. According to Marx, workers will never get ahead if they do not share in the wealth they create.

Why don't workers do something to change their fate? Marx suggested that it was because people had a **false consciousness**, or a lack of understanding of their position in society. Marx proposed that the workers must develop **class consciousness**, or an understanding of one's position in the system. He suggested that most workers do not truly understand how capitalism enslaves them. They think if they work hard, they'll get by and perhaps thrive. Marx argued that these ideas were fantasy.

Marx believed that once workers recognized their positions, they would unite to end the tyranny. He proposed an overthrow of the private ownership of business, and instead suggested socialism. In such a system, the government controls the economic system, ensuring that all people share in the profits generated by their own labor.

Sociologists' opinions on Marxist theory vary. Although some may hope for a type of class consciousness to arise and replace our current system, others think he oversimplified class struggle. His simple system of social class is difficult to apply to a complex postindustrial capitalist society, and even if you try, where would you draw the line between owners and workers? My student actually

owned stock in the company that let her go, so was she a worker or an owner? Seems like both.

Marxist theory clearly remains active in today's discussions of sociology. Marx felt that economic power should be in the hands of the people because wealth corrupts human nature.

These ideas continue to inspire sociologists. Let's next look at the work of four conflict theorists, Martineau, Du Bois, Addams, and Foster, to study how gender, race, and class affect a society.

HARRIET MARTINEAU

Harriet Martineau (1802–1876), like Karl Marx, came from a bourgeois family and received the benefits and status that came with such a class distinction. However, she hoped that capitalism and industrialization would bring greater justice and opportunity. Martineau, one of the first female sociologists, did not just examine the inequalities in the economic system, she also focused on the inequality between the sexes.

In the book *Society in America*, Martineau analyzed the impact of slavery, the position of women in society, and the social customs within U.S. political and economic systems.[26] She points out how these systems favor men who hold the power in society.

Martineau's studies noted hypocrisy and favoritism in the United States. For example, only white men could vote in the United States, despite the nation's democratic ideals. Enslaved people and women did not have equal opportunities for political, economic, and educational involvement. Martineau pointed out that some people did not have the same opportunities as others. She not only paved the way for other female sociologists, but also expanded people's thinking about the world, enlightening what would become the conflict paradigm.[27]

CYCLE OF WEALTH IN A CAPITALIST SYSTEM

The Bourgeoisie

spends their wages in businesses owned by

owns the wealth and exploits

The Proletariat

W.E.B. DU BOIS

W.E.B. Du Bois (1868–1963) was an African American conflict theorist who agreed with a great deal of Marx's thinking. After attending Fisk University, Du Bois moved on to Harvard, where he would eventually complete both his undergraduate and graduate work. His writings are vast, but he is often credited for initiating the study of race in America. He was particularly interested in issues of racial inequality in the United States.[28]

In his book *The Philadelphia Negro*, Du Bois showed that poverty among African Americans in the United States was primarily the result of prejudice and discrimination.[29] In the book, he reviewed the history of African Americans in Philadelphia and connected that history to the problems his contemporaries were facing. Implying that slavery and capitalism led to African Americans' problems, Du Bois pointed out that history was influential over the present. He also noted that African Americans of his time had to live in two worlds, a white one and a black one. In one world, they were second-class citizens, while in the other they were equals. This idea, which Du Bois termed "double consciousness," created tension and conflict for African Americans. He felt that with greater assimilation into the mainstream culture, African Americans would eventually lead better-quality lives.[30]

In many respects, Du Bois was the first and perhaps most influential sociologist to study race in the United States. He was a social activist, and he became more interested in working to improve life on the African continent and less interested in life in the United States. Du Bois eventually came to believe that African Americans would never be equal to whites because the white population would not allow this. For this reason, he left the United States and spent his remaining years in Africa.

When Du Bois saw extreme poverty, oppressive governments, and many wars in Africa, he realized that colonizing Europeans caused many of these problems. **Colonialism was a primary way for European powers to generate wealth for capitalists while doing little to improve the lives of the African poor.** Du Bois increasingly believed that the greed of the United States and western Europe was the cause of war and poverty throughout the world. **To counter this, promoting economic justice and equality helps the world be at peace.**[31]

V
V Early conflict theory studies revealed
V inequality in the U.S. democratic system.
What about today? **Is the U.S. system fair for each person in the photograph below?**

JANE ADDAMS

Laura Jane Addams (1860–1935) was born in Cedarville, Illinois. Addams's father, a businessman and politician who worked to elect Lincoln and strongly opposed slavery, raised her. She earned a bachelor of arts degree from Rockford Women's Seminary in 1882, then traveled to Europe, where she saw things that changed her life.

In Toynbee Hall, Addams witnessed the settlement house movement.[32]

The settlement house movement supported the

©Moodboard/Corbis

THE CONFLICT THEORISTS—AT A GLANCE

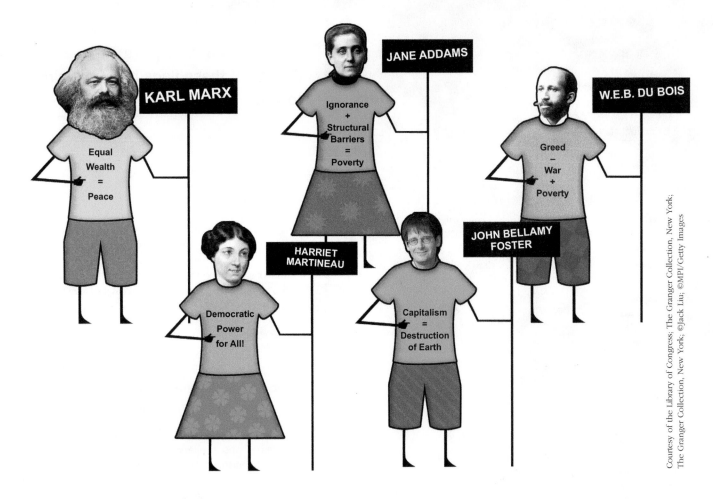

KARL MARX

Equal
Wealth
=
Peace

JANE ADDAMS

Ignorance
+
Structural
Barriers
=
Poverty

W.E.B. DU BOIS

Greed
–
War
+
Poverty

HARRIET
MARTINEAU

Democratic
Power
for All!

JOHN BELLAMY
FOSTER

Capitalism
=
Destruction
of Earth

Courtesy of the Library of Congress; The Granger Collection, New York; The Granger Collection, New York; ©Jack Liu; ©MPI/Getty Images

idea that poverty results from ignorance and structural barriers, not from failings in the morality of the person. The settlement house workers actually lived and worked in the slums. Addams and a friend, Ellen Gates Starr, decided to create a settlement house in Chicago. In 1889, they opened Hull-House with these three principles:

1. Workers would live in the slums to better understand the problems there.
2. Every person has dignity and worth regardless of race/ethnicity, gender, or social class.
3. Dedication, education, and service can overcome ignorance, disease, and structures that perpetuate poverty.

Offering services from medical to educational, Addams also used her position at Hull-House to write articles and books on a variety of topics such as the rights of women and the poor. In many ways, Hull-House became a laboratory for the application of sociological principles. In 1931, Addams won the Nobel Peace Prize for her lifetime of service and dedication to peace.[33]

Through her teaching, writing, and action, Addams embodied the best of sociology principles. Along with Albion Small, she helped found the American Sociological Association and often guest lectured in sociology classes at the University of Chicago. In order to understand the poor, Addams felt that she must live among them. Once she comprehended this situation, she wrote about it to change the system. These theories impacted her work at Hull-House. These are the steps you will take in learning to think like a sociologist.

JOHN BELLAMY FOSTER

John Bellamy Foster, a contemporary professor of sociology, often writes using a conflict paradigm. His work is primarily concerned with the negative effects of capitalism on society and the planet as whole. In his article, "The End of Rational Capitalism," he points out that purely capitalist economies, or economies in which markets are totally free, are disappearing throughout the world.

In free-market capitalism, businesses seek short-term rewards by working to expand markets. They do not care about long-term consequences. As a result, Foster argues that businesses' pursuit of wealth has created environmental and global problems, including the existence of extreme global poverty and inequality.

Foster argues that markets cannot "solve problems" because there are no profits to be had from such an endeavor. Often, people suggest that the United States is the wealthiest country in the world because we have worked harder and used the capitalist system to give opportunity and incentive to people. Foster reminds us that such a perspective ignores important parts of history, namely the period after World War II when most of the "industrialized world" was destroyed (except the United States). The expansion of the U.S. economy was largely related to building up these devastated countries. This had very little to do with the superiority of the American capitalist system. Issues such as the fall of the USSR and the privatization of the Chinese economy seem to indicate that capitalism has won and is "superior" to socialism. However, totally

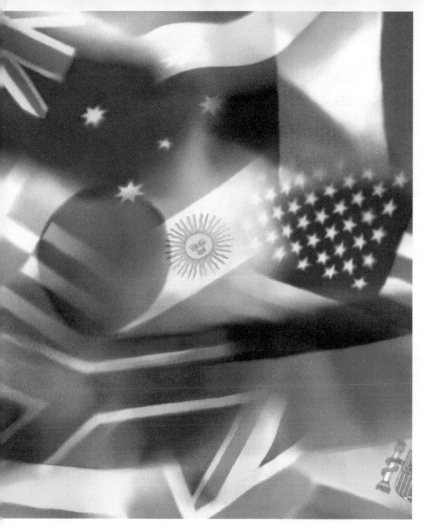

©Reza Estakhrian/Getty Images

<<< This is a collage of flags from many of the world's most populous and powerful nations. **Do any of these flags have meaning to you?**

The Symbolic Interactionist's Worldview

Symbolic interactionism focuses on how communication influences the way people's interactions with each other create the social world in which we live. Symbolic interactionists believe that the root of society comes from its symbols. They suggest that the symbols we use are arbitrary, meaning that they vary from culture to culture.

Do you write with a pen or una pluma? Neither is wrong; one is a label in English, the other in Spanish. **As long as you are with other people who speak the same language, you can interact.**

A long time ago, I enrolled in a language school in Mexico. I lived with a family who spoke no English, and my teachers only spoke to us in Spanish. At first, I was totally lost. I clung to the members of the family with whom I lived as if I were a little child. However, I soon began to learn the language. It is amazing how our need to communicate with others helps us learn. Although the words or accents sound different, communication is central to all human interactions.

Of course, words are not the only symbols. Consider the photograph of flags from countries around the world. The flag that probably has meaning for you is the U.S. flag. However, people from China, Brazil, Belgium, or the United Kingdom probably feel the same way about their flags as you do about yours. These symbols represent entire nations, and yet you cannot identify many of them and they probably don't hold much interest to you. This is because the importance of a symbol is rooted in the culture from which it comes. Just as language varies between people, so, too, do their symbol systems.

As you can see then, for interactionists, society is fluid thing. It is always in a process of change because how we use symbols and what they mean to us is constantly changing. For example, when I was in school, teachers might tell ethnic jokes, such as "Polack" jokes. Of course, now most of you have not ever heard these jokes. Why? Because people began to define such humor as unacceptable.

You can see then, that our definition of what has value depends on our understanding of it. Context and setting affects our understanding of a social event. You certainly behave differently in church than you do in a bar or on a golf course. Social order results when the members of society share common definitions of what is appropriate.

free-market capitalism will result in the destruction of the environment and the exploitation of workers throughout the world.[34] The long and short of it, according to Foster, is that capitalism requires expanding markets. Once the entire planet is developed, the system will collapse.

CRITICISMS OF CONFLICT THEORY

Critics of conflict theory often accuse it of being too radical. This paradigm often becomes synonymous with the idea that powerful people oppress the weak. However, most people seem to agree that the roles and rules of society "make sense." For example, even after we discussed globalization and the depletion of factory jobs in the United States, my student who lost her job still felt that the U.S. system was "fair." She said, "it still makes sense to me, even though I'm being hurt by it." This illustrates the reality that most people in society tend to agree with the status quo. Certainly, some are victimized by racism, sexism, and other prejudices, but most members of society seem to agree that things are generally fine.

A simple reading of conflict theory can also seem to make the notion of conflict seem like a "bad" thing. However, doesn't competition breed excellence? When I played baseball, I never worked harder than when my team got a new member, a young man who also played second base. I worked even harder to maintain my spot on the roster. Starting positions are rare, and the "conflict" actually improved my play.

After examining the works of functionalists and conflict theorists you're probably thinking in a macro manner. Whether you're using functionalism or conflict theory, you are thinking like many sociologists. Yet one more paradigm remains. If you believe that the way to change the world is through the individual, you might find symbolic interactionism appealing.

Disputes arise when we do not share the same definitions. Think about an argument you've had with someone recently. Did the fight stem from a different interpretation of meaning? For example, if your roommate eats your food without asking your permission, you might interpret that behavior as disrespectful and rude. However, he might feel that his behavior shows that the two of you are friends and share everything with one another.

Symbolic interactionism is the most micro of sociological approaches, as it often studies the activities of individuals and then draws connections to larger society from these. Studies of relationships, race, deviance, and even social movements can all use a symbolic interactionist approach.

Interactionists argue that individuals have the power to co-create the world, to make it what they want it to be. People develop standards and norms through a process of interacting with others. This way, we learn what is "normal" and acceptable behavior. Widespread social acceptance of a behavior is the main criterion in declaring it to be "normal," and we quickly learn that different situations allow for different behaviors. For example, if you're dating someone, kissing good night is a perfectly acceptable behavior. However, trying to kiss a co-worker good-bye could result in your being charged with sexual harassment.

Symbolic interactionism is a distinctly American way of looking at the world. In many ways it blends sociology and psychology. Let's take a look at the work of its founder, George Herbert Mead.

GEORGE HERBERT MEAD

Symbolic interactionism was the brainchild of George Herbert Mead (1863–1931), an American sociologist from the University of Chicago. After his death in 1931, Mead's former students were so committed to his legacy that they combined his articles, notes, and lectures into the book *Mind, Self, and Society*. This book introduced a new theory called symbolic interactionism.[35]

In *Mind, Self, and Society*, Mead suggests that the root of society is the symbols that teach us to understand the world. We then use these symbols to develop a sense of self, or identity. It is this identity that we then take into the world and interact with other identities to create society. Thus, the building blocks of society start with our minds, where we interpret symbols.

How do you learn to interpret symbols? Mead suggests that we do this through the micro interactions we have every day. When I was born, my parents named me John. When I got older, if someone

SELF refers to a person's identity and what makes that person different from others.

called, "John," I turned my head. Eventually, I learned nuances of the symbol John. For example, if my mother yelled my name, I knew I was in trouble. Mead argues that all these various symbols enter our minds, where their meaning is interpreted and we are told how to react. Mead suggests that this process is never-ending; therefore, we have a fluid sense of who we are. Our selves can change, and they do change based on how we interpret the symbols thrown our way.

In this way, your self develops. **Self** is your identity. It's what makes you who you are and separates you from others. According to Mead, you couldn't have a self without symbols or without someone to pass those symbols to you. In other words, you learn who you are through others.

In middle school, did you ever feel embarrassed by your parents? Do you feel the same level of embarrassment today? The answer to both questions is probably yes *and* no. When I ask this in class, most of my students report that they don't find their parents nearly as embarrassing as they used to. Why does this occur? It is because when you're young, you don't have a well-developed sense of self. You are anxious, taking your cue from others as to what is "cool" or acceptable. You worry that your parents' actions might reflect upon you. As you grow older, you've experienced thousands of interactions that have taught you who you are. This is why, the older you get, the less embarrassing your parents seem. You know yourself much better now than you did in middle school.

Mead proposed that symbols build society. Symbols have meaning, and meaning directs our lives. The symbols a society uses help us understand the people in that society. In the United States, we have accepted that we need the word "homeless" to discuss people who cannot afford housing. Symbols help us define a situation and determine what we should do about it. For example, Liebow finds that people often assign labels, such as "addict," "alcoholic," or "mentally ill," to the homeless, but not as often to people who have jobs. Some even use addiction as an excuse not to help the homeless—*Oh, he or she is just an addict.* If potential employers believe in these labels, then they will be less likely to hire homeless people, perpetuating a system that keeps them homeless.

▶▶ GO GL◉BAL

Homeless Labels Around the World

Assigning negative labels to the homeless occurs not only in the United States, but also in countries all over the world. In Finland during the 1980s, homelessness became associated with alcoholism. People related the two ideas so closely that the government in Finland had to step in to prevent such negative stereotyping. In China and India, people connect homelessness with a lack of governmental registration, which means that the homeless aren't seen as true citizens. In Peru, children living on the street are called *piranitas*, or little piranhas, which implies that they are dangerous and likely to resort to criminal behavior. People in Bangladesh equate homelessness with having a lack of morals.[36]

Criminal, alcoholic, immoral—these are only a handful of labels that exist for the homeless around the world. As Liebow noted, negative labels make it even more difficult for homeless individuals to rise above their situation. If people who are homeless are given an opportunity and adequate support, they can be just as successful and stable as any other members of society.

HERBERT BLUMER

Symbolic interactionist Herbert Blumer (1900–1987), a disciple of George Herbert Mead and former chair of the University of California, Berkeley sociology department, established three basic premises that define the symbolic interactionist perspective:

1. Human beings behave toward things on the basis of the meanings they ascribe to those things.
2. The meaning of such things is derived from, or arises out of, the social interaction that one has with others and society.
3. These meanings are handled in and modified through an interpretive process used by the person in dealing with the things he or she encounters.[37]

What does he mean? First, we all react to situations and people based on how we perceive them. Have you ever noticed that you can "dis" your mom, but if someone else does, you get defensive? This is because you ascribe meaning to the act of dissing that it's OK for someone in the family, but when outsiders join in, you circle the wagons and defend the group.

How did your feelings emerge? They probably occurred from the many years in which your mother cared for you. While she may drive you crazy sometimes, she certainly fed you, tucked you in at night, and nurtured you when you were sick. In other words, the social interactions you had with her support the meaning you ascribe to who can and cannot dis her.

Blumer proposed that the primary focus of the interactionist approach involves studying individual interactions with symbols. This micro focus places great importance on the idea that symbols have great power to affect society as a whole. The way we talk about something creates the way we deal with it. Consider this example: In the 1950s, many whites spoke using racial slurs. Today, such language is socially unacceptable. Has this change eliminated racism? Certainly not, but the level of racism in the United States has certainly declined. Are these two factors connected? Blumer would suggest that they are. Words convey meaning and meaning creates reality. Eliminating racist language moves society closer to eliminating racism.

Normally, people interpret the words and actions of those around them and determine their behavior based on this interpretation. This results in rational behavior, meaning that we tailor our responses to the setting after we've interpreted the reactions. However, in a group setting our behaviors are somewhat different. Generally, Blumer suggests that in a group setting we react without the same degree of thought we use in an individual decision. At some point, people stop thinking rationally and act in ways that they might not consider acceptable in a different setting. Last football season, our college team was losing an important game. A man in the stands became extremely distraught; four-letter words came from his mouth like steam out of Old Faithful. The stands were filled not with sailors, but with men, women, and children, and I'm sure this man would never have behaved this way at a PTA meeting. So why did this happen? Blumer would suggest that it was the result of collective excitement, an intense emotional behavior that makes it hard for us to think and act rationally. This is what Blumer calls **contagion**, a rapid, irrational mode in which people do not think rationally or clearly. In such a setting, they "lose their heads" and react emotionally. In this way, you can see that individual interactions can create social realities. Eventually, someone told the man to watch his mouth because there were children around. Initially, the foul-mouthed man seemed angry to be scolded in public, but he quickly "cooled down" as he noticed that a number of people around him were watching his behavior closely.

How do we react when others are watching? Sociologist Erving Goffman developed a theory about this.

> **Goffman's primary insight is that we are constantly trying to manage the impressions that others have of us. Impression management is the action we use to control what others think of us.** When the angry man at the football game "calmed down," it was probably because he was a season ticket-holder and he knew that we'd all see him again next week. He didn't want to come off as the "jerk who cusses."

ERVING GOFFMAN

Canadian sociologist Erving Goffman (1922–1982) developed a theory he called **dramaturgy**, a theory of interaction in which all life is like acting. Goffman uses this theory to compare daily social interactions to the gestures of actors on a stage. People are constantly "acting" in order to convince people of the character that they wish to portray to the outside world. Not to say that people are always "faking it," but rather that people are concerned about what the rest of the world will think of them, and they adjust their social interactions accordingly.

Frequently, we alter our behavior without much deliberate thought. For example, if you are on a first date, do you behave differently than the way you do with an old friend? Usually, on a first date you dress differently, talk differently, and eat carefully. You may be nervous, but you will also, without thinking about it, change your behavior. Why? Because you are taking extra care to make a good first impression, even if it means not being completely yourself. Goffman points out that managing impressions involves a complex series of actions and reactions. As a person gets older and has more "practice" in socializing, he or she may be better equipped to gauge the reactions that their actions will receive.[38]

HOWARD BECKER

Howard Becker, a sociologist from Chicago, suggests that human action is related to the labels attached to it. In his book, *Outsiders: Studies in the Sociology of Deviance*, Becker suggests that a label is attached to a certain behavior when a group with powerful social status labels it deviant. He suggests that deviance is rooted in the reactions and responses of others to an individual's acts.

The label of deviant, or conformist for that matter, is applied when people see our behavior and react to it. This sets up a self-fulfilling prophecy for behavior as people seek an identity that will match up to the expectations that others hold of them. Becker applied these ideas to the study of deviant behavior, but the idea of labeling theory applies to all identity issues, including gender, sexual orientation, and personal identity.

CONTAGION is a rapid, irrational mode in which people do not think rationally or clearly.

DRAMATURGY is a theory of interaction in which all life is like acting.

Consider the example of a five-year-old girl who has been labeled a "good girl." The theory would suggest that somewhere along the line, she did what others expected of her and that these people had power over her. Her parents asked her to take a bath and she did. She received a positive reward, "she's a good girl," and through repeated events throughout her life, she developed that sense of self whereby she never does anything remotely "dangerous" or out of line and always takes a bath. However, if this "good girl" becomes a "terrible teen" and her parents label her as a delinquent, she might stop bathing and start smoking. Becker would suggest that the label we ascribe to people has a major influence on their behavior.[39]

THE SYMBOLIC INTERACTIONISTS—AT A GLANCE

GEORGE HERBERT MEAD

To know a society is to understand its symbols.

HERBERT BLUMER

Collective Excitement = Irrational Behavior

ERVING GOFFMAN

"All the world's a stage!"

HOWARD BECKER

"Good girl" "Convict" "Bad boy"

CRITICISMS OF SYMBOLIC INTERACTIONISM

Critics of symbolic interactionism suggest that this perspective ignores the coercive effects of social structure, focusing too much on the power of the individual to co-create his or her world. If, for example, you're a slave, it doesn't matter whether or not you reject the ownership symbol or not. If you try to leave, you'll be punished.

Of course, we are all born into a culture and social setting. We don't create them as we go along. As a result, your parents, neighborhood, and nation of birth all influence how you see things. Had you been born in a different time or in a different culture, you might have believed totally different things.

The Three Paradigms— How Are They Interrelated?

In the sports arena, we tend to associate phenomenal players with the teams on which they play. The player's name and the team name become synonymous. Kobe Bryant and the Los Angeles Lakers. Tom Brady and the New England Patriots. Derek Jeter and the New York Yankees. You get the idea. The same is true of sociologists—we associate the theorist with the paradigm that he or she favored or had a hand in developing. For example, Marx is a symbol of conflict theory, whereas Comte and functionalism go hand in hand. However, sometimes it can be tricky to confine sociologists to such a tight box because they might use parts of each paradigm in their analyses. In fact, I know of no colleague of mine who is a "purist" in anything. That's because no single paradigm perfectly fits every situation. To get a complete picture, many sociologists use all three paradigms. In this way, the three paradigms are interrelated and work together to help us figure out why society is the way it is.

Think about sociologist Robert Merton and his concept of latent and manifest consequences. He takes a functionalist stance, but adds to it the notion that intended and unintended results can arise. Thus, we should ask, for whom is this functional? Can you see a bit of conflict theory here?

Like Merton, symbolic interactionist Howard Becker also blurs the lines between the paradigms. Becker's labeling theory can be linked to conflict theory because the labeling tradition suggests that those with power determine what is and is not labeled as deviant or criminal. In other words, the power of the label influences the outcome of the individual, but people with the ability to get what they want done put the label on us. Like a conflict theorist, Becker acknowledges that a system of inequality exists within our society. Consider this question: Why are cigarettes legal, while marijuana is illegal? Labeling theorists would argue that this is because people with power smoke cigarettes, but not pot. If powerful people ever started smoking pot, the practice would become legal.

We've seen how conflict theory overlaps with both functionalism and symbolic interactionism, but does functionalism ever overlap with symbolic interactionism? When Emile Durkheim suggests that values unify people, he sounds a bit like George Herbert Mead. The solidarity of a society for Durkheim is related to what it values, and he acknowledges that values change as societies become more modern.

The point for you as a student of sociology is to beware that just because a sociologist is classified as a functionalist, conflict theorist, or symbolic interactionist, that doesn't mean that he or she won't use other points of view in making an analysis of the world. In fact, at times, a theorist's point of view can be so eclectic that he can't be pinned down into a single category. This sentiment is especially true of sociologist Max Weber (1864–1920).

Overlapping Theories

Functionalism

Everything in the social world exists because it has both an intended outcome and an unintended outcome.

Power differentials (conflict theory) often indicate for whom things are functional and for whom they are not (functionalism).

Conflict Theory

Inequality exists in the social world because of differences between different groups' wealth and power.

People in power create labels and assign them to others (conflict theory), and these labels influence the outcomes of the individual (symbolic interactionism).

Symbolic Interactionism

Labels are attached to certain individuals; this practice sets up a self-fulfilling prophecy as people try to match their behavior to their labels.

THINK SOCIOLOGICALLY

Max Weber—Theorist Who Transcends Categorization

To me, Max Weber (1864–1920) is the German counterpart of Emile Durkheim because he wrote about a great variety of topics, used data in his analysis, and laid the foundations for high-quality sociological research. In his work, students often see a variety of ideas that seem to blend different schools of thought. Yet, he wrote at a time before many of these "schools" were clearly defined or established.

Because Weber wrote partly as a response to some of Karl Marx's ideas, many consider him a conflict theorist. Weber accepted that social classes influence our outcomes; however, he felt Marx's social class system was too simple. He proposed that all people have economic, political, and cultural conflicts that are related to their relative social position. As a result, being an owner does not necessarily make you important in society. Wealth is important, but political power and social standing are also important.

In other ways, Weber appeared to take a more functional approach, particularly when he discussed how bureaucracies function in society. Bureaucracies are formal organizations that are organized into a hierarchy of smaller departments. You might think of a large corporation or a government agency as a bureaucracy. Weber proposed that rational and ideal bureaucracies naturally occur because we need them. They provide clear lines of authority, divide tasks so that workers can specialize, and clearly define rules and expectations. Under such a type of leadership, societies and large organizations function smoothly and improve the function of society. Although Weber was well aware that few perfect bureaucracies existed, he argued that responsible leadership will tend toward the ideal because Western society is increasingly focused on achieving goals, and a rational bureaucracy is an efficient way to achieve those goals.[40]

Other colleagues of mine have suggested that Weber's ideas seem to lay the foundation for the symbolic interactionist school of thought.

Why? Because he pointed out how values influence our goals and affect our behaviors. In his book, *The Protestant Ethic and the Spirit of Capitalism*, Weber clearly linked a person's religious value to the societal creation of a capitalist economy. For him, capitalism arose in the Western world primarily because a religious value system that he called the "Protestant Ethic" emphasizes the accumulation of wealth as a marker of God's favor on a person.

Furthermore, Weber also discussed how values are important to the study of sociology. For example, he understood that sociologists are at risk of approaching their profession with personal values that might influence the outcome of their study. Weber stressed that sociology should be value-free. In other words, sociologists should study society as it is, not as they would like it to be. They should put their biases aside when analyzing a topic. He implied that personal values may impact social research, and therefore sociologists must strive to put such values aside when they make their analyses.

So, where does your professor put Weber? The more you read about social theorists, the more you will find that most of them blend ideas from all schools of thought.

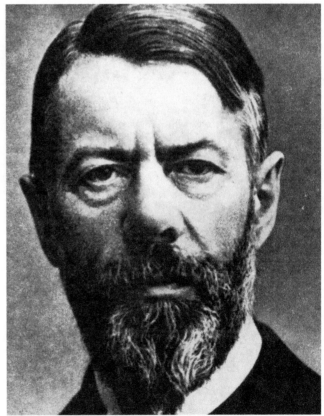

Courtesy of the Library of Congress

>>> Is Max Weber (pronounced *VAY-bur*) a conflict theorist? A functionalist? A symbolic interactionist? Or is he all three? **Sociologists everywhere disagree on how to classify Weber. That's because his views are so varied that he seems to defy categorization.**

APPLYING SOCIOLOGICAL THEORIES

Now it's time to think like a sociologist. Thinking like a sociologist means that you understand the topic, and you examine it from one or more of the three sociological theories covered in this section. Consider the problem of homelessness in a society. How might a functionalist view homelessness? How might a conflict theorist view it? A symbolic interactionist?

WRAP YOUR MIND AROUND THE THEORY

©Jeff Greenberg/PhotoEdit

Functionalists examine the entire social system to see how it works. **Do food banks and homeless shelters solve homelessness or perpetuate it?**

FUNCTIONALISM

Functionalists suggest society works as an inter-related system. Communitarians understand that if society is to run smoothly, the government, the local community, and the business sector must all work together for the well-being of all. The root of society is the local community; it anchors this societal tree. The government carries the will of the people to the economic system, thereby functioning as the trunk of this tree. The leaves of a tree make the sugar that allows the entire plant to live. Of course, leaves without roots blow over, and roots without leaves die.

CONFLICT THEORY

Conflict theorists would view homelessness as a sign of inequality in society. Conflict theorists focus on social class-es and their drastic differences in wealth, power, and prestige. They believe that the upper class controls society's wealth and resources and exploits the lower class. If the upper class shared its wealth, conflict theorists argue, then home-lessness would be cut down dramatically.

WHAT CAUSES HOMELESSNESS IN A SOCIETY?

SYMBOLIC INTERACTIONISM

Because symbolic interactionists view things on a smaller scale, they would explore how home-lessness affects the way individ-uals act toward one another. These theorists would ask: How do individuals behave toward one another? What labels do individuals assign to homeless-ness? How do non-homeless people interact with homeless people?

Conflict theorists look at the role of inequality in society. **Does urban renewal actually increase homelessness by eliminating low-cost housing while lining the pockets of wealthy developers?**

©Anthony Butera/SuperStock

Symbolic interactionists see social interactions as a result of how we define our social interactions. **Would you ignore this person merely because she appears homeless?**

©David Cooper/Toronto Star/ZUMA Press

discover sociology in action: WHY IS COMMUNITY LEARNING IMPORTANT TO A SOCIETY?

Getting Involved in Sociology— Community Learning

COMMUNITY LEARNING occurs when individuals and groups work to identify and address issues of public concern.

In *Tell Them Who I Am: The Lives of Homeless Women*, Elliot Liebow discusses how he often "loaned" money to many homeless women who had absolutely none. He was always careful to consider the money a "loan" because he knew that simply giving it to them would show that he thought of them as nothing more than panhandlers. Liebow figured he wouldn't get the money back, but he didn't mind.[41] His goal was to treat the women with dignity and earn their trust. Liebow was practicing community learning. **Community learning** occurs when individuals and groups work to identify and address issues of public concern.

It's easy for people to believe that social problems are so widespread that there is nothing we can do about them. Often, we feel so out of touch with the world around us that we do not vote, we do not know our neighbors, and we cannot name our town council members. Community learning, however, can help you see things with fresh eyes. Working in the community expands your understanding of sociology and your world.

ACTIVITIES

1. What community learning opportunities are available in your area? Surf the Web to find local shelters, food banks, or other organizations in your community. Choose an organization and volunteer there. Write about your experience.
2. Research your local and state governments. Who are the important government officials? What roles do they play in the government? What policies and issues do they support?
3. Homelessness is just one of many issues that plague today's society. What other social issues do you think are important to address and why? How would you try to solve these problems?

Liebow's study of the homeless showed him that homelessness is a widespread problem, and there is plenty of blame to go around. There are too many people who don't understand the problem, just ignore it, or both. When I worked at a local day shelter during my undergraduate days, I realized I had a lot to learn. One day, while serving lunch, I noticed that one of the patrons became quite irritated. "Hot dogs again!" he screamed. In shock, I thought that he had no right to complain when he could be eating nothing for lunch. An older and more experienced volunteer must have noticed my face because she said to me, "Sometimes, so many people look past them, that they just have to yell so you'll know they're there." That sobering comment brought me back to my senses. When you actually take a minute to view the world from someone else's perspective, you'll find it hard to just sit around and do nothing.

From Classroom to Community } Helping the Homeless

"Homeless people are just a bunch of drug addicts, aren't they?"

I wasn't surprised when Theo, one of my first-year sociology students, made this comment during a lecture. However, I was disappointed because I knew that many people around the world share this view. After a lively debate on the subject, I realized I hadn't changed Theo's mind, so I challenged him to volunteer at a local homeless shelter.

Day after day, Theo worked with the families at the shelter—feeding, clothing, and

talking with them. While at the shelter, he met a homeless mother who had been the victim of domestic violence.

"When I looked into that mother's face and the face of her children, I realized how narrow my viewpoint had been," Theo remarked to me later. "How did I ever think you could label an entire group of people?"

At the end of Theo's volunteer period, he wrote a paper for class revealing how much he had learned about the homeless. He even decided to continue working at the shelter. Volunteering made him feel like he was making a difference in the lives of the people he encountered, and he knew they were making a difference in his. Theo's experiences helped him realize that the people at the shelter were just like him. The only difference was that they had fallen on some bad luck.

Theo's story shows how moving out of the classroom and into the community helps people gain a new perspective. They can get out of their individual boxes and view the world as a sociologist would.

Courtesy of Library of Congress

WHAT IS SOCIOLOGY?

a science guided by the basic understanding that the social matters: our lives are affected not only by our individual characteristics, but by our place in the social world

WHAT ARE THE CHARACTERISTICS OF THE THREE MAJOR SOCIOLOGICAL PARADIGMS?

©Moodboard/Corbis

functionalism: defines society as a system of interrelated parts; primarily a macro orientation because it focuses on larger social structures rather than individuals

conflict theory: views society as an unequal system that brings about conflict and change; focuses on macro issues and supports the idea that the struggle for scarce resources holds a society together; concerned with inequality as it relates to wealth and power

symbolic interactionism: focuses on how individual people interact with other people in their everyday lives; studies how the use of "symbols" influence how people communicate; follows a micro approach because it is concerned with the individual's role in creating society .

WHY IS COMMUNITY LEARNING IMPORTANT TO A SOCIETY?

©Jeff Greenberg/PhotoEdit

provides you with a fresh perspective and expands your understanding of sociology and your world

get the topic: WHAT IS SOCIOLOGY?

Theory

FUNCTIONALISM

- society is a system of connected parts working together to keep society intact
- it is important to consider the function of any issue
- society is fairly stable, which means that things occur in society for a specific function
- suggests society will find a balance point of its own

CONFLICT THEORY

- focuses on social classes and their drastic differences in wealth, power, and prestige

- upper class controls society's wealth and resources and exploits the lower class
- once a group has power, they want to keep it, so they are likely to create advantages for themselves

SYMBOLIC INTERACTIONISM

- believes the root of society comes from its symbols
- society is fluid, meaning it is always in the process of change because the symbols we use and their interpretations change
- disputes arise when people do not share the same definitions of symbols

Key Terms

sociology	fatalistic suicides	social dynamics	proletariat
sociological imagination	anomic suicides	social Darwinism	false consciousnes
micro	paradigm	mechanical solidarity	class consciousness
macro	functionalism	organic solidarity	self
solidarity	conflict theory	functions	contagion
social control	symbolic interactionism	manifest functions	dramaturgy
egoistic suicides	social laws	latent functions	community learning
altruistic suicides	social statics	bourgeoisie	

MY SEARCH LAB

1. ***Invitation to Sociology*** by Peter L. Berger, reprinted from *Invitation to Sociology*, 1963, Anchor/Doubleday & Company, Inc. Copyright by Peter L. Berger, pp. 1–24. www.randomhouse.com

   In this classic 1963 essay, Berger explains the unique aspects of the sociological perspective.

1. Berger calls sociologists "professional peeping Toms." What does he mean by this?
2. What questions do sociologists ask when studying social phenomena? Use those questions to describe your college classroom.

2. *Manifest and Latent Functions*

In this 1957 excerpt, sociologist Robert Merton explains the difference between manifest and latent functions.

1. Explain the difference between manifest and latent functions. Now apply them to a social act. For example, what are the manifest and latent functions of the marriage ceremony?

2. Why is the distinction between manifest and latent functions important to the discipline of sociology?

3. *The Promise* by C. Wright Mills, reprinted from The Sociological Imagination, 1959. Copyright by Oxford University Press. pp. 3–24.

In this classic 1959 excerpt, C. Wright Mills (1916–1962) introduces the concept of the "sociological imagination."

1. Explain what Mills means by the "personal troubles of milieu" and the "public issues of social structure." What is the relationship between the two?

2. In this excerpt, Mills explains public temperament as feelings of well-being, crisis, indifference, and uneasiness. At the time of this writing, Mills believed that it was a time of uneasiness and indifference. How would you characterize the public temperament of society today? Why?

THE THINKSPOT

www.thethinkspot.com

What is the ThinkSpot and why have I chosen to include it in this text? The ThinkSpot is a place I encourage you to go to get more information on topics included in the chapter and to expand your critical thinking skills by looking at text and video that will help you analyze what you have learned.

To start, you can find a link that will take you to the *New York Times* and links to articles that may get you thinking, may help you craft a research paper, or you may want to read just for more information or dare I say "fun"? I've also included links, for this chapter in particular,

that will allow you to learn more about the sociologists we've discussed and how they crafted their theories. Of particular interest will be the short documentary of Karl Marx, a video of which can be found on the ThinkSpot.

It has been said that in the United States, "bigger is better." The same could be said for functionalist Talcott Parsons, not only a "giant" in the field of sociology but a big thinker when it came to how to think about the human experience and how social systems interconnect. A contemporary of Parsons, Robert Merton, set out to bridge the gap between grand theories and the study of individual parts of society. For more on both Parson and Merton, go to the ThinkSpot (www.TheThinkSpot.com).

Sample Test Questions

These multiple-choice questions are similar to those found in the test bank that accompanies this textbook.

1. Which of the following is a criticism of conflict theory?

   a. It overlooks that fact that many willingly accept society's rules.

   b. It does not recognize the differences between social classes.

   c. It fails to acknowledge social inequality.

   d. It is unsympathetic to homelessness.

2. Which of the following questions might a symbolic interactionist ask about the social world?

   a. Why does inequality exist in society?

   b. Why do income disparities occur between the races?

   c. How do social institutions keep society running smoothly?

   d. How does a particular social setting affect a person's behavior?

3. Erving Goffman's theory of dramaturgy suggests that

   a. people behave similarly in a variety of situations.

   b. people change their behavior to fit the setting they are in.

   c. people's behavior has little to do with others' perceptions of them.

   d. people's behavior is not affected by the behavior of others around them.

4. Which could be considered a latent function of slavery in the United States?

   a. The ease in which crops were harvested

   b. The increase in the growth of crops

   c. The mistreatment of African slaves

   d. The wealth farmers generated

5. All of the following are macro orientations *except*

   a. functionalism.

   b. conflict theory.

   c. social Darwinism.

   d. symbolic interactionism.

ESSAY

1. The three sociological paradigms often overlap with one another. Choose a sociologist discussed in the chapter. Discuss how his or her ideas connect to all three sociological paradigms.

2. Why is it important for a sociologist to use a sociological imagination? What consequences might arise if he or she failed to use this way of thinking?

3. What sort of attitudes concerning homelessness might a symbolic interactionist discourage?

4. Why is suicide a compelling sociological issue?

5. Describe possible manifest and latent functions of a law that would legalize drugs.

WHERE TO START YOUR RESEARCH PAPER

To learn more about sociology as a scientific discipline, go to
http://www.asanet.org

To find an in-depth sociology dictionary, go to
http://www.webref.org/sociology/sociology.htm

For more information about sociology departments in the United States, go to http://www.sociolog.com/us_links/

To find a guide for sociological Internet sources, go to
http://www.socioweb.com/

To find an online journal of sociology, go to
http://www.ou.edu/special/freeinq/

To find a Web site dedicated to finding out the truth about urban myths, go to http://www.truthorfiction.com/

To find an excellent source for different information on sociology, go to http://www.trinity.edu/~mkearl/theory.html

ANSWERS: 1. a; 2. d; 3. b; 4. c; 5. d

Endnotes

1. Reprinted with the permission of The Free Press, a Division of Simon & Schuster, Inc., *Tell Them Who I Am: The Lives of Homeless Women* by Elliot Liebow. Copyright © 1992 by Elliot Liebow. All rights reserved.

2. "Health of Sociology," *American Sociological Association*, 2007, http://www.asanet.org/galleries/Research/SocHealthsheet_Intro.pdf (accessed August 25, 2008).

3. C. Wright Mills, *The Sociological Imagination* (New York: Oxford, 1959).

4. Ibid.

5. Ibid.

6. Emile Durkheim, *Suicide*, edited by George Simpson, translated by John A. Spaulding and George Simpson (New York: The Free Press, 1897/1966).

7. Ibid.

8. Ibid.

9. Emile Durkheim, *Suicide*, edited by George Simpson, translated by John A. Spaulding and George Simpson (New York: The Free Press, 1897/1966); Robert Travis, "Halbwachs and Durkheim: A Test of Two Theories of Suicide," *British Journal of Sociology*, 1990. 41: 225–243.

10. Jean Stockard and Robert M. O'Brien, "Cohort Effects on Suicide Rates: International Variations," American Sociological Association, *American Sociological Review*, 2002. 67(6): 854–872.

11. Centers for Disease Control and Prevention, "Suicide: Fact Sheet" Atlanta, GA: Centers for Disease Control and Prevention, 2005, http://www.cdc.gov/ncipc/factsheets/suifacts.htm (accessed August 19, 2008).

12. Elliot Liebow, *Tell Them Who I Am: The Lives of Homeless Women* (New York: Penguin Books, 1995).

13. *Modern Sociological Theory, 6/e*, 2004. George Ritzer and Douglass J. Goodman New York: McGraw-Hill.

14. Jonathan Turner, Leonard Beeghily, and Charles H. Powers, *The Emergence of Sociological Theory* (Albany, NY: Wadsworth Publishing Company, 1998).

15. Kenneth Thompson, *Auguste Comte: The Foundation of Sociology* (New York: Halsted Press, 1975).

16. Jonathan Turner, Leonard Beeghily, and Charles H. Powers, *The Emergence of Sociological Theory* (Albany, NY: Wadsworth Publishing Company, 1998).

17. Emile Durkheim, *The Division of Labor in Society*, with introduction by Lewis A. Coser, translated by W.D. Halls (New York: Free Press, 1893/1997).

18. Ibid.

19. Ibid.

20. Vernon K. Dibble, *The Legacy of Albion Small* (Chicago: University of Chicago Press, 1975).

21. Talcott Parsons, *The Social System* (Glencoe, IL: The Free Press, 1951).

22. Ibid.

23. Robert K. Merton, *Social Theory and Social Structure* (Glencoe, IL: Free Press, 1957).

24. Ibid.

25. CNNMoney.com, "*Fortune 500 Women CEOs*," http://money.cnn.com/galleries/2008/fortune/0804/gallery.500_women_ceos.fortune/index.html (accessed July 6, 2010).

26. Susan Hoecker-Drysdale, *Harriet Martineau: First Woman Sociologist* (New York: St. Martin's Press, 1992).

27. Ibid.

28. "W.E.B. Du Bois," NAACP, http://www.naacp.org/about/history/dubois/ (accessed October 21, 2008).

29. W.E.B. Du Bois (William Edward Burghardt), "The Philadelphia Negro: A Social Study," pp.167–170 in *Readings in Social Theory: The Classical Tradition to Post-Modernism*, 4th edition, edited by James Farganis (New York: McGraw-Hill, 1899/2004).

30. Tukufu Zuberi, "Being Here and Being There: Fieldwork Encounters and Ethnographic Discoveries: W.E.B. Du Bois's Sociology: The Philadelphia Negro and Social Science," *The Annals of the American Academy of Political and Social Science*, 2004. 595: 146–156.

31. Joseph P. DeMarco, *The Social Thought of W.E.B. Du Bois* (Lanham, MD: University Press of American Inc., 1983).

32. Allen F. Davis, *American Heroine: The Life and Legend of Jane Addams* (New York: Oxford University Press, 1973).

33. Mary Jo Deegan, *Jane Addams and the Men of the Chicago School, 1892–1918* (New Brunswick, NJ: Transaction Books, 1988).

34. John Bellamy Foster, "The End of Rational Capitalism," *Monthly Review*, March 2005, http://findarticles.com/p/articles/mi_m1132/is_10_56/ai_n16126168/pg_1? tag5artBody;col1 (accessed September 11, 2008).

35. George H. Mead, *Mind, Self, and Society: From the Standpoint of a Social Behaviorist* (Chicago: University of Chicago Press, 1934/1962).

36. Suzanne Speak and Dr. Graham Tipple, "Perceptions, Persecution, and Pity: The Limitations of Interventions for Homelessness," *International Journal of Urban and Regional Research*, 2006. 30(1): 172–188.

37. Herbert Blumer, "Society as Symbolic Interaction," in Arnold M. Rose, *Human Behavior and Social Process: An Interactionist Approach* (Boston: Houghton-Mifflin, Reprinted in 1969).

38. Erving Goffman, *The Presentation of Self in Everyday Life* (Edinburgh: University of Edinburgh, Social Sciences Research Centre, 1958).

39. Becker, Howard. "Outsiders: Studies in the sociology of deviance." NY: The Free Press, 1991.

40. Jonathan Turner, Leonard Beeghily, and Charles H. Powers, *The Emergence of Sociological Theory* (Albany, NY: Wadsworth Publishing Company, 1998).

41. Elliot Liebow, *Tell Them Who I Am: The Lives of Homeless Women* (New York: Penguin Books, 1995).

SOCIOLOGICAL RESEARCH

From Chapter 2 of *THINK Sociology 2011*. John D. Carl. Copyright © by Pearson Education. Published by Prentice Hall. All rights reserved.

SOCIOLOGICAL RESEARCH

Observation

of the tearoom encounters . . . is made doubly difficult when the observer is an object of suspicion. Any man who remains in a public washroom for more than five minutes is apt to be either a member of the vice squad or someone on the make.

I assumed the role of the voyeur—a role superbly suited for sociologists and the only lookout role that is not overtly sexual . . . By serving as a voyeur-lookout, I was able to move around the room at will . . . and to observe all that went on without alarming my respondents or otherwise disturbing the action.

Identification of the sample was made by using the automobile license registers of the states in which my respondents lived . . . friendly policemen gave me access to the license registers without asking to see the numbers or becoming too inquisitive about the type of "market research" in which I was engaged.

Realizing that the majority of my participant sample were married—and nearly all of them are quite secretive about their deviant activity—I was faced with the problem of how to interview. . . . Clearly, I could not knock on the door of a suburban residence and say, "Excuse me, I saw you engaging in a homosexual act in a tearoom last year, and I wonder if I might ask you a few questions." Having already been jailed, locked in a restroom, and attacked . . . I had no desire to conclude my research with a series of beatings.

My research in tearooms required such a disguise. Does it then constitute a violation of professional ethics?...

Are there, perhaps, some areas of human behavior that are not fit for social scientific study at all? Should sex, religion, suicide, or other socially sensitive concerns be omitted from the catalogue of possible fields of sociological research? . . . [S]everal have suggested to me that I should have avoided this research subject altogether. Their contention has been that in an area of such sensitivity, it would be best to "let sleeping dogs lie." I doubt that there are any "sleeping dogs" in the realm of human interaction . . . Even if there are, sexual behavior in public places is not among them.

The wonder to me is not that some sociologist might endanger his ethical integrity and that of his profession by standing around in public lavatories making mental notes on the art of fellatio. . . . Concern about "professional integrity," it seems to me, is symptomatic of a dying discipline. Let the clergy worry about keeping their cassocks clean; the scientist has too great a responsibility for such compulsions!

I believe that preventing harm to his respondents should be the primary interest of the scientist. We are not, however, protecting a harassed population of deviants by refusing to look at them . . . Our concern about possible research consequences for our fellow "professionals" should take a secondary place to the concern for those who may benefit from our research.[1]

How Do We Learn About Society?

In *Tearoom Trade: Impersonal Sex in Public Places*, Laud Humphreys concludes that men use tearooms because they're bisexual or gay, and the social stigma of being openly gay is too great to endure.

Scandalous sex is nothing new in America. Whether it's Tiger Woods and his dozens of affairs, or U.S. Senator Larry Craig's visits to "tearooms"—public places, a men's room in this case, that serve as locations for sex acts between men[2]— sexual liaisons make news. When sociologists heard the news of Senator Craig, they immediately pointed to research by Laud Humphreys, detailed in his book, *Tearoom Trade*.[3] His findings showed that many married men have secrets; 54 percent of the men participating in tearooms were married and living with their wives and children, while only 14 percent were openly gay men.

Although Humphreys's research calls into question many ethical concerns, his studies prove that it's only through the use of sound scientific research that sociologists can learn. In our ongoing quest to think like a sociologist, this chapter will arm you with a precise understanding of research method weapons.

get the topic: WHAT ARE RESEARCH METHODS?

RESEARCH METHODS are the scientific procedures that sociologists use to conduct research and develop knowledge about a particular topic.

When students hear the term "sociological research" or "statistical analysis," they often feel dread. Visions of crunching numbers and memorizing formulas can strike fear in even the most committed of students. However, learning research methods is very different from that. Although it's true that research requires dealing with data and measurements, it also allows you to delve into the behaviors of your society. **Research methods** are the scientific procedures that sociologists use to conduct research and develop knowledge about a particular topic. So, to fully understand what sociology is, you have to be aware of what a sociologist *does*. And that means learning to think and act like a sociologist.

The first step in thinking like a sociologist is to comprehend the topic, and part of this involves understanding certain terms and research methods.

Research Methods

are the scientific process by which sociologists conduct research in an effort to develop knowledge

key concepts are

Objectivity
means by which research is conducted without bias
Variables
factors being studied
Causes
something that brings about change in something else
Correlation
measure of how two or more factors vary under certain circumstances

which help you understand

Step 6
Share and Publish Results

now you can complete

Qualitative
words, pictures, or photos
Quantitative
numeric form

which can be

Objectivity

The first concept in a sociologist's repertoire should be objectivity, the foundation for all sociological research. For sociologists, **objectivity** is the ability to conduct research without allowing personal biases or prejudices to influence them. They must put their own opinions and preconceived notions aside to study human behavior objectively. Being objective may seem simple, but it can be very difficult in practice. We all have our own opinions and prejudices, which can skew an objective point of view. For example, if you're studying the implication of ethics violations among NBA referees, your research might be swayed if you feel a particular referee has treated your favorite team unfairly. In that case, it's probably unwise to start this study after a bad call just cost your team a playoff game.

©Thomas Knuesselman/Corbis

Whether you're studying NBA referees or researching tearoom encounters in your area, it's important to be objective. Sociologist Max Weber (1864–1920) applied the term *verstehen*—understanding the meaning of action from the actor's point of view—to his research.[4] Weber argued that only when a researcher completely detaches himself or herself from a subject could accurate conclusions be drawn. When conducting a sociological study, you must enter your subject's world and check your personal prejudices at the door.

> **OBJECTIVITY** is the ability to conduct research without allowing personal biases or prejudices to influence you.
>
> **INDEPENDENT VARIABLES** are variables that are deliberately manipulated in an experiment.
>
> **DEPENDENT VARIABLES** are the response to the manipulated variable.
>
> **CONTROL VARIABLES** are variables that are kept constant to accurately test the impact of an independent variable.

Variables

It may be impossible to erase your own biases, but you can become aware of them and train yourself to see beyond them. Once you've accounted for your prejudices, you can then focus on the variables you will observe. Two types of variables exist in all kinds of research: independent and dependent. **Independent variables** are variables that are deliberately manipulated to test the response in an experiment, and **dependent variables** are the response to the manipulated variable. In other words, the dependent variable *depends* on the independent variable. Let's say you want to know if there's a connection between playing a musical instrument and doing well in school. In this case: playing an instrument = the independent variable, and your GPA = the dependent variable. When testing these two variables, a person's academic success, or lack thereof, is dependent upon whether or not he or she plays a musical instrument.

To determine the effect of playing an instrument on GPA accurately, though, you'll need to control these variables. **Control variables** are variables that are kept constant to accurately test the impact of an independent variable. These variables must be controlled because they might influence the results, which would lead the researcher to a false conclusion. If you compare the GPAs of students who play instruments to the GPAs of students who don't play instruments, you have to make sure that all other factors are equal. If all the students who don't play instruments also have learning disabilities, then you'll get skewed results. You'd have no way of determining whether the students' disability caused the poor GPA or if it was the absence of a musical gift. Control variables ensure that you are testing *only* the independent variable.

> ∧
> ∧ Max Weber's idea of *verstehen* suggested that **sociologists step out of**
> ∧ **their own shoes and into their subject's shoes when conducting a study.**

CAUSAL RELATIONSHIP is a relationship in which one condition leads to a certain consequence.

CAUSATION is the relationship between cause and effect.

CORRELATION is an indication that one factor might be the cause for another factor.

POSITIVE CORRELATION includes two variables that move in a parallel direction.

NEGATIVE CORRELATION occurs when variables move in opposite directions.

SPURIOUS CORRELATION occurs when two variables appear to be related, but actually have a different cause.

SOCIAL RESEARCH is investigation conducted by social scientists.

LITERATURE REVIEW is a study of relevant academic articles and information.

THEORY is a comprehensive and systematic explanation of events that lead to testable predictions.

HYPOTHESIS involves a suggestion about how variables relate.

CONCEPTS are abstract ideas that are impossible to measure.

OPERATIONALIZING is turning abstract ideas into something measurable.

Cause and Correlation

A **causal relationship** is one in which a condition or variable leads to a certain consequence. To understand causal relationships, you need to recognize the difference between causation and correlation. **Causation** is the relationship between cause and effect. Suppose I let go of a pencil. Gravity *causes* the pencil to fall to the floor. According to the law of gravity, the same cause results in the same effect every time. Correlations, unlike causes, are not laws because they do not guarantee a certain effect. Instead, a **correlation** is an indication that one factor *might* be a cause for another factor. Consider this correlation using the variable we discussed: Students who play musical instruments generally have higher GPAs than students who don't play an instrument. There is a correlation between the study of music and one's GPA. However, that doesn't mean that playing an instrument will always result in a higher GPA. There are other factors that come into play, such as how much you study and whether you apply what you learn. Unlike gravity, the correlation between instrumental music and grades is not a *law*.

Causes always create the same effects; correlations don't. Although it's likely that there is a relationship between getting good grades and playing an instrument, it's not a sure thing.

There are three types of correlations—positive, negative, and spurious. A **positive correlation** involves two variables moving in a parallel direction. In other words, you can find a positive correlation when variables increase or decrease together. Take the relationship between one's level of education and income. It has been observed that people with higher levels of education earn higher incomes.[5] This is a positive correlation because both variables trend in the same direction. A second type of relationship between variables is called a **negative correlation**, which occurs when the variables move in opposite directions. So, if you notice your grades slip as your Internet surfing or TV watching increases, that is a negative correlation. The third type is a spurious correlation. Spurious means not genuine or authentic, so a **spurious correlation** occurs when two variables appear to be related, but actually have a different cause. So, if you're looking at statistical data and notice that ice cream sales and the drowning rate are both increasing, that doesn't mean that someone eating a hot fudge sundae is destined to drown in a swimming pool. Another

factor is probably affecting these statistics. In this case, these increases are likely occurring in the hot summer months, when more people happen to be buying ice cream and going swimming. This proves that researchers should always be wary of spurious correlations.

Scientific Method: What Are the Six Steps of Social Research?

Doing sociological research follows many of the same procedures as any type of scientific research. After all, sociology is the scientific study of society. By requiring a logical and organized series of steps, sociologists ensure accurate results. In the next section of this chapter, we will review the six steps of **social research**, or investigation conducted by social scientists. As with any type of research, you first need to decide what topic you want to find out more about.

1 **Decide on a Topic** The first stage of the research model involves determining what you want to study. In order to take this step, researchers bring to light a question they want answered. Sociologists select topics on the basis of importance, personal interest, or the availability of research.

2 **Review the Literature** After you select a topic, you'll need to perform a **literature review**, which is a study of relevant academic articles and information. This is essentially an organized effort to research your topic. Literature reviews let you know what other researchers think about a particular topic and what they have discovered through their research. For example, if you were still examining how playing instruments affects one's GPA, you might review scholarly articles written by sociologists who've examined the same idea. Viewing their methodology will help you improve upon their work and avoid making any of the same mistakes they made.

3 **Develop a Hypothesis** After you have completed the initial research of your topic, it is time to formulate a hypothesis. It is important not to confuse a hypothesis with a theory. A **theory** is a comprehensive and systematic explanation of events that lead to testable predictions. These testable predictions are the basis for what we call a hypothesis.[6] A **hypothesis** involves a suggestion about how variables relate. For example, my hypothesis that students who play a musical instrument will have high GPAs is dependent on the theory that students who earn good grades are more likely to play an instrument than students who earn bad grades, and that music is part of the reason they do better. My hypothesis is a way for me to test that theory by manipulating variables. In this case, the two variables are playing an instrument and the students' grades.

Concepts and Operationalizing Variables

So how are we supposed to measure these variables anyway? You might notice that the two variables above are not very specific. What does it mean to *play* an instrument? Will playing once a week be enough? Do you have to be an exceptional musician, or can your music be mediocre? Also, what does a *good* GPA entail exactly? Is 3.1 a good GPA? In order to create a testable hypothesis, we'll need to be a bit more specific. Right now, "playing a musical instrument" and getting a "good grade" are just **concepts**, or abstract ideas that are impossible to measure. Turning these abstract ideas into something measurable is called **operationalizing** the variables. If you operationalize "playing an instrument" into "hours spent playing the instrument," you now have a variable that's measurable in minutes. Likewise, we can change the relative idea of "a better grade" into a more measurable "grade of A." Now that we have a hypothesis, we can move on to designing a research strategy.

4 **Collect Data** You have a hypothesis, so now what? Now you'll have to test that hypothesis to see whether data support or refute your idea. Collecting data means using a research design to help you. A **research design** refers to the process used to find information. Designs need to be both logical and orderly so that the research is reliable and valid. A logical, orderly design isn't the only thing that'll guarantee your research is up to snuff. For research to be **reliable**, or able to be trusted, you must measure things the same way, every time. If you alter your measuring technique in any way, your results could easily change. **Validity** assures that you're actually measuring the thing you set out to measure in the first place. In our example, you wouldn't want your professor to use your musical taste to determine what kind of grade you get in class. To collect data that are both reliable and valid, sociologists use a variety of strategies, which include conducting studies.

Comparative, Cross-Sectional, and Longitudinal Studies

Comparative studies use data from different sources in order to evaluate them against each other. International comparisons often use data from different countries and put them side by side. You should be aware, though, that comparative data across cultures might have methodological problems. For example, the definition of a drug offense differs greatly between the Netherlands and the United States. What passes as taboo in one country might be perfectly permissible in another.

The majority of available data in sociology are the result of cross-sectional studies. Like a camera capturing a singular moment,

> **RESEARCH DESIGN** refers to the process used to find information.
> **RELIABLE** means able to be trusted.
> **VALIDITY** assures that you're actually measuring the thing you set out to measure in the first place.
> **COMPARATIVE STUDIES** use data from different sources in order to evaluate them against each other.
> **CROSS-SECTIONAL STUDIES** look at one event at a single point in time.
> **LONGITUDINAL STUDIES** include data from observations over time using a cohort.
> **COHORT** is a specific group of people used in a study.

cross-sectional studies look at an event at a single point in time. Researchers may use a variety of cross-sectional studies to try to track trends in society. However, these may not always include data gathered from the same people. To learn how specific people change over time with the changes in society, researchers conduct longitudinal studies.

Longitudinal studies include data from observations over time using a specific group of people called a **cohort**. These types of studies allow the researcher to provide measures of the same group over a period of time. The period of time can be extensive, and researchers frequently take multiple measures over a period of years. Although this longitudinal information can be expensive and time-consuming to gather, it is useful in illustrating trends and showing how segments of society change.

MAKE CONNECTIONS

Country Music and Suicide

Back in 1992, researchers wanted to study the relationship between country music and its listeners. Researchers Steven Stack and Jim Gundlach found positive correlations between country music airplay and white male suicide rates in metropolitan areas.[7] According to their research, common themes in country music created a subculture that essentially led men to suicide. These themes include problems with personal relationships, including divorce and infidelity, alcohol consumption, and general hardships like work problems or death. Sara Evans's *Cheatin'*, Toby Keith's *Get Drunk and Be Somebody,* and Johnny Paycheck's *Take This Job and Shove It* are all songs that fit these themes.

The researchers took data from 49 different metropolitan areas in the United States. To prevent a spurious conclusion, they used poverty, divorce, gun availability, and region of the country as control variables. For example, because divorce has a strong influence on the suicide rate, the researchers had to make sure that this variable didn't affect their results. In their analysis, they showed that the white male suicide rates

positively correlated with the amount of radio airtime of country music.

The conclusion was that country music contributed to an ideology that supported suicide. Because people tend to listen to songs many times, the power of their thematic message is stronger than other media. These themes help create a subculture in which individuals perceive a world full of sadness, drinking, and exploitation.

Following this research, a statistical and methodological debate raged. Sociologists Maguire and Snipes tried to retest the data, but failed to duplicate Stack and Gundlach's 1992 results.[8] Maguire and Snipes claimed the original authors were mistaken because they did not take into account how other factors in their subjects' lives might have contributed to their actions. Stack and Gundlach stuck by their research. In a series of articles, each designed to respond to the other, these two camps argued over which side's research was valid.

Can you see problems with the research, particularly as associated with spuriousness and correlation? Is it possible that there is another relationship being depicted? For example, since white men are more likely to listen to country music than other ethnic groups, perhaps more

country music is aired in metropolitan areas with higher concentrations of white men.[9]

>>> **ACTIVITY** Pick three songs within a particular genre (i.e., hip-hop, rock, pop), and examine their lyrics. Do these songs express anything about the culture in which we live? If so, how do you think this affects people who listen to this type of music? Is there a spurious correlation?

©Angelo Cavelli/Corbis

∧ **Could country music**
∧ have **led** this man **to**
the edge?

International Voting Statistics

In the United States, media messengers often talk about how few people actually turn out to vote. But does the United States actually have fewer people involved in voting than other nations do? The International Institute for Democracy and Electoral Assistance is a nongovernmental organization that keeps track of democracy and voting worldwide. In a study of voter turnout from 1945 to 2001, they found that Australia ranks first in voter turnout, boasting almost 95 percent of registered voters voting in 22 different elections during that time. The United States, in 17 national elections, saw only 66 percent of registered voters actually vote. Our ranking was 120th out of possible 169 different countries.[10] However, many of these nations listed are relatively recently created democratic governments. Thus, they do not have the same ratio of elections over time. Do such statistics provide you with an insight as to how the American people view their democracy compared to other residents of democratic nations? Check out the graphic to the right, which provides data from nations with at least 15 elections over the same period of time.

Country	Percentage turnout of registered voters
1. Australia	94.5
4. Liechtenstein	92.8
5. Belgium	92.5
10. Austria	91.3
13. New Zealand	90.8
15. Italy	89.9
18. Iceland	89.5
23. Thailand	88.3
26. Netherlands	87.5
27. Sweden	87.1
32. Denmark	85.9
36. Argentina	84.2
48. Norway	80.4
50. Israel	80.3
53. Greece	79.9
71. Finland	76.0
76. United Kingdom	75.2
83. Canada	73.9
84. France	73.8
87. Ireland	73.3
109. Japan	69.5
120. United States	66.5
122. Mexico	65.2
154. Guatemala	51.6
161. Colombia	47.6

Source: The International Institute for Democracy and Electoral Assistance, "Voter Turnout Since 1945: A Global Report," http://www.idea.int/publications/vt/upload/VT_screenopt_2002.pdf.

Survey

A **survey** is an investigation of the opinions or experience of a group of people by asking them questions. In sociological research, surveys are necessary to gauge valuable information. Institutions ranging from government agencies to marketing teams rely on survey responses to determine how the general public feels about their policies or their products. Surveys include interviews and questionnaires. Seeing as how it would be nearly impossible to survey every single individual within a specific population, researchers need to be more focused.

How to Conduct a Survey

Sociologists generally use the following seven steps to conduct a survey:

1. Clarify Your Purpose—What do I want to find out?

2. Define Your Population—Who do I want to study?

3. Choose a Sample—I can't study everyone so I have to choose a few people to represent the entire population.

4. Prepare Questions—Do my questions really ask what I think they are asking?

5. Decide How to Collect Data—Do I want to conduct face-to-face interviews or handout surveys?

6. Collect the Data—What procedures must I follow?

7. Record, Analyze, and Interpret the Data—What do these data mean?

Populations

For starters, researchers need to determine the specific **populations**, or target groups, from which they wish to gain information. Perhaps you're interested in discovering what commuter students think about the parking situation on campus. Ideally you'd ask every student with a car on campus, but that would take a lot of time and money. Because researchers also have limits on their resources, they have to practice **parsimony**, or extreme unwillingness to use resources, so that they get the most for their effort.

Samples

To get the most bang for their buck, sociologists only give surveys to a **sample**, or subset of the population, selected for research. In order to produce a reliable result, samples should represent an accurate picture of the population.

When sociologists study a part of the population, the percentages in the sample should reflect the percentages of women, racial minorities, and other groups that exist in the population. In short, the sample needs to look like the population so we can generalize the findings. **Generalization** is the extent that what is learned from a sample can be applied to the population from which the sample is taken. Would it be fair to take the results of Humphreys's research and apply it to every male who enters a bathroom in the United States? Certainly not. Why? Humphreys's research was conducted in the St. Louis area, meaning that his findings may or may not reflect bathroom behavior in California, Texas, or New York. Humphreys did not claim that one could take the results of his study and apply them to the entire country. To do that would require a special type of sampling.

A **random sample** is a group of subjects arbitrarily chosen from a defined population. This type of sample increases the chances that the sample represents the population. Randomness means that everyone in the population has an equal chance of selection for the sample. However, few true random samples exist, especially if the entire country is the target population. But, random samples are the true research method that allows a social scientist to know his or her sample looks like the population.

SURVEY is an investigation of the opinions or experience of a group of people by asking them questions.

POPULATIONS are target groups from which researchers want to get information.

PARSIMONY is extreme unwillingness to use resources.

SAMPLE is a subset of the population.

GENERALIZATION is the extent that what is learned from a sample can be applied to the population from which the sample is taken.

RANDOM SAMPLE is a group of subjects arbitrarily chosen from a defined population.

OVERSAMPLING is the process of taking a bigger sample if the group you wish to study makes up a small percentage of the whole population.

SAMPLE OF CONVENIENCE is a nonrandom sample available to the researcher.

SELECTION EFFECTS are the likelihood that a nonrepresentative sample may lead to inaccurate results.

Many national surveys, therefore, rely on random samples and can, with as few as 1,000 people, make predictions about what Americans think about specific issues. Although sample size can affect the power of the predictions, after a certain point, the advantage of a bigger sample becomes almost irrelevant. Thus, samples are usually as small as possible. However, if you want to use the survey for a variety of purposes, it might be a smart practice to make the sample bigger. This is called **oversampling**. You need to oversample if the group you wish to study makes up a small percentage of the whole population. Let's say you want to understand how race and ethnicity affect the way people vote. Because Latinos make up approximately 13 percent of the U.S. population, and blacks make up 12 percent, a random sample of 1,000 people would correlate to roughly 130 Latinos and 120 blacks. A sample of 1,000 might be large enough if you were not interested in studying race; however, these numbers would be too small to help a researcher understand how blacks and Latinos vote. Therefore, the researcher might draw a much larger sample to capture the information of minority groups and thus be able to answer the research question about how minority status affects voting.

Selection Effects and Samples of Convenience

Even though random samples are preferred, other types of samples are often used. Researchers may use a **sample of convenience**, which is a nonrandom sample available to the researcher. These are simply people we can find to study. These samples often suffer from **selection effects**; that is, the likelihood that a nonrepresentative sample may lead to inaccurate results.

Think back to Laud Humphreys's study of tearooms. His results showed that 54 percent of men involved in tearooms were married. Does that mean over half of all men participating in tearooms were married? No, it only signals that 54 percent of men he spoke to were married. To suggest that his findings would imply that most men who frequent tearooms are married is overstating the power of the research. Why? Because Humphreys used a sample of convenience. Of course, nonrandom samples can be quite valuable because they help illustrate a problem, illuminate issues, and test theories, but one cannot generalize the findings from them to the larger population. Therefore, all men who frequent tearooms probably don't look like the men in Humphreys's study.

Experiments

Like any good scientist, a sociologist uses experiments to test ideas. In an experiment, researchers hope to control variables in order to test causes and effects. Sociological experiments do the same thing, but some may test people's interactions or other social causes of human behavior. Read the *Think Sociologically* feature to learn about a series of experiments Stanley Milgram conducted in the 1960s.

THINK SOCIOLOGICALLY

Milgram Obedience Study

Social psychologist Stanley Milgram created a series of experiments to test a subject's ability to reject the orders of a perceived superior. In the experiment, two subjects enter a room where a man in a lab coat meets them. This individual, called "the experimenter," takes on the role of the authority figure. The subjects are told they are going to be a part of a study to test the effects of punishment on learning. One of the subjects role-plays as the "teacher," while the other—who is secretly one of Milgram's assistants—is the "learner."

The subjects are then led into a room where the "learner" is strapped into a chair with electrodes attached to him. The experimenter assures both subjects that while pain will result, no permanent damage will occur.

The teacher is placed in front of an electroshock machine and separated from the learner. If the learner failed to recall a series of paired words, the teacher was supposed to administer an electric shock. With each error, the teacher was instructed to increase the voltage. In reality, the learner was only acting and never received a shock, unbeknownst to the teacher.

Throughout the experiment, some subjects would pause when they heard learners cry "ouch" or "I want to quit." The scripted responses also included groans, screams, and even silence. When teachers questioned whether they should continue to inflict pain on the learner, they were told, "Please go on" and/or "You must go on."

Milgram found that 65 percent of the teachers administered up to 450 volts, even when there was no reply and despite the fact that the dial on the machine for this voltage read "danger."

Milgram points out that subjects would shock others to unconsciousness and even death on the command of a stranger who represented authority. Thus, Milgram suggests that when faced with an authority figure, most people follow orders even if those orders go against their better judgment.[11]

Courtesy of Alexandra Milgram. Copyright 1968 by Stanley Milgram. Copyright renewed 1993 by Alexandra Milgram. From the film OBEDIENCE, distributed by Penn State Media Sales

If you were the teacher in Milgram's research, **what action would you have taken based on the learner's response?**

Hawthorne Effect

The seminal Milgram experiment documented what happens when a subject is unaware that he is being experimented on. But what about people who are cognizant of the experiment? In the 1930s, an electric company hired researchers to test worker productivity in its Hawthorne Works factory outside Chicago. After pretesting worker performance, researchers made the lighting brighter. They quickly noticed that brighter lights seemed to make people work harder. However, when they later turned down the lights, productivity increased once again. In fact, every step the researchers took helped boost the workers' productivity.

Why did every change, even ones that seemed like it might hinder productivity, have the same effect? Researchers believed it was because the subjects knew they were being studied. Thus, the **Hawthorne effect** was coined for occurrences in which people behave differently because they know they are part of an experiment.[12] Unlike the experiment at the Hawthorne factory, Milgram's experiment used subjects who did not know they were being studied. When conducting experiments and studies, sociologists must make sure that the Hawthorne effect does not influence their findings.

FIELD RESEARCH

It would be difficult to study society without actually mingling with the people you're observing. Therefore, researchers need to venture out and conduct studies in a natural setting. This **field research** takes the sociologist out into the streets. There are three common methods of field research—participant observation, case studies, and ethnography.

Participant Observation

In *Tearoom Trade,* Laud Humphreys describes how he "assumed the role of the voyeur" by observing the men who engaged in public sex without actively participating himself. Humphreys practiced **participant observation**, a type of field research in which the researcher poses as a person who is normally in the environment. Participant observation decreases the chances of the Hawthorne effect because subjects do not know they're being studied.

As a voyeur, Humphreys learned signals to use to inform participants of police presence or accidental passersby. Eager to find out more information about the men, Humphreys needed to expand the sample further. This led him to secretly record some participants' personal information. About a year later, posing as a health survey researcher, Humphreys visited many of the men in their homes. By becoming a participant in the men's activities and misleading them to gain access to their personal lives, Humphreys gained the men's trust and was able to conduct his study more freely.

Case Studies

Unlike participant observations, **case studies** investigate one person or event in detail. Such a study is able to illuminate a complex issue through the lens of an individual case. Isabelle, a feral child who had spent most of her six years in a dark room with minimal human contact, is an example of a case study.[13] This case study includes not only a history of neglect both emotionally and physically, but also provides a compelling tale about experts who worked to develop her potential. When Isabelle was discovered, she could communicate using only grunts and invented gestures. Remarkably, Isabelle was able to improve her social skills and fully integrate into mainstream society. Some critics believe case studies are subjective because it's tricky to generalize the findings of an individual case to fit a larger group.[14] For example, the findings in Isabelle's case don't fit *all* feral children because some might not be able to fully develop.

Ethnography

An **ethnography** is a research method that aims to understand the social perspective and cultural values of a particular group by participating with or getting to know their activities in detail. In 1991, Ralph Weisheit articulated the complex nature of Illinois's illegal marijuana crop

HAWTHORNE EFFECT occurs when people behave differently because they know they are part of an experiment.

FIELD RESEARCH is research conducted in a natural setting.

PARTICIPANT OBSERVATION is a type of field research in which the researcher poses as a person who is normally in the environment.

CASE STUDIES are investigations of one person or event in detail.

ETHNOGRAPHY is a research method that aims to understand the social perspective and cultural values of a particular group by participating with or getting to know their activities in detail.

SECONDARY DATA are data that others have already collected and published.

SECONDARY DATA ANALYSIS is the process of using and analyzing data that others have collected.

economy, showing that often there is more involved than simply a desire to support the illegal drug trade. Interviewing about 30 marijuana farmers in rural Illinois, Weisheit presented a context for this phenomenon by showing that growers often have different motives for their illegal deeds. Marijuana farmers fall into one of three groups—*hustlers*, *pragmatists*, and *communal cultivators*. Hustlers grow marijuana for the large profits and are clearly driven by a desire for the money. Pragmatists, the largest group of growers, generally don't use the drug. Instead, they farm marijuana because they are in financial trouble often caused by poor prices of legitimate cash crops or a desire to provide better support for their families. Communal growers cultivate marijuana because they wish to use the drug themselves, and this is a method to secure access to it. They sell their surplus, but their primary goal is personal use. In each case, the threat of incarceration is not a great enough deterrence to cause any of the growers to stop their illegal activity.[15]

Secondary Data Analysis

Sociologists don't always have to collect new data. Instead, sociologists sometimes need to access **secondary data**, or data that others have already collected and published. The process of using and analyzing data others have collected is known as **secondary data analysis**. A variety of data sources exist for sociologists to use. Not surprisingly, the World Wide Web contains many of these sources. Census data, crime statistics, journal entries, and transcripts of speeches are just a few of the examples of secondary data found on the Web.

	Research Methods: How Do They Measure Up?		
Method	Example	Pros	Cons
Survey	Interview	• Sampling process lets researcher apply data from a few subjects to an entire population	• Time-consuming • Difficult to find participants
Experiments	Manipulation of variables to study human behavior	• Gives researcher specific quantitative data	• Ethical concerns put restrictions on the way human subjects can be used
Field Research	Case study	• Can study behavior in a natural environment • Can be inexpensive	• Time-consuming • Ethical concerns put restrictions on the way human subjects can be used
Secondary Data Analysis	Another sociologist's analysis of population data	• Inexpensive • Reduces time spent to collect data	• Data not collected for the purpose in which you are using it • Data could be biased by the collector

5 **Analyze Results** The fifth step of the scientific method, analyzing results, involves the dreaded "S-word." No, not *that* word. The term I'm thinking of is *statistical* analysis. Because sociological research can delve into very complex statistics, it's important that you learn a few basics that will help you confidently confront any statistics you encounter now or in the future.

MEASURES OF CENTRAL TENDENCY

You know how news outlets report on the national price of a gallon of gasoline? Sometimes, the price you hear on the radio ends up being lower—or higher—than the one at the pump. This is because the reporters were only finding a measure of **central tendency**. To put it simpler, researchers look at an

> **John's Test Scores**
>
> Test 1: 90
> Test 2: 70
> Test 3: 80
> Test 4: 20
> Test 5: 80

array of numbers and find the ones that are in the middle. There are three measures of central tendency—mean, median, and mode. Imagine that a student received the test scores listed above. How would you calculate the mean, median, and mode?

Mean

A **mean** is an average. You add up all the scores and then divide by the number of scores. John's mean score is 68. Does this average accurately measure his performance? He failed one exam, but received a C or better on all other tests. It doesn't seem fair that one bad grade leaves John with a D average for the class. That's the problem with calculating mean scores. Extremely high or low scores can have dramatic impact on statistical means.

$$90 + 70 + 80 + 20 + 80 = 340$$
$$340 \div 5 = 68$$
$$Mean = 68$$

Median

When you're cruising down the highway—after blowing your savings on that full tank of gas—you might notice the northbound lanes are separated from southbound ones by a median. In statistical analysis, the **median** refers to the midpoint in a distribution of numbers. If you line up the numbers from lowest to highest, the median is the one in the middle. The median does not vary when you have extremely high or extremely low values in the distribution. John's median score is 80.

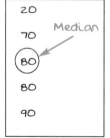

Mode

The **mode** refers to the most common value in a distribution of numbers. Extremely high or low scores do not impact this measure either. It's possible to have more than one mode in a distribution of numbers. In our simple example, 80 is the mode because it occurs twice. You will notice that the modal score in this example is the same as the median. Both give John a final grade of a B. Which measure of central tendency best shows John's performance?

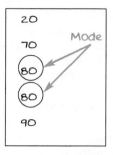

Most colleges have a policy of using averages to calculate grades. However, when I review grades at the end of the semester, I frequently take all three measures of central tendency into account. In most cases, the mean is close to the median and the mode. However, an extreme score can alter the mean score dramatically, as in John's case. If you have a low score on an exam, consider asking your professor to consider other measures of central tendency to calculate your performance. It might just raise your grade!

EVALUATING DATA

Evaluating and interpreting data are important parts of conducting research. What's the use of gathering data if you don't know what to do with them? It's vital to be able to make sense of the data you collect. The tables and graphs you will encounter during the research process may seem daunting at first. But it's really not as complicated as you might think, as long as you know what steps to take.

HOW TO READ A TABLE

The table to the right provides statistics from the Centers for Disease Control and Prevention. These data can give you a snapshot of fertility and abortion trends in the United States. If at first you look at this table and it makes no sense, don't worry. Fortunately, there are four simple steps that you can follow to help you read this and all tables.

If you struggled to make sense of the table, don't worry. You're not alone. Fortunately, the four simple steps that follow will help make reading this and other tables second nature to you.

1. Carefully read the title of the table. Ask yourself: What do I expect the table to show me? The title of this table is Fertility Trends in the United States. That is what you are supposed to see.

2. Notice the structure of the table. This one is made up of columns and rows. The columns represent a specific category, or in this case, years. The rows give you a list of the categories studied, such as total pregnancy, total fertility, and abortion rates.

3. This table has an important subheading. In italics, you see the phrase, "*rates = per 1,000 women.*" In a table with rates, it is quite common to tell the reader how that rate was calculated.

4. Read any text and notes provided below the table.
   • The note at the bottom of the table tells you where the author found these data. In this case, the numbers come from the Centers

for Disease Control and Prevention, part of the U.S. Department of Health & Human Services, and the official repository for health data in the United States.

Now review the table again. Do the data make more sense now?

6 **Share and Publish Results** Doing research is important; however, if we don't share what we learn with others, our work is meaningless. Sharing allows others to read and use your findings in their own research, which ultimately expands the base of knowledge.

CENTRAL TENDENCY is the numbers in the middle of an array of numbers.

MEAN is an average.

MEDIAN refers to the midpoint in a distribution of numbers.

MODE refers to the most common value in a distribution of numbers.

Publishing requires an appropriate writing style. Most sociology research follows the American Sociological Association style. In the ASA style guide, you'll find standards for using language and directions on how to cite sources appropriately. If you need a quick style guide, be sure to visit their Web site at http://www.asanet.org/.

Fertility Trends in the United States. Rates = per every 1,000 women				
	2005	2000	1996	1990
TOTAL PREGNANCY RATE	3.17	3.24	3.18	3.42
White	2.65	2.72	2.68	2.93
Black	4.18	4.58	4.56	5.21
Hispanic	4.26	4.17	4.26	4.53
TOTAL FERTILITY RATE	2.05	2.06	1.98	2.08
White	1.84	1.87	1.78	1.85
Black	2.02	2.18	2.14	2.50
Hispanic	2.88	2.73	2.77	2.95
TOTAL ABORTION RATE	.6	.97	.71	.83
White	.33	.38	.44	.61
Black	1.55	1.75	1.78	1.92
Hispanic	.77	.87	.91	.97

Source: "Estimated Pregnancy Rates for the United States, 1990–2005: An Update," National vital statistics reports: Vol 58, Number 4 Centers for Disease Control and Prevention, http://www.cdc.gov/nchs/data/nvsr/nvsr58/nvsr58_04.pdf.

ETHICS is a system of values or principles that guide one's behavior.

QUANTITATIVE DATA refer to data based on numbers.

QUALITATIVE DATA include words, pictures, photos, or any other type of information that comes to the researcher in a nonnumeric form.

CONTENT ANALYSIS is a type of research in which the sociologist looks for common words or themes in newspapers, books, or structured interviews.

ETHICAL CONCERNS

Have you ever had to do something that violated your personal beliefs or values? Of course you have. Sociologists struggle with this issue all the time. Sometimes, a sociologist's findings have the potential to hurt or embarrass the human subjects of a particular study. Deciding how to protect human subjects is a major concern for sociological researchers. In *Tearoom Trade*, Humphreys addressed some of the ethical questions that surrounded much of his research.

Ethics is a system of values or principles that guide one's behavior. For some, it means following the law, and for others, trusting one's gut. The American Sociology Association's code of ethics lays down standards for sociological research. Five general principles make up ethical practice in sociology.[16]

1 **Professional competence** refers to the obligation to limit our research, teaching, and other activities to our area of expertise. Sociologists ensure competence in their work through ongoing professional training. Competent researchers know their limits and consult with others who have greater expertise when necessary.

2 **Integrity** suggests that when researching, teaching, and providing service, sociologists act in an honest and fair manner. Misleading subjects or deliberately making false statements is unethical.

3 **Professional and scientific responsibility** is a researcher's obligation to treat others with professional courtesy. When reviewing other sociologists' work, we confront theoretical or statistical issues in a manner that is honest, not hostile.

4 **Respect for people's rights, dignity, and diversity** is a foundational sociological belief. Sociologists believe that discrimination based on differences between people is contrary to the core values of the discipline.

5 **Social responsibility** is a professional responsibility to serve the community. Understanding that sociology is more than an activity in a classroom or the research lab, we take what we know and apply it for the good of all people.

>>> Although the media had a field day with Tiger's sexual indiscretions, **the study of such intimate activities can create problems for sociologists who wish to practice ethicality.**

THE ETHICS OF HUMPHREYS

After reviewing the five pillars of ethical behavior, do you think Humphreys engaged in unethical practices? Humphreys used tearoom subjects without their knowledge. Sociological researchers are not supposed to behave like the paparazzi tracking down Tiger Woods. By going to the homes of observed tearoom participants, he risked violating their anonymity and thus damaging their reputations. Humphrey suggests that this is justified in order to gain this knowledge. Others might suggest he failed to respect his subjects' dignity and worth.

In Humphreys's defense, the code of ethics was not in place when he conducted his research. This code, in fact, was the result of studies like Humphreys's investigation of the tearoom trade. Studies like Humphreys's also prompted the federal government to play a role in research ethics. The government established an institutional review board, which must review all grant applications from colleges and universities that want federal funding to conduct research using human subjects.

Nonetheless, researchers who study deviant behaviors suggest that deception is essential in collecting accurate information. The issue of how to use deception is a critical question in field research. If you fully disclose what you are doing, how can you be sure the Hawthorne effect is not affecting your results? If you deceive, how can you protect the subjects' dignity and worth? That's why a debate on ethics rages on within the sociological research community today.

So the question is how can you avoid ethical dilemmas? One way is to get the consent of your subject. Hand out an informed consent form before the study begins. Informed consent means that the research subject understands the general purpose of the study and its main features. If the researcher is using deception, subjects deserve to know when they will find out the truth. Subjects must know that they can cease their participation at any time without risk to themselves.

©Lori Moffett/Bloomberg, Pool, Retna Ltd./Corbis

think sociologically: HOW DO SOCIOLOGISTS USE RESEARCH METHODS?

No single research method applies only to functionalism, conflict theory, or symbolic interactionism. But these theoretical frameworks do lend themselves to using types of data in different ways. The basis for these differences is often quantitative and qualitative data.

Quantitative and Qualitative Methods

If you were asked to rank your motivation on a scale of 1–5, with 5 being highly motivated, your response would be an example of quantitative data. Simply put, the term quantitative data refers to data based on numbers. Often, **quantitative data** include data gathered from national sources such as the United States Census. When Humphreys conducted his study, he used the information he received from his subjects to create quantitative data. After interviewing his subjects, Humphreys calculated their responses and found that a much lower number than he expected—only 14 percent—of his total subjects were openly gay men.

Qualitative data may include words, pictures, photos, or any other type of information that comes to the researcher in a nonnumerical form. When Humphreys posed as a market researcher and interviewed his subjects in their homes, he was collecting qualitative data. One common type of qualitative data is a **content analysis**—a type of research in which the sociologist looks for common words or themes in newspapers, books, or structured interviews.

Both quantitative and qualitative data require evaluation. The way in which the evaluation is measured is different, but both allow sociologists to better understand an issue.

The choice to use either qualitative or quantitative data pertains to all three theoretical perspectives, but there are some general trends that appear. Functional and conflict theorists tend to address more structural issues, and so they often use quantitative measurements. Conversely, symbolic interactionists might prefer qualitative data because they deal with the words and meanings attached to events. Whichever way you slice it, there is no hard and fast rule that connects a particular theoretical paradigm to a singular research method. Both qualitative and quantitative data can be appropriate.

Think about the research methods we discussed earlier in the chapter. How would you classify those methods? Are they quantitative or qualitative?

©Fotocrisis/Shutterstock; ©NatUlrich/Shutterstock; ©Karel Broz/Shutterstock

METHODS OF QUANTITATIVE ANALYSIS

CROSS-SECTIONAL STUDIES

COMPARATIVE STUDIES

LONGITUDINAL STUDIES

SURVEYS

EXPERIMENTS

TRIANGULATION is the process of using multiple approaches to study a phenomenon.

NEEDS ASSESSMENT is an analysis that studies the needs of a specific group and presents the results in a written statement.

Triangulation

Triangulation is the process of using multiple approaches to study a phenomenon. Just as a centrist politician triangulates by co-opting issues from both sides of the political spectrum, sociologists often use triangulation to include aspects of both qualitative and quantitative analysis. For example, if you want to study the influence of hip-hop music on white, teenage, suburban culture, you might look at the quantitative data of hip-hop CD sales among white teens. Afterward, you'd conduct in-depth qualitative interviews with the consumers who buy hip-hop to gauge how the music influences their lives. When you follow this process, you're triangulating the issue, or studying it from multiple points of view. Triangulation allows you to better explain a social event because you use two or more methods to study it.[17]

If you relied on only one method, you might draw an inappropriate conclusion about a social issue because all the facts are not available.

Triangulation helps researchers use **the strengths of one approach** to **compensate for the weaknesses in another.**

Research Methods and the Three Paradigms

Although our theoretical paradigm does not dictate the research method we use, it does affect how we interpret data. Conflict theorists and functionalists can look at the same data and come to different conclusions. Imagine that a conflict theorist and a functionalist studied data showing the rise of income inequality in a community. In other words, the gap between the "haves" and the "have-nots" in the community is widening. How might the two sociologists interpret the data? Remember, both functionalists and conflict theorists have a macro-orientation, so they study how a certain issue affects the whole society and not individual people. However, functionalists examine how a certain issue functions in a society, whereas conflict theorists study how the unequal distribution of goods affects society.

Functionalists studying the data might suggest that income inequality serves the society well, as more rich people are able to start businesses and invest in long-term projects that will one day make society better for everyone. These businesses might one day be able to employ the poor members of the community and help them rise above their situation. Functionalists would not view the income inequality as a negative phenomenon. Conflict theorists, meanwhile, might suggest that the same numbers show that the rich exploit the poor and that this exploitation is only getting worse. You can see how two researchers look at the same data and come to different conclusions.

Because symbolic interactionists have a micro-orientation, they might focus more on how the income inequality affected people at an individual level. These researchers might study wealthy individuals' perceptions of the poor and low-income individuals' perceptions of the rich. They might examine how being poor affects an individual's lifestyle. For example, how does the lack of money affect the kind of clothes that a person wears or the place he or she lives? Here too, you can see, the same set of data can be interpreted differently depending on the theoretical lens through which the data are viewed.

Using Triangulation to Examine the Tearoom Trade

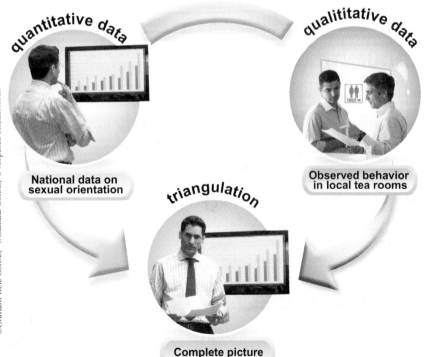

quantitative data

National data on sexual orientation

qualititative data

Observed behavior in local tea rooms

triangulation

Complete picture

<<< Using both qualitative and quantitative data helps approach a subject from all angles. **It helps us gain what Weber called *verstehen*. Here's how Humphreys would have used it in his study.**

discover sociology in action:
HOW IS RESEARCH INVOLVED IN SOCIAL POLICY AND COMMUNITY LEARNING?

The American Sociological Association's code of ethics calls sociologists to take action in their communities. Working on social policies and participating in community-learning projects are just two of the ways sociologists can better the community.

Social Policy and Statistics

Social policies arise because people recognize a problem and take action to deal with it. Often the first step is to get more information about the problem, which involves analyzing statistics. When consuming statistical evidence, it's important that you:

• **Beware the Headline.** News organizations titillate the public with sensational headlines such as "Airline Accident Rate is Highest in 13 Years." The problem here is that the rate of airline accidents was really declining. In this instance, the writer misused the word "rate." Instead, the writer should have stated that the *gross number* of airline accidents had increased.[18]

• **Check Term Definitions.** Each researcher makes decisions about how to measure certain constructs. Beware of any study using value-laden terms such as "conservative" or "liberal" without properly defining them. What you consider "liberal" might not be interpreted the same way by your neighbor or a community in another state.

• **Find Out Who Funded the Study.** Groups who fund research often have an interest in the outcome. You should always consider the possibility that stakeholders want to use research to support their positions.

Remember, objectivity is the foundation of sociological research. Be on the lookout for groups or individuals with ulterior motives.

• **Look for Spuriousness and Selection Effects.** When reading research, ask yourself: Could something else be causing this result? Has the researcher really looked at every possible angle?

• **Look for Agendas.** Agendas are often political in nature. Many times politicians quote statistics, but that doesn't mean they're true. Regardless of party affiliation, many politicians choose to manipulate statistics to make their claims appear stronger than they actually are.[19]

ACTIVITIES

1. Check out the online resources at your college library. Which search engines does your college suggest are best for sociological research? Make a list. Then write a paragraph evaluating each one.
2. Conduct a class survey. Talk with your professor and create a 10-question survey to give to your classmates about something that interests you.
3. Have a class discussion about Humphreys's claim that the end justifies the means. How can a researcher truly hope to find out about a subculture without deception?

Community Learning— Needs Assessments

As you consider how to assist your local communities, one research method might be exceptionally valuable: a needs assessment. A **needs assessment** is an analysis that studies the needs of a specific group and presents the results in a written statement. There are three key questions to ask when you're doing a needs assessment:

1. What information is needed?
2. What is the background of this situation?
3. How will we collect this information?

Your methodological training can help you help others in your community. But don't forget, statistics are everywhere, and you need to understand them in order to evaluate research accurately.

From Classroom to Community } Volunteering at the Rec Center

"I can't believe the building has changed so much within a year,"
Kathryn, one of my first-year sociology students, remarked at the grand reopening of a local recreation center that provided after-school and weekend activities for troubled youth. As a volunteer at the center last year, Kathryn noticed that many of the center's rooms were empty and unused. She knew that if the rooms were put to use, the kids' attendance would skyrocket. Since she didn't know why the rooms were unused or even how the center should use them, Kathryn decided to conduct a needs assessment.

"I met with the directors of the center and learned that they didn't have the funds necessary to renovate the empty rooms," she said. "But the directors agreed that giving the kids more options at the center might beef up their interest."

After meeting with the board, Kathryn spoke to staff members to find out how they proposed to use the empty rooms. She met with potential investors and found several interested parties. A quick examination of the public records found that 40 percent of the city's population was within the recreation center's target age group. Armed with this information, Kathryn met with the board of directors again. This time she proposed her own ideas for how to renovate the space and how the center could fund the renovations. Kathryn worked alongside the board to create two computer rooms and a game room. Like many sociologists, Kathryn identified a need, analyzed data, and found a way to meet that need in the end.

WHAT ARE RESEARCH METHODS?

the scientific procedures that sociologists use to conduct research and develop knowledge about a particular topic

HOW DO SOCIOLOGISTS USE RESEARCH METHODS?

through analysis of quantitative data using cross-sectional studies, comparative studies, longitudinal studies, surveys, and experiments; through analysis of qualitative data using participant observation, case studies, and ethnographies

HOW IS RESEARCH INVOLVED IN SOCIAL POLICY AND COMMUNITY LEARNING?

through analysis of statistics and by conducting needs assessments

get the topic: WHAT ARE RESEARCH METHODS?

Objectivity
Variables
Cause and Correlation
Scientific Method: What Are the Six Steps of
Social Research?

Quantitative and Qualitative Methods
Triangulation
Research Methods and the Three
Paradigms

Social Policy and Statistics
Community Learning—Needs
Assessments

Key Terms

research methods
objectivity
independent variables
dependent variables
control variables
causal relationship
causation
correlation
positive correlation
negative correlation
spurious correlation
social research
literature review

theory
hypothesis
concepts
operationalizing
research design
reliable
validity
comparative studies
cross-sectional studies
longitudinal studies
cohort
survey
populations

parsimony
sample
generalization
random sample
oversampling
sample of convenience
selection effects
Hawthorne effect
field research
participant observation
case studies
ethnography

secondary data
secondary data analysis
central tendency
mean
median
mode
ethics
quantitative data
qualitative data
content analysis
triangulation
needs assessment

MY SEARCH LAB

1. *Use of Black English and Racial Discrimination in Urban Housing Markets* by Douglas Massey and Garvey Lundy, from *Urban Affairs Review*, volume 36. Reprinted by permission of Sage Publications, Inc.

INTRODUCTION

This 1999 experiment, in which college students call prospective landlords on the phone to find out about rental property, led the authors to conclude that racial discrimination is alive and well in the urban housing market in Philadelphia.

DISCUSSION QUESTIONS

1. Do you think that this study does a good job of demonstrating discrimination? Is there another research method that could be used to find this type of subtle discrimination?
2. An interesting aspect of this experiment is that most people making calls about rentals would never know that

discrimination had occurred. If this is true, what is the solution to this type of discrimination?

2. *If Hitler Asked You to Electrocute a Stranger, Would You? Probably* by Philip Meyer, reprinted from *Esquire*, February 1970. Reprinted by permission of Philip Meyer.

INTRODUCTION

This article explains the shocking and controversial study on obedience to authority conducted by Stanley Milgram in the 1960s.

DISCUSSION QUESTIONS

1. Explain what is meant by a "state of autonomy" versus a "state of agency." How does each state change a person's behavior?
2. Do you think that this experiment is ethical? Why or why not?
3. Are there other research methods a person could use to find this same information?

THE THINKSPOT

We spent a good deal of time talking about the scientific method in this chapter and now you know what sociologists do when they conduct research. You might be surprised to know that others use the scientific method when conducting research but does that make them scientists? Go to the ThinkSpot and look at a brief clip from a recent ComicCon convention where the stars of the popular cable TV show "Mythbusters" discuss the question "Are you scientists?"

We also discussed Stanley Milgram's controversial experiment on obedience to authority. Just why did people—who normally wouldn't be considered violent or who lack judgment—seemingly put others in harm's way just because they were told? Go to the ThinkSpot and watch a video that explores the Milgram experiment and its impact.

Sample Test Questions

These multiple-choice questions are similar to those found in the test bank that accompanies this textbook.

1. "Children who participate in organized sports are less likely to suffer from obesity later in life." This statement is an example of a
   a. causal relationship.
   b. positive correlation.
   c. negative correlation.
   d. spurious correlation.

2. Which of the following research steps requires developing a logical research design?
   a. Collecting data
   b. Analyzing results
   c. Deciding on a topic
   d. Developing a hypothesis

3. What kind of study tells you what other researchers think about a particular topic?
   a. Literature review
   b. Longitudinal study
   c. Comparative study
   d. Cross-sectional study

4. The ethical principle that refers to staying within one's area of expertise is
   a. integrity.
   b. social responsibility.
   c. professional competence.
   d. professional and scientific responsibility.

5. Which measure of central tendency is not affected by extreme high or low scores?
   a. Mean
   b. Mode
   c. Average
   d. Median

ESSAY

1. How could you argue that Humphreys's study of the tearoom trade violated ethical standards of sociological study?

2. What caveats should you keep in mind when reading statistical evidence?

3. Suppose you were conducting a study of how people of different racial and ethnic backgrounds felt about a particular political candidate. How might you collect quantitative data for this study? How might you collect qualitative data?

4. How could the Hawthorne effect influence the results of a study on office productivity?

5. Provide an example of a theory. Next, explain how you would use that theory to form a hypothesis.

WHERE TO START YOUR RESEARCH PAPER

For more information on all countries, including maps and profiles, go to http://www.cia.gov/cia/publications/factbook/index.html

To find United Nations data on children, go to http://www.unicef.org/statistics/index.html

To find more information on national and international population projections and reports as well as inequality and poverty numbers, go to http://www.census.gov

To learn more about the World Values Survey (which includes data from surveys of 66 countries), go to http://www.worldvaluessurvey.org/

To find religious data on the Web, go to http://www.adherents.com/

For comparison data on education, go to http://nces.ed.gov/

For more information on the world population report, data, and trends, go to http://www.un.org/esa/population/unpop.htm

To find summary data on topics related to population growth, go to http://www.prb.org/

To find information on health indicators, international comparisons or health care systems, and health-related data, go to http://www3.who.int/whosis/en/

To find international data and analysis of poverty and wealth throughout the world, go to http://www.worldbank.org/

ANSWERS: 1. c; 2. a; 3. a; 4. c; 5. d

Endnotes

1. From Laud Humphreys, *Tearoom Trade: Impersonal Sex in Public Places*. Copyright © 1970. Reprinted by permission of Transaction Publishers.

2. Carl Hulse and David Stout, "Guilty Plea Stands, but Craig Won't Quit Senate," *New York Times*, sec. A, October 5, 2007.

3. Laud Humphreys, *Tearoom Trade: Impersonal Sex in Public Places* (Chicago: Transaction Publishing Co., 1970).

4. Max Weber, "Class, Status, Party," in *Readings in Social Theory: The Classical Tradition to Post-Modernism* 4th edition, ed. James Farganis (New York: McGraw-Hill, 1978/2004).

5. Elizabeth Lanthier, PhD, "Correlation," Elizabeth Lanthier, http://www .nvcc.edu/home/elanthier/methods/correlation.htm (accessed August 26, 2008).

6. Earl Babbie, *The Practice of Social Research 8th edition* (Belmont, CA: Wadsworth Publishing Company, 1998).

7. Steven Stack and Jim Gundlach, "The Effect of Country Music on Suicide," *Social Forces* 1992. 72: 211–218.

8. Jeffery B. Snipes and Edward R. Maguire, "Reassessing the Link Between Country Music and Suicide," *Social Forces* 1994. 72: 1239–1243.

9. Jeffery B. Snipes and Edward R. Maguire, "Reassessing the Link Between Country Music and Suicide," *Social Forces* 1994. 72: 1239–1243; Jeffery B. Snipes and Edward R. Maguire, "Country Music, Suicide, and Spuriousness," *Social Forces* 1995. 74: 327–330; Steven Stack and Jim Gundlach, "The Effect of Country Music on Suicide," *Social Forces* 1992. 72: 211–218; Steven Stack and Jim Gundlach, "Country Music and Suicide, A Reply to Maguire and Snipes," *Social Forces* 1994. 72: 1245–1248; Steven Stack and Jim Gundlach, "Country Music, Suicide—Individual, Indirect, and Interaction Effects: A Reply to Snipes and Maguire," *Social Forces* 1995. 74: 331–336.

10. The International Institute for Democracy and Electoral Assistance, "Voter Turnout Since 1945: A Global Report," http://www.idea.int/publications/vt/upload/VT_screenopt_2002.pdf.

11. Stanley Milgram, *Obedience to Authority: An Experimental View* (New York: Harper and Row, 1974).

12. Fritz J. Roethlisberger and William J. Dickson, *Management and the Worker* (Cambridge, MA: Harvard University Press, 1939).

13. Anthony R. Ward, "Isabelle," Feral Children, http://www.feralchildren.com/en/showchild.php?ch5isabelle (accessed August 26, 2008).

14. Robert Yin, *Applications of Case Study Research, 2nd edition* (Thousand Oaks, CA: Sage Publishing, 2003).

15. Ralph A. Weisheit, "The Intangible Rewards from Crime: The Case of Domestic Marijuana Cultivation," *Crime and Delinquency* 1991. 37: 506–527; Ralph A. Weisheit, "Marijuana Subcultures: Studying Crime in Rural America," in *Ethnography at the Edge: Crime, Deviance, and Field Research*, ed. Jeff Ferrell and Mark S. Hamm (Boston: Northeastern University Press, 1998).

16. American Sociological Association, "Code of Ethics," Washington D.C.: American Sociological Association, http://www.asanet.org/page.ww?section5 Ethics&name5 Ethics (accessed August 26, 2008).

17. Norman K. Denzin, *The Research Act in Sociology* (Chicago: Aldine Publishing Company, 1970).

18. Barry Glassner, *The Culture of Fear: Why Americans Are Afraid of the Wrong Things: Crime, Drugs, Minorities, Teen Moms, Killer Kids, Mutant Microbes, Plane Crashes, Road Rage, and So Much More* (New York: Basic Books, 1999).

19. Factcheck.org, "Misstatement of the Union: The President Burnishes the State of the Union through Selective Facts and Strategic Omissions," http://factcheck.org/article376.html (accessed August 26, 2008).

CULTURE

CULTURE

At different

times in our history, different cities have been the focal point of a radiating American spirit. In the late 18th century, for example, Boston was the center of a political radicalism that ignited a shot heard round the world—a shot that could not have been fired any other place but the suburbs of Boston. At its report, all Americans, including Virginians, became Bostonians at heart. In the mid-19th century, New York became the symbol of the idea of a melting-pot America—or at least a non-English one—as the wretched refuse from all over the world disembarked at Ellis Island and spread over the land their strange languages and even stranger ways. In the early 20th century, Chicago, the city of big shoulders and heavy winds, came to symbolize the industrial energy and dynamism of America. If there is a statue of a hog butcher somewhere in Chicago, then it stands as a reminder of the time when America was railroads, cattle, steel mills and entrepreneurial adventures. If there

is no such statue, there ought to be, just as there is a statue of a Minute Man to recall the Age of Boston, as the Statue of Liberty recalls the Age of New York.

Today, we must look to the city of Las Vegas, Nevada, as a metaphor for our national character and aspiration, its symbol a thirty-foot-high cardboard picture of a slot machine and a chorus girl. For Las Vegas is a city entirely devoted to the idea of entertainment, and as such proclaims the spirit of a culture in which all public discourse increasingly takes the form of entertainment. Our politics, religion, news, athletics, education, and commerce have been transformed into congenial adjuncts of show business, largely without protest or even much popular notice. The result is that we are a people on the verge of amusing ourselves to death.[1]

A Framework
for the Individual

In his book *Amusing Ourselves to Death* professor and social commentator Neil Postman sounds a sociological alarm, warning readers that a culture based purely on technology and TV is not necessarily a culture worth enjoying.

We are rapidly becoming a society that focuses on trivia. We all know who's dating who in Hollywood and which TV star recently got arrested, but can we name the vice president? If we become caught up in a culture of mindless entertainment, he argues, we spend our time thinking about insignificant trivia and ignoring important issues. We are at risk of killing our culture because people are too busy focusing on the insignificant.

Is Postman's warning nothing more than hyperbole? Not necessarily. Recently, I watched a family sitting at a table eating frozen custard. The mother listened to her iPod as a Nintendo DS game hypnotized her son. The father talked on his cell phone, and the five-year-old daughter seemed totally bored because she had no electronic toy or anyone to talk to. This technophilic family was clearly caught up in our country's culture of instant, constant entertainment.

Entertainment is not all bad, as Postman points out, but pursuing entertainment at all costs affects our relationships and our nation. Of course, there's more to culture than movies, slot machines, and electronic gizmos. In fact, culture forms the foundation of society and frames our perception of life.

get the topic: WHAT IS CULTURE?

CULTURE is the language, beliefs, values, norms, behaviors, and material objects that are important enough to pass on to future generations of a society.

The languages we speak and the behavioral codes we follow may seem perfectly natural to us, but there's nothing "natural" about culture: It is a framework built by and for human societies. We adopt our **culture** from those who came before us.

If you want to think like a sociologist, you'll need to understand not only the definition of culture but also how culture affects our lives. Because we see the world through the lens of our culture, it's easy for us to take our cultural orientation for granted, accepting it without much thought. In fact, we're often not even aware of the ways in which culture guides (or misguides) our thoughts and actions. The fact that you may only speak English, for example, is indicative of the culture in which you grew up. Had the Spanish or French run the English out of the United States in the 1600s, you might greet your friends, "¡Hola!" or "Bonjour!" The tangible and intangible aspects of culture have a significant impact on your daily life.

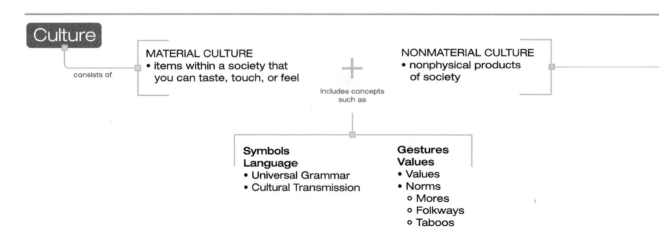

Culture

consists of

MATERIAL CULTURE
• items within a society that you can taste, touch, or feel

includes concepts such as

NONMATERIAL CULTURE
• nonphysical products of society

Symbols
Language
• Universal Grammar
• Cultural Transmission

Gestures
Values
• Values
• Norms
  ○ Mores
  ○ Folkways
  ○ Taboos

Material Culture

One category of culture is **material culture**: items within a society that you can taste, touch, or feel. The jewelry, art, music, clothing, architecture, and crafts a society creates are all examples of material culture. Of course, the natural resources available to a culture can influence that culture's creations. For example, while seven countries (the United States, Japan, Russia, Canada, Germany, France, and the United Kingdom) use more than 46 percent of the world's electricity and oil, these countries combined hold only about 12 percent of the world's population. What do these statistics tell you about material culture? On a tour of these countries, you'd be likely to stumble across plenty of cars, air conditioners, heaters, blow dryers, and a host of other modern conveniences. If you took a trip to Nigeria, though, you'd notice that a lack of access to energy also influences material culture. Nigeria is the ninth largest country in the world, yet it ranks 71st in the world's electricity use and 42nd in the world's use of oil. Few people own a car, and many live without regular access to electricity.[2]

Nonmaterial Culture

Not all elements of culture are items you can touch, see, or buy at your local mall. **Nonmaterial culture** consists of the nonphysical products of society, including our symbols, values, rules, and sanctions.

SYMBOLS

What do you think of when you see the U.S. flag? To most of us, it's more than just a piece of cloth—it's a symbol. **Symbols** represent, suggest, or stand for something else. They can be words, gestures, or even objects, and they often represent abstract or complex concepts. For example, wedding rings represent a legal bond of marriage and an emotional bond of love between two people. Each culture determines the meaning of its own symbols and uses these symbols to share thoughts and concepts with others. Have you ever seen the symbol shown above? You probably recognize it as the German swastika, a symbol of Nazi power used by Adolph Hitler

©vario images GmbH & Co.KG/Alamy

> **MATERIAL CULTURE** consists of items within a culture that you can taste, touch, and feel.
> **NONMATERIAL CULTURE** consists of the nonphysical products of society, including our symbols, values, rules, and sanctions.
> **SYMBOLS** represent, suggest, or stand for something else.
> **LANGUAGE** is a system of speech and/or written symbols used to convey meaning and communicate.

and the Nazi Party in the 1920s. Did you know that Hitler actually borrowed this symbol from other cultures? For example, Hindus see the symbol as a representation of holiness. To Buddhists, the symbol represents balance and harmony because of its symmetry. However, in modern times, Westerners view the symbol as a sign of racism and oppression. Clearly, symbols have great power.[3]

LANGUAGE

Language is a system of speech and/or written symbols used to convey meaning and communicate. Some languages exist only in the oral tradition, while other languages are expressed through both speech and writing systems, but all cultures use some form of language. The United Nations reports that currently, there are more than 6,000 different languages on the planet. Due to conquest, commerce, and failure to write down some languages, about half of these are in danger of extinction.[4]

Two main factors determine the number of speakers of a language: population size and colonial history. China and India are the world's largest countries by population, a fact that single-handedly explains the large percentage of people who speak Mandarin Chinese and Hindi. The English language is widely spoken throughout the world, but this has little to do with Great Britain's population size. If you've ever heard the phrase, "The sun never sets on the British Empire," you know that the British Empire once owned territory on every continent. As Great Britain colonized countries around the world from the 1700s to the 1900s, English was introduced to these places.

The Study of Culture

may be influenced by
- Ethnocentrism
- Xenophobia
- Xenocentrism
- Cultural Relativism

and should focus on
- **Ideal Culture**—the values to which a culture aspires
- **Real Culture**—the way people actually behave

and might discuss

- **Multiculturalism**—concept that supports the inherent value of different cultures in a society
- **Assimilation**—process by which minority groups adapt to the dominant culture

+

- **Subcultures**—subsets of the dominant culture that have distinct values, beliefs, and norms
- **Countercultures**—subcultures whose values and/or beliefs are in opposition to the dominant group

<<< **Language influences how we perceive things,** which in turn influences our experience of the world. Our experiences help up develop language, but **our use of language also influences our experiences.** How might you give directions if you had no sense of "left" or "right"?

Universal Grammar

The famous linguist Noam Chomsky suggests that human beings' ability to use language comes from common roots.[5] All languages contain what Chomsky calls a "universal grammar." This term refers not to particular language rules but to the way in which languages are constructed. Chomsky theorizes that, among other things, commonalities in sentence construction and word pronunciation connect languages throughout the world. Furthermore, he says, universal grammar begins in children at about the same age, regardless of culture. Chomsky's observations suggest that humans have an innate need for language.

Research by Coppola and Newport supports much of Chomsky's theory. In their study of deaf subjects who were isolated and knew no official sign language, Coppola and Newport found that these people's "home sign language" (i.e., language that they developed themselves) follows a predictable grammatical style.[6] For instance, the subject of a sentence generally appears at the beginning of the statement. Such findings point to an innate logic in the construction of language and support Chomsky's theory of universal grammar.

Cultural Transmission

Language is a useful tool, but is it culturally crucial? There's plenty of evidence to support the idea that a system of communication is, in fact, a critical aspect of culture. Culture often passes from

>>> Lifestyles and lyrics of rappers often celebrate the "bling" of American society. **How does such language influence our attitudes?**

one generation to the next through language. We call this phenomenon **cultural transmission**. Thanks to cultural transmission, you can use information others have learned to improve your own life. Cultural transmission also helps spread technology: Scientific studies of electricity and the development of microwave technology and the microchip made today's cell phones and computers possible.

Language not only advances our knowledge; it also brings us together by helping us create social consensus, or agreement. If you and I were to meet, we could use language to exchange ideas, debate, or decide on a course of action. Language is inherently social: It serves as a tool for sharing past memories, making plans, and building relationships.

The Sapir-Whorf Hypothesis

It's difficult to overstate the importance of language in our lives. Benjamin Whorf, a student of anthropologist Edward Sapir, suggested that language and thinking patterns are directly connected. Sapir and Whorf reached this conclusion, known as the **Sapir-Whorf hypothesis**, after studying many different languages and the people who spoke them.[7] The Sapir-Whorf hypothesis proposes two key points:

1. The differences in the structure of language parallel differences in the thinking of the people who speak languages.

2. The structure of a language strongly influences the speaker's worldview.

Have you ever considered how much language actually influences our thinking? Imagine that the English language had no words for right, left, front, or back. Would you still be able to understand these concepts? Probably not. An aboriginal group from Cape York Peninsula in Australia has no words for relative locations; instead, the group has words for absolute location, such as east, west, north, and south. Most members of the group do learn English, so they have an understanding of relative location. However, if they do not learn English at an early age, they struggle when asked to describe their location in relative terms.[8] Ongoing research into the Sapir-Whorf hypothesis suggests that because language influences thinking, it also influences culture.

GESTURE

Although language is a primary component of nonmaterial culture, it's not the only one. Another symbol system that differs by culture is gesture. **Gestures** are symbols we make using our bodies, such as facial expressions, hand movements, eye contact, and other types of body language. A gesture's symbolic meaning can vary widely between cultures: When I worked as a counselor to a Native American man, I interpreted my client's refusal to make eye contact with me as a sign of distrust until I learned that in his culture, looking someone in the eye is considered rude.

VALUES

Values, part of a society's nonmaterial culture, represent cultural standards by which we determine what is good, bad, right, or wrong.

CULTURAL TRANSMISSION is culture passing from one generation to the next through language.

SAPIR-WHORF HYPOTHESIS is a hypothesis, first advanced by Edward Sapir in 1929 and subsequently developed by Benjamin Whorf, that the structure of a language determines a native speaker's perception and categorization of experience.

GESTURES are symbols we make using our bodies, such as facial expressions, hand movements, eye contact, and other types of body language.

VALUES are a part of a society's nonmaterial culture that represent cultural standards by which we determine what is good, bad, right, or wrong.

VALUE PAIRS help us define values, usually in terms of opposites.

VALUE CLUSTERS are two or more values that support each other.

VALUE CONFLICT occurs when two or more values are at odds.

©Eduardo Miller/Shutterstock; ©Andy Z./Shutterstock

Sometimes, these values are expressed as proverbs or sayings that teach us how to live. Do you recognize the phrase, "Life is like a box of chocolates—you never know what you're going to get"? This modern-day saying is popular today among those who embrace life's unpredictability. Cultures are capable of growth and change, so it's possible for a culture's values to change over time.

Value pairs help us define values, usually in terms of opposites. For every positive value, we have a negative one. We may also hold values that support or contradict our other values. **Value clusters** are two or more values that support each other. Let's say you value both equality and tolerance. These values form a value cluster because they are similar concepts that strengthen each other. When two or more values are at odds, however, a **value conflict** occurs. For example, equality and racism are conflicting values.

▶▶ GO GL◉BAL

International Gestures Quiz

Think you know what it means to give a high five in Honduras or a thumbs-up in Thailand? Test your body language IQ to find out if you're culturally savvy.

1. How would you let a French person know he's boring you to tears?
   a. pat your mouth and let out a giant yawn
   b. mime playing an imaginary flute
   c. push your nose with your middle and index fingers

2. Your Puerto Rican friend wiggles her nose at you. What's she saying?
   a. "What's going on?"
   b. "I smell a rat—literally."
   c. "My nose itches!"

3. Which gesture is considered offensive in Egypt?
   a. using the right hand for eating
   b. showing someone the sole of your shoe
   c. walking hand in hand with someone

ANSWERS: 1. b; 2. a; 3. b

Gestures provide us with informal means of communication and can be extremely effective. Although many road rage incidents start with an infuriated gesture, **the power of the gesture is related to the receiver's ability to understand it.** You can't anger someone with a gesture that the person doesn't understand.

55

Fifteen U.S. Values According to Sociologist ROBIN WILLIAMS

If someone asked you to list the values of people in today's society, what would you include? Famous sociologist Robin Williams (*not the comedian*) suggests there are fifteen dominant values in the United States.[9]

1 **Achievement and Success.** What do you want to accomplish with your life? Each of us has our own definition of success. For some, it's a college degree; for others, it may mean making piles of money. Americans value winners and forget losers. Michael Phelps won a record-breaking eight gold medals at the 2008 Summer Olympics. But do you remember who his competition in the swimming pool was?

2 **Activity and Work.** It's what you might call the American dream: With enough hard work, anyone can pave a path to success. Thanks in part to this widely held belief, work has become a strong cultural value in the United States. In fact, we spend more time on the job than most people in the industrialized world.[10]

3 **Moral Orientation.** U.S. citizens have a tendency toward absolute ethical judgments regarding what is good, bad, right, or wrong. For example, when former President George W. Bush suggested in 2003 that North Korea, Iran, and Iraq formed an "axis of evil," he was using an absolute moral orientation that many Americans understood.

4 **Humanitarianism.** In the United States, many people are generous and value philanthropy. In times of crisis, we are willing to help. After the earthquake in Haiti in January 2010, Americans raised millions of dollars to support the victims. Internationally, the United States donated about 20 percent of the total money raised, and it led the world with more than 400 million dollars donated.[11]

5 **Efficiency and Practicality.** People in the United States seek the most benefit for the least effort. We believe that efficiency helps us achieve goals quickly and easily. When students ask for detailed study guides, they want to study efficiently and hope study guides prove a practical way to get a good grade.

6 **Progress.** People who value progress believe in "moving forward" by making changes and proposing ideas designed to improve society. For example, you (and most of the people you know) probably believe that, to some extent at least, new technology improves life. This belief is one motivator behind the One Laptop per Child program, which sends kid-friendly, wireless-enabled laptops to developing countries in an attempt to increase children's educational opportunities.[12]

7 **Material Comfort.** If you've ever felt like you have too much "stuff"—and yet you still want more—you're far from alone. The desire for material comfort drives many of us to buy bigger homes and fill them with recliners, TVs, and computers to make our lives easier.

8 **Equality.** Since the Declaration of Independence was penned, people in the United States have embraced the notion that all people should be treated equally regardless of race, gender, social class, or religious background. However, we don't always put our egalitarian values into practice. For example, female CEOs ran only 12 Fortune 500 companies in 2007. This gender disparity reflects women's struggle to achieve equality in the workplace.

9 **Freedom.** Generally, U.S. citizens place high value on civil liberties and the rights of the individual. Civil liberties limit the power of the government in our daily lives. We have the freedom to speak our minds. Freedom, for most Americans, means that we should be able to do what we want, so long as it doesn't hurt other people.

10 **External Conformity.** Don't underestimate the power of a group to influence your choices. If you value external conformity, you're probably eager to fit in with those around you. Fads in fashion show our desire to conform to those around us. When you were in high school, for example, other students probably influenced your desire to have the latest and greatest clothes, shoes, or haircut.

©Jupiterimages/Comstock Images/Getty Images

<<< Judging from their large house and nice clothes, it's safe to say that **this family places a high value on material comfort.**

v
v Many churches in the United
v States fly American flags. **What does this tell us about how patriotism, nationalism, and religion mix?**

©James R. Martin/Shutterstock

11 **Science and Secular Rationality**. In the United States, scientific proof and rational thought aren't concepts to be sneezed at. The essence of the scientific method is to use logic, order, and rational thought to attain knowledge. Many of us believe that logic and science can solve any problem that arises, including complex issues such as a cure for cancer or a solution to global warming.

12 **Nationalism and Patriotism.** We use the term civil religion to describe national pride and patriotism when it takes on an almost religious context.[13] In our everyday lives, you and I might engage in ritualistic patriotism without much thought. For example:

- **What** does singing the national anthem before sporting events have to do with sports?
- **What** does starting the school day with the pledge of allegiance have to do with learning?

13 **Democracy.** As any politician running for elected office would be happy to tell you, voting is a valuable aspect of civic engagement in our democracy. For a significant number of U.S. citizens, inspiring democratic systems of government in other nations is valuable, too. In the past 18 years, the number of electoral democracies in the world has doubled. Although more than half of the countries in the world have democracies, not all of those countries give their residents the freedoms U.S. citizens take for granted. In 2009, Freedom House reported that only 47 of the 89 independent electoral democracies are "free" in the same sense as the United States is.[14]

14 **Individual Personality.** When Williams discusses "individual personality," he's talking about individualism, or the tendency to look at the world through the lens of the individual rather than the lens of family or community. If you have an individualist worldview, you believe that people are autonomous—in other words, people's choices and actions are not predetermined by their positions in society. Individualism in extreme forms suggests that all individuals can overcome any negative event. Because individualists tend to place personal goals ahead of group goals, tension often develops in groups of individualists.[15]

15 **Racism and Related Group Superiority.** According to Williams, racism is a value in the United States, though not a positive one. Historical examples of racism toward non-Caucasian citizens abound, but racism is very much a contemporary issue. In a recent survey published in the Washington Post, only 22 percent of whites suggested that racism was a large problem, while double that percentage of blacks thought it remained a big problem. Both these percentages are much lower than they were in the past, and yet both groups acknowledged that race continues to be a problem. In fact, 28 percent of whites felt race was no longer even an issue, while only 15 percent of blacks felt that this was true.[16]

▶▶ GO GL🌐BAL

Individualistic and Collectivistic Views

When researches look at various cultures, they often compare the differences between what are termed "individualistic" and "collectivist" countries. Generally speaking, individualist nations are those whose core values are associated with a European history, while collectivist nations tend to be more closely linked to values developed in Asia. Thus, people in countries such as Japan are more apt to see things through the lens of collectivism.[17] In a collectivist culture, interdependence is valued over independence, group goals valued over individual wants and needs.[18]

How do our individualist or collectivist views affect us in practical terms? For starters, let's consider how we respond to questions. Research has shown that people from more collective societies, such as China and Japan, are less likely to answer with extremes on surveys. On a survey that allows participants to strongly agree, agree, disagree, and strongly disagree, U.S. citizens are more likely to choose "strongly agree" and "strongly disagree," whereas Chinese and Japanese participants tend to choose the less extreme responses.[19]

Important cultural differences like these can inform business situations. For example, research has found that a culture's orientation, whether individualistic or collectivist, does influence economic development, and vice versa. When individualist U.S. businesses enter collectivist countries without well-established legal codes, regulations, and court systems, these U.S. companies are likely to find that their business strategies don't succeed as well. Collectivist nations' business styles often differ from those of U.S. companies; In China, for example, businesspeople greatly value *guanxi*, or relationship development. While people working in the United States might not be used to building strong interpersonal relationships with potential business partners before even starting to work on a project, this type of in-depth relationship cultivation is critical in China. U.S. companies must be sensitive to cultural differences and adapt their business practices accordingly to be successful.[20]

NORMS are rules developed for appropriate behavior based on specific values that are conditional; they can vary from place to place.

SANCTION is a prize or punishment you receive when you either abide by a norm or violate it.

FOLKWAYS are informal types of norms.

MORES are norms that represent a community's most important values.

TABOO is an act that is socially unacceptable.

ETHNOCENTRISM occurs when a person uses his or her own culture to judge another culture.

XENOPHOBIA refers to fear and hostility toward people who are from other countries or cultures.

XENOCENTRISM is perceiving other groups or societies as superior to your own.

CULTURAL RELATIVISM means making a deliberate effort to appreciate a group's ways of life without prejudice.

NORMATIVE RELATIVISM is the evaluation of a society based on that society's norms.

CULTURAL LAG occurs when social and cultural changes occur at a slower pace than technological changes.

Additional Values

Because Williams' list of U.S. values is more than 30 years old, I believe that today's society warrants the addition of two new values. Look at any magazine cover, and you will see images of youthful, physically fit bodies and people in sexy, intimate poses. That's because today's society values these traits.

1 **Physical Fitness and Youthfulness.** People in the United States value a youthful appearance and a physically fit body. This is perhaps strange in a country that has increasingly high rates of obesity.[21] Yet, if you describe beauty, it's likely to be in terms of being young and physically fit.

2 **Sexuality and Romance.** John D'Emilio and Estelle B. Freedman detail the history of sexuality in the United States.[22] Reviewing data about sex over time, they conclude that we are becoming an increasingly sexualized society. This claim shouldn't be surprising—music, television, and magazines all tend to glorify sexuality. Linked to feelings about sexuality is romantic love, which involves sexual attraction and feelings of affection. In our society, nothing speaks to our value of romance like Valentine's Day. Every February 14th, about half of adult consumers buy 13 billion dollars of roses and other gifts to show their love.[23]

Norms and Sanctions

How can people uphold and enforce their values in everyday life? First of all, they might develop rules for appropriate behavior based on those values. We call these rules norms. **Norms** are conditional; they can vary from place to place. The way you behave at a football game is certainly different from the way you behave at a funeral. Our behaviors are linked to the situation. It is normal to cry at a funeral, and not so acceptable to cry at a football game.

Norms provide the justification for sanctions. A **sanction** is a prize or punishment you receive when you either abide by a norm or violate it. If you do what you are supposed to do, you get a positive sanction; if you break the rules, you earn a negative sanction.

Most sanctions are informal, like when your friend rolls her eyes at your terrible joke. However, if we violate a law or some formal written rule, we receive a formal negative sanction. A speeding ticket is one example of a formal sanction. Sanctions, both positive and negative, can reinforce a culture's values by rewarding people who hold those values and punishing those who have opposing values.

FOLKWAYS

Folkways are informal types of norms. They provide a framework for our behavior and are based on social expectations. Because they are less serious types of norms, the sanctions applied are less severe than for other types of norms. For example, if you see a person struggling with packages, you will hold the door for him or her. If you let the door slam on the person, you might be considered rude, but you won't go to jail. Folkways are often social customs that, when violated, call for minor, informal negative sanctions.

MORES

Although folkways are informal norms, mores (pronounced MORE-ayes) are more serious. **Mores** are norms that represent a community's most important values. A **taboo** is an act that is socially unacceptable. For example, if you murder a person, you've violated one of society's mores. People who violate mores are given a particularly serious type of formal negative sanction. Acts that lead us to feel revulsion, such as murder, are taboos.[24]

The Study of Culture

When you study culture, it's a good idea to consider whether a particular behavior or event is a cultural universal, or common to all cultures. For example, funeral rites are a cultural universal because all cultures have methods of disposing of the dead. Many specific cultural norms surround funerals and death, however, these norms vary widely

<<< **Advertising for youthfulness and fitness often contains before and after images.** Usually, it focuses on an unhappy, "unfit" person who in the after photo has the world by the tail.

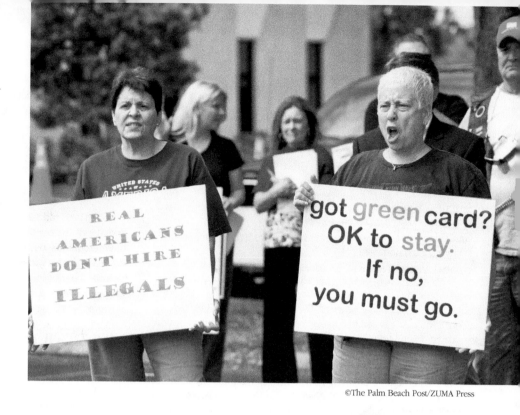

>>> In recent years, anger over illegal immigration has intensified in the United States. Often, such protests contain racial overtones.

from culture to culture. In what is now known as Micronesia, anthropologist Bronislaw Malinowski witnessed a funeral ritual in which native islanders ate part of the dead person to maintain a connection.[25] After eating, they would vomit in an attempt to create distance from the deceased. This Micronesian funeral norm probably differs greatly from your own culture's norm.

ETHNOCENTRISM AND CULTURAL RELATIVISM

When studying culture from a sociological perspective, you must not allow your personal biases to complicate your understanding. **Ethnocentrism** occurs when a person uses his or her own culture to judge another culture. Nearly all people in the world are ethnocentric, but ethnocentrism is potentially dangerous to sociologists because it can lead to incorrect assumptions about different cultures.[26]

Xenophobia refers to fear and hostility toward people who are from other countries or cultures. The United States has a long history of xenophobia. When the United States entered World War II after Japan bombed Pearl Harbor in 1941, people in the United States began to fear Japanese Americans and locked many in internment camps.

Perspectives of a Central American Hotel Room

No TV in my hotel room? This place is a dump!

Do hotels in Central America normally have a TV in every room?

Ethnocentrism   **Cultural relativism**

©Dmitriy Aseev/Shutterstock

When **traveling in Central America**, I noticed that even in very nice hotels there was **rarely a television in the room**. I viewed this observation through an **ethnocentric** lens based on my **cultural expectations**, but I was also able to view it through an **objective, prejudice-free lens of cultural relativism**.

Not all personal biases result in a negative view of foreign cultures. Sometimes, we engage in **xenocentrism** when we perceive other groups or societies as superior to our own. When living in Mexico, I noticed that my host family watched very little television. Instead, the family spent time discussing ideas. I remember wishing that people in my own culture would follow suit and interact with one another more.

Thinking like a sociologist means striving to practice cultural relativism when studying other cultures. **Cultural relativism** consists of a deliberate effort to appreciate a group's ways of life in its own context, without prejudice. Philosophers sometimes refer to this effort as **normative relativism** because it bases the evaluation of a society on that society's own norms. In some Islamic countries, for instance, women are not encouraged to seek education. Within the context of these countries, this practice could be interpreted as a normal function of that culture. However, if women in the United States were not allowed to get an education, the practice would seem unfair because it would violate U.S. cultural norms. When we engage in normative relativism, we evaluate acts within their cultural contexts.

Some people, however, argue that there are universal human values that are standards by which we should evaluate cultures.[27] According to this argument, women in every culture should be educated, and any culture that does not allow this is inferior and exploitive of women.

CULTURAL LAG AND CULTURE SHOCK

Cultural lag happens when social and cultural changes occur at a slower pace than technological changes. This is often the case when new technology enters and changes a culture. In the late 1970s, scientists were concerned with the deforestation of poorer regions of the world. People used most of the felled lumber to heat stoves for cooking. To combat this problem, solar stoves were developed. However, initial tests in Africa and Haiti showed that people were reluctant to use these stoves. After learning of the stoves' benefits, people's reluctance waned, and today more than 120 million solar stoves are used around the world.[28]

CULTURE SHOCK occurs when a person encounters a culture foreign to his or her own and has an emotional response to the differences between the cultures.

SUBCULTURE is a subset of the dominant culture that has distinct values, beliefs, and norms.

COUNTERCULTURES are groups with value systems that are in opposition to the dominant group's values.

MULTICULTURALISM is a concept that supports the inherent value of different cultures within society.

ASSIMILATION is the process by which minority groups adopt the patterns of the dominant culture.

GLOBAL VILLAGE refers to the "shrinking" of the world through immediate electronic communications.

Have you ever traveled to a foreign country and been stunned by how the culture differed from your own? If so, you were probably experiencing culture shock. **Culture shock** occurs when a person encounters a culture foreign to his or her own and has an emotional response to the differences between the cultures. During my time in Mexico, the electricity went out every afternoon. My host family planned their cooking schedule around the predictable power outages. It took some time, but I eventually got used to this cultural difference.

IDEAL VERSUS REAL CULTURE

Is there a difference between culture as we'd like it to be and culture as it really is? Often, the answer is yes. Ideal culture represents the values to which a culture aspires, and real culture represents a culture's actual behaviors. Our society aspires to equality, and yet a brief look at the data shows that minorities still suffer from inequality in the United States. They experience more poverty, lower incomes, and less access to health insurance.[29]

SUBCULTURES AND COUNTERCULTURES

Groups with a common interest may form a subculture. A **subculture** is a subset of the dominant culture that has distinct values, beliefs, and norms.

In complex societies, subcultures allow people to connect with other people who have similar interests. Churches, civic organizations, clubs, and even online communities can become subcultures.

When a subculture expresses values or beliefs that are in direct opposition to the dominant group's values, it becomes a counterculture.

When you read the term counterculture, images of mafia organizations and violent motorcycle gangs might come to mind. These groups are **countercultures** because their value systems are in opposition to the dominant group's values. Sometimes, countercultures can merge with and change the dominant culture. For example, in the Roman Empire, Christianity was once banned and practicing Christians were persecuted. However, Christianity later became the official religion of the empire.

MULTICULTURALISM AND ASSIMILATION

If you move to a new country, you'll bring along not only material belongings but also concealed cultural baggage. It can be tricky to "unpack" that baggage, but you'll need to find a way to adapt to your new culture. **Multiculturalism** is a concept that supports the inherent value of different cultures within society. Proponents of multiculturalism think that immigrants should maintain links to aspects of their original culture—such as language, cultural beliefs and traditions, and religion—while also integrating into their new culture. However, opponents of multiculturalism worry that this practice keeps groups from adapting to the dominant culture.

Assimilation is the process by which minority groups adopt the patterns of the dominant culture. If a minority group completely abandons its previous culture in favor of a new one, that group is likely to experience rapid assimilation. One method by which the U.S. government tried to force rapid assimilation involved taking Native American children from their parents and placing them in boarding schools to teach them "white ways." However, many Native American students left the boarding schools unprepared to live in either the dominant culture or their own culture.[30]

MAKE CONNECTIONS

The Subcultures of Facebook

Are you a member of a Facebook subculture? Considering that Facebook use continues to explode, many colleges and universities (and even stores and restaurants) now have pages. Facebook is perhaps the most widely used social networking site around, its number of online visitors per week surpassing even the Google homepage.[31] Unsurprisingly, my students often have it up on their laptops as I enter class. Facebook helps you stay connected to others who share your interests. When you use this site, your friends always seem to be available.

When you join Facebook, you create a profile that includes personal information, interests, beliefs, or hobbies. The more information you include, the larger your world can become, because Facebook connects you to others in the system who have similar characteristics. For example, you can connect to people who have the same class schedule or belong to the same fraternity and/or sorority. You're linked to people who have similar values, or your subculture of friends.

Like any culture or subculture, Facebook has norms and sanctions. Many Facebook users believe that the more friends you have, the more popular you are. One norm for interacting with friends on the site is to post a message to a person's wall. The person you contact may write you back or ignore your remark. An informal sanction might occur if your message goes unanswered. A formal sanction can occur if a friend deletes you from his or her friends list. Although nontraditional, Facebook creates a virtual community in which people interact with others who share norms and values.

>>> **ACTIVITY** Log on to a social networking site, like Facebook, and identify a culture.
- **MAKE** a list of the values of that culture.
- **HOW** are these values distinct from the values discussed earlier?
- **HOW** are they similar?

Global Village

In the 1960s, Marshall McLuhan popularized the term "**global village**," which refers to the "shrinking" of the world through immediate electronic communications.[32] McLuhan's work suggests that time and space differences are rapidly becoming irrelevant as a result of technology. But is technology really bringing people closer together?

Before the advent of the Internet, Stanley Milgram conducted an experiment in an attempt to determine whether it really is a small world after all.[33] Milgram found people from different areas of the United States and sent them on a hunt for strangers. He asked them to mail a letter to a target person, whom they did not know, using only their social networks. He provided only the subject's name and town of residence but nothing else. After passing through the hands of between two and ten people, the letters eventually found their targets. Now that the Internet plays such a large role in our lives, could our separation be even shorter than it was in the 1960s? How many links would it take you to connect with a student in Japan?

Dodds et al. used the Internet to conduct a similar study.[34] Through e-mail, Dodds sent more than 60,000 people on a target hunt to find 18 people in 13 different countries. Their results were astonishingly similar to Milgram's results. Although these findings certainly support the notion of a small world, they do not suggest that the world is any smaller today than it was in Milgram's time.

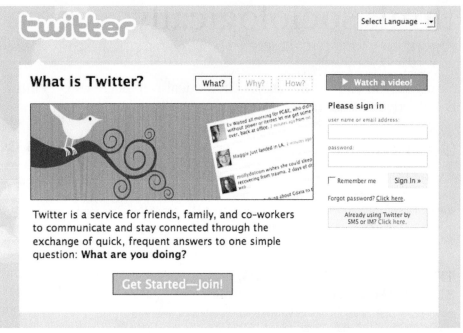

Public Citizen

Twitter, a social-networking/micro-blogging device, allows users to alert their friends (with "Tweets") to their current activities via instant message or RSS feed. Twitter, in effect, encourages users to know all the actions of their friends in real time. **Do programs like Twitter make the world feel smaller? Why or why not?**

THINK SOCIOLOGICALLY

Technology and Cultural Change

In *Amusing Ourselves to Death: Public Discourse in the Age of Show Business*, Neil Postman discusses television's impact on U.S. culture. Television is the primary means of communication for news and information in the United States. Fewer people read newspapers and magazines. Do the media affect the message?

Marshall Fishwick would say that they do. According to him, many aspects of life that make us human are not computable.[35] Your laptop cannot feel, create beauty, or think. Your MP3 player talks to you; it does not listen. Like Fishwick, Postman argues that technology, such as television, provides a passive type of engagement for the user. Postman suggests that this creates a nation of people who cannot think. This inability increases the odds that we will accept overly simple solutions to extremely complex problems, which will destroy our culture in the long run.

Of course, not everyone believes that technology will destroy our culture. In *Culture and Technology*, Andrew Murphie and John Potts claim that technology has improved society. For example, Murphie and Potts argue that the technology of writing "transformed human consciousness" because it brought about new ways of thinking. Technological advancements, such as the Internet and television, inspire creativity and innovation, and open up a world of opportunity for a society. They argue that technology does not limit a society, as Fishwick and Postman suggest, but it gives people the tools to continue to improve their lives.[36] Is our culture becoming a technopoly? A technopoly is a society that values technological change for its own sake. In such a culture, having the latest upgrade is most important. Fishwick suggests that our culture is experiencing a tyranny of technology, while Murphie and Potts argue that culture and technology are so tightly linked that we can't really separate one from the other. What do you think? Has technology really improved society?

think sociologically: WHAT DIFFERENTIATES ONE CULTURE FROM ANOTHER?

Now we will turn to the major theoretical perspectives on culture. The theoretical perspectives affect how sociologists view language, gestures, and values in a culture.

Symbolic Interactionism— A Crisis of Values

Symbolic interactionists explore how language, gestures, or values affect a culture. If a symbolic interactionist were to study values in U.S. society, he or she might ask: How are values defined in the United States? Are U.S. values weakening? Is the United States experiencing a moral decline?

TRADITIONAL VALUES VS. SECULAR VALUES

In *America's Crisis of Values*, author Wayne Baker investigates whether a crisis of values really exists.[37] Baker surmises that proponents of a decline of values usually support one of three arguments: the trend hypothesis, the comparative hypothesis, or the distribution hypothesis. He compares traditional and secular values over time.

Traditional values include the importance of religion and God, absolute standards of good and evil, importance of the family, deference to authority, male dominance in economic and political life, and intolerance of certain moral issues such as abortion, homosexuality, divorce, and suicide. Secular values emphasize reason and logic. Ignoring religion and custom when determining government and social decisions, accepting low levels of religious beliefs and relative standards of good and evil, and questioning authority are all examples of secular values.

THE THREE HYPOTHESES

The comparative hypothesis suggests that the values in U.S. society are inferior to those found in other modern democracies. The argument proposes that our individualist and traditional values result in higher rates of murder, poverty, and out-of-wedlock births. When Baker compared value statements from a variety of countries, he found more similarities than differences, which lends no support to the comparative hypothesis.

The distribution hypothesis or, as Baker also refers to it, "the culture war thesis" suggests that the United States is involved in a culture war. According to this theory, two morally opposed groups (one liberal, one conservative) fight for control of the media, government, and society. Here again, Baker finds no evidence to support the idea that the United States is divided into two opposed groups fighting for moral high ground.

BAKER'S CONCLUSION

Using data gathered from the U.S. public over a 30-year span, Baker concludes that U.S. citizens are becoming more traditional and less secular. Baker's results may come as a surprise to pundits who love to chatter about culture wars. His findings suggest that U.S. citizens have more similar values today than they did 30 years ago. In fact, the country's traditional values have become stronger over time. Yet, many who espouse these values suggest that secular rational values are "winning," when in fact they are not. Baker suggests that the United States' purported "crisis of values" is nothing more than an illusion fueled by rhetoric.

©Tomislay Forgo/Shutterstock; ©Jonas Staub/Shutterstock; ©T-Design/Shutterstock; ©Shutterstock; ©Junial Enterprises/Shutterstock; ©James Steidl/Shutterstock

The Three Trends
How Do They Measure Up?

U.S. Values — Values of Modern Democracies
The Comparative Hypothesis

Values of U.S. Liberals — Values of U.S. Conservatives
The Distribution Hypothesis

U.S. Secular Values — U.S. Traditional Values
The Trend Hypothesis

>>> The trend hypothesis asserts that **traditional values are losing ground to secular ones.**

Functionalism—Communitarianism

When functionalists look at the importance of culture, they often consider how culture works to hold society together. Functionalists suggest that culture binds society through shared values and norms and the interaction of social structures. Noted sociologist Amitai Etzioni has explored these systems in U.S. society.

Amitai Etzioni is one of the foundational creators of communitarianism—a functional approach to the understanding of culture in the United States.[38] This theory suggests that for society to function properly, it must have a balanced relationship between the community, the market, and the government. Etzioni stresses that to build a society that works, its members must see themselves as individuals and as part of a community. Communitarians are not communists. Unlike communists, communitarians believe in free markets and private ownership of business. However, they stress that a sense of community must exist to check excesses of either the government or the market place.

Conflict Theory—The McDonaldization of the United States

Conflict theorists suggest that society is united in a struggle for scarce resources. Unequal distribution of wealth means that some people win and others lose. But how do you win? Are there predictable patterns of interaction that can bring about financial success? McDonald's restaurant is successful because it prizes efficiency, practicality, and affordability. Sociologist George Ritzer suggests that U.S. society models itself after a McDonald's restaurant through a process he calls "McDonaldization."[39]

Using a conflict theory rooted in the work of economist/sociologist/political scientist Max Weber, Ritzer notes that efficient bureaucracies succeed in business. In a capitalist system, those who follow the McDonaldization process are likely to be financially successful.

1 **Efficiency.** When a business practices efficiency, consumers benefit from the low prices that the business offers. The McDonaldization of efficiency means customers do the employees' work. If you go to McDonald's, you usually carry the food to the table yourself, and in some parts of the country, you might fill your own drink as well.

2 **Calculability.** McDonald's counts every item, from the pickles on the hamburger to the number of chicken tenders in a box. Quantity is valued, and quality is less relevant. McDonaldized societies measure success by the number of tasks completed on time. If the quality of the task is mediocre, we often accept it as long as it is finished on schedule.

3 **Predictability.** Finding a product that is predictable decreases the risk of business failure. In this way, our culture has taken a page from the fast-food industry. Food from Taco Bell tastes the same whether you purchase it in San Antonio or Boston. Predictability increases reward and decreases risk to both the business owner and the consumer.

4 **Technology.** Businesses gain more control over their products when they use technology to limit human error. This trend helps increase profits because business owners are able to hire fewer people.

NEGATIVE EFFECTS OF MCDONALDIZATION

Ritzer warns that the use of technology dehumanizes our culture. People use ATMs or self-checkout lines for convenience. However, using these forms of technology shows that society values speed through a checkout line over human interaction. In the long run, is this healthy for today's society?

McDonaldization trades convenience for high quality and ensures high profits for business owners. Innovation and creativity suffer, but short-term profits rise. By replacing workers with technology, wages drop and inequality increases, leading to conflict between business owners and workers.

©AP Wide World Photos

Morgan Spurlock's 2004 documentary *Super Size Me* showed how his eating McDonald's food every day for one month negatively affected his health. **Even though McDonald's is a perfect example of efficiency, calculability, and technology, does the common experience of a Big Mac really improve our society?**

WRAP YOUR MIND AROUND THE THEORY

©Petr Jilek/Shutterstock

For society to function effectively, it must be like a tree, with each part—the government, the market, and the local community—doing its job. What happens to the tree if one part gets too weak?

FUNCTIONALISM

Functionalists suggest society works as an interrelated system. Communitarians understand that if society is to run smoothly, the government, the local community, and the business sector must all work together for the well-being of all. The root of society is the local community; it anchors this societal tree. The government carries the will of the people to the economic system, thereby functioning as the trunk of this tree. The leaves of a tree make the sugar that allows the entire plant to live. Of course, leaves without roots blow over, and roots without leaves die.

IS YOUR COUNTRY LOSING TRADITIONAL VALUES TO SECULAR ONES?

CONFLICT THEORY

Conflict theorists point out that members of society struggle for what is scarce. In our society, that usually involves wealth and power because of the McDonaldization process. Short-term rewards increase power and wealth of the few. The costs to society are irrelevant. Las Vegas casinos, for instance, frequently make money off people who are not wealthy. These consumers gamble for the entertainment value and because they believe gambling will make them rich. In reality, it's the casino owners who become wealthier. Fast food chains may please customers with dependable food and low prices, but originality is lost.

SYMBOLIC INTERACTIONISM

Interactionists suggest that culture is rooted in the values expressed by the people who live within it. Politicians use symbols to articulate that which they believe is important. Successful candidates are able to attract votes from a wide variety of people; so, in general, they do not have extreme values. Many people in today's society get their information about politicians from television news, giving the media enormous power. In 2009, chairman of the Republican National Committee Michael Steele publically apologized for calling radio host Rush Limbaugh an "entertainer."[40] Neil Postman would argue that this exemplifies America's preference for amusement and celebrity over important social concerns.

©Jeff Greenberg/PhotoEdit

©Ethan Miller/Getty Images

Conflict theorists point out that **McDonaldization increases profits for those with money and power.** Does it make our lives more meaningful or interesting?

Symbolic interactionists note the importance of verbal and nonverbal communication. **What does it mean that a talk show host can get apologies from national leaders?**

discover sociology in action: HOW DOES CULTURE INFLUENCE SOCIOLOGICAL THEORY AND STUDY?

Social Policy—Multiculturalism and Assimilation

In recent years, more than 15 states in the United States have passed laws that require immigrants to understand English in order to use public services. Some "English-only" laws simply state that English is the official state language, while others prohibit giving state applications, forms, and driver's license exams in any language other than English.[41]

When discussing the social polices related to the English-only movement, sociologists often use the terms "multiculturalism" and "assimilation." Supporters of multiculturalism believe that people should be allowed to adapt to a new culture. People who favor assimilation often criticize multiculturalism because they believe that immigrants should adapt to society. Society does not need to adapt to immigrants.

Is one theory better than the other is? Sociologist Ruben Rumbaut explores immigrant assimilation by reviewing a variety of studies.[42] Traditionally, experts believed that assimilation occurred in a linear process. Immigrants began to assimilate by learning the language and then incorporated other parts of the culture into their lives. Rumbaut finds that this linear idea is not valid. Assimilation varies based on the immigrant's time of entry into the country and country of origin. Many of today's immigrants come from countries with little understanding of industrialization and democracy, which limits the process by which they assimilate. Under these conditions, coerced rapid assimilation has a negative impact on successful immigrant adaptation. Recent research shows that immigrants improve their chances of successful adaptation if they remain tied to their own culture and remain bilingual.[43]

Those who support aggressive assimilation policies view the policies as a way to functionally support the country's unity and ease the fear that a bilingual society would negatively affect the country. Interestingly, as an individual's education level increases, the likelihood of supporting "English only" laws decreases. Therefore, college graduates are more likely to realize that successful immigrant adaptation occurs slowly and cannot be forced.[44]

ACTIVITIES

1. Research the laws in your state. In what languages other than English can a person take a driver's license test?
2. Imagine that you moved to another country and were banned from speaking English. How might you feel? What would you do to adapt?
3. Visit an English as a Second Language classroom in a school in your community. Ask the teacher about the importance of language in cultural transmission.

From Classroom to Community ⟩ Assisting Immigrants

"I didn't know what I was getting into."

Sonya, a 22-year-old, bilingual, United States born Latino student uttered these words when reflecting on an experience she had while working on a civic engagement project. When Sonya began volunteering at a local Latino development organization that offered legal, medical, and psychological help to Spanish-speaking immigrants, she could not imagine the life lessons she would learn.

"After the first week, I was given a case of an immigrant woman who needed help **getting medical care for her children,**" Sonya recalled. The woman spoke very little English, and her husband had left her and her children about a year earlier. As a legal citizen of the United States, the woman was entitled to public assistance. However, she did not know how to get it.

The process was long and arduous, but Sonya did not falter. She followed the woman through the system and appealed each rejection along the way. Eventually, Sonya was able to help the woman find daycare assistance and food stamps, and she helped the woman collect child support from her ex-husband. The experience taught Sonya how not speaking English cripples many immigrants in the United States.

"If you can't speak English very well, you cannot really negotiate the system. Even legal immigrants suffer in such an environment.

Fortunately, the Latino society is closely knit and more collective. This helped her to survive.

Without her community's support she would have had no hope to make a new and better life for herself and her children."

WHAT IS CULTURE?

the language, beliefs, values, norms, behaviors, and material objects that are important enough to pass on to future generations of a society

WHAT DIFFERENTIATES ONE CULTURE FROM ANOTHER?

language, gestures, values, perception and categorization of experiences, actions, norms, interaction of social structures, and struggle for scarce resources

HOW DOES CULTURE INFLUENCE SOCIOLOGICAL THEORY AND STUDY?

culture: affects how we perceive things; guides our thoughts and actions; must be studied while keeping these differences in mind

get the topic: WHAT IS CULTURE?

Material Culture
Nonmaterial Culture
Additional Values
Norms and Sanctions

The Study of Culture
Symbolic Interactionism—A Crisis of Values
Functionalism—Communitarianism
Conflict Theory—The McDonaldization of the
  United States

Social Policy: Multiculturalism and Assimilation

Theory

FUNCTIONALISM

- culture (shared values and norms) holds society together through shared values and norms
- interaction of social structures
- society must have a balanced relationship between the community, the market, and the government
- communitarians (free markets and private ownership of businesses)

CONFLICT THEORY

- society struggles for resources
- societies win resources by using McDonaldization process (efficiency, calculability, predictability, and technology)

- convenience over quality
- only the wealthy benefit: wages drop, inequality increases, short-term profits rise

SYMBOLIC INTERACTIONISM

- traditional vs. secular values
- three hypotheses: trend, comparison, and distribution
- individualist and traditional values result in higher rates if murder, poverty, and out-of-wedlock births
- U.S. citizens becoming more traditional, not secular

Key Terms

culture
material culture
nonmaterial culture
symbols
language
cultural transmission
Sapir-Whorf hypothesis
gestures
values
value pairs

value clusters
value conflict
norms
sanction
folkways
mores
taboo
ethnocentrism
xenophobia
xenocentrism

cultural relativism
normative relativism
cultural lag
culture shock
subculture
countercultures
multiculturalism
assimilation
global village

MY SEARCH LAB

1. **The Amish: A Small Society** by John Hostetler, *Amish Society,* third edition. pp. 3–12. © 1980 The Johns Hopkins University Press. Reprinted with permission of The Johns Hopkins University Press.

INTRODUCTION

Hostetler describes the Amish—a unique subculture that has maintained many of its traditions and customs in modern society—as a simple, unified, traditional, and religious community.

DISCUSSION QUESTIONS

1. What does the author mean by "commonwealth"? Do you believe that a sense of commonwealth is lost in society today?
2. Amish society in modern times has increasing contact with the larger society through tourism. How do you think this will affect their culture in the future?

2. **The McDonaldization of Society** by George Ritzer, reprinted from *The McDonaldization of Society*, 1996. Copyright by Pine Forge Press. pp. 35–58, 121–142, 177–204.

INTRODUCTION

In this excerpt, George Ritzer—who coined the term "McDonaldization"—demonstrates how the principles of the fast-food restaurant (speed, efficiency, and standardization) have come to dominate all areas of American society.

DISCUSSION QUESTIONS

1. At the end of this excerpt Ritzer argues that citizens should fight against the McDonaldization of society. Is it possible to do so?
2. In addition to the examples in this excerpt, what other areas of social life have become "McDonaldized"?

THE THINKSPOT

www.thethinkspot.com

Who knew sociology could be entertaining? Go to the ThinkSpot to find a group of young people who alternately take their sociology seriously but have also found a way to discuss it in a casual manner. They do a particularly good job of discussing sociology and culture. Take a look.

What does a list of "friends" say about you? What about the fact that you have a social life online? Go to the ThinkSpot and listen to what Harvard University fellow Danah Boyd has to say on the subject. Do you agree with what she has to say about "public" versus "private" lives and the Internet's relationship to culture?

Sample Test Questions

These multiple-choice questions are similar to those found in the test bank that accompanies this textbook.

1. Norms include all of the following *except*
   a. folkways.
   b. mores.
   c. rules for behavior.
   d. definitions of beauty.

2. Which of the following statements is *false*?
   a. Values may cluster, but they cannot contradict.
   b. Values remain the same over time.
   c. Values are often defined by their opposite.
   d. Values exist in all societies.

3. Gestures are part of
   a. assimilation.
   b. material culture.
   c. nonmaterial culture.
   d. multiculturalism.

4. How does a counterculture form?
   a. When a subculture's values differ from the dominant group's values
   b. When a group maintains likes to aspects of their original culture
   c. When the dominant culture does not accept part of the group
   d. When the subculture adopts the values of the dominant culture

5. In order for sociologists to practice cultural relativism when studying polygamists in the United States, they must consider
   a. U.S. laws.
   b. U.S. norms.
   c. polygamist norms.
   d. cultural universals.

ESSAY

1. What aspects of Las Vegas culture may lead to the city's culture death?
2. How does culture influence sociological theory and study?
3. How might individualism lead to conflict?
4. How can a business benefit from the McDonaldization process?
5. How did Wayne Baker determine whether a crisis of values really exists in the United States?

WHERE TO START YOUR RESEARCH PAPER

To learn more about the McDonaldization of America, go to http://www.mcdonaldization.com

To find more information about attending college while traveling the world, go to http://www.semesteratsea.com

To learn more about the Small World project (the online experiment to test the idea that any two people in the world can be connected through only six others), go to http://smallworld.columbia.edu

To learn more about the communitarian movement, go to http://www.gwu.edu/~ccps/index.html

To find urban legends and myths as well as their origins and why they are not true, go to http://www.snopes.com

For more information on international study options, go to http://www.studyabroad.com, http://www.studyabroadlinks.com

To find vital information to consider before studying abroad, go to http://travel.state.gov/travel/living/studying/studying_1238.html

For more information on international volunteering, go to http://www.crossculturalsolutions.org

To learn more about the Peace Corp, go to http://www.peacecorps.gov

ANSWERS: 1. a; 2. b; 3. c; 4. a; 5. c

Endnotes

1. "The Medium is the Metaphor," from *Amusing Ourselves to Death* by Neil Postman, copyright © 1985 by Neil Postman. Used by permission of Viking Penguin, a division of Penguin Group (USA) Inc.

2. The World Factbook, "Rank Order—Electricity—Consumption," Central Intelligence Agency, https://www.cia.gov/library/publications/the-world-factbook/rankorder/2042rank.html (accessed March 30, 2006); The World Factbook, "Rank Order—Oil—Consumption," Central Intelligence Agency, https://www.cia.gov/library/publications/the-world-factbook/rankorder/2174rank.html (accessed March 30, 2006); The World Factbook, "Rank Order—Population," Central Intelligence Agency, https://www.cia.gov/library/publications/the-world-factbook/rankorder/2174rank.html (accessed March 30, 2006).

3. Quinn, Malcolm. 1994. *The Swastika: Constructing the symbol.* New York: Routledge.

4. Jan Kavan, "International Mother Language Day: Address to the Fifty-seventh Session of the United Nations General Assembly," Office of the President of the General Assembly, http://www.un.org/ga/president/57/pages/speeches/statement210203-MotherTongue.htm (accessed September 18, 2008).

5. Noam Chomsky, *Reflections on Language* (New York: Pantheon Books, 1975).

6. Marie Coppola and Elissa L. Newport, "Grammatical Subjects in Home Sign: Abstract Linguistic Structure in Adult Primary Gesture Systems without Linguistic Input," *Proceedings of the National Academy of Sciences of the United States,* 2005. 103(52): 19249–19253.

7. Benjamin L. Whorf, *Language, Thought, and Reality* (New York: Wiley, 1956)

8. Richard Monastersky, "Speak Before You Think," *Chronicle of Higher Education,* 00095982, 2002. 48(29): A17–A19.

9. Robin M. Williams, Jr., *American Society: A Sociological Interpretation*, 3rd ed., (New York: Alfred A. Knopf, 1970).

10. Organization for Economic Cooperation and Development, "Employment Outlook Statistical Annex—2008," OECD, http://www.oecd.org/searchResult/0,3400,en_2649_201185_1_1_1_1_1,00.html (accessed September 18, 2008).

11. guardian.co.uk, "Haiti earthquake aid pledged by country," http://www.guardian.co.uk/news/datablog/2010/jan/14/haiti-quake-aid-pledges-country-donations (accessed April 18, 2010).

12. One Laptop Per Child Foundation, http://laptopfoundation.org/en/program/ (accessed September 5, 2008).

13. Robert N. Bellah, Richard Madsen, William M. Sullivan, Ann Swidler, and Steven M. Tipton, *Habits of the Heart, Individualism and Commitment in American Life* (Berkley, CA: University of California Press, 1996).

14. Freedom House, "Combined Average Ratings: Independent Countries 2009," http://www.freedomhouse.org/template.cfm?page=475&year=2009 (accessed April 18, 2010).

15. Harry C. Triandis, *Individualism and Collectivism* (Boulder, CO: Westview, 1995).

16. Michael A. Fletcher and Jon Cohen, "Far Fewer Consider Racism Big Problem; Little Change, However, at Local Level," The Washington Post, January 19, 2009.

17. Peijia Zha, Jeffrey J. Walczyk, Diana A. Griffith-Ross, Jerome J. Tobacyk, Daniel F. Walczyk, "The Impact of Culture and Individualism-Collectivism on the Creative Potential and Achievement of American and Chinese Adults," *Creativity Research Journal,* 2006. 18(3): 355–366.

18. B. Quiroz, P. M. Greenfield, and M. Altchech, "Bridging Cultures with a Parent-Teacher Conference," *Educational Leadership,* 1999. 56 (7): 68–70.

19. Chuansheng Chen, Shin-ying Lee, and Harold W. Stevenson, "Response Style and Cross-cultural Comparisons of Rating Scales Among East Asian and North American Students," *Psychological Science,* 1995. 6(3): 170–175.

20. Richard Ball, "Individualism, Collectivism, and Economic Development," *Annals of the American Academy of Political and Social Science,* 2001. 573: 57–84.

21. CDC, "Overweight and Obesity: Obesity Trends: U.S. Obesity Trends 1985–2004," Centers for Disease Control and Prevention, http://www.cdc.gov/nccdphp/dnpa/obesity/trend/maps/index.htm (accessed September 18, 2008).

22. John D'Emilio and Estelle B. Freedman, *Intimate Matters: A History of Sexuality in America* 2nd ed. (Chicago: University of Chicago Press, 1997).

23. NRF, "Cupid Strikes Again as Valentine's Day Spending Set to Top $13 Billion: More Than Half of Consumers to Celebrate on Feb. 14," National Retail Federation, http://www.nrf.com/content/default.asp?folder5press/release2005&file5valentines0105.htm (accessed September 18, 2008).

24. William Sumner, *Folkways and Mores* (New York: Schocken Books, 1911/1979).

25. Bronislaw Malinowski, *Magic, Science, and Religion and Other Essays* (Garden City, NY: Doubleday, 1954).

26. Elizabeth Cashdan, "Ethnocentrism and Xenophobia: A Cross-cultural Study," *Current Anthropology,* 2001. 42(5): 760–765.

27. Robert B. Edgerton, *Sick Societies: Challenging the Myth of Primitive Harmony* (New York: Free Press, 1992).

28. Daniel M. Kammen, "Cookstoves for the Developing World," *Scientific American,* 1995. 273(1): 72–76.

29. U.S. Census Bureau, "Income, Poverty, and Health Insurance Coverage in the United States: 2008," http://www.census.gov/prod/2009pubs/p60-236.pdf (accessed April 18, 2010).

30. David Wallace Adams, *Education for Extinction: American Indians and the Boarding School Experience* (Lawrence, KS: University of KS Press, 1995).

31. The Denver Post, March 18, 2010, http://www.denverpost.com/headlines/ci_14696630.

32. Marshall McLuhan, *The Gutenberg Galaxy: The Making of Typographic Man* (Toronto: University of Toronto Press, 1962).

33. Stanley Milgram, "The Small-World Problem," *Psychology Today,* 1967. 1: 61–67.

34. Peter Sheridan Dodds, Roby Muhamad, and Duncan J. Watts, "An Experimental Study of Search in Global Social Networks," *Science,* 2003. 301(5634): 827–829.

35. Marshall Fishwick, *Probing Popular Culture: On and Off the Internet* (Binghamton, NY: The Haworth Press, Inc, 2004).

36. Andrew Murphie and John Potts, *Culture and Technology* (New York: Palgrave McMillian. 2003).

37. Wayne Baker, *America's Crisis of Values: Reality and Perception* (Princeton, NJ: Princeton University Press, 2005).

38. Amitai Etzioni, *The Spirit of Community: The Reinvention of American Society* (New York, Simon & Schuster, 1994).

39. George Ritzer, *The McDonaldization of Society: Revised New Century Edition* (Thousand Oaks, CA: Pine Forge Press, 2004).

40. Adam Nagourney, "R.N.C. Chairman Apologizes to Limbaugh in Flap Over His Role," *The New York Times,* March 2, 2009.

41. Wayne A. Santoro, "Conventional Politics Takes Center Stage: The Latino Struggle against English-Only Laws," *Social Forces,* 1999. 77(3): 887–909

42. Rubén G. Rumbaut, "Assimilation and its Discontents: Between Rhetoric and Reality," *International Migration Review,* 1997. 31: 923–968.

43. Alejandro Portes and Rubén G. Rumbaut, *Immigrant America: A Portrait* (Berkeley: University of California Press, 1996).

44. Valerie Barker and Howard Giles, "Who Supports the English-Only Movement? Evidence for Misconceptions about Latino Group Vitality," *Journal of Multilingual and Multicultural Development,* 2002. 23(5): 353–370.

SOCIAL STRUCTURE AND INTERACTION

From Chapter 4 of *THINK Sociology 2011*. John D. Carl. Copyright © by Pearson Education. Published by Prentice Hall. All rights reserved.

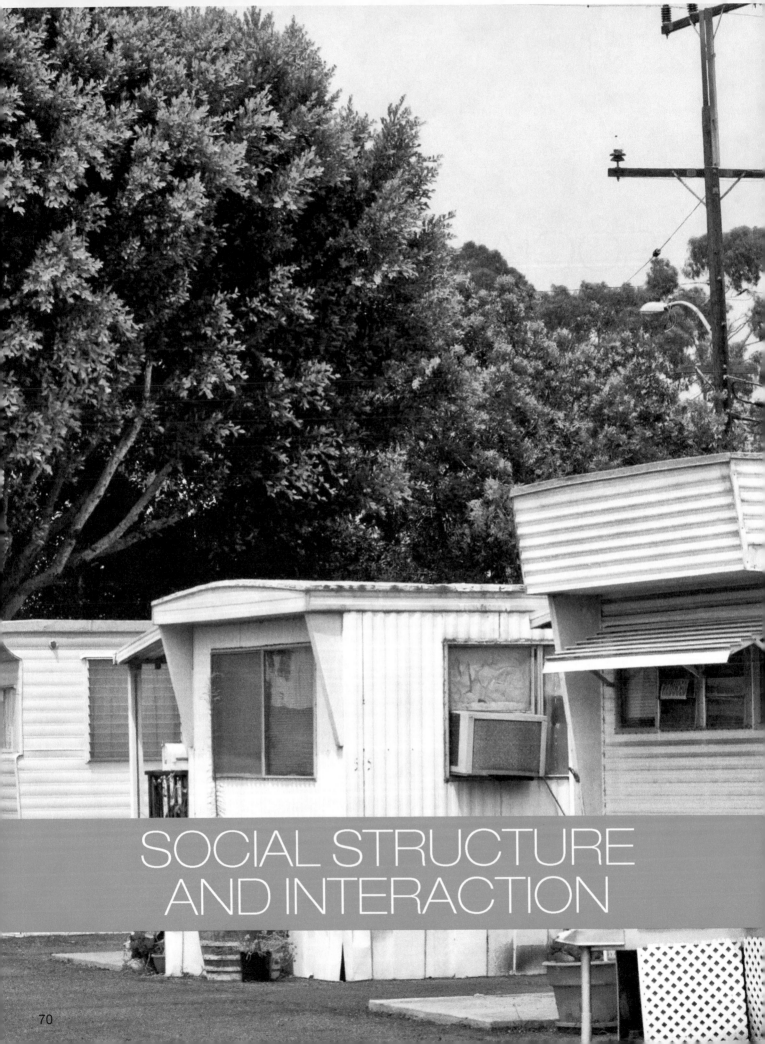

SOCIAL STRUCTURE
AND INTERACTION

Being

poor is worse in the United States than it is in France. First, the French poor are less poor: The French welfare state is better equipped to redistribute income, and it has not experienced the rise in poverty seen in the United States in recent years. Second, poverty is mostly associated with long-term unemployment in France, whereas in the United States the minimum wage is so low as to create a large segment of impoverished workers. Third, the French poor are less isolated than the American poor because the French public housing projects are more racially and ethnically diverse and bring together employed and unemployed people. By contrast, American public housing projects tend to contain a relatively homogenous population of unemployed urban blacks. French workers also have a less negative image of the poor than American counterparts, given the presence among the poor of many native-born whites, their lesser geographic concentration, and the weaker stigmatization of public project dwellers. Also, American mass media reinforce the association between poverty and blackness by underrepresenting whites in reporting on the poor.[1]

Micro *and* Macro Orientations

By studying workers in the United States and France, Michèle Lamont illustrates that there is a clear link between the small-scale and large-scale components of a society.

I've had many different jobs, from bicycle repairer to landscaper. In these labor-intensive jobs, I witnessed firsthand the link Lamont describes in *The Dignity of Working Men: Morality and the Boundaries of Race, Class, and Immigration*. Few of my co-workers had taken any college classes, and many hadn't finished high school. Most of the men with whom I worked had high school diplomas, but none had any hope of having a career that did not include manual labor. Although we were all poor, I noticed a distinct difference between the ways whites interpreted their life chances compared with members of minority groups. One day, a panhandler came by and asked for a dollar. A white co-worker immediately launched into a vicious rant about the man's lazy lifestyle before he stormed off. I continued to watch as a Mexican American worker reached into his pocket and gave the man a dollar. I remember wondering about this disparity. Now I see that it's related to Lamont's claim that individual decisions are related to large-scale issues; in this case, it was race.

One's race, Lamont argues, colors his or her opinions of general social issues like poverty. Whites in the United States, for example, are more likely to ascribe economic success or failure to individual or moral causes, while African American workers view poverty as related to failures within the structures of the society. As you view any society, you'll find that the small interactions and the large components combine to create the social world.

get the topic: WHAT ELEMENTS CREATE A SOCIAL STRUCTURE?

Macrosociology and Microsociology

When Oceanic Flight 815 first crashed in the middle of the ocean on the hit TV show *Lost*, the survivors found themselves washed up on the shores of a seemingly uncharted desert island. After recovering from the initial shock of the crash, some survivors searched the island for signs of life or danger. Another group scoured the wreckage for food and water.

Still others battled mysterious clouds of black smoke and fended off polar bears; this *was* a fictional TV show after all, but you get the idea. Very quickly, fixed social positions were established. The survivors became hunters, warriors, builders, and cooks. Whether it's *Survivor*, *Lost*, or *Gilligan's Island*, television shows provide illustrations of individuals who create social structures to form societies. In this chapter, we investigate the interaction between micro and macro to understand better how societies are formed.

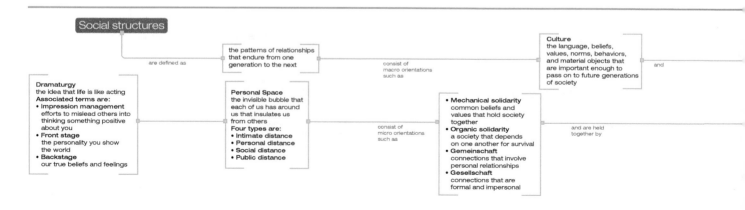

Social structures

are defined as **the patterns of relationships that endure from one generation to the next** consist of **macro orientations such as** ... **Culture** the language, beliefs, values, norms, behaviors, and material objects that are important enough to pass on to future generations of society **and**

Dramaturgy the idea that life is like acting
Associated terms are:
• **Impression management** efforts to mislead others into thinking something positive about you
• **Front stage** the personality you show the world
• **Backstage** our true beliefs and feelings

Personal Space the invisible bubble that each of us has around us that insulates us from others
Four types are:
• **Intimate distance**
• **Personal distance**
• **Social distance**
• **Public distance**

consist of micro orientations such as

• **Mechanical solidarity** common beliefs and values that hold society together
• **Organic solidarity** a society that depends on one another for survival
• **Gemeinschaft** connections that involve personal relationships
• **Gesellschaft** connections that are formal and impersonal

and are held together by

There are two important components of society: the macro (large) elements and the micro (small) elements. On the *Lost* island, the survivors developed both macro structures to accomplish needed tasks and micro orientations to ensure that their society would run smoothly. **Macrosociology** is the study of large-scale society, focusing on the social structures that exist within a society and examining how those structures create the social world. **Microsociology** deals primarily with the small interactions of daily life.

SOCIAL STRUCTURE

You've probably never had to think too hard about the way a society functions. That's because we often have an inherent understanding of how our society is structured. **Social structures** are patterns of relationships that endure from one generation to the next. They are the arrangement of systems—such as marriage, education, and work—by which people in a society interact and are able to live together.

Consider your position at work. When you first arrived on the job, you noticed certain roles. There's a boss, customers, and co-workers. The patterns of these relationships dictate their function. Your boss hires and fires you, while your customers pay your salary, and your co-workers help you learn the ropes. Customers and co-workers can't fire you, but they can influence how your boss sees you. The pattern of these relationships does not vary much over time or place; if you take another job in another state, you'll likely still see these patterns. They become a part of work culture.

Culture

Culture is the language, beliefs, values, norms, behaviors, and material objects that are important enough to pass on to future generations of a society. The embedded structure of culture touches every aspect of our lives and is a large part of our society.

Groups

Groups are any number of people with similar norms, values, and behaviors who frequently interact with one another. Knitting clubs, government agencies, religious cults—all of these are groups. Residents living in the same apartment complex aren't necessarily a group because they may rarely hang out together.

Sociologist Charles H. Cooley suggests that we divide ourselves into two types of groups: primary and secondary.[2] **Primary groups** are small, intimate, and enduring. Your family and close friends are primary groups to which you belong. **Secondary groups** are formal, superficial, and temporary. Your relationship to your classmates is probably a secondary group. The line between these two types of groups is not always clear-cut, but we have far more secondary groups than primary ones.

MACROSOCIOLOGY is the study of large-scale society, focusing on the social structures that exist within a society and examining how those structures create the social world.

MICROSOCIOLOGY is the study of the small interactions of daily life.

SOCIAL STRUCTURES are patterns of relationships that endure from one generation to the next.

GROUPS are any number of people with similar norms, values, and behaviors who frequently interact with one another.

PRIMARY GROUPS are groups that are small, intimate, and enduring.

SECONDARY GROUPS are groups that are formal, superficial, and temporary.

SOCIAL CLASS is a group with similar access to power, wealth, and prestige.

Social Class

Social class refers to a group with similar access to power, wealth, and prestige. The importance of social class varies depending upon the society. In the United States, for example, the working class makes up about 30 percent of the population.[3] The members of this social class are often the swing voters at election time. Although they are often treated as a unified group, Michèle Lamont's research finds that the working class frequently remains divided along racial lines.

Your social class can have a profound impact on your life, especially the length of it. Studies have shown that one's social class can affect his or her health, happiness, and life span. In England, researchers have found that the life expectancy of professional women is far longer than women who are unskilled laborers.

©Thomas Barwick Lifesize/Getty Images;
©Kablonk!/photolibrary.com

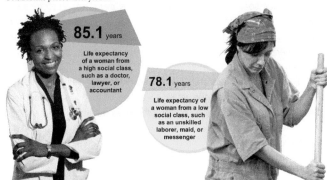

85.1 years
Life expectancy of a woman from a high social class, such as a doctor, lawyer, or accountant

78.1 years
Life expectancy of a woman from a low social class, such as an unskilled laborer, maid, or messenger

Source: Data from the "Wealthy, Healthy, and Aged 85: The Women Living Even Longer" by Jill Sheerman.

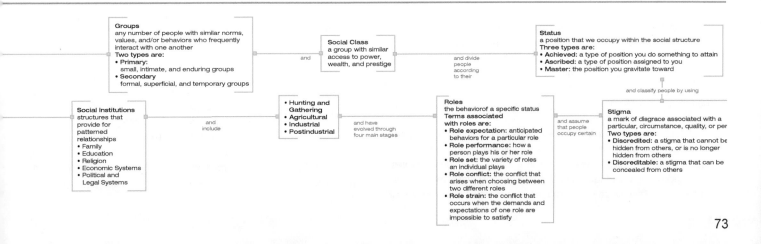

Groups
any number of people with similar norms, values, and/or behaviors who frequently interact with one another
Two types are:
• Primary:
small, intimate, and enduring groups
• Secondary
formal, superficial, and temporary groups

and

Social Class
a group with similar access to power, wealth, and prestige

and divide people according to their

Status
a position that we occupy within the social structure
Three types are:
• Achieved: a type of position you do something to attain
• Ascribed: a type of position assigned to you
• Master: the position you gravitate toward

and classify people by using

Social Institutions
structures that provide for patterned relationships
• Family
• Education
• Religion
• Economic Systems
• Political and Legal Systems

and include

• Hunting and Gathering
• Agricultural
• Industrial
• Postindustrial

and have evolved through four main stages

Roles
the behavior of a specific status
Terms associated with roles are:
• Role expectation: anticipated behaviors for a particular role
• Role performance: how a person plays his or her role
• Role set: the variety of roles an individual plays
• Role conflict: the conflict that arises when choosing between two different roles
• Role strain: the conflict that occurs when the demands and expectations of one role are impossible to satisfy

and assume that people occupy certain

Stigma
a mark of disgrace associated with a particular, circumstance, quality, or per
Two types are:
• Discredited: a stigma that cannot be hidden from others, or is no longer hidden from others
• Discreditable: a stigma that can be concealed from others

►►► GO GL🌐BAL

Social Class in China

While some cultures don't have a rigid social class system, others have a well-established system. Take, for example, the Hukou system used in China immediately after the Communist Revolution. Under this system, once a person registered in a specific geographic area—rural or urban—he or she was not allowed to move far beyond the area. This fixed system gave city dwellers the advantages of better access to education and more opportunity for advancement than those living in rural areas.

Today, groups of workers in rural areas are predominantly male and make up emerging social classes. In the rural areas of modern China, being connected to the government is far less important than it is in urban areas where Communist party membership can be vital to a person's success. Therefore, in urban areas class systems are significantly different than they are in rural areas. For one thing, they're much more fluid and allow for more movement than rural divisions do.

In the rigid rural class system, people do not have much freedom to move up and down the hierarchy. The rural system from top to bottom includes cadres, capitalists, managers, household business owners, professionals, wage laborers, and peasants.

For the urban class, the system is more flexible. The urban social class system from top to bottom includes capitalist entrepreneurs, intellectuals and professionals, members of the middle and working class, and the poor.

Because of the increasing fluidity of China's social systems, people are able to change the social class in which they belong. Receiving an education and owning a business are two ways that people raise their social standing.[4]

Social Status

Visit a trendy Hollywood hotspot like Ecco, and you'll probably wait hours for a table, if you can get in at all. Of course, if you're famous, like the Kardashians, you'll be whisked in through the front door with an army of paparazzi chronicling your every move. So what's the difference? Kim and Khloé Kardashian have high social status, and you probably do not. In our fame-obsessed society, celebrities—even the Kardashians, who are simply famous for being famous—have reached a certain social status. **Status** refers to the position that a person occupies within the social structure and is often closely linked to social class. The wealthier and more powerful you are, the higher your social status will be. Often, a person's value to society does not determine his or her social status. For example, lawyers enjoy high social status, while construction workers have lower status. However, if we had no more construction workers, buildings would fall down.

Sociologists divide status into two different types: achieved and ascribed. **Achieved status** refers to a type of position that someone earns or does something to attain. When you get a promotion at work, you have *achieved* a new status. **Ascribed status** describes a position in society that is given or assigned. For example, socialite Paris Hilton's fame is an ascribed status. Because she was born into a wealthy and famous family, she draws attention at red-carpet events and enjoys the privileges of a celebrity. Paris didn't choose to be wealthy, just like you didn't choose your gender, race, or ethnicity. Ascribed statuses are given to us at birth—we do not make a decision to choose them.

Most of us occupy a number of positions in our lives. For example, I am an author, college professor, husband, father, son, and brother, just to name a few. Since we all occupy more than one status in life, we will gravitate toward one that we call a **master status**. The master status may be what is most important to us, such as our status as a parent, or what is most important to others, such as one's race or economic standing.

People often perceive individuals who have high status to be experts in fields other than their professions. Oldmeadow et al. find that personal status impacts others' perceptions.[5] In a study of student athletes, Oldmeadow found that team captains have a higher status than the rest of the team.[6] Thus, team members are likely to follow the advice of their captains even in areas unrelated to their particular sport.[7] Other research suggests that this is particularly true when a hierarchical status is known. Individuals with lower perceived status are highly likely to follow the lead of a high-status person, even if to do so conflicts with the interest of the lower status person.[8] For example, although a student may have more knowledge in a particular area, he or she may defer to the professor's wisdom on the topic because the professor has achieved a certain status and is deemed wise.

Status is an important social construct because **the positions we occupy lead to the roles we play.**

Social Roles

When you enter a classroom, you sit in the chairs designated for students. You don't go to the front of the room and stand behind the podium. You understand that your status is that of a student and so you play the role of student, not teacher. A **role** is the behavior of a specific status, and your status affects the role you play. If the professor asked you to lecture without any advance notice, you'd probably think something was wrong. This is because the roles we play come with certain expectations about how to play those roles.

Role expectations are the anticipated behaviors for a particular role. When you go to the doctor, you do as the doctor says, even if you have never met him or her before. This is because the statuses of doctor and patient define the roles. However, if the doctor is rude or obviously uninterested in your care, you'll say he or she has a "bad bedside manner." We tend to view people as less capable when they do not fill their role expectations as socially gracefully as we would hope.

Role expectations are extremely powerful. When you refer to a "bad date," it's usually because you expected one thing and got another. We evaluate **role performance** on whether or not a person plays the role in a manner we expect. These expectations can be reasonable or unreasonable. A student once negatively evaluated my class because I "expected work to be turned in on time." If you expect college to be a cakewalk, you're probably going to be disappointed.

Robert Merton clarifies other important components of roles.[9] We all play a variety of roles, which makes up our role set. As a college student, you might also play the role of child, employee, parent, or spouse, and when playing these multiple roles, you might find you have to choose between the competing demands of those roles—a phenomenon known as **role conflict**. This happens often when parents return to college. A sick child quickly becomes more important than studying for a test, and grades can suffer. Why? Because the role of student and parent often conflict.

At other times, we may feel **role strain**. This occurs when the demands and expectations of one role are impossible for us to satisfy. You might feel role strain when deciding whether to go out to a party on Saturday night or cram for the midterm that Monday.

The ways in which status and roles influence our lives often goes unnoticed. We expect the cashier at the grocery store to take our money and send us on our way. If he or she talks too much, we might get annoyed. The setting influences our expectations. The way you behave at a church service is certainly different than the way you behave at a frat party. Although both events have crowds of people and a common reason for being at the event, they're not the same. If you dress for a party and attend church, you're likely to be judged negatively.

Stigmas

Any convict who's been released from prison will tell you that life on the "outside" is no picnic. That's because people who serve time for a crime and then rejoin society carry with them the label of "ex-con" for the rest of their lives. In other words, we attach a **stigma**, or a mark of disgrace associated with a particular status, quality, or person, to the ex-convict. Sometimes, one's age, religion, sexual orientation, economic status, or race can result in a stigma.

STATUS is the position that you occupy within the social structure, which is often closely linked to social class.

ACHIEVED STATUS is a type of position that you earn or do something to attain.

ASCRIBED STATUS is a position in society that is given or assigned.

MASTER STATUS is the status toward which we gravitate.

ROLE is the behavior of a specific status.

ROLE EXPECTATIONS are the anticipated behaviors for a particular role.

ROLE PERFORMANCE is the degree to which a person plays the role in a manner we expect.

ROLE CONFLICT is a phenomenon occurring when one is forced to choose between the competing demands of multiple roles.

ROLE STRAIN occurs when the demands and expectations of one role are impossible for us to satisfy.

STIGMA is a mark of disgrace associated with a particular status, quality, or person.

DISCREDITED STIGMA is a stigma that cannot be hidden from others or is no longer hidden from others.

DISCREDITABLE STIGMA is a stigma that can be concealed from others.

Sociologist Erving Goffman suggests that we all have a positive ideal identity that we hope others will accept.[10] Unfortunately, a stigma points out the differences between our ideal and real selves. There are two types of stigma—discredited stigma and discreditable stigma. A **discredited stigma** is a stigma that cannot be hidden from others, or is no longer hidden from others. A person with a physical handicap has a discredited stigma. A **discreditable stigma** is a stigma that can be concealed from others, such as sexual orientation, STDs, and criminal history.

For example, in *The Dignity of Working Men*, Lamont describes how white and African American workers stigmatized others. Many white workers were more likely to hold the poor in contempt and view African Americans as lazy, unmotivated individuals, whereas many African American workers viewed whites as domineering, controlling, and lacking warmth.

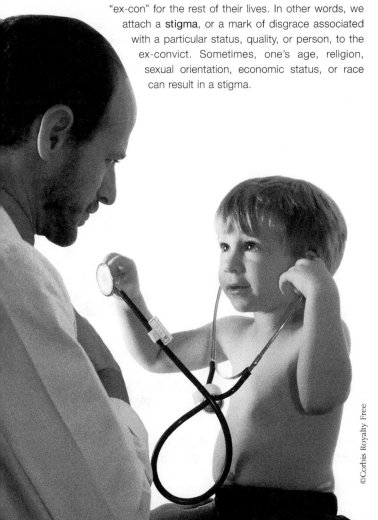

©Corbis Royalty Free

<<< Here, the roles seem to have reversed. We'd normally expect the adult to play the role of the doctor, while the child plays the role of the patient.

STAGES OF SOCIETAL CHANGE

As societies change over time, the complexity of social interaction also changes. With increasing population and technological advancement, societies have become more diverse, which leads to changes in the social structures. American sociologist Gerhard E. Lenski is one of the few theorists who maintain an evolutionary view of society. According to Lenski et al., the evolution of society consists of four main stages—hunting and gathering, agricultural, industrial, and postindustrial.[11]

Hunting and Gathering Societies

Have you ever wondered how you might survive if you were forced to become a hunter-gatherer? Recently, some friends and I took a camping trip to the Boundary Waters Canoe Area in northern Minnesota. In such a place, you have only what you bring with you. And if you want to eat, you'd better learn how to fish. I can't say we had much luck living off the land; the one fish I did manage to catch was hardly enough to feed us all. Luckily, the dehydrated food in our backpacks was enough to sustain us.

Of course, the first hunter-gatherers didn't rely on dehydrated food to survive, but they did live off the land and focused most of their efforts on finding food. Archeological evidence supports the idea that Homo sapiens lived as hunters and gatherers approximately 50,000 years ago. Beginning in the Neolithic period, hunters and gatherers existed in small groups of approximately 150 people for about 2,000 generations. Over this period, their culture and population changed slowly.[12]

In hunting and gathering societies, an individual's status and role were closely linked. Thus, the status of tribal leader was often given to the strongest person or the best hunter. Because there were few roles for people to play in these types of societies, Lenski suggested that the division of labor in hunting and gathering societies was very limited.[13] Everyone in the society had to be involved in the production of food for survival.

Successful hunters and gatherers adapted to their environment. Geography professor Jared Diamond shows that food supply and available natural resources dictate a great deal about the form of society.[14] People living in areas with abundant food were able to hunt and gather for longer periods than those living in cold climates. Geological differences fostered human innovation. For example, farming and raising animals occurred in areas that supported crop growth and had a suitable climate for animals. This transition ushered in the agricultural stage of society.

Agricultural Societies

Approximately 10,000 years ago, people began to move from hunting and gathering to agrarian-based societies.[15] With this change, society became more complex. Lenski et al. divided agricultural societies into two groups: (1) pastoral and horticultural societies and (2) agricultural groups.[16]

Pastoral and horticultural societies appeared when humans learned to domesticate plants and animals. Members of these societies learned to use simple hand tools to till the soil and plant seeds in order to grow grains for food. They figured out that certain grains could be planted in soft ground. Likewise, they developed ways to raise certain types of animals in captivity, such as cows, goats, and chickens, which increased their food supply and allowed them to become less nomadic.[17]

Around 5,000 to 7,000 years ago, some groups took yet another step in the evolution of society. With the invention of the plow, agricultural societies arose. The simple technology of the animal-drawn plow—a sharp, hard piece of stone, wood, or metal that tills the soil—helped people cultivate lands that were previously unusable. The dramatic increase in food production promoted the growth of cities.[18] These agrarian city-states were often quite large, with up to one million people. Humans lived for approximately 500 generations in agrarian cultures.[19]

The Stages of Societal Change

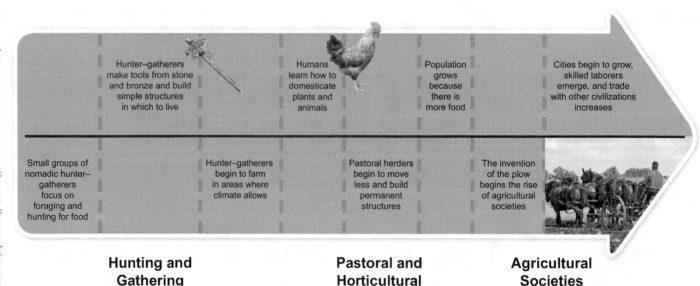

Hunter–gatherers make tools from stone and bronze and build simple structures in which to live

Humans learn how to domesticate plants and animals

Population grows because there is more food

Cities begin to grow, skilled laborers emerge, and trade with other civilizations increases

Small groups of nomadic hunter–gatherers focus on foraging and hunting for food

Hunter–gatherers begin to farm in areas where climate allows

Pastoral herders begin to move less and build permanent structures

The invention of the plow begins the rise of agricultural societies

Hunting and Gathering Societies

Pastoral and Horticultural Societies

Agricultural Societies

Industrial Societies

During the 17th and 18th centuries, the Western world experienced an industrial revolution. Complex machines, such as the steam engine, encouraged the growth of industry. Steam-powered machines made human labor more efficient because the machines could perform a simple task quickly and repeatedly without rest.[20] The steam engine revolutionized the clothing industry, for example, because fabric no longer had to be hand-woven. Machines mass-produced fabric, which reduced the cost of labor.

This basic idea, using technology to create goods, greatly expanded the surplus of industrial societies. Farming techniques improved through mechanization, and early tractors expanded the farmable land even more. Fewer people were required to produce sufficient food for the population, which allowed for even more specialization of labor. As a result, more new types of jobs were created that ultimately led to new statuses and roles.

Lenski et al. suggested that industrial societies actually have less social inequality than agrarian societies.[21] This is largely because the increasing technology and surplus improve the standard of living. Even the poorest people in industrial societies have access to goods and services that are unavailable in agrarian societies. Working-class men, like the group Lamont studies in *The Dignity of Working Men*, exist in industrial societies.

The industrial society lasted only nine generations in some parts of the world, although it continues in others. The change occurred in some areas as a new form of society began—the postindustrial society.[22]

Postindustrial Societies

The term *postindustrial society* refers to the societal change that occurs when people move from an economy based on manufacturing to one based on service and technology. Such societies still require basic food and manufactured goods, but seek them from other countries. Before this stage, it's possible for a society to live off its natural resources. Since postindustrial societies can no longer meet their own needs, energy, food, and goods must be imported. These societies have become societies vested in a technology that grew exponentially with the invention of the microchip.

Sociologist Daniel Bell suggested three key characteristics of a postindustrial society: (1) a shift from manufacturing to services, (2) the centrality of the new science-based industries, and (3) the rise of new technical elites. These characteristics bring about changes in status and power.[23] The creation of wealth is no longer rooted in controlling land or building factories. Power and wealth are associated with who controls and develops the latest technology. Thus, Bill Gates became the richest man in the world by developing computer software.

Postindustrial societies have great surpluses of wealth and goods. Their material culture is the most developed of all societal forms. Consider the fact that even the poorest person in your neighborhood probably owns a phone or a television. Although these societies do not provide dramatic changes in where people live or how they are governed, the advances of technology expand divisions of labor and increase international interdependence.

SOCIAL INSTITUTIONS

Although hunting and gathering, agricultural, industrial, and postindustrial societies are very different, they all share—social institutions. **Social institutions** are structures that provide for patterned relationships.

> **SOCIAL INSTITUTIONS** are structures that provide for patterned relationships.

©Dave Wetzel/Shutterstock; ©Stephanie Maze/Corbis; ©Jim Sugar/Corbis

New occupations, such as scientists, arise that expand knowledge of the physical world

Migration to urban areas leads to safety, waste management, and resource

Economy moves from one based on manufacturing to one based on service and technology

Nations struggle for natural resources— whoever controls the technology holds the power

Inventions of technology, such as the steam engine, allow for machines that replace human labor

Increased food production and understanding of disease increases life expectancy

Increased industry leads to a greater need for natural resources and energy

The microchip brings about changes in biomedicine and genetic engineering, which expands life expectancy

Industrial Societies

Postindustrial Societies

GEMEINSCHAFT refers to community connections involving personal relationships based on friendship and kinship ties, such as family.

GESELLSCHAFT refers to societal connections that are more formal and impersonal.

In other words, the roles and statuses are already established and the members of society merely need to step into them. It's important to note that the specifics of these institutions change with the type of society and the culture of the people being studied.

Family

Families are a cultural universal and a social structure. The form of the family may have changed a great deal throughout human history, but the institution of family has remained constant.[24] Families teach the value of sharing and mutual support. They provide safety and security needs for their members, pass on important values, and offer a safe haven for raising children and caring for the elderly.

Educational and Religious Systems

These are two more structures that are universal to all societies. Educational systems transfer the knowledge and information of the society to new members and can be both formal and informal.

Every region has some type of educational system, even though every child does not always participate in that system.

Secondary School Net Enrollment Rate in World Regions, 2006	
Developed Regions	**92%**
Developing Regions	**54%**
Sub-Saharan Africa	25%
Oceania	33%
Southern Asia	54%
Western Asia	58%
Northern Africa	60%
Southeastern Africa	63%
Latin America & the Caribbean	67%
Eastern Asia	68%
Transitional Countries in South and Eastern Europe	84%

Source: Data from the United Nations, *The Millennium Development Goals Report, 2007.*

Religious practice varies a great deal depending upon a person's culture, but most religions unify people through an organized system of beliefs. By bringing people together, religion stabilizes society and provides a framework for people to live their lives.

Economic Systems

From the time of the earliest hunters and gatherers to today, societies have needed a system that helps people get what they need. Economic systems allow for the consumption, production, and orderly transition of goods from one person to another. If, for example, you want the new iPad, you have to trade money to get it. Without an economic system, people either do without, make the goods themselves, or steal.

Early economic systems involved bartering—the trading of goods from one person to another. As societies became more complex, the currency of coins and money became the default value source, allowing for quicker and easier transitions of goods and services.

To keep a society's economic system running smoothly and efficiently, rules must be established. That's why every society has political and legal systems to help establish rules for society at large.

Political and Legal Systems

Ever since the first chief in the first hunter-gatherer tribe was named, people have been involved in politics. Political systems distribute power in a society, and power is the key component of any political system, whether a dictatorship or democracy. As you consider the importance of political systems, it's crucial to understand how power is used.

Political power is used to create laws or rules that dictate right and wrong in society. So, the political and legal systems are integrally linked. When someone with power sees something that's wrong, he or she is likely to create a law to fix it. The legal system serves the vital function of enforcing those laws to maintain social order and promote unity.

Although the form may vary, family, education, religion, economics, politics, and legislation exist in every form of society. That makes these institutions social facts. As we have seen, societies become more complex as they develop; this complexity witnesses the replacement of many of the old ways of living and thinking.

HOLDING SOCIETY TOGETHER

When natural disasters strike, people reach out to help. Whether it's giving aid to earthquake victims in Haiti or helping rebuild a city after Hurricane Katrina, it is always refreshing to see the extent of people's generosity. Why does this happen? Disasters tend to unify people.

What exactly holds a society together? Solidarity. That's the "glue" that binds a society.

Mechanical and Organic Solidarity

Emile Durkheim suggested that simple forms of society have mechanical solidarity, whereas organic solidarity holds more complex societies together. In societies with mechanical solidarity, people's common beliefs and practices help bind them together. On the other hand, the interdependence of the people is what holds societies with organic

©Gautier Willaume/Shutterstock; ©AP Images/ The Ledger Independent, Terry Prather;
©Yuri Arcurs/Shutterstock; ©Anders Ryman/Alamy; ©AP Images/Jessica Kourkounis;
©Blend Images/SuperStock; ©Liv friis-larsen/Shutterstock

<<< Since people have virtually the same job, **mechanical solidarity** creates a common moral order that **holds people together.**

societies. In such a society, social status, role, and social class become very important. Are you interested in knowing the janitor who cleans the classroom? You're probably only aware that the seats and floor are clean. Tonnies suggested that as societies grow more complex, many of our interactions invariably become more impersonal.

As you review these ideas, you can see that large cities tend toward *Gesellschaft* relationships, while smaller ones tend to be more *Gemeinschaft*. That means the size of your immediate area influences your daily life.[26] This idea leads sociologists to look for other common behavior patterns. To do this, we turn from large-scale observations and review the sociological study of small orientations.

society together. Durkheim's idea led German sociologist Ferdinand Tonnies to investigate how the form of society affects the interactions that we might have.

Gemeinschaft and *Gesellschaft*

Society can be classified into two distinct groups: *Gemeinschaft* (or community) and *Gesellschaft* (or society).[25] **Gemeinschaft** connections involve personal relationships based on friendship and kinship ties, such as the family. A society's form can also influence the type of group. For example, small bands of hunters and gatherers live in communal societies because they have very little division of labor. This creates a group that exists with shared values, goals, and beliefs.

Often we also engage in groups considered as **Gesellschaft**. These relationships are more formal and impersonal. Urban life is filled with many impersonal interchanges, so groups living here are more likely to occur in industrial and postindustrial

Gemeinschaft

The common work and life experience of an Amish community is more *Gemeinschaft* than a group of businesspeople working together in an office.

The form of society also influences family sizes. *Gemeinschaft* family units are larger and more connected than *Gesellschaft* ones.

Gesellschaft

Religious expression is influenced by the size and form of society. How do *Gemeinschaft* expressions of religion differ from *Gesellschaft* ones?

THINK SOCIOLOGICALLY

Social Class and Character Traits

In *The Dignity of Working Men: Morality and the Boundaries of Race, Class, and Immigration*, Michèle Lamont describes how working-class men view members of the upper class. Many believe that a person's class connotes specific traits. For example, an "auto mechanic describes himself as

middle class because he shares, '[T]his whole idea of being concerned a little more about other things rather than your immediate self. That for me starts to define middle class.'"[27] Working-class men pick up on this feeling from middle-class workers that they are somehow morally inferior. Working-class men believe middle-class workers purposefully distance themselves from people "who are not

their own kind."[28] They point out specific attributes they associate with middle-class behavior, such as insensitivity, snobbery, and narrow-mindedness.

Generally, when people hear the terms working, middle, and upper class, they think of occupation and salary, not necessarily character. But do these terms also connote specific personal characteristics?

PERSONAL SPACE is the invisible bubble that each of us has around us that insulates us from others.

INTIMATE DISTANCE is distance reserved for those with whom we are very close.

PERSONAL DISTANCE is distance that ranges from 18 inches to 4 feet; this distance is for normal conversations.

SOCIAL DISTANCE is distance that ranges from about 4 feet to 12 feet and is usually reserved for formal settings.

PUBLIC DISTANCE is the zone of interaction that is used in highly formal settings; this distance includes everything greater than 12 feet.

IMPRESSION MANAGEMENT is management of the impression that the performer makes on others.

FRONT STAGE is what the audience sees, or the part of ourselves that we present to others.

BACKSTAGE is the demeanor that incorporates our true feelings and beliefs.

> ∨
> ∨ Just as you adjust the personal dis-
> ∨ tance between yourself and others depending on the situation, you probably also adjust your behavior so that it's appropriate for the setting you're in. **When you're in public, you often show off your best self to others and hide what you don't want them to see.**

Micro Orientations: Social Interactions

Generally, macro orientations take for granted that societal structures exist. Additionally, less emphasis is placed on the ways in which societies are held together. Thus, symbolic interactionists tend to study the "how" of society, as opposed to the "what." Instead of observing what binds a society together, these sociologists seek to discover how that society is held together.

Communication is one component of the "how" of the social world. However, communication involves more than simply having conversations. From verbal interaction to physical distance, effective communication requires knowledge of the things that inform how we communicate with one another. One of those things, **personal space**, refers to the invisible bubble that each of us has around us that insulates us from others.

PERSONAL SPACE

How do you feel when someone stands very close to you during a conversation? It's a little uncomfortable, right? Even if the person is a friend, your natural impulse is to back away.

Our feelings about personal space often depend upon the setting and the person with whom we are interacting. For example, in order for a doctor to properly examine you, she needs to enter your personal space. In a different setting, you would never allow such behavior. Although socially appropriate amounts of personal space vary between cultures, Edward Hall suggests that people in the United States have four discrete zones of personal space.[29]

1 We reserve **intimate distance** for those with whom we are very close. This zone covers roughly from 0 to 18 inches. We generally reserve this distance for intimate encounters, but these conditions may vary depending on setting.

2 **Personal distance** ranges from 18 inches to 4 feet. Normal conversations occur at a personal distance. When you share secrets with a friend, you automatically lean in to an intimate distance. Once the whispering is over, though, you will automatically return to a personal distance.

Zones of Personal Space

Intimate Distance 0- 18″

Personal Distance 18″- 4′

Social Distance 4′- 12′

Public Distance 12′ or greater

3 **Social distance** ranges from about 4 feet to 12 feet and is usually reserved for formal settings. When you go on a job interview, for instance, you generally sit at what sociologist Edward Hall called "social distance."[30] Social encounters at this distance are not very personal. This distance allows the speaker to be heard, but does not presume any friendship.

4 **Public distance** refers to the zone of interaction that is used in highly formal settings. This distance includes everything greater than 12 feet. When you sit in the back of the classroom, you guarantee that you will maintain a public distance from your professor. Public distance also occurs during political speeches, at churches, and at formal events. Speakers are separate from the listener, and, generally, the audience shows respect and deference to the speaker.

DRAMATURGY

"All the world's a stage," Shakespeare wrote in *As You Like It*. Though he wasn't technically a sociologist, the Bard may have been more accurate than he realized. Erving Goffman developed a theory of interaction called dramaturgy, which suggests that life is like acting.[31] Social actors enter

> **EMBARRASSMENT** is a state that occurs when we realize our act has failed.
>
> **FACE-SAVING WORK** is a reaction to embarrassment in the form of either humor, anger, or retreat.

every situation with two possible selves. The first, the performer, attempts to manage the impressions that he or she makes on others. Goffman termed this effort **impression management**.

For example, if you think someone having an iced mocha at the corner coffee shop is attractive, you might want to make contact with him or her. As you approach, hoping to look "cool," you are entering the **front stage**. This is what the audience sees. Most of us live our lives on the front stage.

Of course, we are more than our front stage acts. **Backstage** demeanor incorporates our true feelings and beliefs. Most people do not show their backstage personas very often. We usually save that version of ourselves for our very closest family and friends.

Returning to our coffee shop example, let's assume that as you approach this person, you trip and fall. Obviously, you'll be embarrassed. **Embarrassment** occurs when we realize our act has failed. It's hard to pull off looking "cool" and tripping at the same time. When this type of mismatch happens, we engage in **face-saving work**. People generally choose one of three different options when they engage in face-saving work: humor, anger, or retreat.

Using humor, you can turn an embarrassing situation into a self-deprecating joke. This gives you the chance to impress upon the person that you have your act together because you can laugh at yourself.

In an angry reaction to this embarrassing situation, you may start cussing. This reaction is an attempt to say to the audience, "I'm powerful, even though I'm on the floor."

Efforts to retreat when we become embarrassed involve simply an attempt to escape. After all, our act has failed, and we want to leave the stage as soon as possible.

Goffman suggests that we would be wise to distrust most of what we see in other people because almost every interaction is front stage behavior. A wise student of Goffman can use impression management to get ahead in the world. Look at the Make Connections box and review the research there by Wayne and Liden.[32]

©Andrew Gombert/Photoshot

> > > > **On Friday, November 27th, 2009, life changed for Tiger Woods. A suspicious late night car crash led to a news conference in which he admitted to cheating on his wife.** After years of carefully crafting an image of the all-American athlete and role model, Woods faced a real problem of impression management. **Politicians and famous people caught in sex scandals face incredible scrutiny when their backstage behavior conflicts with the front stage image that consultants try to present.**

MAKE CONNECTIONS

Using Impression Management to Get Ahead in the Workplace

No matter where you start your career, you probably hope to climb the ladder of success while you're there. You can impress your boss and chart your course to the corner office of your dreams by following the simple steps below.

Wayne and Liden showed that successful impression management techniques positively affect an employee's performance rating.[33] They found three components that influence successful performance reviews:

demographic similarity, supervisor-focused impression management, and self-focused impression management. **Demographic similarity** means that you share characteristics such as race, gender, or age, with your boss, coworkers, or others you encounter. **Supervisor-focused impression management** techniques involve flattering your boss and agreeing with your boss's opinions (or at least avoiding disagreements whenever possible). **Self-focused impression management** techniques include acting modest about your accomplishments (even if that modesty is false), boasting occasionally about your successes, and showing your

friendliness and self-assuredness through smiles and eye contact.

Most of us like people who are like us, and bosses are no different. By using either self-focused or supervisor-focused impression management techniques, you can advance your career and look forward to the day when your employees use impression management techniques to impress *you*.

>>> ACTIVITY The next time you hang out with a friend, act as though your friend is your boss and use the impression management techniques listed above. Record how he or she responds and share it with your class.

think sociologically: HOW DO THE THREE PARADIGMS VIEW SOCIAL STRUCTURES?

Now let's turn our attention from the specific terms and concepts of the macro/micro world, and look at it through the lens of the three sociological paradigms.

An Example of Symbolic Interactionism: The Thomas Theorem and the Social Creation of Reality

From the interactionist point of view comes the Thomas Theorem: "If men define situations as real, they are real in their consequences."[34] This statement describes the social construction of reality.

Think back to the chapter opener about how race can help dictate your own personal reality. White workers are more apt to view success as a personal achievement and are less concerned with issues such as equal opportunities or affirmative action. Many African Americans also believe in the "American Dream," but they are more likely to see obstacles that must be overcome in order to get there. Both groups believe that success is possible, but they have different opinions on what it takes to be successful. The social creation of reality emphasizes personal power; however, it does not deny the importance of social structures and their effect on us. We attach the meaning of events to them.

An Example of Functionalism: Studying Essential Features of Functional Social Structures

When functionalists study a topic, they often ask how various elements fit together. Social institutions and structures serve essential functions in a society. As you study social structures in later chapters, you will see a general functional framework that applies in virtually all cases. Durkheim (1858–1917) called these essential features "functional requisites."[35] Consider the five primary tasks of society that create social structures: (1) adaptation and replacement, (2) orientation and socialization, (3) production and economy, (4) social order, and (5) unity and purpose.

Adaptation and Replacement Effective and functional societies must get their needs met to survive. Jared Diamond suggests that

societies collapse unless they can accomplish certain tasks, including adapting to changes in the environment.[36] Adaptations are also essential for accommodating the changing relationships that a society has with the world around it.

Besides adapting to environmental and political changes, societies must also replace people who either die or leave the group. Without continually replacing people, societies cannot carry on.

Socialization and Orientation Closely tied to replacement are socialization and orientation of new members. When children are born, they need to be socialized into the group. Socialization and orientation are vital to the continuation of a society because these processes allow new members to join and assign them roles. In "traditional societies," this assigning of roles might include gender-specific tasks such as men hunting or women caring for children. In a postindustrial society, socialization and orientation can be much more formal and include teaching related social norms.

©Corbis/SuperStock

∧
∧ **According to Durkheim, there are**
∧ **"functional requisites" that hold**
society together. Think of the five
tasks listed as puzzle pieces; if
you're missing one, the puzzle
isn't complete.

Socialization is not possible without some means to communicate. Societies create a system of symbols that include language and gestures to orient new members and to pass on information to the next generation. Socialization takes place in schools and families as well as through media, religion, and other structures found in various forms of society.

Production and Economy Production The ability of a society to meet its needs through its environment is the most important idea associated with this task. Simple societies create a material culture based on the resources at hand, whereas more complex societies trade with other groups to get the goods and services they need.[37] People within complex societies require an economic system to simplify the trading of goods and services. Although the exact nature of the economic system differs between societies, people always need a way to make or acquire the goods and services they need.

Social Order Because every society has people who cannot follow the rules, social norms and sanctions must be created to deal with these lawbreakers. In simple societies, force and strength might rule the day, whereas in complex societies, people settle disputes through legal battles. Not all societies have written laws, but they all socialize their members to promote social order.

Unity and purpose unity is achieved through common thoughts, beliefs, and attitudes. The United States is built on common ideals, not common heritage. Those shared thoughts united people, leading them to create a new country. Unity is also achieved through a sense of purpose, which gives a society some goal to achieve. This purpose holds people together, causing them to work together in times of trial.[38]

DEMOGRAPHIC SIMILARITY refers to shared characteristics such as race, gender, or age.

SUPERVISOR-FOCUSED IMPRESSION MANAGEMENT refers to techniques that involve flattering your boss and agreeing with your boss's opinions (or at least avoiding disagreements whenever possible).

SELF-FOCUSED IMPRESSION MANAGEMENT refers to techniques that include acting modest about your accomplishments (even if that modesty is false), boasting occasionally about your successes, and showing your friendliness and self-assuredness through smiles and eye contact.

An Example of Conflict Theory: Deliberate Efforts to Weaken the Structure and Culture of Native Americans

In order to understand the interaction of micro and macro components, consider the conflict perspective of the interaction of Native Americans with European settlers. Be aware that the connections Native Americans had with whites varied, which makes historical sociological generalizations very difficult.

Long before whites arrived in North America, a variety of different Native American cultures emerged. Although tribal societies did fight between themselves, Native Americans clashed violently with the influx of Europeans in the country. Eventually, the newcomers assumed that every inch of land was open for settlement, and conflict increased.

After the so-called Indian Wars, the remaining Native Americans endured a process known as Americanizing. Striving to change both micro and macro components of Native American life, the goal was to teach them "white ways." The acculturation of Native Americans involved deliberate efforts to make them a part of the "melting pot" of the United States.[39]

When whites dominated various Native American cultures, they generally did so out of a desire to control land and gain wealth. Policies such as the Dawes Act were purportedly enacted to help Native Americans. However, the Dawes Act allowed whites guardianship over Native American lands. These policies did little more than dismantle the reservations in an effort to turn Native Americans into farmers.

Perhaps the most abusive form of Americanization involved the use of boarding schools. These schools existed to "educate" Native Americans by trying to destroy their culture and teach them to be "white" instead. The schools took children from their parents early in life and barred them from speaking their native tongue. Frequently, these children were not allowed to visit their parents at all. The misguided motivation behind the Americanization effort was supported by the desire to change the next generation of Native Americans into good citizens of the United States. Without any power to control their own lives, these children fit into neither the white world nor their own.[40]

The structures of family and the entire Native American population were weakened because the children were removed, thus leaving parents with no role to fill and children without the support they needed. Consequently, a generation of people was unschooled in their own culture. Whites saw the efforts to Americanize natives as a social program designed to help them assimilate, but Native Americans saw it as an example of cultural genocide.[41]

WRAP YOUR MIND AROUND THE THEORY

Race can define our reality. **How do you think these different characters** from *The Blind Side* might **define their situations?**

SYMBOLIC INTERACTIONISM

Symbolic interactionists believe that a person's social creation of reality may take into account social issues such as job opportunities, welfare policies, and unemployment. Experiences with these issues can have an effect on people, causing them to alter their creation of reality. Recall how impression management can be used to help you get ahead on the job. Bosses may take demographic differences into account. The 2009 film *The Blind Side* provides a look at how racial definitions can influence our perceptions. When the affluent Tuohys adopt struggling African American teen Michael Oher, friends of the family react with mixed feelings, both applauding the Tuohys for offering Michael a safe home, and warning them that he is likely to steal or abuse their other children. Race influences our opinions of people, as well as our definitions of what is real and what is not.

FUNCTIONALISM

Social institutions and structures are essential functions for society. Sociologists believe that there are five basic structures necessary for a society to function. However, just because society is getting its needs met, this does not mean individual members of society are also having their needs fulfilled. The United States has a stable social structure, but millions and millions of people are living at or below the poverty level. Functionalists might suggest that for both the rich and poor, the economic system rewards those with ability and drive, while the system allows those who are less motivated to fall behind of their own merits. In Lamont's book, white factory workers tend to be functionalist while minorities see things differently. Why do you think there is a difference? Should people rethink the causes of poverty?

WHY IS THERE SUCH A DISTINCTION BETWEEN THE WORKING CLASS AND OTHER CLASSES IN THE UNITED STATES?

CONFLICT THEORY

Conflict theorists often look at how the structures of society favor one group over another. After Hurricane Katrina hit the Gulf Coast in 2005, money flowed into New Orleans to help the city rebuild. However, research by the Brookings Institute shows that the rebuilding process is closely linked to the wealth of the area. Wealthy areas of flooded New Orleans have generally been rebuilt, while poorer neighborhoods still remain unlivable.[42] Did the citizens' social class really affect their treatment? In Michèle Lamont's *The Dignity of Working Men*, she points out that the current isolation of the U.S. poor from the rest of society applies nationwide. Conflict theorists suggest that the scales of opportunity are not balanced between the rich and poor. They favor the rich.

Even though we are living in a stable society, millions of Americans are living in poverty. **How should society adapt to help these individuals?**

Social structures favor the affluent. **How does society tip the scales in certain segments?**

discover sociology in action: HOW CAN SOCIAL POLICIES IMPROVE SOCIETY?

In our culture, social policies are applied in an effort to improve society. High-quality preschool is one such policy that provides an interaction between macro and micro components.

Social Policy— The Perry Preschool Project

Does early intervention assist children in negotiating the macro and micro components of American society? One study set out to find the answer by following students at Michigan's Perry Elementary School from 1960 to the present day.[43] Students enrolled in the preschool program there attended school for two and a half hours each morning, five days a week. Each child also received a weekly home visit from a teacher, during which the teacher worked with students on academic skills and guardians on parenting skills. All of the children were living in poverty at the time of the project.

The cost of this program was high when compared with standard preschool programs, mostly because teachers were extremely well qualified and were paid accordingly. The results support the notion that high-quality early childhood education improves students' lives in the long term, despite the students' socioeconomic backgrounds.

In 2002, when the original Perry Preschool participants were about 40 years old, Lawrence Schweinhart examined their lives. The students who had participated in the revolutionary program reported better educational outcomes, higher salaries, and fewer arrests compared to those who did not participate. Furthermore, although the program was expensive to run, it actually saved money over the 42-year period. Most students in the program did not ultimately require special education, welfare, or incarceration, so fewer tax dollars were spent on these programs. Schweinhart's study shows that high-quality early childhood intervention can create significant positive changes in students' lives, the communities where they lived, and our society as a whole.[44]

Social policies, like preschool, help improve society. However, the quality of implementation drastically affects the outcome of the programs.

ACTIVITIES

1. Visit a Head Start program in your area. Talk to the staff and the clients, and learn why early intervention is important. Consider spending some time helping them as a student volunteer.
2. What type of public funding does your state provide for preschool education? Does the state rank day care centers based on quality? If so, how?
3. Aside from preschool, what features act to strengthen U.S. society? What features weaken it?

From Classroom to Community } Giving Kids a Head Start

Janet, a student in a sociology course, decided to volunteer at Head Start, a national educational program similar to the Perry Preschool Project that, largely due to a lack of funding, has never attained Perry's level of success.

She told our class, "The first thing I noticed was that the entire program was about socialization. The teachers taught the kids about rules and how to fit in. The children and parents both attend different classes designed to help them adapt to school and eventually be successful in it."

During her time as a volunteer, Janet helped set up classrooms, file necessary papers, and supervise the children during free time. "Playing with the kids was my favorite thing to do. I discovered that many of the things with which I was raised are rare for these children. For example, their clothes and toys were often used and torn. Some came to Head Start for lunch because their parents could not always afford food for them."

Janet saw her time at Head Start through the lenses of both functionalists and conflict theorists. "I couldn't help but think that this program was really there to help teach children how to fit into school and the larger society. In that way, it supports social control components of society and socializes children.

"However, the lack of staff and funding seemed to be the major issue facing my placement. I couldn't help but wonder why the program was so underfunded. It seems like people should be able to do more to help these kids learn."

WHAT ELEMENTS CREATE A SOCIAL STRUCTURE?

macrosociology and microsociology

HOW DO THE THREE PARADIGMS VIEW SOCIAL STRUCTURE?

functionalism: social institutions and structures serve essential functions in a society

conflict theory: the structure and culture of the underprivileged are deliberately weakened for the benefit of the dominant group

symbolic interactionism: social construction of reality: "If men define situations as real, they are real in their consequences"

HOW CAN SOCIAL POLICIES IMPROVE SOCIETY?

high-quality preschool programs: improve the lives of the participants; decrease the amount of funding needed for other social programs (special education, welfare)

get the topic: WHAT ELEMENTS CREATE A SOCIAL STRUCTURE?

Macrosociology and Microsociology
Micro Orientations: Social Interactions
An Example of Symbolic Interactionism:
   The Thomas Theorem and the Social
   Creation of Reality

An Example of Functionalism: Studying
   Essential Features of Functional Social
   Structures

An Example of Conflict Theory: Deliberate
   Efforts to Weaken the Structure and Culture
   of Native Americans
Social Policy—The Perry Preschool Project

Theory

FUNCTIONALISM

- social institutions and structures are essential functions for society
- five primary tasks of society that create social structures: (1) adaptation and replacement, (2) orientation and socialization, (3) production and economy, (4) social order, (5) unity and purpose
- just because society is having its needs met, this does not mean individual members of society are also having their needs fulfilled

CONFLICT THEORY

- study issues such as race, social class, and inequality

- conflict theorists perceive a pattern of inequality for the U.S. poor that does not occur on an international level, such as Hurricane Katrina relief

SYMBOLIC INTERACTIONISM

- a person's social creation of reality may take into account social issues such as job opportunities, welfare policies, unemployment, and access to a living wage
- experiences with these issues can have an effect on people, causing them to alter their creation of reality

Key Terms

macrosociology	master status	Gemeinschaft	embarrassment
microsociology	role	Gesellschaft	face-saving work
social structures	role expectations	personal space	demographic similarity
groups	role performance	intimate distance	supervisor-focused impression management
primary groups	role conflict	personal distance	
secondary groups	role strain	social distance	self-focused impression management
social class	stigma	public distance	
status	discredited stigma	impression management	
achieved status	discreditable stigma	front stage	
ascribed status	social institutions	backstage	

MY SEARCH LAB

1. *Names, Logos, Mascots, and Flags: The Contradictory Uses of Sport Symbols* by Stanley D. Eitzen, from *Fair and Foul: Beyond Myths and Paradoxes of Sport.* Copyright 1999 by Rowman & Littlefield Publishers, Inc. Reprinted with permission.

INTRODUCTION

This 1999 article by Eitzen demonstrates the importance of language and symbols in society.

DISCUSSION QUESTIONS

1. Some people argue that changing sexist language in sports will not change the way people feel about female athletes or result in more support for female athletics. Do you agree or disagree?
2. Make a list of examples of sexist or racist symbols and language in the area of jobs/employment.

©Corbis Royalty Free
©Corbis/SuperStock
© JP Laffont/ Sygma/Corbis

2. *The Social Construction of Reality* by Peter L. Berger, reprinted from *Invitation to Sociology*, 1963, Anchor/Doubleday & Company, Inc. Copyright by Peter L. Berger. pp.1-24. www.randomhouse.com

INTRODUCTION

In their 1966 book *The Social Construction of Reality: A Treatise in the Sociology of Knowledge*, Berger and Luckmann introduce the idea that social reality emerges through the process of interaction.

DISCUSSION QUESTIONS

1. According to the authors, there are elements that provide the scene and tools to understand reality that predatess the individual. What are they?
2. Explain how face-to-face interactions are both predictably patterned and highly flexible.

3. *Suspended Identity: Identity Transformation in a Maximum Security Prison* by Thomas J. Schmid and Richard S. Jones, reprinted from *Symbolic Interaction*, Vol. 14, No. 4, 1991 by permission of University of California Press.

INTRODUCTION

In this 1991 ethnographic analysis of prison, the authors use participant observation to show how individual prisoners go through identity transformation as an adaptation to incarceration.

DISCUSSION QUESTIONS

1. Explain what "impression management" means. How does impression management become increasingly important to a prison inmate?
2. How does an inmate's identity shift and change through the duration of imprisonment? Explain the pre-prison, middle, and post-prison identities.

THE THINKSPOT

Can social media be considered a corporate structure? Is social media taking the place of government? These are some interesting questions, to say the least. Go to the ThinkSpot to watch Dan Robles of the Ingenesist Project discuss these very questions and why he thinks the answers to both questions may be "yes." Robles, the founder of the site, states that "The Ingenesist Project provides complete specification for an innovation economy built on a platform of social media." After watching this video, do you agree?

Now that you've read the chapter and thought long and hard about social interactions, go to the ThinkSpot and watch the clip from "The Big Bang Theory" in which Leonard, Sheldon, and Penny have an interaction in their apartment building's lobby that illustrates just how differently people interact at the social level. Think about what symbolic interactionists, functionalists, and conflict theorists would say about this interaction.

Sample Test Questions

These multiple-choice questions are similar to those found in the test bank that accompanies this textbook.

1. In what kind of society is the economy based on service and technology?

   a. Industrial
   b. Agricultural
   c. Postindustrial
   d. Hunting and gathering

2. Craigslist is an example of a modern-day

   a. social institution.
   b. political system.
   c. barter system.
   d. religious group.

3. Which of the following systems distributes power in a society?

   a. Legal
   b. Political
   c. Economic
   d. Educational

4. Which of the following groups is the best example of a *Gemeinschaft* relationship?

   a. A large city
   b. A soccer team
   c. A government
   d. A large corporation

5. Which of the five tasks of society allows new members to join and assigns roles to the new members?

   a. Socialization and orientation
   b. Adaptation and replacement
   c. Production and economy
   d. Unity and purpose

ESSAY

1. What are the differences between an industrial society and a post-industrial society?
2. How do societies demonstrate adaptation and replacement for survival? Give examples.
3. Why is it important to observe the conventions of personal space?
4. Explain how a group might change from a *Gemeinschaft* to a *Gesellschaft*.
5. Which systems would a conflict theorist target when addressing the issue of poverty? Why?

WHERE TO START YOUR RESEARCH PAPER

For more information on sociological theories, especially the works of Durkheim and Marx, go to http://www2.uwsuper.edu/HPS/MBALL/DEAD_SOC.HTM

To learn more about the agricultural revolution and its transition from hunting and gathering, go to http://www.wsu.edu/gened/learn-modules/top_agrev/agrev-index.html

For a detailed view of hunting and gathering in New Guinea, go to http://www.climatechange.umaine.edu/Research/projects/NewGuinea.html

To learn more about how elevated social status may help people live longer lives, go to http://www.newscientist.com/article/dn10972-social-status-helps-you-live-longer.html

For more information on impression management as an important factor in business success, go to http://changingminds.org/index.htm http://www.impressionmanagement.com/ http://www.salesvantage.com/article/view.php?w5857&Using_Impression_Management_to_Excel_in_Your_Career/

To learn more about Head Start, go to http://www.acf.hhs.gov/programs/hsb/hsweb/index.jsp

ANSWERS: 1. c; 2. c; 3. b; 4. b; 5. a

Endnotes

1. Reprinted by permission of the publisher from *The Dignity Of Working Men: Morality and the Boundaries of Race, Class, and Immigration* by Michèle Lamont, p. 234, Cambridge, Mass.: Harvard University Press, Copyright © 2000 by the Russell Sage Foundation.

2. Charles H. Cooley, *Human Nature and Social Order*, Revised ed. (New York: Scribner and Sons, 1922).

3. Dennis Gilbert, *The American Class Structure in an Age of Growing Inequality*, 6th ed. (Belmont CA: Wadsworth, 2003).

4. Yanjie Bian, "Chinese Social Stratification and Social Mobility." *Annual Review of Sociology*, 2002. 28: 91–116.

5. Julian A. Oldmeadow, Michael J. Platow, Margaret Foddy, and Donna Anderson, "Self-categorization, Status, and Social Influence," *Social Psychology Quarterly*, 2003. 66(2): 138–152.

6. Ibid.

7. Ibid.

8. Kwaadsteniet, Erik W. and Eric van Dijk, "Social status as a cue for tacit coordination," *Journal of Experimental Social Psychology* 46 no. 3 (2010): 515–524.

9. Robert K. Merton, "The Role-Set: Problems in Sociological Theory," *British Journal of Sociology*, 1957. 8: 106–120; Robert K. Merton, *Social Theory and Social Structure*, Revised and Enlarged ed. (New York: The Free Press, 1968).

10. Erving Goffman, *Stigma: Notes on the Management of Spoiled Identity* (Englewood Cliffs, NJ: Prentice-Hall, 1963).

11. Gerhard Lenski, Jean Lenski, and Patrick Nolan, *Human Societies* (New York: McGraw-Hill, 1990).

12. Douglas S. Massey, "A Brief History of Human Society: The Origin and Role of Emotion in Social Life: 2001 Presidential Address," *American Sociological Review*, 2002. 67(1): 1–29.

13. Gerhard Lenski, *Power and Privilege: A Theory of Social Stratification* (Chapel Hill, NC: University of North Carolina Press, 1966).

14. Jared Diamond, *Collapse: How Societies Choose to Fail or Succeed* (New York: Viking Penguin Press, 2005).

15. Douglas S. Massey, "A Brief History of Human Society: The Origin and Role of Emotion in Social Life: 2001 Presidential Address," *American Sociological Review*, 2002. 67(1): 1–29.

16. Gerhard Lenski, Jean Lenski, and Patrick Nolan, *Human Societies* (New York: McGraw-Hill, 1990).

17. Ibid.

18. Ibid.

19. Douglas S. Massey, "A Brief History of Human Society: The Origin and Role of Emotion in Social Life: 2001 Presidential Address," *American Sociological Review*, 2002. 67(1): 1–29.

20. Gerhard Lenski, Jean Lenski, and Patrick Nolan, *Human Societies* (New York: McGraw-Hill, 1990).

21. Ibid.

22. Douglas S. Massey, "A Brief History of Human Society: The Origin and Role of Emotion in Social Life: 2001 Presidential Address," *American Sociological Review*, 2002. 67(1): 1–29.

23. Daniel Bell, *The Coming of Post Industrial Society: A Venture in Social Forecasting* (New York: Basic Books, 1973, 1999).

24. Stephanie Coontz, *Marriage, A History: How Love Conquered Marriage* (New York: Penguin Publishing, 2005).

25. Ferdinand Tonnies, *Community and Society (Gemeinschaft und Gesellschaft)*. Translated and edited by Charles P. Loomis, (East Lansing, Michigan: Michigan State University Press, 1887).

26. Steven Brint, "Gemeinschaft Revisited: A Critique and Reconstruction of the Community Concept," *Sociological Theory*, 2001. 19(1): 1–23.

27. Michèle Lamont, *The Dignity Of Working Men: Morality and the Boundaries of Race, Class, and Immigration* (Cambridge, Massachusetts: Harvard University Press, 2000).

28. Ibid.

29. Edward T. Hall, *The Hidden Dimension* (New York: Anchor Books, 1966, 1982).

30. Ibid.

31. Erving Goffman, *The Presentation of Self in Everyday Life* (Edinburgh: University of Edinburgh, Social Sciences Research Centre, 1958).

32. Ibid.

33. Sandy J. Wayne and Robert C. Liden, "Effects of Impression Management on Performance Ratings: A Longitudinal Study," *The Academy of Management Journal*, 1995. 38(1): 232–260.

34. W. I. Thomas and Dorothy Swaine Thomas, *The Child in America: Behavior Problems and Programs* (New York: Alfred A. Knopf, 1928).

35. Emile Durkheim, *Rules of Sociological Method*, Edited by George E. G. Catlin, Translated by Sarah A. Solovay & John H. Mueller, (New York: The Free Press of Glenco, 1895).

36. Jared Diamond, *Collapse: How Societies Choose to Fail or Succeed* (New York: Viking Penguin Press, 2005).

37. Jared Diamond, *Guns, Germs, and Steel: The Fates of Human Societies* (New York: W.W. Norton and Company, 1999).

38. Emile Durkheim, *Rules of Sociological Method*, Edited by George E. G. Catlin, Translated by Sarah A. Solovay & John H. Mueller. (New York: The Free Press of Glenco, 1895); D. F. Aberle, A. K. Cohen, A. K. Davis, M. J. Levy Jr., and F. X. Sutton, "The Functional Prerequisites of a Society," *Ethics*, 1950, 60(2): 100–111; Raymond W. Mack and Calvin P. Bradford, *Transforming America: Patterns of Social Change*, 2nd ed. (New York: Random House, 1979); Jared Diamond, *Guns, Germs, and Steel: The Fates of Human Societies* (New York: W.W. Norton and Company, 1999); Jared Diamond, *Collapse: How Societies Choose to Fail or Succeed* (New York: Viking Penguin Press, 2005).

39. Evon Z. Vogt, "Acculturation of American Indians." *Annals of the American Academy of Political Science*, 1957. 311: 137–146.

40. Colin G. Calloway, *First Peoples: A Documentary Survey of American Indian History*, 2nd ed. (Boston: Bedford/St. Martin's, 2004).

41. Ibid.

42. Brookings, "Concentrated Poverty in New Orleans and Other American Cities," http://www.brookings.edu/opinions/2006/0804cities_katz.aspx (accessed June 4, 2010).

43. David P. Weikart, "An Early Education Project that Changed Students' Lives: The Perry School Program, 20 Years Later," *Education Digest*, 1985. 51: 32–35.

44. Lawrence J. Schweinhart, The High/Scope Perry Preschool Study through Age 40: Summary, Conclusions and Frequently Asked Questions, *High/Score Educational Research Foundation*, http://www.highscope.org/productDetail.asp?intproductID52164 (accessed October 11, 2006).

SOCIALIZATION

SOCIALIZATION

©Michael Newman/Photo Edit

When

I was a child, summers were spent outside. I went fishing at the lake, played baseball in the street, and ran through the sprinkler to cool off. I rarely watched television because, with no Disney Channel or Nickelodeon, there was no daytime TV directed at me. My toys were sticks, rocks, balls. When I think about how my own children are being raised, it's very different.

My children stay inside in the summer because it's "too hot." They are not free to imagine and create their own fun because we send them to organized activities where adults supervise or coach them. At home, they play on the computer or vegetate in front of the TV. They say they get "bored" easily, because they are passive receivers of information and stimulation.

In the book *Consuming Kids: Protecting Our Children from the Onslaught of Marketing & Advertising,* Susan Linn points out that corporations understand this, and therefore are targeting children as a way to influence adult spending. Advertisers spend more than $15 billion each year on direct marketing to children. That's a lot of Happy Meals. Advertisers know that a child customer today will likely become a loyal adult consumer later. However, Linn shows that this socialization is damaging to kids emotionally and intellectually. It even negatively affects their health.[1]

The Process of Fitting *into* Society

Have you ever wondered how your life would have been different had you been born at another time, in another country, with different parents? Lots of things influence a child's life. In *Consuming Kids: Protecting Our Children from the Onslaught of Marketing & Advertising*, Susan Linn looks at the role of media and advertising on the life of a child. Children no longer spend their days playing outside or pretending with friends. Today, their highly structured lives include a great deal of created imagery.

Even the most popular of children's books quickly become movies filled with created imagery limiting a child's own ability to think and create. When parents try to eliminate the influence of video games, movies, and advertising, the task is almost impossible. Parents are confronting the deliberate efforts of corporate America to woo their children to gain them as customers for life. The younger the target market, the trickier the ad campaign. Linn shows how advertisers often use cute, animated characters and stories to draw children into influencing their parents to buy the product for them. In this way, children are becoming integrated into the consumer culture of the United States. Children are often essentially trained or socialized into patterns of consumption. What long-term behavioral patterns will these children learn? In this chapter, we look in depth at how people are socialized and how different socialization affects people.

get the topic: WHAT IS SOCIALIZATION?

SOCIALIZATION is the process that teaches the norms, values, and other aspects of a culture to new group members.

Had you been born in another time, in another place, you might speak a different language, salute a different flag, and celebrate a different religion. The language, values, and beliefs we all have are passed down to us through a process of socialization.

Socialization is the process that teaches the norms, values, and other aspects of a culture to new group members. As such, it is a lifelong process of creating and maintaining group membership. Countless sociologists and psychologists have studied how people become socialized, which has led to the development of several socialization theories.

Socialization theory claims that the person we become is the result of our environment. According to sociologist Talcott Parsons,

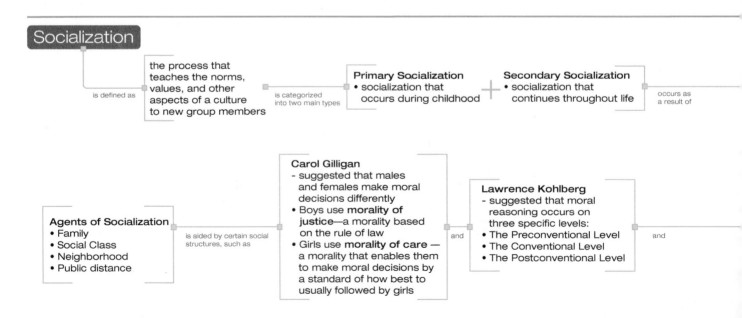

Socialization

— is defined as → the process that teaches the norms, values, and other aspects of a culture to new group members — is categorized into two main types → **Primary Socialization** • socialization that occurs during childhood + **Secondary Socialization** • socialization that continues throughout life — occurs as a result of

Agents of Socialization • Family • Social Class • Neighborhood • Public distance — is aided by certain social structures, such as → **Carol Gilligan** - suggested that males and females make moral decisions differently • Boys use **morality of justice**—a morality based on the rule of law • Girls use **morality of care** — a morality that enables them to make moral decisions by a standard of how best to usually followed by girls — and → **Lawrence Kohlberg** - suggested that moral reasoning occurs on three specific levels: • The Preconventional Level • The Conventional Level • The Postconventional Level — and socialization requires people to learn and internalize society's values.[2] In other words, we accept and integrate the values of the group as our own. These social values constantly surround us, but they often go unexamined.

At what point in our lives does socialization take place? Parsons and Bales argue that most socialization occurs during childhood.[3] Orville Brim refers to this early socialization as **primary socialization**.[4] Parents are their children's first teachers; they pass on values, rules, language, religious beliefs, and an unending list of social norms. However, socialization is also reciprocal because children also influence their parents. Before I had children, I thought I knew about parenting, but each child teaches me something new as I try to socialize them. Because socialization is an unending cycle, we are at times the "socializer" and at other times the "socialized."[5] This dynamic, whereby socialization continues throughout our lives is considered **secondary socialization**.[6] As you experience life-changing events—like going to college, beginning a career, or getting married—new socialization occurs. At each stage of life, we encounter new norms, values, and expectations. We learn to accept and integrate them as we adapt to our environment. In a sense, the socialization process makes us who we are. How might primary socialization that includes repeated advertising efforts influence a child?

The Nature vs. Nurture Debate—What Makes Us Who We Are?

As one theorist said, "We, and all other animals, are machines created by our genes."[7] Pure "**nature**" theorists believe that the genes we get from our parents at conception are the primary causes of human behaviors—in short, our genetic makeup determines who we are. Few geneticists would suggest we are born to consume, but we may be born to do other things.

In the 20th century, social scientists began to fight biologists' belief that nature is the sole determinant of who we are. Those who believe in "nurture," like philosopher John Locke, propose that our environment influences the way we think, feel, and behave.[8] Supporters of this idea assert that socialization molds us like pieces of clay, particularly during early childhood. Many nurture theorists believe that a social process teaches people who they are and how they fit into their world.

PRIMARY SOCIALIZATION is socialization that occurs during childhood.

SECONDARY SOCIALIZATION is the dynamic whereby socialization continues throughout our lives.

NATURE THEORY states that the genes we get from our parents at conception are the primary causes of human behaviors.

NURTURE THEORY states that our environment influences the way we think, feel, and behave.

Extreme proponents on both sides of the nature/nurture debate have difficulty sorting out this issue. Although it is true that our genes do not necessarily dictate our destiny, it's also true that our biological makeup is what interacts with the environment in the first place. Noted biologist and author Paul Ehrlich supports a blended point of view. In Ehrlich's book he notes, "We can't partition the responsibility for aggression, altruism, or charisma between DNA and upbringing. In many such cases, trying to separate the contributions of nature and nurture to an attribute is rather like trying to separate the contributions of length and width to the area of a rectangle, which at first glance also seems easy. When you think about it carefully, though, it proves impossible."[9]

©Tarhill Photos Inc/Corbis

∧∧∧ **Does our genetic makeup really determine who we will become? Or do other factors come into play, such as the way our parents care for us?** Where do you stand on the nature vs. nurture debate?

Nature
• the belief that genetic and biological heredity are the primary causes of human behaviors

or

Nurture
• the belief that the way in which we think, feel, and behave are the results of our environment

has inspired many theorists to explain how people become socialized, such as

Charles H. Cooley
• proposed the theory of "looking-glass self," which states that the self develops through a process of reflection

and

George Herbert Mead
- proposed that the self consists of two parts the "I" and the "Me"
- suggested that the self develops in three stages:
• The Imitation Stage
• The Play Stage
• The Game Stage

and

Jean Piaget
- proposed that people go through a four-stage process of cognitive development:
• The Sensorimotor Stage
• The Preoperational Stage
• The Concrete Operational Stage
• The Formal Operational Stage

and

Erik Erikson
- proposed that people develop a personality in eight psychosocial stages
- at each stage we experience a crisis that upon resolving will have an effect on our ability to deal with the next one

The Eight Stages:
• Infancy
• Toddlerhood
• Preschooler
• Elementary School
• Adolescence
• Young Adulthood
• Middle Adulthood
• Late Adulthood

THINK SOCIOLOGICALLY

Rhesus Monkey Study

Which is more important to our survival—nature or nurture? To find out, researchers Harry and Margaret Harlow conducted numerous experiments with rhesus monkeys.[10] One of the most famous was designed to test which need is greater: the need for physical contact or the need for biological sustenance. The Harlows raised monkeys in isolation and eventually presented them with two artificial "mothers." The first "mother"—which was simply a hard wire frame with a wooden head—provided food. The other "mother" provided no food at all but was made of soft, cuddly material. The Harlows noticed that frightened baby monkeys sought comfort with the soft "mother" and not with the "mother" that fed them. They drew the conclusion that the key component of infant–mother bonding is not the providing of food, but the presence of comfort. The Harlows' findings, while not directly applicable to human development, support the idea that socialization, i.e., nurture, is a key building block in normal development.

The Harlows' conclusion somewhat confounds Susan Linn's suggestion that children today are being led away from the traditional support systems of family, toward entertainment and consumption as a means of support. The need for support is particularly important in the early years of life. A lack of primary socialization can lead to long-term problems for a child.

FERAL AND ISOLATED CHILDREN

Tales of **feral**, or wild, children raised by animals are not limited to works of fiction like *Tarzan* or *The Jungle Book*. Newspapers and tabloids often feature sensational headlines about the discoveries of such children. Unfortunately, there are also too many stories about children held captive at the hands of abusive and/or mentally unstable parents. Although these stories are staples on the nightly news, we rarely explore or even think about what happens to these children as a result of their isolation. How does human contact, or the lack thereof, affect the people we become?

In April 2008, the story of Josef Fritzl — an Austrian father who had imprisoned his daughter in a basement dungeon for 24 years—attracted worldwide coverage on all the cable news networks. During this time, Fritzl repeatedly abused and raped his imprisoned daughter Elisabeth, even impregnating her seven times. One child died, Fritzl and his wife were raising three children, and the remaining three were left in the dungeon with little human contact. Until the rescue, the three isolated children had never seen the light of day, and they communicated using only simple grunts and gestures.[11] Having never seen sunlight, received proper nutrition, or nor gotten exercise or normal human interaction, Elisabeth and the Fritzl children, aged 19, 18, and 5 when rescued, faced intense physical and psychological therapy and likely will continue to undergo it for the rest of their lives.[12] Will the children ever become socialized?

Some clues might be found when looking at the story of Genie, a girl who was discovered in California in 1970. When authorities found Genie, she had literally been raised in her parents' attic strapped to an infant's potty chair and isolated from almost all socialization. Once removed from her home, doctors and researchers immediately began to care for her.[13] A group of experts, known as "the Genie team," observed that Genie could not walk normally and understood only a few words. Additionally, she had problems eating solid food and still needed diapers. However, after her rescue, Genie made rapid progress. She quickly learned to dress and go to the toilet herself. She also learned to walk more normally. Her language skills began to develop, and within a few months, her vocabulary of only 5 to 10 words had expanded to more than 100 words.[14]

Unfortunately, despite the massive efforts to help Genie, she never caught up with her peers. "The Genie team" concluded that her delayed progress was the result of missing key points in her primary social development. Because this lack of socialization kept her brain

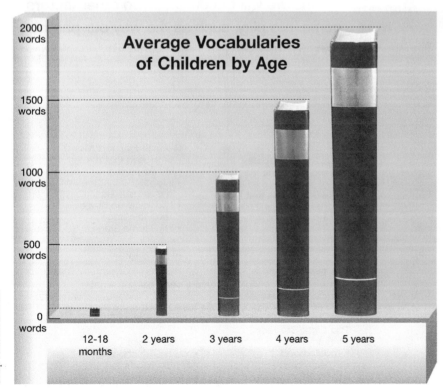

Average Vocabularies of Children by Age

2000 words — 1500 words — 1000 words — 500 words — 0 words

12-18 months | 2 years | 3 years | 4 years | 5 years

©Filip Fuxa/Shutterstock

Source: Based on *Stages of Language Development* by Louis De Maio.

<<< **Shortly after Genie's rescue, she developed a vocabulary of more than 100 words.** How does Genie's vocabulary compare to children raised in a more "typical" way?

from fully developing, Genie must now live in a home for mentally retarded adults, despite having been born mentally healthy.[15]

Not all feral children have such difficulty becoming socialized. Isabelle, a feral child whose grandfather locked her in a darkened room with her deaf–mute mother, was discovered at age six. She communicated only through gestures, which her mother taught her. Experts put Isabelle through a rigorous socialization process. Surprisingly, Isabelle learned quickly. After two months, she was able to speak in sentences, and after about 18 months she had a vocabulary of 1,500–2,000 words. Ultimately, Isabelle was able to go to school and function normally with children her own age.[16]

Humans need other humans in order to live and to develop normally. Our human nature is not necessarily instinctual. If it were, Genie would have been able to catch up developmentally to her peers.

Deprivation of human interaction is perhaps more detrimental to humans than being underfed or physically abused. If we are to achieve our full potential, we need others to socialize us. The nurturing we experience in our early lives ultimately affects who we are and who we will become.

Theorists on Socialization

Socialization is a process that theorists have been studying for decades. Many of these theorists, from sociologists to psychologists, have made significant contributions to our understanding of the development of self and the development of morality. Like a never-ending college course, we're enrolled in "socialization" until the day we die. In that sense, we're constantly learning about ourselves.

COOLEY'S LOOKING–GLASS SELF

Charles H. Cooley is one of the central theorists of the development of the self. His notion of the **"looking-glass self"** proposes that, like a mirror, the self develops through a process of reflection. That said, one's self is also established through interactions with others. According to Cooley, this process contains three steps:

1. We imagine how our behaviors will look to others.
2. We interpret others' reactions to our behaviors.
3. We develop a self-concept.[17]

Although Cooley's ideas were developed more than a century ago, modern scholars remain interested in them. King-To Yeung and John Levi Martin, contemporary sociologists who study the processes of the "looking-glass self," used Cooley's theory to test the internalization of self-understanding.[18] Their research found general support for the theory that our self-concept involves interpreting and internalizing others' perceptions about us. Yeung and Martin showed that the importance of our relationships is the key factor in determining how we internalize others' perceptions of us. This is why our parents influence us more than our local bank tellers do.[19]

GEORGE HERBERT MEAD—THE THREE STAGES OF THE "I-ME" SELF

Another theory about how humans develop the self was explored in symbolic interactionist George Herbert Mead's *Mind, Self, and Society*. For

---

FERAL means wild.

LOOKING-GLASS SELF is the theory that the self develops through a process of reflection, like a mirror.

"I" SELF is the subjective part of the self.

"ME" SELF is the objective part of the self.

IMITATION STAGE is Mead's first stage of development, which is the period from birth to about age 2, and is the stage at which children merely copy the behaviors of those around them.

PLAY STAGE is Mead's second stage of development, which occurs around the ages of 2-4 years, during which children play roles and begin to take on the characteristics of important people in their world.

GAME STAGE is Mead's third stage of development that never truly ends, and is the stage in which we begin to understand that others have expectations and demands placed upon them.

THE GENERALIZED OTHER is our sense of others.

Mead, the self is that part of personal identity that has both self-awareness and self-image.[20] Like Cooley, Mead agreed that the development of self involves interaction with others.

For Mead, though, the self consists of two parts: the "I" and the "Me." These two parts essentially create the self through their interaction. The **"I" Self** is the part of us that is an active subject, our subjective sense of who we are. It seeks self-fulfillment, asking, "What do *I* want?" In contrast, the **"Me" Self** is the objective part of the self; the part of our self-concept that questions how others might interpret our actions. The "Me" understands the symbols that others give us, and seeks to find favorable reactions to our behaviors from others.[21]

According to Mead, the self develops in three stages. The first is the **imitation stage**, which is the period from birth to about age 2. At this stage, children merely copy the behaviors of those around them. They don't attribute meaning to their actions, nor do they understand the implications of their behavior. For instance, when you see your baby sister clapping her hands, she's probably just imitating something she's seen and not actually giving you a round of applause.

Children enter the **play stage** around the ages of 2–4 years. Here, children play roles and begin to take on the characteristics of important people in their world. By playing roles, children see others as separate from themselves. They understand that their actions can affect other people, and vice versa. Mead claimed that, through play, children learn to find a sense of who they are and how to best interact with others in their society. At this stage, you're likely to see little boys tie blankets around their necks and pretend to be superheroes.

During our early school years, we enter what Mead called the **game stage**, a stage that never truly ends. It is in the game stage that we begin to understand that others have expectations and demands placed upon them. Mead termed this sense of others **"the generalized other."**

Through understanding others we are able to adjust or evaluate our own behavior based on factors such as culture and society. Developing a concept of the generalized other helps us understand other people's roles, norms, and expectations. This concept is important if we are to fit into society and live intimately with others.[22] The idea of little league sports best represents this stage.

When children are involved in a team sport like baseball or basketball, they must understand each position's roles and responsibilities in order to play the game. Not everyone can hit or shoot; everyone has a job to do or we can't play the game.

PSYCHOSOCIAL CRISIS is a crisis occurring during each of Erikson's stages that will be resolved either positively or negatively, and each outcome will have an effect on our ability to deal with the next one.

COGNITIVE DEVELOPMENT is a person's ability to think and reason.

SENSORIMOTOR STAGE is the stage (birth to 2 years) at which infants learn to experience and think about the world through their senses and motor skills.

PREOPERATIONAL STAGE is the stage (ages 2 through 7 years) at which the ability to speak grows rapidly.

CONCRETE OPERATIONAL STAGE is the stage (ages 7 through 12 years) at which children can think about objects in the world in more than one way and start to understand causal connections in their surroundings.

FORMAL OPERATIONAL STAGE is the stage (ages 12 years and above) at which people become able to comprehend abstract thought.

Erik Erikson's Eight Stages of Development

Erik Erikson proposed that humans develop a personality in eight psychosocial, or psychological and social, stages. During each stage, we experience a particular **psychosocial crisis** that will be resolved either positively or negatively, and each outcome will have an effect on our ability to deal with the next one.[23]

According to Erikson, the crisis at each stage of development must be resolved positively before you can successfully master subsequent stages. Think back to Genie. She was imprisoned from the infancy stage through the elementary school stage, so did she ever truly become socialized? The answer is no. Although Genie did make some initial progress, she regressed after her first foster parents severely punished her for vomiting. Genie refused to open her mouth for fear it might happen again and responded in the only way she knew how: silence.[24] Genie's case helps illustrate Erikson's theory that failing to master one stage can mean that a person will fail the subsequent stages.

Jean Piaget's Theory of Cognitive Development

While Erikson's research focused on personality development, the work of Jean Piaget focused on **cognitive development**, which relates to a person's ability to think and reason. Since the way we think helps shape our self-concept, cognition (thinking) plays a significant role in socialization. Simply put, Piaget found that children don't think like adults. His four-stage theory of cognitive development has become an important basis for much educational theory, particularly as it applies to teaching young children.

When my daughter was an infant, nearly everything she touched went directly into her mouth. It didn't matter if it was a stuffed panda, board book, or a long red millipede. If she could reach it, it was going in her mouth. According to Piaget, this is the way babies learn. At the **sensorimotor stage** (birth to age 2 years), infants learn to experience and think about the world through their senses and motor skills. During this period, children develop a sense of "object permanence," the understanding that objects outside themselves still exist even when they are not in view.[25] For example, play "peek-a-boo" with an infant and you'll notice that the baby expresses surprise when you cover your face, followed by great joy when you reveal it. Near the end of the sensorimotor stage, peek-a-boo loses its allure and object permanence exists.

At the **preoperational stage** (ages 2 through 7 years), the ability to speak grows rapidly. Although children have already learned some words and phrases, their ability to use and interpret symbols is limited. Children will generally identify objects by a single characteristic. If you show a child the letters *C-A-T*, for example, the child is likely to read each individual letter aloud. It is unlikely that she will link them together into the word *cat*. Linking multiple symbols together is difficult for a preoperational thinker. By the end of this stage, however, a child can say the word *ball*, draw a picture of a ball, point to a ball on the floor, and understand that all of these mean the same thing.[26]

During the **concrete operational stage** (ages 7 through 12 years), children can think about objects in the world in more than one way and start to understand causal connections in their surroundings. They can think logically about some objects and events. For example, they learn that even though a plain sheet of white paper is folded into a paper airplane, it is still that same piece of white paper. Children at this stage can also imagine what other people might be thinking or feeling. Piaget believed we can't understand the "position" of others until we have passed through some developmental state. Children gain this ability during the concrete operational stage.[27]

Only at the **formal operational stage** (ages 12 years and above) do people become able to comprehend abstract thought. Because they're testing their ability to reason and comprehend the complexities of their world, children at this stage often argue with those in authority. Unsure of themselves, they're testing their thinking. Understanding abstract mathematical principles, such as algebra, becomes possible at this stage, and we become able to understand more deeply the interactions of concrete reality with abstract ideals.[28]

Piaget argued that it could be frustrating and traumatizing to force children to learn ahead of their cognitive capacities. In other words, it serves no purpose to try to teach geometry to a first-grader. Expecting a child to act like an adult is both impossible and unfair.[29]

Each of the theorists—Cooley, Mead, Erikson, and Piaget—provides a different view of the development of self. **All these theorists agree that a person's development continues throughout life. These theories present human development as a type of staircase process.** Children who miss one or more stages of socialization generally fail to reach successful completion of their development.

Erikson's Eight Stages of Development

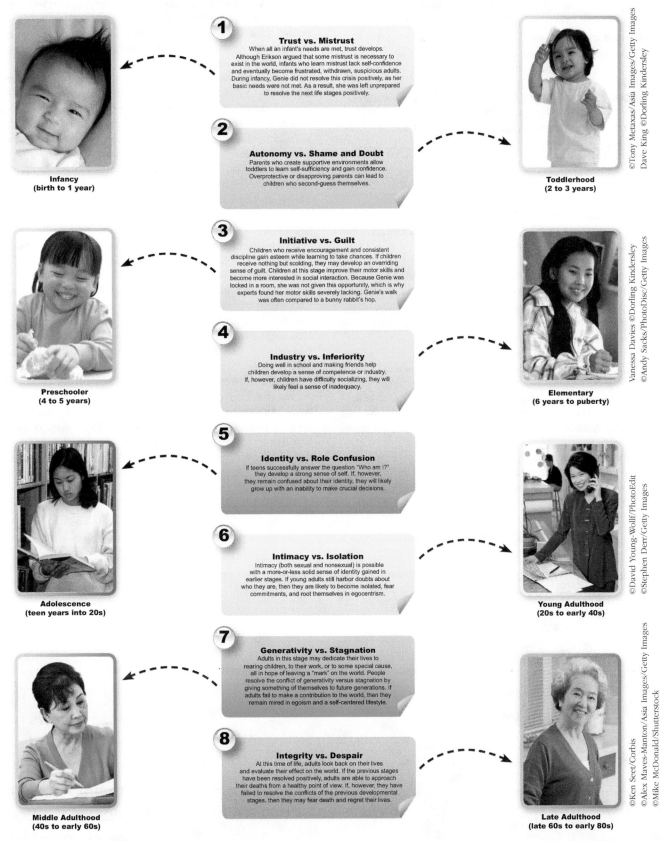

1 Trust vs. Mistrust
When all an infant's needs are met, trust develops. Although Erikson argued that some mistrust is necessary to exist in the world, infants who learn mistrust lack self-confidence and eventually become frustrated, withdrawn, suspicious adults. During infancy, Genie did not resolve this crisis positively, as her basic needs were not met. As a result, she was left unprepared to resolve the next life stages positively.

2 Autonomy vs. Shame and Doubt
Parents who create supportive environments allow toddlers to learn self-sufficiency and gain confidence. Overprotective or disapproving parents can lead to children who second-guess themselves.

3 Initiative vs. Guilt
Children who receive encouragement and consistent discipline gain esteem while learning to take chances. If children receive nothing but scolding, they may develop an overriding sense of guilt. Children at this stage improve their motor skills and become more interested in social interaction. Because Genie was locked in a room, she was not given this opportunity, which is why experts found her motor skills severely lacking. Genie's walk was often compared to a bunny rabbit's hop.

4 Industry vs. Inferiority
Doing well in school and making friends help children develop a sense of competence or industry. If, however, children have difficulty socializing, they will likely feel a sense of inadequacy.

5 Identity vs. Role Confusion
If teens successfully answer the question "Who am I?" they develop a strong sense of self. If, however, they remain confused about their identity, they will likely grow up with an inability to make crucial decisions.

6 Intimacy vs. Isolation
Intimacy (both sexual and nonsexual) is possible with a more-or-less solid sense of identity gained in earlier stages. If young adults still harbor doubts about who they are, then they are likely to become isolated, fear commitments, and root themselves in egocentrism.

7 Generativity vs. Stagnation
Adults in this stage may dedicate their lives to rearing children, to their work, or to some special cause, all in hope of leaving a "mark" on the world. People resolve the conflict of generativity versus stagnation by giving something of themselves to future generations. If adults fail to make a contribution to the world, then they remain mired in egoism and a self-centered lifestyle.

8 Integrity vs. Despair
At this time of life, adults look back on their lives and evaluate their effect on the world. If the previous stages have been resolved positively, adults are able to approach their deaths from a healthy point of view. If, however, they have failed to resolve the conflicts of the previous developmental stages, then they may fear death and regret their lives.

Infancy
(birth to 1 year)

Toddlerhood
(2 to 3 years)

Preschooler
(4 to 5 years)

Elementary
(6 years to puberty)

Adolescence
(teen years into 20s)

Young Adulthood
(20s to early 40s)

Middle Adulthood
(40s to early 60s)

Late Adulthood
(late 60s to early 80s)

Source: Based on *Childhood and Society* by Erik Erikson.

PRECONVENTIONAL LEVEL is the first stage of moral development that lasts through the elementary school years; at this level, children make their moral judgements within a framework of hedonistic principles.

HEDONISM is seeking pleasure over pain.

CONVENTIONAL LEVEL is the second stage of moral development that arises before puberty and uses the lens of norms and rules to determine what is right and wrong.

POSTCONVENTIONAL LEVEL is the third stage of moral development that refers to a morality based on abstract principles.

MORALITY OF JUSTICE is morality based on the rule of law.

MORALITY OF CARE is morality decided by a standard of how best to help those who are in need.

Theories of Moral Development

How do we know what's right and what's wrong? Do girls learn about morals differently from boys? These are just two of the questions that theories of moral development seek to answer.

Kohlberg's Theory of Moral Development

Building upon the work of Piaget, the prominent theorist Lawrence Kohlberg suggested that moral reasoning occurs on three specific levels: preconventional, conventional, and postconventional. Each level describes different ways in which we make moral decisions.[30]

During the **preconventional level**, which lasts through the elementary school years, children make their moral judgments within a framework of **hedonism**—seeking pleasure over pain.[31] In other words, children judge right from wrong on the basis of what feels good or right to them. If a little boy notices that drawing on the walls results in a visit to the "naughty stool," chances are he won't take the crayons to the walls again.

The **conventional level** arises before puberty and uses the lens of norms and rules to determine what is right and wrong.[32] Basically, what is "right" is obedience to the rules. Rather than question the logic behind why those rules were established, a child simply does what he or she is told. The child may not understand *why* kicking his sister is wrong; he just understands that he shouldn't do it because "Mommy says so." Following the expectations of the family or group is valuable in and of itself. Doing your duty and respecting authority are the hallmarks of this level of development.

Kohlberg's third stage of moral development, the **postconventional level**, refers to a morality based on abstract principles. These may be rooted in political beliefs, religious beliefs, or a combination of both. Kohlberg suggests that the "good" includes adherence to agreed-upon principles rather than rules.[33] Such principles guide all decisions and provide a seamless web of morality for us all. For example, during the civil rights movement of the 1950s and 1960s, countless African American college students held sit-ins at segregated lunch counters, museums, libraries, and many other public places. Although their behavior broke the Jim Crow laws of the time, these students believed their behavior was "right" because they were drawing attention to laws that were morally wrong.

Although Kohlberg's own research supported his theory, more recent scholars question some of his assumptions. For example, Charles Helwig and Urszula Jasiobedzka found that children's moral judgments about law and lawbreaking occur earlier in life than Kohlberg's theory proposed.[34] Preschoolers may abide by the rules because they believe rule-breaking is wrong. In addition, moral reasoning doesn't always correlate with moral behavior. Using Kohlberg's schema, Colby and Damon showed that people at the highest levels of moral development act the same as people at lower levels of moral development. Instead, the situation influences people's behavior.[35] Take speeding, for example. Although everyone knows it's against the law, many people speed when they believe they won't be caught. These and other questions about Kohlberg's theory of moral development led Carol Gilligan to propose another point of view in 1982.

<<< It's hard to imagine that the simple act of sitting at a lunch counter could be illegal. **The unfairness of laws such as these led many students of all races to hold peaceful sit-ins across the South in hopes of abolishing Jim Crow laws.**

Carol Gilligan and the "Morality of Care"

Carol Gilligan suggested that Kohlberg's theories were valid, though only when discussing the development of male morality. To Gilligan, his conclusions were biased against women because Kohlberg only studied men initially.[36] This, in turn, led him to erroneously assume men and women developed moral decisions similarly without actually studying women. Do men and women approach moral decisions differently?

I recently faced a moral decision while shopping at my local discount store. The cashier gave me $10 too much change. Being a bit of a miser, I immediately noticed her mistake. I'm human, so I considered keeping the money, but then I began to wonder what might happen if I took the money. Was it my fault that the cashier made a mistake? Would she get in trouble when she came up short at the end of her shift? All of these thoughts ran through my mind. Of course, I gave her the money back. Gilligan would argue that my gender influenced the way I approached my decision; women would follow a slightly different process.

After investigating women's experiences with morality, Gilligan concluded that moral decisions arise from two different principles: the morality of justice and the morality of care. She agreed that boys primarily follow what she called a **morality of justice**, a morality based on the rule of law. However, girls learn a **morality of care**, which enables them to make moral decisions by a standard of how best to help those who are in need.[37]

To study the differences between moral development in boys and girls, Gilligan proposed a real-life moral dilemma to young male and female subjects. Gilligan used the story of "Mr. Heinz and the Druggist," a tale that Kohlberg also used in his research. The general idea of the story is this: Mr. Heinz's wife is sick with a potentially fatal disease. Luckily, their small-town pharmacy is the only place around that carries the life-saving medication that his wife needs. The problem is the drug costs an astronomical $10,000, and the druggist refuses to sell it for any less. Should Mr. Heinz steal the drug?

Gilligan found that most male subjects used logic when answering the question. Many boys believed that Mr. Heinz should steal the medication, even though it's legally wrong. Boys reasoned that the judge would likely be lenient on Mr. Heinz because of the circumstances. In short, the boys answered the question like a math problem: $x + y = z$. The girl subjects, however, considered the personal relationships involved. Girls worried that Mr. Heinz might go to jail, which could make his wife sicker and leave no one around to care for her or provide her with medicine. They also tried to think of other ways for Mr. Heinz to get the drug so that he would not have to leave his wife. Girls were more concerned about how Mr. Heinz's actions would affect the dynamic between him and his wife.

Modern research provides mixed support for Gilligan's assertion of gender differences in moral reasoning. In short, it appears that girls and boys learn *both* morality of care and morality of justice. The two types of morality are not exclusive to one gender over the other.[38] Some findings show that since girls advance through the stages of moral development faster than boys, they actually develop postconventional morality at earlier ages.[39] The most important aspect, perhaps, is the link between ego development and the moralities of care and justice. Because girls develop faster than boys, they present a morality of care more quickly than boys.[40]

Either way, Gilligan and Kohlberg both agree that moral reasoning follows a developmental process and that the surroundings affect that process. Although the precise gender differences may not be as clearly distinguished as Gilligan initially believed, and Kohlberg's age groups may be more flexible than he proposed, both theories show that we learn to make moral decisions in different ways.

Kohlberg and Gilligan's Theories of Moral Development

Agents of Socialization

We learn socialization with outside help from different **agents of socialization**, which are the people and groups that shape our self-concept, beliefs, and behavior. So what social structures, or agents, help us become socialized?

THE FAMILY: PARENTING STYLES AND RECIPROCAL SOCIALIZATION

Few things in life shape us more than our parents. Because both my parents worked full time, I learned at an early age that one must work to live. I started working at 13 and am still working today, as evidenced by my writing this book on nights, weekends, and summer vacations. My parents also valued education. Although they never completed college, they encouraged us kids to go. Sometimes, I wonder what my life would have been like if I had had different parents. What if my parents were drug addicts? Or illiterate? Or members of the wealthiest elite in the country (my personal favorite)? My point is merely that children don't select their parents, and yet family is one of the most important agents of socialization.

When parents socialize their children, they do so in two different ways. First, they create safe environments by providing emotional support through love, affection, and nurturing. Second, parents provide social control by teaching their children appropriate behaviors. Parents do this by using force, coercion, threats, or rewards.[41] If parents are not successful at providing these things for their children, the results can be disastrous. Linn suggests that parents overtly work to limit the influence of corporate advertising on their children while at the same time encouraging independent thinking. The role of the parent in this endeavor is key.

Sociologist Diana Baumrind explored how parental discipline affects children. Although disciplining children is a cultural universal, the manner in which it occurs varies by culture and family style. Baumrind observed that parenting styles have a substantial effect on individual socialization outcomes.[42] Parents who practice an **authoritative style** listen to their children's input while consistently enforcing the preset rules. Children reared in such an environment integrate into the world with the most ease because they exhibit high levels of self-esteem and possess the capacities for independence and cooperation with others.

Whereas authoritative parents practice a balanced style of child-rearing, permissive and authoritarian parents represent opposite extremes, and neither produces positive outcomes. **Permissive style** parents provide high levels of support but an inconsistent enforcement of rules. This results in a child who does not understand boundaries and expectations. The teenagers on MTV's *My Super Sweet 16* who are showered with lavish gifts and extravagant parties by their affluent parents may be ill-equipped to deal with the disappointments and responsibilities that are sure to come later in life. Conversely, children reared by **authoritarian style** parents experience high levels of social control but low levels of emotional support. Such children understand the rules but have no relational reasons to obey them when their parents are not looking. Often, the most rebellious youths are by-products of very strict households. Baumrind suggests that these two styles of parenting produce children with lower self-esteem and less self-assurance.[43]

Three Parenting Styles

Three Parenting Styles

Permissive Style | **Authoritative Style** | **Authoritarian Style**

©Shutterstock

Source: Based on *Current Patterns of Parental Authority* by Diana Baumind.

Parenting in Asian Cultures

Do the parenting styles that Baumrind describes apply in all cultures? Ruth Chao studied how the parenting styles of Chinese families affected children.[44] In order to explore the perception of Chinese school-children as successful and well behaved, Chao observed how parents interacted with their children.[45] The mothers she observed provided high levels of control, but also high levels of sacrifice and personal closeness to their children. Parents in China expect their children to meet high standards of both individual achievement and social conformity. In general, Chinese children meet these standards. The parents in this culture are authoritative; children receive adequate emotional support and know that their hard work will gain the family's approval.

In another study, sociologist Min Zhou proposed that Confucian philosophy, with its emphasis on family loyalty, acts as a social control mechanism that supports Asian children's success.[46] Studies of Vietnamese immigrant children living in enclaves in the United States show similar findings to those of Chao. They show that second-generation immigrant children who remain linked to their families and culture have better outcomes with regard to educational attainment and the likelihood that they will stay in school.[47] Culture plays an important role in psychologists' and sociologists' interpretations about family socialization.

SOCIAL CLASS: OPPORTUNITIES FOR SOCIALIZATION

Family isn't the only agent of socialization; our social class also affects us. Numerous studies show connections between social class and socialization. Melvin Kohn's research found that working-class parents focus on their children's obedience to authority, whereas middle-class parents showed greater concern about the motivations for their children's behavior.[48] Because working-class parents are closely supervised at their jobs, they are more likely to demand this same conformity from their children. Therefore, the mother who is used to punching a clock at the assembly line is more likely to expect a home environment in which her children do their chores at set times.

Our social class affects us in many ways that we do not anticipate and may not even recognize. The availability of piano lessons, art classes, and little-league sports teams all socialize children; however, these experiences are typically available only to middle- and upper-income families. Children of less affluent families tend to miss these socialization opportunities. Social class affects not only the type of experiences we have, but also their quality and quantity.

NEIGHBORHOOD

Anyone who's ever visited a dormitory building before making a decision to live there believes that the "right" dorm matters. The same is true of choosing a neighborhood in which to live because your social class is often tied to the kind of neighborhood you live in. Noted sociologist William J. Wilson looked at how inner-city poverty brought with it the disadvantages of poor schools, weak social structures, high crime rates, and rampant drug use.[49] Wilson argued that poor people are truly disadvantaged because their community offers few role models for anything else. Children who grow up in these communities are likely to make poor decisions. Studies have shown that neighborhood has significant negative effects on IQ, teen pregnancy, and high school dropout rates.[50]

Neighborhoods also influence economically privileged children. Children who grow up in more affluent neighborhoods often do better in

AGENTS OF SOCIALIZATION are the people and groups who shape our self-concept, beliefs, and behavior.

AUTHORITATIVE STYLE is a parenting style in which parents listen to their children's input while consistently enforcing the preset rules.

PERMISSIVE STYLE is a parenting style in which parents provide high levels of support but an inconsistent enforcement of rules.

AUTHORITARIAN STYLE is a parenting style with which children experience high levels of social control but low levels of emotional support.

RESOCIALIZATION is the process of learning new norms, values, attitudes, and behaviors, and abandoning old ones.

TOTAL INSTITUTIONS are places in which the most effective forms of resocialization can occur because they isolate people from outside influences so they can be reformed and controlled.

school, have lower rates of teen pregnancy, and higher IQ scores.[51] Neighborhoods can also predict how far you may go in school, showing that the higher the socioeconomic status of the neighborhood, the higher the educational attainment.[52] Neighborhood effects also apply to voluntary associations for children. A predicting factor in the sport children will play is correlated to their neighborhoods.[53] For example, children of well-to-do families are more likely to take up a sport like skiing that requires expensive equipment because they can afford the upkeep and travel to the slopes.

Of course, just because parents are affluent does not mean that they will be great parents or that their children will be successfully socialized. The reverse is also true; a parent who has very limited financial means may be a very good parent.

Can We Be "Resocialized"? Experiencing the Total Institution

Resocialization is the process of learning new norms, values, attitudes, and behaviors and abandoning old ones. This process involves more than the kinds of secondary socialization that occur when we marry or take a new job. Yoda, the noted Jedi philosopher, says it best in the film *The Empire Strikes Back*; sometimes, "You must unlearn what you have learned."

The most effective forms of resocialization occur in **total institutions** that isolate people from outside influences so they can be reformed and controlled.[54] People may enter total institutions voluntarily, as in the case of non-draftees that enlist in military boot camps, or involuntarily, as in the case of inmates in mental institutions and prisons. Regardless, total institutions have certain characteristics:

1. There is one authority, and activities take place in specific locations.

2. Carefully structured activities control the participants.

3. Authorities carefully screen all information from outside the institution.

4. Rules and roles are clearly defined.

5. A strict hierarchy exists within the institution.

6. Total institutions restrict individual choice.

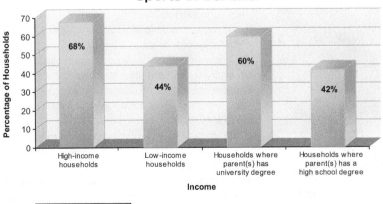

The Effect of Income and Education on Children's Participation in Organized Sports in Canada

- High-income households: 68%
- Low-income households: 44%
- Households where parent(s) has university degree: 60%
- Households where parent(s) has a high school degree: 42%

Y-axis: Percentage of Households
X-axis: Income

Legend: Participation in Organized Sports

Source: Based on "Organized Sports Participation Among Children," 2005.

think sociologically: HOW DO THE THREE THEORETICAL PARADIGMS VIEW SOCIALIZATION?

Symbolic Interactionism and Resocialization

We've seen how symbolic interactionists interpret society's symbols as a means for people to create a sense of self. We've also learned how the self develops under ordinary conditions. But how might development inside a total institution affect a person's sense of self?

Sociologist Harold Garfinkel explored the similarities in the ways prison inmates and military enlistees are resocialized upon entering those total institutions.[55] Garfinkel points out that these institutions "welcome" new members through some form of degrading ceremony designed to humiliate the person. This humiliation is required to "break them down" so that resocialization is possible. Inmates and enlistees may both have their heads shaved and their "street clothes" taken away. After putting on uniforms, their individual style of dress is erased in order to look like everyone else. In boot camp and under the control of the institution, the new recruit has no choice in when he or she will eat, sleep, or bathe. Similarly, inmates receive numbers to replace their names, are given uniforms to wear, and are told where they will sleep, when they will eat, and how they will spend their allocated "free" time. In both cases, the goal is to strip away former identity and resocialize the person into someone who will be obedient to commands.

Through resocialization, the institution controls all aspects of a person's life.[56] The techniques that total institutions use change the inmate's or soldier's internal thinking, which in turn changes his or her sense of self.

©Stephen Ferry/Liaison/Getty Images

∧∧∧ **Prison inmates are stripped of their individual identities so that they can be transformed into people who willingly follow the orders** of those in authority.

Functionalism

While symbolic interactionists study the effect of institutions on individuals, functionalists examine how certain institutions, specifically religion and education, function in society. An institution's function, and the individual's relationship to that institution, helps determine what role it plays in the development of self.

RELIGION

In every U.S. election, Christian fundamentalists are a key voting bloc that politicians court by campaigning on "family values." Though the idea of such values is malleable depending on the issues, it's clear that the members of this group share a common set of beliefs that finds its foundation in religion.

From Muslim practitioners to Orthodox Jews and Buddhist monks, all world religions provide frames of reference for believers. These frameworks include beliefs, values, and behaviors in keeping with the teachings of that religion. Religions teach about life, death, and all of life's transitions in between. The religious socialization that results from this teaching process has measurable effects.

Sociologists Charles Tittle and Michael Welch studied the links between religiosity and juvenile delinquency and found that they were inversely related. The more religious the juvenile, the less likely he or she is to be delinquent.[57] Harold Grasmick and colleagues found weaker, but similar, results with respect to adults and behaviors such as tax cheating and littering.[58] This research shows that religion can play a role in forming our behavior.

EDUCATION

Out of a typical seven-hour school day, students in secondary schools in the United States spend only about three hours doing academic activities.[59] Instead, students are learning the "**hidden curriculum**"—lessons taught in school that are unrelated to academic learning. School teaches you to deal with peers who are sometimes cruel.[60] If students successfully negotiate the dangers of their neighborhoods and the various power struggles that go on in their schools, they feel a sense of satisfaction. Mock elections and saluting the flag help foster citizenship among students. Schools also socialize children by setting regulations that structure the school day. Students must show up on time, get along with others, follow teachers' expectations, wait in lines, and follow the rules.[61]

When families and schools cooperate to teach children to follow the rules, they help create a society that has fewer lawbreakers. When neighborhoods support these ideals, children grow up feeling part of something important. In the event that the family is dysfunctional, or the school does not work, or the neighborhood is infecting them with negative ideas about the society, this too socializes children. Negative outcomes usually result. Society functions best when social institutions cooperate.

Conflict Theory—What Forces Socialize Us?

Recall that conflict theory suggests that power relationships influence our perceptions. To guide our actions, societies use **gender socialization** to teach their members how to express their masculinity or femininity. **Gender** refers to the expectations of behavior and attitude that a society considers proper for males and females. If and when these expectations limit one gender in favor of the other, it usually occurs as a result of differences in power.

> **HIDDEN CURRICULUM** refers to the lessons taught in school that are unrelated to academic learning.
>
> **GENDER SOCIALIZATION** teaches members of society how to express their masculinity or femininity.
>
> **GENDER** is the expectations of behavior and attitude that a society considers proper for males and females.
>
> **MASS MEDIA** include any print or electronic resource that is used to communicate to a wide audience.

Conflict theorists often argue that **men use their power to dominate and limit women.**

MAKE CONNECTIONS

Fictional Tales and Gender

From *Aesop's Fables* to the Brothers Grimm, folktales symbolize the innocence of childhood. But a closer analysis shows how these folktales shape how children perceive gender. Most folktales follow a typical pattern in which a dependent woman relies exclusively on a strong man to save her from harm. Think about the story of Rapunzel—the girl with the long, golden hair who is trapped in a tower by a witch. In the story, Rapunzel is merely a piece of property, given away by her father in exchange for his life. While trapped in the tower, Rapunzel is dependent on the witch and unable to escape. Rapunzel, afraid of the witch's wrath, remains in the tower alone and refuses the prince's help to escape. The prince goes blind because he is unable to save the beauty. Young children, especially young girls, who read these tales internalize the idea that being submissive and reliant on men is a desired trait.

These stereotypes are not just a part of archaic folktales; they also appear in modern works of fiction. Television programs like *Grey's Anatomy* and *Desperate Housewives* feature female characters who reinforce generalizations about gender roles. That said, there are a number of stereotype-breaking characters like those featured on Law and Order: SVU and Nurse Jackie. Even in the *Harry Potter* series, Hermione Granger, Harry's sidekick, is a secondary character and yet she is always saving the day. Real life does not work as it does in fiction. Not all men can be heroes, and passivity and dependency rarely bring women success in the modern world.

>>> **ACTIVITY** Think about a movie or TV show you've seen or a book you've read recently. What gender stereotypes, if any, are depicted on the screen or the page? Does the work defy any traditional gender stereotypes? Write a paragraph analyzing the work you chose.

GENDER BIAS IN THE MEDIA

When Senator Hillary Clinton ran for the Democratic nomination in the 2008 presidential race, one of the major issues involved how the pundits and politicos treated the first viable woman to run for the highest office in the land. Clinton's supporters pointed to the disproportionate amount of attention given to their candidate's appearance and noted a perceived gender bias in the coverage of her campaign.

Any print or electronic resource that is used to communicate to a wide audience is referred to as **mass media**.

Products of mass media—books, magazines, television, radio, movies, music, and newspapers—are everywhere, and their influence on culture is inescapable. **The media play a role in our socialization because they transmit stories, values, and attitudes.**

Consider the effect the media have in determining gendered stereotypes through sexual imagery. Kirstie Farrar and her colleagues reviewed the sexual images that aired during "prime-time" television hours. They found that images on shows like *The Bachelor* and *One Tree Hill* tended to reinforce the notion that women are primarily sexual objects.[62] These and other images supported the dominant male/submissive female paradigm. They also found that 64 percent of the television shows during the 2000–2001 season contained sexual messages, and that sexual intercourse occurred in 14 percent of the shows. For conflict theorists, these findings suggest that such imagery is an effort by those in power to maintain it. Men are the primary decision makers for large media corporations, so are they responsible for perpetuating these ideas about gender roles?

Because of the way gender roles are defined in society, it can take several years to see through the generalizations. I can remember realizing during my freshman year in college that my father and I had never hugged, primarily because of gender ideals about men touching each other. The next time I returned home, I gave him a big hug as soon as he answered the door. From that day forth, hugging was no longer taboo at our house. In this simple way, my father and I changed our gender socialization.

WRAP YOUR MIND AROUND THE THEORY

For a society to function, norms, values, and institutions must be passed onto future generations. **How do agents of socialization, like religion, influence the people we become?**

Gunter Marx ©Dorling Kindersley

FUNCTIONALISM

According to functionalists, socialization occurs when people internalize society and enact its norms, values, and roles. In high schools across the country, students struggle with the choice to conform and practice "normal" behavior or to think outside the box. Those who step outside the box are often stigmatized and labeled as "different." These individuals are not "functioning" because they don't conform to the rules set by the society's institutions. Institutions, such as religion and education, serve their function. To keep a society running smoothly, people adapt to the norms and values of their particular institutions. In short, people become socialized when they learn and accept what a society expects of them.

CONFLICT THEORY

Conflict theorists believe that the "haves" and the "have-nots" are socialized differently. Children who come from middle- and upper-class backgrounds are more likely to participate in organized sports, take music or art lessons, and have Internet access in their homes. Taking part in activities such as these teaches children how to interact with others and learn what society expects of them. Impoverished children sometimes find themselves at a disadvantage because they are less likely to have these experiences. Of course, material wealth is not the only determinant of whether one becomes socialized. However, parents' material wealth does put some children at an advantage.

HOW DO PEOPLE BECOME SOCIALIZED?

SYMBOLIC INTERACTIONISM

Symbolic interactionists believe that socialization is the major determinant of human nature. People develop their sense of self by incorporating how others interpret their behavior. The symbols we encounter, such as other people's interpretations of our behavior, help shape who and what we become. Genie, the feral child discovered in 1970, was not given the opportunity to interact with others during her formative years. As a result, she was unable to fully develop her own identity when she was thrust into the social world. As we saw in Mead's theory of the "I" and the "Me," people develop their sense of self though their interaction with others.

©Steve Skjold/Alamy

©Nick White/Thinkstock

Children who participate in organized sports learn how to interact with others in the social world. **How might this influence children whose parents are poor and cannot afford to have them participate?**

Students in class might snicker when another child gives a report. How might the child interpret these symbols? How might he feel about himself?

discover sociology in action:
HOW DOES UNDERSTANDING SOCIALIZATION HELP US IMPROVE THE COMMUNITY?

Applying Sociological Thinking in the World, Social Policy, and Title IX

Auguste Comte, the founder of sociology, urged us to use our knowledge about society to improve society. Lawmakers have used that philosophy to enact various **social policies**, deliberate strategies designed to correct recognized social problems. The 1972 educational amendment, commonly known as **Title IX**, is one such attempt to implement sociological knowledge. Named the Patsy T. Mink Equal Opportunity in Education Act in honor of its principle author—a Hawaiian congresswoman who felt that gender discrimination in public schools must be stopped—the act prohibits the exclusion of any person from participation in an educational program on the basis of gender.[63]

Title IX became important when it was used to allocate funding for extracurricular activities like sports. Before 1972, very few girls were involved in sports partly because few sports existed for girls. In the three decades since Title IX, however, those numbers have skyrocketed:

- Female participation in high school sports has increased 800 percent.
- Female participation in intercollegiate athletics has increased 400 percent.
- Girls now make up 42 percent of high school athletes.

SOCIAL POLICIES are deliberate strategies designed to correct recognized social problems.

TITLE IX is a 1972 educational amendment that prohibits the exclusion of any person from participation in an education program on the basis of gender.

- Women now make up 42 percent of Division I varsity college athletes.
- Women receive 43 percent of Division I athletic scholarship dollars.
- Women's college sports receive about one dollar for every two spent on men's programs.[64]

ACTIVITIES

1. How does your college deal with Title IX? Are male and female scholarships equal? Are they in compliance?
2. What agents of socialization influenced you the most when you were growing up? What influences you the most now?
3. Read stories of feral children, like the Fritzls. What is the importance of early socialization on development? Have researchers made any strides in socializing feral children?
4. Visit a developmental disability hospital in your area and talk to the staff and parents. Can the best efforts at socialization overcome nature? Write about your findings.

You can see that a social policy designed to give equal opportunities to both genders has increased women's athletic participation. However, these numbers also indicate that the goal of actual equality has not yet been met. Today, girls may have many more athletic role models than they did 30 years ago, but they do not yet receive equal funding for sports programs in their schools. Although women outnumber men on college campuses, funding remains largely in the hands of male sports. A quick look at the difference in television budgets between the men's and women's NCAA Final Four basketball tournaments demonstrates the disparity. Sports play a big role in a child's socialization, and both genders should have the opportunity to participate equally.

From Classroom to Community } Preschool

When Karen, one of my sociology students, decided to do her service learning project at a local preschool that specializes in working with developmentally disabled children, she was almost overwhelmed. "I guess I never really thought about how easy I had it growing up. Almost everything was hard to do for these kids," she said.

"After studying the socialization process, I began to wonder how you would appropriately deal with the primary socialization for these children."

Karen was amazed at how many children with severe limitations also had attachments to consumer goods. "From Barney dolls to Disney clothing, these kids were covered in consumer goods. The socialization of children into consumption applies to all kids in the United States."

Working with these children taught Karen a great deal about herself and the process of socialization. "Some children had physical delays, while others had cognitive ones," she recalled. "I couldn't help but see the interaction between nature and nurture. Most of these kids were deeply loved by their families, and yet their life opportunities are limited by their biology."

Karen found working with the kids to be rewarding and challenging, all at the same time. "It really struck at my heart to see these kids, and I couldn't help but wonder if there would ever be a way for them to experience all the things I've done. It didn't seem very likely."

WHAT IS SOCIALIZATION?

the process that teaches the norms, values, and other aspects of a culture to new group members

HOW DO THE THREE THEORETICAL PARADIGMS VIEW SOCIALIZATION?

functionalism: institutions, like religion and education, are useful in socializing individuals
conflict theory: societies use gender socialization to teach members how to express their femininity and masculinity
symbolic interactionism: total institutions are successful in resocializing people by altering their sense of self

HOW DOES UNDERSTANDING SOCIALIZATION HELP US IMPROVE THE COMMUNITY?

through social policies that are designed to give equal opportunities to both genders

get the topic: WHAT IS SOCIALIZATION?

The Nature vs. Nurture Debate—
    What Makes Us Who We Are?
Theorists on Socialization
Agents of Socialization

Can We Be "Resocialized"? Experiencing the
    Total Institution
Symbolic Interactionism and Resocialization
Functionalism

Conflict Theory—What Forces Socialize Us?
Applying Sociological Thinking in the World,
    Social Policy, and Title IX

Theory

FUNCTIONALISM

* socialization occurs when people internalize society and enact its norms, values, and roles
* people who don't internalize norms are stigmatized and labeled as "different"
* people become socialized when they learn and accept what society expects of them

CONFLICT THEORY

* the "haves" and the "have-nots" are socialized differently

* taking part in activities teaches children how to interact with others and learn what society expects of them
* children who come from middle- and upper-class backgrounds are more likely to participate in organized activities than some impoverished children who are unable to participate

SYMBOLIC INTERACTIONISM

* socialization is the major determinant of human nature
* people develop their sense of self by incorporating how others interpret their behavior

Key Terms

socialization	play stage	hedonism	total institutions
primary socialization	game stage	conventional level	hidden curriculum
secondary socialization	the generalized other	postconventional level	gender socialization
nature theory	psychosocial crisis	morality of justice	gender
nurture theory	cognitive development	morality of care	mass media
feral	sensorimotor stage	agents of socialization	social policies
looking-glass self	preoperational stage	authoritative style	Title IX
"I" self	concrete operational stage	permissive style	
"me" self	formal operational stage	authoritarian style	
imitation stage	preconventional level	resocialization	

MY SEARCH LAB

1. *What Does it Mean to Be Human?:* *Human Nature, Society, and Culture* from Ten Questions: A Sociological Perspective, 7th Edition, Joel M. Charon, Minnesota State University, Moorhead. © 2010 Wadsworth, a part of Cengage Learning, Inc. Reproduced by permission. http://www.cengage.com/permissions.
This excerpt is from the 1998 book *Ten Questions: A Sociological Perspective*. In this excerpt, Charon asks us to consider what it means to be human.

1. Charon argues that we become who we are because of a complex mixture of heredity and socialization. Explain this point further using the example of a child who grows up to be a drug dealer.
2. Charon argues that individual qualities are really social qualities. What does this mean? Do you agree or disagree with this statement?

2. *Parents' Socialization of Children* by D. Terri Heath, reprinted from *Families in Multicultural Perspective*, edited by Bron

Ingoldsby and Suzanna Smith, 1995, pp. 161–186. Reprinted by permission of Guilford Publications.

In this 1995 selection, Heath summarizes studies from a range of countries to compare parenting styles and socializing effects on children.

DISCUSSION QUESTIONS

1. Explain the difference between authoritative, permissive, and authoritarian parenting styles. How does each result in different outcomes of child behavior?
2. How do differences in social class result in different expectations and outcomes for children? Use the Wisconsin Model to explain.

3. **"Final Note on a Case of Extreme Isolation"** by Kingsley Davis, reprinted from *American Journal of Sociology*, vol. 52, 1947. pp. 432–447.

In this excerpt, sociologist Kingsley Davis explores the importance of primary socialization and raises interesting questions regarding the role that nature and nurture play in human behavior.

DISCUSSION QUESTIONS

1. What evidence points to congenital defects as the cause of Anna's behavior? What evidence points to socialization as the cause of her behavior?
2. What do these two cases tell us about the role of nature versus nurture in the development of personality?

THE THINKSPOT

How would you describe your parents' parenting style? If you're a parent, how would you describe yours? As you've learned from reading the chapter, our parents' influence is one that has a truly profound effect on us. They are agents of socialization. Go to the ThinkSpot and read the information provided on different parenting styles and watch the videos that accompany the text. Although the videos use amateur actors, it is interesting to see how the different styles are portrayed, along with the reactions of the "children." How does an authoritarian parenting style affect nutrition? The answer might surprise you.

And what happens when two people in a relationship do not agree on a unified parenting style? Go to the ThinkSpot to the "He Said/She Said" video to get a real take on parenting in the United States today. Do you agree with the wife or the husband in this clip? Neither? Why? Based on what you've learned in the chapter about parenting styles, how would you classify his style? Hers?

Sample Test Questions

These multiple-choice questions are similar to those found in the test bank that accompanies this textbook.

1. During which of Erikson's eight stages would a person develop a strong sense of self?
   a. Trust vs. mistrust
   b. Initiative vs. guilt
   c. Industry vs. inferiority
   d. Identity vs. role confusion

2. According to Piaget, at what stage of cognitive development does a child's ability to speak grow rapidly?
   a. Sensorimotor stage
   b. Preoperational stage
   c. Concrete operational stage
   d. Formal operational stage

3. The preconventional level, conventional level, and postconventional level are stages of
   a. moral development.
   b. social development.
   c. creative development.
   d. language development.

4. Which of the following is *not* an example of a total institution?
   a. A prison
   b. The military
   c. A university
   d. A rehabilitation clinic

5. Which researcher developed the morality of care and the morality of justice?
   a. Erik Erikson
   b. Carol Gilligan
   c. Lawrence Kohlberg
   d. George Herbert Mead

ESSAY

1. How did Piaget describe the stage at which a child learns to speak?
2. What is the difference between authoritative style and authoritarian style parenting?
3. Why is resocialization important in total institutions?
4. Conflict theorists often argue that men use their power to dominate and limit women. Provide an example of gender bias in the media and explain how it supports this theory.
5. In the terms of Erikson's theory, how was Genie's development stunted?

WHERE TO START YOUR RESEARCH PAPER

For in-depth articles on the field of evolutionary psychology, relating the development of the brain and how social settings influence a person's development, go to http://www.psych.ucsb.edu/research/cep/

For more information on child socialization, go to http://www.childdevelopmentinfo.com/parenting/socialization.shtml

For more information on education and health care for parents and children, go to http://www.kidsource.com/

To learn more about how media influences society (particularly the sociological perspective on media and society), go to http://www.public.asu.edu/~zeyno217/365/notes1.html

To find more information on Mama Feeta and her work in caring for the children of war-torn Liberia, go to http://www.shinefoundation.org/

For more information on centers that work with people who have developmental delays, go to http://www.miusa.org/ncde/

ANSWERS: 1. d; 2. b; 3. a; 4. c; 5. b

Endnotes

1. Susan Linn, *Consuming kids: Protecting our children from the onslaught of marketing & advertising* (NY: First Anchor Books, 2005).

2. Talcott Parsons, *The Social System* (New York: Free Press, 1951).

3. Talcott Parsons and Robert Bales, *Socialization and the Interaction Process* (New York: Free Press, 1955).

4. Orville G. Brim, Jr., "Socialization Through the Life Cycle," In: Orville Brim and Stanton Wheeler (eds.), *Socialization after Childhood: Two Essays* (New York: Wiley, 1966).

5. Theodore E. Long and Jeffrey K. Hadden, "Reconception of Socialization," *Sociological Theory.* 1985. 3(1): 39–49.

6. Orville G. Brim, Jr., "Socialization Through the Life Cycle," In: Orville Brim and Stanton Wheeler (eds), *Socialization after Childhood: Two Essays.* (New York: Wiley, 1966).

7. Richard Dawkins, *The Selfish Gene* (Oxford: Oxford University Press, 1989).

8. W. L. Reese, *Dictionary of Philosophy and Religion: Eastern and Western Thought* (Atlantic Highlands, NJ: Humanities Press Inc., 1987).

9. Paul R. Ehrlich, *Human Natures: Genes, Cultures, and the Human Prospect* (Island Press. Washington, D.C., 2000), p. 6, at http://books.google.com/books?id5mHFsScY8ewMC&dq5Human﹍Natures﹍Paul﹍Ehrlich&pg5PP1&ots5XW4w7TDMLU&sig5MjKy9QADe0TPCKe0fZZ8h﹍ahKLM&hl5en&sa5X&oi5book﹍result&resnum51&ct5result.

10. Harry F. Harlow and Margaret Harlow, "Social Deprivation in Monkeys," *Scientific America,* 1962. November: 137–146.

11. Susan Donaldson James, "Wild Child Speechless After Tortured Life," *ABC News*, May 7, 2008, at http://abcnews.go.com/Health/story?id54804490; "What Drove Father Who Built House of Horror?" *CNN News*, April 29, 2008, at http://www.cnn.com/2008/WORLD/europe/04/29/austria.cellar.profile/ (accessed November 12, 2008).

12. Allan Hall, "Fritzl's victims face life in care," *The Age*, August 21, 2008, http://www.theage.com.au/world/fritzls-victims-face-life-in-care-20080820-3yvt.html?page=-1.

13. Russ Rymer, *Genie: An Abused Child's Flight from Silence* (New York, NY: Harper-Collins Publishers, 1993).

14. Ibid.

15. Ibid.

16. Louis De Maio, "Stages of Language Development," at www.mnstate.edu/pccp/stages%20of%20%20language%20development.pdf (accessed June 5, 2008); "Isabelle," http://www.feralchildren.com/en/showchild.php?ch5isabelle (accessed June 26, 2008).

17. Charles H. Cooley, *Human Nature and the Social Order* (New York: Schocken Books, 1902, 1964).

18. King-To Yeung and John L. Martin, "The Looking Glass Self: An Empirical Test and Elaboration," *Social Forces*, 2003. 81(3): 843–879.

19. Ibid.

20. George Herbert Mead, *Mind, Self, and Society*, Charles W. Morris, ed. (Chicago: University of Chicago Press, 1934, 1962).

21. Ibid.

22. Ibid.

23. Erik Erikson, *Childhood and Society* (New York: Norton Press, 1963).

24. "Secret of the Wild Child," *Nova*, March 4, 1997, http://www.pbs.org/wgbh/nova/transcripts/2112gchild.html (accessed November 12, 2008).

25. Jean Piaget and Barbel Inhelder, *The Psychology of the Child* (New York: Basic Books, 1969, 2000).

26. Ibid.

27. Ibid.

28. Ibid.

29. Ibid.

30. Lawrence Kohlberg, *The Psychology of Moral Development: The Nature and Validity of Moral Stages* (New York: Harper & Row, 1981).

31. Ibid.

32. Ibid.

33. Ibid.

34. Charles Helwig and Urszula Jasiobedzka, "The Relation Between Law and Morality: Children's Reasoning about Socially Beneficial and Unjust Laws," *Child Development,* 2001. 72: 1382–1394.

35. Anne Colby and William Damon, *Some Do Care: Contemporary Lives of Moral Commitment* (New York: Free Press, 1992).

36. Carol Gilligan, *In a Different Voice: Psychological Theory and Women's Development* (Cambridge, MA: Harvard University Press, 1982).

37. Ibid.

38. Elliott Turiel, "The Development of Morality," In: W. Damon (ed.), *Handbook of Child Psychology*, 5th ed., Vol. 3, 863–932 (New York: Wiley, 1998).

39. Eva A. Skoe and Alethia Gooden, "Ethics of Care and Real-Life Moral Dilemma Content in Male and Female Early Adolescents," *Journal of Early Adolescence*, 1993. 13(2): 154–167.

40. Eva A. Skoe and Rhett Diessner, "Ethics of Care, Justice, Identity and Gender: An Extension and Replication," *Merrill–Palmer Quarterly*, 1994. 40: 102–119. Eva A. Skoe and Anna L. von der Lippe, "Ego Development and the Ethics of Care and Justice: The Relations Among Them Revisited," *Journal of Personality*, 2002. 70(4): 485–508.

41. Andrew J. Cherlin, *Public and Private Families: An Introduction*, 2nd ed. (Boston: McGraw–Hill College, 1999).

42. Diana Baumrind, "Current Patterns of Parental Authority," *Developmental Psychology Monographs*, 1971. 4(1, pt. 2):103; Diana Baumrind, "Parental Disciplinary Patterns and Social Competence in Children," *Youth and Society*, 1978. 9: 239–276. Diana Baumrind, "The Discipline Controversy Revisited," *Family Relations*, 1996. 5(4): 405–415.

43. Ibid.

44. Ruth K. Chao, "Beyond Parental Control and Authoritarian Parenting Style: Understanding Chinese Parenting Through the Cultural Notion of Training," *Child Development*, 1994. 65(4): 1111–1119.

45. Ibid.

46. Min Zhou, *Chinatown: The Socioeconomic Potential of an Urban Enclave* (Philadelphia, PA: Temple University Press, 1992).

47. Min Zhou and Carl L. Bankston, III, "Social Capital and the Adaptation of the Second Generation: The Case of Vietnamese Youth in New Orleans," *The New Second Generation*, Alejandro Portes (ed.), (New York: Russell Sage Foundation, 1996), 197–220.

48. Melvin L Kohn, "Social Class and Parent-Child Relationships: An Interpretation," *American Journal of Sociology*, 1963. 571–580.

49. William J. Wilson, *The Truly Disadvantaged: The Inner City, The Underclass, and Public Policy* (Chicago: University of Chicago Press, 1987).

50. Jeanne Brooks–Gunn, Greg Duncan, Pamela Klebanove, and Naomi Sealand, "Do Neighborhoods Influence Child and Adolescent Development?" *American Journal of Sociology*, 1993. 99(2): 353–395.

51. Ibid.

52. Gary Solon, Marianne Page, and Greg J. Duncan, "Correlations Between Neighboring Children and Their Subsequent Educational Attainment," *Review of Economics and Statistics*, 2000. 82(3): 383–393.

53. John D. Carl, "Social Capital and Sport Participation," Ph.D. dissertation, Department of Sociology, University of Oklahoma, Norman, OK, 2002.

54. Erving Goffman, *Asylums: Essays on the Social Situation of Mental Patients and Other Inmates* (Chicago: Aldine, 1961).

55. Harold Garfinkel, "Conditions of Successful Degradation Ceremonies," *American Journal of Sociology*, 1956. 61(2): 420–424.

56. Howard S. Becker, "The Politics of Presentation: Goffman and Total Institutions," *Symbolic Interaction*, 2003. 26(4): 659–669.

57. Charles Tittle and Michael Welch, "Religiosity and Deviance: Toward a Contingency Theory of Constraining Effects," *Social Forces*, 1983. 61(3): 653–682.

58. Harold Grasmick, Karyl Kinsey, and Kent Smith, "Framing Justice: Taxpayer Evaluations of Personal Tax Burdens, *Law and Society Review.* 1991. 25: 845–873.

59. "Prisoners of Time," Education Commission of the States, April 1994, www.eric.ed.gov/ERICDocs/data/ericdocs2sql/content_storage_01/0000019b/80/1b/b9/60.pdf (accessed November 12, 2008).

60. Annette Hemmings, "The 'Hidden' Corridor Curriculum," *High School Journal*, 2000. 83(2): 1–10.

61. Philip Jackson, *Life in Classrooms* (New York, NY: Holt, Rinehart, and Winston, 1968).

62. Kirstie Farrar, Dale Kunkel, Erica Biely, Keren Eyal, Rena Fandrich, and Edward Donnerstein, "Sexual Messages During Primetime Programming," *Sexuality & Culture*, 2003. 7(3): 7–38.

63. "Patsy T. Mink Equal Opportunity in Education Act," *K12 Academics*, http://www.k12academics.com/patsy_t_mink_equal_opportunity_education_act.htm (accessed June 27, 2008).

64. NWLC: National Women's Law Center, "Quick facts on women and girls in athletics," June 2002, http://www.nwlc.org/pdf/quickfacts_June2002.pdf; NWLC: National Women's Law Center, "The Battle for Gender Equity in Athletics: Title IX at Thirty," 2002, http://www.nwlc.org/pdf/Battle%20for%20Gender%20Equity% 20in%20Athletics%20Report.pdf.

GROUPS AND SOCIETIES

©Stephan Gladieu/Getty Images

GROUPS AND SOCIETIES

WHAT ARE THE CHARACTERISTICS
OF SOCIAL GROUPS?
HOW DO SOCIOLOGISTS VIEW GROUP
LEADERSHIP?
HOW DOES A PARENT'S CIVIC ENGAGEMENT
AFFECT A CHILD'S FUTURE POLITICAL
INVOLVEMENT?

We will

consider an extraordinary subculture, the Oneida community, sharing an unusual set of religious beliefs and following an individual with unusual personal magnetism, John Humphrey Noyes. He exercised what is referred to as charismatic authority. This refers to the power made legitimate by a leader's exceptional personal or emotional appeal to his or her followers . . . Noyes was able to lead and inspire without relying on established rules or traditions.

Noyes acquired a reputation for being a radical, and although he was granted his license to preach in 1833, he was not a success. At one point . . . he declared himself to be without sin. . . . For the next few years [Noyes] traveled through New York and New England . . . spreading the doctrine of Perfectionism: People could live without sin. . . . Given the proper environment, therefore man could lead a perfect or sinless life. . . .

In 1844 . . . the Perfectionists adopted economic communalism as a way of life. They commenced to share their work, their food, their living quarters, and their resources. . . . In 1846, the group began to share spouses. As might have been predicted, once the Perfectionists began the practice of spouse sharing, the word soon spread. . . . Amidst rumors of mob violence, John Humphrey

Noyes was indicted . . . on the grounds of adultery. He was released pending trial . . . and on the advice of his lawyer . . . fled to New York . . . [O]ther Perfectionist centers were available to him. One such spot was a fairly large tract of land along Oneida creek in New York State. . . .

With several hundred people living under one roof, the Oneidans had an interesting problem in human relations. . . . Practically everything the Perfectionists did was designed to play down the "I" in favor of the "we." Members ate . . . worked . . . and played together. They shared their property, they shared their sexual partners. And they shared their children . . .

The religious practices of the Oneidans also served to reinforce primary-group association. . . . Perfectionists dispensed with most of the formal aspects of religion. They maintained no church, held no prayer services. . . . Neither baptismal nor communion services were utilized. . . . At the same time, religion was a central part of the Oneidan's daily lives . . . rather than special religious celebrations. . . . Perfectionists believed that every day should involve religious awareness. . . . And they believed that by listening to John Humphrey Noyes—and his followers' teachings—they were listening to the voice of God.[1]

Understanding Our Environment

*I*n a world without sin, where polygamy reigns and formal religion is shunned, one man, believed by his followers to be God, leads with an iron fist. This sounds like the deep voice of a movie trailer, but instead it's the real life story of John Humphrey Noyes.

Even if you aren't familiar with Noyes and his Oneida group, the remnants of this group have crept into your daily life. Any time you've eaten with Oneida silverware, you're using utensils that come from a community that believed it could live without sin and where monogamy was unnatural for both men and women. All that remains of the community, which dissolved in 1879, is the famous Oneida silverware corporation.

We only need examine Noyes's leadership, the members' interactions with one another, and their ultimate dissolution to understand what can make a group triumph or flop.

get the topic: WHAT ARE THE CHARACTERISTICS OF SOCIAL GROUPS?

SOCIAL GROUPS are groups that consist of two or more people who interact with one another and share a common identity.

In the 2010 NCAA Basketball Final Four Championship, 142,000 people bought tickets, making it the second highest attendance record for the men's tournament.[2] At the same time, thousands of soldiers faced redeployment in Afghanistan. There is certainly a difference between a crowd that gathers to watch basketball and a unified military group. For one, the values and goals of the army are unified, while those of the basketball fans are rather diverse. In this chapter, we'll take an in-depth look at the role of **social groups** in our lives.

Whether we're aware of it or not, we all belong to a social group in some way or another—families, close friends, teammates, classmates, clubs, and organizations are all examples of groups to which we belong. Few of us could live totally self-reliant lives, so we find groups on which to depend. Of course, not all groups are the same. For all intents and purposes, your membership in your family is permanent, but you might not work with the same people for the rest of your life. Although no two groups are alike, they do have two

© Keith Brofsky/Getty Images

<<< These people work in the same building, maybe even in the same office. But **are these people a social group?**

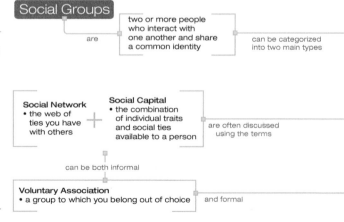

Social Groups are two or more people who interact with one another and share a common identity — can be categorized into two main types

are often discussed using the terms

Social Network
• the web of ties you have with others

+

Social Capital
• the combination of individual traits and social ties available to a person

can be both informal

Voluntary Association
• a group to which you belong out of choice

and formal

commonalities; the members of the group share something in common, and they identify each other as members of that group.

PRIMARY AND SECONDARY GROUPS

We've already established that classmates qualify as a social group with shared goals and values. If you have this relationship with your classmates, why might you refrain from spilling your guts to your chemistry lab partner? Because we have different types of groups that dictate how we interact within them.

According to sociologist Charles H. Cooley, groups can be divided into two main categories—primary and secondary. *Primary groups* are small, intimate, and long-lasting.[3] Our most immediate relationships, such as relationships with family members and close friends, form primary groups. The Oneida community created a primary group by sharing everything, including spouses and children. Oneidans had a communal society in which all adults were married to each other and the community collectively raised the children.

More importantly, primary groups help us to determine who we are. Because our primary groups are usually made up of our relatives and closest friends, their presence and influence are constant reminders of how we see ourselves. It is through these relationships that we create our

©Rick Gomez/Corbis
©Jim Craigmyle/Corbis

PRIMARY VS. SECONDARY GROUPS

Primary relationships are not easily replaced.

Primary relationships play a variety of roles.

Secondary relationships have specialized roles.

Primary relationships are filled with emotion and involve open communication.

Secondary relationships are impersonal and unemotional and involve limited communication.

"looking-glass selves." By reflecting their perceptions back to us, primary relationships provide valuable feedback.

Secondary groups, on the other hand, are formal, superficial, and last for a short or fixed time.[4] These groups generally come together to meet some specific goal or purpose. If you join a civic organization in order to help put on a parade, you are joining a secondary group. Such groups provide **bounded relationships** that exist only under specific conditions. For example, you and your co-workers might "do lunch," but you probably wouldn't invite them to a family function. Co-workers form a group that is usually of secondary importance to you.

Formal types of social norms heavily influence the way we interact in secondary groups. These norms direct our actions and frame our communication. For example, you might ask your mailman about the weather, but you probably wouldn't get into a debate about climate change. Moreover, the types of norms we follow when interacting affects the way we feel about the group. If we are close and informal, we may fit in with the group, making it feel more like a primary one. If not, we can easily feel like outsiders.

IN-GROUPS AND OUT-GROUPS

As the character Cady learns in the classic teen movie *Mean Girls*, the social groups to which we belong can have a huge impact on our lives. You might have acknowledged different "cliques" back in high school, such as the jocks, the artists, or the theater kids. If you've ever had to wait for what seemed like hours on the sidelines—while all the popular kids were getting chosen for the team—you were hoping to be welcomed into an in-group.

An **in-group** is a group to which we feel an affinity or closeness. For this reason, we often have a strong sense of loyalty to an in-group. Most people hold an **in-group bias**, the feeling that their in-group is superior to others.[5] Have you ever noticed that it is OK for you to talk bad about your family but if someone else insults them, you get angry? That's because most people hold an in-group bias toward their own family, and if someone who is not part of that group attacks it, they defend the group.

An **out-group** is a group from which we are disconnected. We often hold negative biases toward out-groups and may even feel very competitive toward them. We see this all the time in sports. Ask any member of Red Sox Nation about the Yankees, and you're likely to be met with unvarnished vitriol. The same will probably happen if you ask

Yankees fans about the Red Sox. In both cases, each respective fan group holds an out-group bias toward the other fan group. This is especially true in partisan politics in which skirmishes between Democrats and Republicans can erupt over the most mundane issues. The members of the Oneida community came together to form a type of in-group. Members of the group were fiercely loyal to one another and shunned those who lived in the "outside" world.

Sociologist Robert Merton suggests that our biases come from our position in society.[6] We see the traits of our group as acceptable while we hold the views of out-groups as unreasonable. Generally, people hold a bias toward out-groups; however, there are a number of factors that impact whether these biases are positive or negative.[7] For example, social outcasts in high school can hold either a positive or negative bias toward the "popular" group. If the outcasts know that nothing can change their outsider status, then they're likely to hold the cool kids in contempt. If, on the other hand, an outcast hopes to one day penetrate the cool group, he or she holds a positive bias toward them. In a sense, outcasts place the in-group on a pedestal if they think they can join them, and they knock this group down if they feel joining the group is impossible.[8]

Sociologists Tajfel and Turner suggest that everyone seeks a positive social identity.[9] This pursuit is the root cause of in-group and

∧ The 2004 movie *Mean Girls* depicts the **in-groups and out-groups** of
∧ high school society.

out-group biases. We may point out the negative differences in others to elevate our own identity, even if the differences are insignificant. Go to an Internet message board where posters are discussing a hypothetical battle between Superman and the Incredible Hulk, and you might observe some heated wrath being spewed as each camp takes sides. This seemingly innocuous conversation can quickly devolve into a flame-throwing contest between angry fanboys. By poking fun at the other, the groups make themselves feel superior.

Position and power are other factors that can impact our perception of in-groups and out-groups. The workplace is common ground for these biases. Courtney Von Hippel studied temporary employees' out-group biases.[10] Temps who actually wanted a full-time job desired their co-workers' acceptance.[11] Meanwhile, temps who didn't expect permanent employment resented full-time employees because they didn't need to feel accepted.[12] In other words, it was highly unlikely that full-timers were taking these temps out to lunch.

IN-GROUP is a group to which we feel an affinity or closeness.

IN-GROUP BIAS is the feeling that a person's in-group is superior to others.

OUT-GROUP is a group from which we are disconnected.

REFERENCE GROUP is the group that you use to evaluate yourself.

REFERENCE GROUPS

In nearly every situation, we compare ourselves to another person or group. For example, you might not have a need for a new cell phone, but if one of your best friends keeps going on and on about his new iPhone, you might find yourself visiting your local wireless phone dealer so you're not left out. Since we cannot make judgments about our own behavior in isolation, we often use others to assess our behavior.[13] Sociologists refer to the group you use to evaluate yourself as a **reference group**.

REFERENCE GROUPS, though, are not necessarily in-groups because we don't have to belong to them. **If, for example, you are studying to be a neurosurgeon,** you might talk to surgeons at your local hospital **about the duties and challenges of the career.** But simply thinking like a surgeon doesn't make you one. **They're just a reference group to help guide who you are and who you will become.**

©Jodnen Sands/Digital Visions/Getty Images
©Kiselev Andrey Valerevich/Shutterstock

>>> GO GLOBAL

In and Out in Japan

Xenophobia, the fear of outsiders, is a powerful example of out-group bias. In Japan, only those with 100 percent Japanese lineage are considered Japanese.[14] Foreigners who move to Japan and live there for years might eventually be able to gain citizenship, but will never "become Japanese," nor will their children.[15] In this way, Japanese society alienates itself from other cultures. "True" Japanese people in Japan form an in-group,

whereas all other nonnative or different peoples form an out-group.

Throughout history, it's been customary for the Japanese to create out-groups, ostracize them, and then hold that group responsible for current social problems.[16] During the early 1900s, many Korean people were brought into Japan as migrant workers to meet the nation's industrialization needs.[17] Japanese society immediately began to look at the Korean population as outsiders. Association with the population was frowned

upon, and cultural integration was impossible. In fact, in present-day Japan, Koreans cannot gain full citizenship. However, leaders are working to change laws in order to recognize Koreans as full-fledged Japanese citizens.

>>> ACTIVITY Research a country other than Japan. What in- and out-groups are part of that country's society? How are members of the out-groups treated? Discuss your findings with a classmate.

DYAD is a group consisting of only two people.

TRIAD is a group consisting of three people.

LEADERSHIP STYLE is a behavioral mode that leaders use to influence group members.

AUTOCRATIC LEADERS are leaders who determine the group policies and assign tasks.

DEMOCRATIC LEADERS are leaders who strive to set group policy by discussion and agreement.

LAISSEZ-FAIRE LEADERS are leaders who lead by absence and may in fact not want to be leaders at all.

CONFORMITY is the degree to which we will alter our behavior, attitudes, and points of view to fit into our perceived expectation of what is appropriate.

GROUPTHINK is the term for group decisions that are made without objective thought.

GROUP SIZE, STRUCTURE, AND INTERACTION

Groups come in all shapes and sizes. When the Oneida group began in 1849, there were 87 original members.[18] The group grew to a total of 306 members before dissolving in the late 1800s. Part of the reason the Oneida community broke up was due to its size—the large group size led to infighting among its members. As a group gets larger, maintaining in-group feelings becomes harder. Smaller groups tend to be more intimate and less official, making them easier to maintain.

The smallest and strongest form of a group is a **dyad**, a group consisting of only two people. The two members become very close, intimate, and connected. Think of a happy marriage as an example of a strong dyad. Such closeness is not possible in larger groups. Paradoxically, a dyad can also be unstable because either member can unilaterally decide to dissolve the group.[19] If someone has ever dumped you, you probably understand this principle.

When a third member enters a twosome, a **triad**, or group of three, forms. In a triad, mediation, alliances, and competition are likely. For example, if two members of the triad are at odds, the third member can act as a mediator to resolve the conflict. Triads can also allow for alliances between two of the members, potentially against the third, which weakens the group. If two friends ever teamed up against you, then you understand this principle. When alliances occur, the chance for competition among the members increases, which can lead to dissolution of the group. As a result, sociologist Georg Simmel referred to the triad as the weakest group size.[20]

As group size grows, there are greater opportunities for potential interactions, but also more formality and less intimacy. Family gatherings are great places to see this theory play out in real life. At a recent family gathering, I closely watched the interactions taking place as people slowly began to arrive. When the group size was small, people remained together, sitting in the same room and holding a single conversation. However, as the size grew to greater than ten, having one large conversation became impossible. I noticed people breaking off into subgroups. Some played games, others went outside, and still others stayed in the kitchen sampling the holiday goodies. Such divisions are normal even among close families. The group was simply too large to allow for one conversation.

If you attend a concert in a large arena, you'll probably talk only to those with whom you came, right? You and others are sandwiched into tight surroundings, and you may be actually physically touching someone you don't know, yet you probably won't talk to that person. Ironically, our sense of group often gets smaller when we're in large crowds. As a population increases in size and becomes denser, our perception of group size becomes smaller.[21] As crowds get larger, they become more stressful to us. In order to reduce the stress, we retreat into smaller, safer groups, thus limiting the interactions in the group and the stress of being in the crowd.

LEADERSHIP STYLES

In many groups, there are always those individuals who stand apart from the crowd and become leaders, either officially or unofficially. If sociologists made TV shows, they might have created the show *Survivor*. If you watch, you know that tribe leaders often emerge. Tribe leaders provide food for the group, instructions for building shelter, and unity among the tribe members. Since leadership makes others more conscious of the person, leaders on *Survivor* often have a huge target on the backs even though their contributions are usually crucial to the tribe's success.

According to Lewin et al., leadership can be summarized by three distinct styles.[23] **Leadership style** refers to a behavioral mode that leaders use to influence group members. Leadership style varies between autocratic, democratic, and laissez-faire styles. **Autocratic leaders** determine the group policies and assign tasks.[24] These strict authoritarians inform you, "It's my way or the highway." Conversely, **democratic leaders** strive to set group policy by discussion and agreement.[25] They hope for consensus and are likely to ask for your opinion on matters. Finally, **laissez-faire leaders** lead by absence and may in fact not want to be leaders at all.[26] They set few goals and do only what must be done.

Whichever style you've encountered, there are some important points to remember about leadership style as it applies to social groups:

1. There is no "right" type of leadership style.
2. Successful leaders adapt the style to the situation.
3. The process of leadership impacts both the group members and the leader.
4. Leadership styles are learnable.
5. Different styles can be effective in certain situations and/or with certain groups of people.[27]

> According to Hamburger et al., **the size of the group affects the group's ability to cooperate in a task.[22]** This phenomenon explains why reducing class size in public schools is a major issue in education policy. **Smaller groups accomplish more in less time than larger ones do.**

CONFORMITY

Because it takes the rare individual to stand out and be a leader, most members of a group are followers in some way. **Conformity** refers to the degree to which we will alter our behavior, attitudes, and points of view to fit into our perceived expectation of what is appropriate. Everyone hopes to "fit in," but would you change your opinion of what you think is true in order to fit into a group?

Psychologist Solomon Asch wanted to test the impact of groups on people's perception in 1952.[28] Asch set up groups so that only one member was not aware that the rest were actors. Then, he showed the pseudo-group a series of cards like those shown below. He asked them to match the lines on card 2 to the line they saw on card 1. At first, the confidants chose correctly and the group could easily make unified decisions. However, over time the confidants began to make deliberate mistakes in order to test the desire to achieve group conformity. Amazingly, about a third of the participants went along with the group, even though it was in error. Such a phenomenon is more common than you might think. When people are in a group, they often want to conform to the majority and don't offer an opinion that goes against the grain.

Groupthink

At times, group conformity becomes so strong that a group will not consider other ideas or influences. Extremely cohesive groups or

©John Berry/Syracuse Newspapers/The Image Works

∧ When you're with a crowd, **do you** find that
∧ you **change your behavior to match everyone?**
Or do you march to your own drummer?

ASCH'S CARDS

CARD 1

CARD 2

A   B   C

ones with very strong leaders might make decisions using groupthink.[29] **Groupthink** is the term for group decisions that are made without objective thought. When a group is in this mode, people conform to what they believe is the consensus of the rest of the group. They often make decisions that they would not make as individuals. Extreme group conformity leads to groupthink. It frequently results in bad decisions that people later agree were a mistake. Groupthink is more likely when the following conditions are present:

- **Cohesiveness:** Groups that are highly connected are more likely to engage in groupthink. If, for example, you were to join a board of directors that the same people had led for 10 years, odds are groupthink is occurring. This group is likely to be very interconnected and to think they have ironed out all the possible solutions to the potential problems.
- **Threats:** When groups encounter an external threat, solidarity increases because common enemies unify groups.
- **A Strong Leader:** If the leader has a domineering style or is charismatic enough, groups will usually accept the leader's will. Although a strong leader is important to a group's progress, it can also increase the odds of groupthink because few will want to take on the leader.[30]

MAKE CONNECTIONS

A History of Groupthink

Sociologist Irving Janis pinned down eight shortcomings that are likely to result from groupthink decisions.[31] We can use these criteria as standards to evaluate any decision and determine if groupthink was involved. Groupthink in U.S. politics is hardly anything new. Janis points out that political leaders often run the risk of making poor decisions because of this phenomenon. The failed U.S. invasion of Cuba, known as the Bay of Pigs, fits the bill.[32] Think about past U.S. leaders' decisions to invade nations such as Iraq. Was groupthink behind these decisions?

1 **Illusion of invulnerability.** Groupthink creates excessive optimism that the desired outcome will occur. Some have suggested that the 2003 invasion of Iraq arose from an illusion of invulnerability. When the United States launched its "Shock and Awe" campaign in 2003, media coverage gave citizens the impression that the war would be easily won.[33] The military was supposed to dominate Iraq rapidly, quickly winning the war on terror and suffering few casualties in the process.

2 **Collective rationalization.** Members ignore warnings as irrelevant and will not reconsider the assumptions of the decision. Some have suggested that the 2003 invasion of Iraq arose from collective rationalization. Critics point to President Bush's "Bring 'em on" and Vice President Cheney's proclamation that "We'll be greeted as liberators" as examples of such thinking.[34]

©Reuters/Corbis

∧ ∧ ∧ **What conditions** do you think **contributed to groupthink** during the beginning of the war with Iraq?

3 **Belief in inherent morality.** People in the group believe their cause is just and right. In a 2001 speech, President George W. Bush claimed, "Either you are with us, or you are with the terrorists."[35] This led many citizens to reconsider their opposition to the war.

4 **Stereotyped views of out-groups.** Groupthink is likely when members view themselves as the "good guys" and their opponents as the "bad guys." When the United States invaded Iraq to overthrow the government of Saddam Hussein, many of my students held negative stereotypes of the Iraqi people, believing them to be "cold-blooded terrorists."

5 **Direct pressure on dissenters.** Members of the group who disagree are under pressure to keep quiet if they dissent. Frequently, the group will not allow any voicing of disagreement. In his 2004 book *Plan of Attack*, journalist Bob Woodward suggests that members of President George W. Bush's presidential cabinet effectively isolated dissenters of the war in Iraq.[36] Moreover, many critics of the administration were labeled "unpatriotic" and accused of "not supporting the troops" if they expressed contradictory opinions.

6 **Self-censorship.** Group members squelch their doubts and fail to express reservations they may have about the proposal. When group members see dissenters punished or isolated, they will self-censor in order to avoid punishment from a strong leader. In the time leading up to the war in Iraq, many media outlets, such as *The New York Times* and NBC News, tended to downplay anti-war stories due to pressure from the Bush administration.[37]

7 **Illusion of unanimity.** The group leadership in particular mistakes a pressured majority view for unanimity. For example, in an interview with ABC News, former Secretary of State Colin Powell admitted that his public support for the war in Iraq came from his loyalty to President Bush and not his personal convictions.[38] When Powell silenced his personal convictions, he gave the appearance of unanimity.

8 **Self-appointed mind guards.** Certain members play the role of protector of the leader, shielding him or her from information and ideas that might be contradictory to the group's decision. Many television media stations could be considered mind guards because they rarely, if ever, aired views that could be considered counterproductive to the war.

>>> ACTIVITY Think about your own life. How has groupthink played a role in a past decision you've made? Do you regret that decision now? Evaluate your choice using the eight shortcomings of groupthink. Did all eight factor into your decision?

SOCIAL CAPITAL AND SOCIAL NETWORKS

When you think of all the possible things that brought you to this point in your life, you're basically thinking about social capital. **Social capital** is a sociological concept that refers to the individual and collective resources available to a person. Social capital includes the institutions, relationships, attitudes, and values that influence interactions among people and contribute to economic and social development. Coleman suggests that social capital impacts all aspects of our lives and affects the choices and options available to us.[39]

Most of us use this kind of capital to find jobs, colleges, and other opportunities. For example, my first job was repairing bicycles in a local bike shop. I got the job because my mother knew the owner. Later on, a friend helped me find my second job at a fast-food chicken restaurant. Of course, I had to do the work and keep the job, but my friends and family were a part of my social capital that helped me gain employment.

Although Coleman suggests that social capital is functional for society and individuals, Bourdieu, a conflict theorist, views it as an economic resource.[40] Consider legacy admissions: A policy in which applicants to a highly touted private university are admitted based on their family's history with the school. Such a practice tends to benefit wealthier students because they are more likely to have family members who are alumni. In short, our social and familial contacts can help us get a foot in the door of a place to which we might have otherwise been denied access.

The social contacts that people make, when culled together, comprise a social network, which is one component of social capital. Basically, a **social network** is the web of ties you have with others. Networks usually include people with similar values, beliefs, and identities. They allow us to gain important information and may even open doors of opportunity. In the 21st century, social networking has taken on an even greater importance for Web-savvy individuals. Sites such as MySpace, Facebook, and LinkedIn serve as virtual alternatives to traditional networks. The power of the Internet allows people to expand their network exponentially.

> **SOCIAL CAPITAL** is a sociological concept that refers to the individual and collective resources available to a person.
>
> **SOCIAL NETWORK** is the web of ties you have with others.

Social Capital

JOB

Family

EDUCATION

Professors

SOCIAL CLASS

MOTIVATION

Friends

Acquaintances

Employers

Co-workers

GENDER

RACE

Classmates

©Monkey Business Images/Shutterstock; ©Monkey Business Images/Shutterstock; ©Brian Chase/Shutterstock; ©Dmitriy Shironosov/Shutterstock; ©Yuri Arcurs/Shutterstock; ©Andresr/Shutterstock

> ∧∧∧ Your **social capital** is a combination of **internal and external** resources.

To see the value of a social network, look at how recent immigrants are able to use it to their advantage. Sociologist Carlos Garcia shows that immigrants to the United States from Mexico often use social networks to get jobs and find housing.[41] Garcia found that networks allow immigrants to succeed even when they may not have much personal capital.[42] For example, a good network may help an immigrant overcome illiteracy and/or a lack of understanding of the English language. Immigrants use three different forms of networking:

1 **Traditional networks:** These include primary group relationships with family and close friends. Often Mexican immigrants obtain job leads from family and friends, which can impact decisions they make about where they will live.[43]

2 **Church networks:** These networks connect people based on their religious affiliation and offer many of the same benefits as a traditional one. Mexican immigrants often use church affiliations in order to expand the scope of their networks.[44]

3 **Contract networks:** These involve employers seeking workers. During Garcia's research, meatpacking plants sent agents to Mexico to contract with potential laborers, guaranteeing them work if they could get to the United States. Contract networks provide necessary economic resources, whereas traditional and church networks provide social and emotional support.[45]

Sometimes, you don't have to depend on a strong network to succeed. Weak ties can also be immensely valuable to us. For example, you may hear about a job opening from someone sitting next to you in class. Even though your classmate isn't necessarily in your primary group, this tip could prove much more valuable than information from your family or friends. Granovetter suggests that weak ties play a vital role in social capital because they expand our networks, thus expanding our possibilities.[46]

<<< Our view of an organization depends upon our involvement with it. For example, a prison can be a **utilitarian organization** for the prison guards, **a normative organization** for people who volunteer to lead Alcoholics Anonymous groups with the inmates, **and a coercive organization** to the inmates themselves.

Formal Organizations

When you hang out with friends or family, you let your guard down and forget about all the rules. That's because these social groups are informal. Other groups you're affiliated with, such as your local bowling league or country club, are probably formal organizations. **Formal organizations** are groups created for a certain purpose and built for maximum efficiency.

VOLUNTARY ASSOCIATIONS

Through joining a team, singing in a choir, or helping in a soup kitchen, you can make a **voluntary association**. In 1995, political scientist Robert Putnam showed that participation in these kinds of associations is declining.[47] Take bowling leagues, for example. The number of bowling leagues is decreasing, while the number of people bowling has not changed. People are joining organizations less frequently, creating a more individual and isolated society. The social capital of our entire society may be suffering from shrinking social networks, despite our using networks to increase our outcomes and improve our lives.

Voluntary associations have life-changing effects on communities. For example, in an area of Nepal where high fertility rates were an increasing problem, more individuals became involved in voluntary associations—like credit bank groups, women's groups, agricultural groups, and youth groups. As memberships increased, the likelihood of Nepalese people using contraception also increased.[48] People who lived in neighborhoods that had a number of possible voluntary associations were more likely to use contraceptives than people who lived in relatively isolated communities. Through fostering a better sense of community among individuals, voluntary associations helped control fertility rates.

ORGANIZATIONS AND BUREAUCRACIES

Organizations come in a variety of types and sizes. Some organizations are formed to help a cause, such as the ASPCA. Others, like the retail chain Best Buy, serve to make money. All organizations are alike in that they are formal groups that exist to achieve a desired goal. Sociologist Amitai Etzioni suggested that the type of organization ultimately determines our membership in it.[49] For example, when you get a job at a department store or office building, you're joining a **utilitarian organization**.[50] Members join utilitarian organizations because they receive wages in exchange for work. **Normative organizations**, though, exist in order to achieve a worthwhile goal.[51] If you volunteer at normative organization, such as a soup kitchen, you do so because you believe feeding the homeless serves an essential purpose in society.

While we willingly join utilitarian and normative organizations, we do not join **coercive organizations** by choice.[52] Members of coercive organizations, like prison inmates or rehab patients, don't join voluntarily; outside forces of authority bring them into the organization.

Whether utilitarian, normative, or coercive, organizations have some important qualities that keep them running smoothly.

- **Division of labor:** Tasks are clearly defined and divided, and members understand their roles and expectations.
- **Concentration of power:** Organizations concentrate power in the hands of a few, who can then use that power to control the institution.
- **Methods of succession:** Membership in the organization allows for the replacement of all roles, including leaders.[53]

Within all organizations, a structure exists, though some may be more formal than others. **Formal structure** refers to the explicit rules, goals, and guidelines of the organization. Organization charts, policy and procedure manuals, and established titles and roles are all part of the formal structure of an organization. You can see such formal structures develop in any student organization that elects presidents, vice presidents, and other officers. **Informal structures** consist of friendships, allegiances, and loyalties among members of the organization. All organizations have informal structures, and these often make the organization run smoothly.

CHARACTERISTICS OF BUREAUCRACY

If you've ever had to wait in line for hours to renew your driver's license, only to hear "I can't help you. You'll have to wait over there," then you know some of the frustrations that come with a large bureaucracy. **Bureaucracies** are formal organizations that are organized into a hierarchy of smaller departments. Bureaucracies often have an impersonal feel when one department doesn't have much contact with another. Since a better method of organization has not yet been found, it looks like they are here to stay.

Max Weber was one of the early sociologists to discuss the idea of bureaucracy.[54] Weber proposed that no matter what a formal organization's purpose might be, all ideal bureaucracies display certain characteristics.

Weber and the Iron Cage

For Weber, bureaucratization was a logical extension of formal rational thought.[55] **Formal rationality** refers to the reasonable actions organizations and bureaucracies take to achieve goals in the most effective way. If Weber's theory sounds familiar, it's because George Ritzer used the same theory in his discussion of the McDonaldization of the United States.[56]

According to Weber, any organization that grows large enough will inevitably strive toward formal rationality and bureaucracy. However, such a highly structured bureaucracy can cause the members to feel trapped in a dehumanizing "**iron cage**" that turns them into little more than robots accomplishing tasks. Weber proposed that this iron cage, while problematic from a personal level, is actually a good thing because it helps the organization thrive and places its needs above the needs of the individual.

The power of the bureaucracy often moves from the top down, meaning that leaders of the group make decisions, and those lower on the organizational chart complete these tasks. This setup forces leaders to be accountable for the actions of the bureaucracy and increases their control. However, this hierarchy strips workers of having a say in decision making.

With all the decision-making power at the top, inefficiencies can occur. If leaders don't understand what is happening at the lower levels of the organization, they can easily lead it astray. Japanese car manufacturing is known for its use of teams and quality control activities that ensure the quality of the cars they build. A line worker who sees a problem with a part can stop the line. Meanwhile, American car manufacturers tend to practice a top-down management style in which workers are largely independent and not focused on the final product. The difference between these management strategies leads to fewer quality problems in Japanese cars. American car companies have since adopted many of these techniques to improve their quality control.[57]

The division of labor in a bureaucracy can also be a negative. Workers may become alienated from the organization's purpose and only focus on their specific tasks. For example, a factory worker who

FORMAL ORGANIZATIONS are groups created for a certain purpose and built for maximum efficiency.

VOLUNTARY ASSOCIATION is the act of joining an organization that offers no pay and that expands social networks through interaction.

ORGANIZATIONS are formal groups that exist to achieve a desired goal.

UTILITARIAN ORGANIZATION is an organization in which people receive wages in exchange for work.

NORMATIVE ORGANIZATIONS are organizations that exist to achieve a worthwhile goal.

COERCIVE ORGANIZATIONS are organizations that people are forced to join.

FORMAL STRUCTURES are the explicit rules, goals, and guidelines of an organization.

INFORMAL STRUCTURES are friendships, allegiances, and loyalties among members of an organization.

BUREAUCRACIES are formal organizations that are organized into a hierarchy of smaller departments.

FORMAL RATIONALITY is the reasonable actions that organizations and bureaucracies take to achieve goals in the most effective way.

IRON CAGE is a concept introduced by Max Weber that refers to the way in which bureaucracies make workers feel trapped and turn them into little more than robots accomplishing tasks.

spends hours putting tires on cars might notice a broken windshield but not say anything because "it's not his job." Such a feeling arises from an impersonal organizational culture.

Although written rules and regulations let workers know what is expected of them, strict enforcement of these rules stifles creativity and imagination. Workers might not be inclined to speak up in order to implement a new idea or to perform tasks that do not fall under their job description.

Now that we have discussed the role of groups and group interaction in society, it's time to think sociologically about these groups.

Weber's Characteristics of Bureaucracy

Division of Labor: Workers are assigned specific, specialized tasks.

Hierarchy of Authority: Decision-making power moves from the top (supervisors) down to workers in lower positions.

Rules and Regulations: Rules and regulations guide a bureaucracy's actions to ensure that tasks are performed uniformly.

Technical Qualifications: Hiring and promotions are based on a worker's ability to perform a task.

Impersonality: Workers perform "without hatred or passion," meaning that all clients are treated equally.

©Yuri Arcurs/Shutterstock

think sociologically: HOW DO SOCIOLOGISTS VIEW GROUP LEADERSHIP?

Functionalism and Leadership

What makes someone a good leader? Influential functionalism theorist John C. Maxwell provides a model of leadership made up of five levels.[58] Think about leaders you know who exhibit these qualities.

LEADERSHIP 101: WHAT EVERY LEADER NEEDS TO KNOW

The true measure of leadership is influence on others. If you lack this ability, no one will follow you. The style of leadership—autocratic, democratic, or laissez-faire—you employ does not directly affect your level of leadership. An autocratic leader can be just as influential as a democratic leader. However, Maxwell suggests that all leaders begin at the most basic level.[59]

Level 1: *Positional leaders: People follow the leader because they must.*

This level serves as the most basic type of leadership. Simply put, other people give positional leaders the reins of leadership. They don't rely on vision or charisma to lead others; instead, people follow them because of their title. When you enter the workforce, the hierarchy of your company determines who your supervisor will be, and it is part of your job to follow that person's lead. In the overall scheme of things, though, the positional leader and the people he or she oversees are just cogs in a machine. This type of leader has the least amount of influence.

Level 2: *Permission leaders: People follow because they want to.*

Successful leaders eventually understand that there is more to leadership that merely being the boss.

Although positional leaders often lack personal relationships with their followers, permission leaders take the opposite tack. These leaders generate followers willingly precisely because they develop personal relationships with them. A permission leader doesn't merely view workers as a means to an end; instead, they work together because they enjoy each other's company. Such a leader has considerably more influence because his or her followers are actually invested in the relationship, and, by extension, the task that is to be completed.

Level 3: *Production leaders: People follow because of what you have done.*

At this level of leadership, goals are met with minimum effort because the leader sets the example. Production leaders spur a sense of accomplishment in the people who follow them and clearly communicate a vision of what can be. They then go out and perform just as hard as everyone else. Production leaders are also willing to make difficult decisions and take the blame for failures. Kobe Bryant is known to be quiet and introspective off the basketball court. But on the court, he is unquestionably his team's leader because his effort and skills inspire the rest of his teammates to perform better.

Level 4: *People development: People follow because they are empowered.*

Rather than demonstrating their own skills to set an example, empowering leaders help people meet their potential by encouraging them to accomplish tasks they might have previously felt were impossible. By developing people, an empowering leader accomplishes tasks more easily because the team feels they are capable and competent. An example of this type of leadership is demonstrated in President John F. Kennedy's famous words, "Ask not what your country can do for you; ask what you can do for your country."

Level 5: *Personhood: People follow because of who you are.*

It can take many years for people to attain this highest level of influence. Such leaders must spend a lot of time cultivating relationships with people and developing communication skills. But once this level is reached, they will be able to inspire their followers to exceed their potential and willingly sacrifice for them.

Maxwell suggests that all leaders have the potential to climb this ladder of influence, but every new leader starts at the first level. Successful leaders eventually understand that there is more to leadership than merely being the boss.

THINK SOCIOLOGICALLY

Leadership in the Oneida Community

John Humphrey Noyes displayed each of Maxwell's levels of effective leadership in the way he oversaw the Oneida community. Since Noyes was the founder of the community, anyone who joined had to follow his lead.

Both Noyes and his early followers believed that he had "divine commission," or was sent by a higher power to lead the group. Noyes believed so strongly in his right to lead that he said, "I would never connect myself with any individual or association in religion unless I were acknowledged leader," and many did acknowledge him.[60] Similar to Maxwell's first level of leadership, Noyes' followers were influenced by his title as divine leader. As more members joined, Noyes formed personal relationships with each of them and cultivated a more loyal following.

Noyes was able to sustain his leadership by practicing the "sinless life" he often preached. This influenced his followers to believe in the collective cause of the community. There was no question that the Oneida community was governed as an absolute monarchy. In this society, authority came from Noyes at the top and the members supported his decisions.

Noyes did not completely rule on his own, though. Like Maxwell suggested, leaders succeed because they empower others. Once Noyes discovered loyal individuals, he often employed them as his advisors. At the height of his power, Noyes had climbed to the top of the leadership ladder. His followers were willing to make whatever sacrifices were necessary to remain members of this community.

©Jim West/Alamy

©Tom Merton/OJO Images/Getty Images

∧
∧ Weber believed that **bureaucracy was actually a "hierarchy of knowledge."** The
∧ **leaders trust workers** to handle all the details, while the **workers trust the leaders** to
handle the general outcome. **Marx,** on the other hand, **believed each side
deceived the other,** which ultimately **benefited the bourgeoisie.**[61] Do you agree
with Marx or Weber? Why or why not?

Conflict Theory—Marx, Bureaucracy, and Democratic Organizations

While Weber saw both the positive and negative aspects of bureaucracy, Karl Marx believed that "bureaucracy [was] a circle from which one [could not] escape." For Marx, bureaucracy provided no essential function for society. It was just another way for the bourgeoisie to exploit workers more efficiently and gain more wealth and control for themselves.

You'd probably expect workers to fight against bureaucratic systems. However, Marx's theory suggests that employees who oppose a bureaucracy's leadership are easily discovered, reprimanded, or fired. Is this the most beneficial for productivity? Studies show that a democratic, instead of an autocratic leadership style, actually increases worker productivity. Democratic leaders encourage workers to participate in production decisions, and this participation increases profits and productivity.[62] It seems that a more inclusive leadership style helps both the workers and the owners.

Greater labor participation in leadership roles does not mean that the company will succeed. In studies by Hammer et al., increased laborer participation on boards of directors does not translate to increased profits.[63] In fact, such involvement is counterproductive for future planning because workers and management tend to have differing points of view. Workers focus primarily on job protection, while managers are interested in appeasing stockholders.

Symbolic Interactionism— Creating a Just and Democratic Workplace

After graduating from college, you probably have high hopes of landing your dream job. The sad fact is that for four out of five people in the United States, their daily grind is a nightmare.[64] It appears that U.S. citizens hate their jobs more than ever before.

Negative feelings like these have symbolic interactionists wondering: How do workers' attitudes toward their jobs impact productivity and job satisfaction? This is a question that can keep a human resources administrator up at night. When people have a level of personal control over the outcomes of their jobs, they are more connected to their work.[65] For example, if a programmer has designed a software prototype that catches her supervisor's eye, she is more likely to feel a stronger connection to the company.

Joyce Rothschild suggests that traditional bureaucracies create ineffective work environments because workers are disconnected.[66] Studying Eastern European capitalist and communist countries in the late 1970s and early 1980s, Rothschild found similar feelings of disconnection in both environments.[67] Workers experienced little ability to innovate and change their work environment in the centrally organized government-owned businesses of Eastern Europe. This top-down management style is very similar to that of Western capitalist bureaucracies. Rothschild's conclusion was clear—restrictive work environments equal inefficient and unproductive workers.[68]

In contrast, team approaches in management encourage democracy in the workplace.[69] Teams in the workplace are likely to be more connected to their jobs because individuals can connect to other team members. From the perspective of an interactionist, such a change could be linked to a changing definition of business success. As workers become more educated, they expect to have more input in the work they do. After completing your degree, you'll probably seek a job that includes you in the process of deciding how to do your work. It's a good position to strive for. Jobs like these allow people to have a sense of satisfaction both at work and in their personal lives.

WRAP YOUR MIND AROUND THE THEORY

©Newscom

Today, Oprah Winfrey is one of the most influential women in the world, expanding her audience so much that people have described her influence to be greater than most political and religious leaders, aside from the Pope.[70] **How much of her success is due to her leadership style?**

FUNCTIONALISM

When studying groups, functionalists might examine the group's values and behaviors, particularly those of the group's leader. Successful groups often have successful leaders, so studying a group's leadership and how it impacts other members is important. John Maxwell points out that while anyone can be a "boss," only specific people can become a leader. He created a model outlining the five levels of leadership and proposed that each level depicts an increase in influence and empowerment in workers. Even Oneida community founder John Humphrey Noyes went through these steps before he was able to become powerful. Eventually, he was able to influence hundreds of people to follow him and start his own community of loyal followers.

CONFLICT THEORY

Since conflict theorists focus on macro issues and their relationship to society, they would take note of the arguments surrounding bureaucracy. While Weber saw bureaucracy as an extension of formal rational thought, Marx viewed it as a tool of the rich to keep the working class down. Critics of Marx have pointed out that democratic environments actually improve productivity and profits. However, if a democratic environment is not implemented, then bureaucracy can be stifling for the worker and the organization. To keep control over the Oneida group, Noyes created 48 departments for community organizations and 21 committees to supervise these departments.[71] While Weber may have viewed this system as rational, Marx would claim it as a tool used to keep control.

HOW DO DIFFERENT PERSPECTIVES VIEW GROUP LEADERSHIP?

SYMBOLIC INTERACTIONISM

Symbolic interactionists realize that along with leadership, personal attitude has a big effect on job performance and satisfaction. People feel good about themselves and their jobs when they feel they have a certain level of control over their actions. Rothschild suggests that workers feel disconnected under traditional bureaucracies, which create unproductive environments. Symbolic interactionists view a democratic work environment as more satisfactory for workers because it helps them feel connected to their jobs. Noyes tried to create a sense of connection in the Oneida community through criticism sessions in which people could release their aggression. Although these sessions seemed to be therapeutic, they were actually useful in controlling the community through shame.[72] People gained a sense of power over the community when they could take part in disciplining its members.

Leaders who focus only on the bottom line can be oppressive, often not caring about the quality of the work environment. **What do you see when you look at this picture?**

©PhotoDisc/Getty Images

When people have a certain level of control over their jobs, they are much more likely to feel connected and satisfied. How might this make an organization more productive?

©Tom Wagner/Corbis

discover sociology in action: HOW DOES A PARENT'S CIVIC ENGAGEMENT AFFECT A CHILD'S FUTURE POLITICAL INVOLVEMENT?

I always vote. Why? Primarily because my parents did. During my childhood, they stressed the importance of being involved in my government and community. My mother always said, "If you don't care, why should anyone else?"

Adult Civic Engagement and Childhood Activities

Since the 1960s, civic organizations have witnessed a sharp decline in participation, which could certainly lead to a society that is less interconnected and has a lower level of social capital.[73] As a result, a number of social problems can arise, one of which is voter apathy.

Could participation in voting and politics be related to what you did when you were younger? Daniel McFarland and Reuben Thomas suggest your involvement as a child impacts your willingness to engage in political action in the future.[74] The authors tested children and controlled for a variety of factors, including the parents' socioeconomic status and education.[75] They found that involvement in activities that encouraged public speaking and/or community service increased the likelihood of political involvement in adult life.[76] Perhaps this is because participants become involved in communities and see the benefits of such involvement.

These findings have direct implications on social policies and civic engagement. Schools that encourage students to become involved in their communities build active citizens. Not only does service learning help you take what you learn in the classroom and use it in the community, but you are also more likely to remain civically engaged.

ACTIVITIES

1. Visit with a professor and discuss your ideas about leadership in the classroom and on your college campus. What does your professor do to inspire followers to his or her discipline?
2. Does your college offer courses or clubs to train you in leadership skills? If so, what are they? If not, where in your local community can you find such opportunities?
3. Do you vote? Do your classmates vote? Why or why not?
4. Read other stories from *Extraordinary Groups: An Examination of Unconventional Lifestyles*. What sociological components make groups last? What happens to the group to cause it to die out?

Leading Groups

As you take your learning from the classroom to the community, you may find yourself leading groups. Effective group work practice requires you to have an understanding of how groups work and a level of comfort with group leadership. How do you gain these things?

The first thing you should ask is, "What are the group's goals?" Depending on the group's goals, your work may be quite different. If you are supervising a call center for a political campaign, your goal may be as simple as monitoring the hours other volunteers work, or you may need to keep their motivation up. No matter what type of group you lead, you need to be able to provide direction if the group gets offtrack.

From Classroom to Community } Registering Voters

Janice, a student in my class, was also studying political science. She earned extra credit by helping to register voters for an upcoming election. In a report for her poli-sci class, she detailed how people reacted when asked if they were registered to vote.

"Lots of people just walked by the table and tried to ignore me. Some people actually got mad if I asked them why they weren't registered to vote.

I couldn't understand that. My parents always voted, and so the thought that college students wouldn't care shocked me. Of course, my sociology class helped shed light on the problem. The U.S. government is such a large bureaucracy that many people feel like they don't matter. I guess they're too busy with their primary groups to care much about secondary groups."

WHAT ARE THE CHARACTERISTICS OF SOCIAL GROUPS?

two commonalities: the members of the group share something in common, and they identify each other as members of that group

HOW DO SOCIOLOGISTS VIEW GROUP LEADERSHIP?

functionalism: leaders are measured by their influence on others

conflict theory: for Marx, bureaucracy was a way to exploit workers, so the bourgeoisie could gain wealth

symbolic interactionism: workers' attitudes toward their jobs impact productivity and job satisfaction

HOW DOES A PARENT'S CIVIC ENGAGEMENT AFFECT A CHILD'S FUTURE POLITICAL INVOLVEMENT?

increases the likelihood of political involvement in adult life

©Monkey Business Images/ Shutterstock

©Keith Brofsky/PhotoDisc/ Getty Images

get the topic: WHAT ARE THE CHARACTERISTICS OF SOCIAL GROUPS?

Formal Organizations
Functionalism and Leadership
Conflict Theory—Marx, Bureaucracy, and
   Democratic Organizations

Symbolic Interactionism—Creating a Just and
   Democratic Workplace
Adult Civic Engagement and Childhood

Activities
Leading Groups

Theory

FUNCTIONALISM

- examines the group's values and behaviors, particularly the group's leader
- successful groups often have successful leaders
- Maxwell's five levels of leadership

CONFLICT THEORY

- democratic leadership styles increase worker productivity
- if a democratic environment is not implemented, then bureaucracy can be stifling for the worker and the organization

- greater participation in leadership roles does not mean the company will succeed

SYMBOLIC INTERACTIONISM

- along with leadership, personal attitude has a big effect on job performance and satisfaction
- people feel good about themselves and their jobs when they feel they have a certain level of control over their actions
- democratic work environments help people feel connected to their jobs

Key Terms

social groups	autocratic leaders	organizations
bounded relationships	democratic leaders	utilitarian organization
in-group	laissez-faire leaders	normative organizations
in-group bias	conformity	coercive organizations
out-group	groupthink	formal structure
reference group	social capital	informal structures
dyad	social network	bureaucracies
triad	formal organizations	formal rationality
leadership style	voluntary association	iron cage

MY SEARCH LAB

1. *Fraternities and Collegiate Rape Culture: Why Are Some Fraternities More Dangerous Places for Women?* by A. Ayers Boswell and Joan Z. Spade, reprinted from Gender & Society, 1996, 10(2): 133–147.

INTRODUCTION

In this article, Boswell and Spade go beyond individual/psychological explanations for rape and instead focus on how social settings can influence the incidence of rape.

DISCUSSION QUESTIONS

1. What are the general conditions that contribute to a "rape culture"?
2. If the authors' findings are correct, what can universities do to reduce the incidence of rape on campus?

2. *Dyads, Triads, and Larger Groups* by Georg Simmel, reprinted from *The Sociology of Georg Simmel*, translated by Kurt H. Wolff, 1950. Copyright by Free Press. pp. 118–144.

INTRODUCTION

In this excerpt, Max Weber explains the unique characteristics of bureaucracy.

DISCUSSION QUESTIONS

1. Have modern bureaucratic organizations changed in their organizational style, or do they still fit the characteristics listed in this excerpt?
2. In his writings, Weber has argued that bureaucracy acts as an "iron cage" that dehumanizes its participants. Do you believe this is true? Why or why not?

THE THINKSPOT

What happens when groupthink becomes extreme? Go to the ThinkSpot to watch video of members of the People's Temple Agricultural Project, otherwise known as the Jonestown cult. Led by Jim Jones, this group is known for the tragic mass suicide that took place in 1978 when 918 members were found dead, apparently from poisoning. As you watch the video, think about what you learned about the history of groupthink in this chapter and how one man was able to lead so many people to their deaths.

Tony Dungy was a professional football coach and a successful one at that. Go to the ThinkSpot and access the video around the 3:15 mark, where Dungy begins discussing his time coaching a losing team and how he made them winners. What characteristics of a leader, as discussed in the chapter, do you think Tony Dungy had to become a successful football coach?

Sample Test Questions

These multiple-choice questions are similar to those found in the test bank that accompanies this textbook.

1. What type of leader sets few goals and does only what must be done?
   a. Totalitarian leader
   b. Autocratic leader
   c. Democratic leader
   d. Laissez-faire leader

2. A soup kitchen is an example of a
   a. coercive organization.
   b. utilitarian organization.
   c. normative organization.
   d. democratic organization.

3. Which of the following is *not* a characteristic common to all properly functioning organizations?
   a. Division of labor
   b. Methods of succession
   c. Voluntary participation
   d. Concentration of power

4. Which organization did Weber call a logical extension of formal rational thought?
   a. Democracy
   b. Bureaucracy
   c. Coercive organization
   d. Informal organization

5. By a functionalist's standard, the greatest measure of a leader is
   a. influence.
   b. charisma.
   c. authority.
   d. intimidation.

ESSAY

1. How and why are social networks of great use to immigrants?
2. Why is groupthink a potentially dangerous method of decision making?
3. What are the potential pitfalls of the three leadership styles discussed in this chapter?
4. Which leadership style did John Humphrey Noyes employ as leader of the Oneida group? Explain.
5. Why is a dyad considered the strongest form of a group?

WHERE TO START YOUR RESEARCH PAPER

To find out how you can be a leader, go to
http://www.holsteinfoundation.org/pdffile/EGL02.pdf

To learn more about the skills needed for leadership, go to
http://www.livingskillslibrary.com/html/Leadership%201%20Models.html

To find Max Weber's notes and original texts, go to
http://www.sociosite.net/topics/weber.php

For more information on the sociology of Georg Simmel, go to
http://www.sociosite.net/topics/sociologists.php#simmel

For information on America Reads and how you can become a school volunteer, go to http://www.ed.gov/inits/americareads/index.html

ANSWERS: 1. d; 2. c; 3. c; 4. b; 5. a

Endnotes

1. From *Extraordinary Groups: An Examination of Unconventional Lifestyles, 8th Edition* by Richard T. Schaefer and William W. Zellner. © 2007 by Worth Publishers. Used with permission.

2. Inside Indiana Business with Gerry Dick, "2010 Final Four Comes Close to Attendance Record," http://www.insideindianabusiness.com/newsitem.asp?ID=40998 (accessed April 26, 2010).

3. Charles H. Cooley, *Human Nature and the Social Order* (New York: Schocken Books, 1902/1964).

4. Ibid.

5. Henry Tajfel, "Social Categorization, Social Identity, and Social Comparison," in *Differentiation between Social Groups: Studies in Social Psychology of Intergroup Relations,* ed. Henry Tajfel (London: Academic Press, 1978), 61–76; Robert K. Merton, *Social Theory and Social Structure* (New York: Free Press, 1968).

6. Robert K. Merton, *Social Theory and Social Structure* (New York: Free Press, 1968).

7. Daan Scheeners, Russell Spears, Bertjan Doosje, and Antony S.R. Manstead, "Diversity in In-group Bias: Structural Factors, Situational Features, and Social Functions," *Journal of Personality and Social Psychology*, 2006. 90(6): 944–960.

8. B. Ann Bettencourt, Kelly Charlton, and Nancy Dorr, "Status Differences and InGroup Bias: A Meta-analytic Examination of the Effects of Status Stability, Status Legitimacy, and Group Permeability," *Psychological Bulletin*, 2001. 127(4): 520–542.

9. Henry Tajfel and John Turner, "The Social Identity Theory of Intergroup Behavior," In: S. Worschel and W.G. Austin, Eds, *Psychology and Intergroup Relations,* (Chicago: Nelson-Hall, 1986), pp. 7–24.

10. Courtney D. Von Hippel, "When People Would Rather Switch Than Fight: Out-group Favoritism Among Temporary Employees." *Group Processes and Intergroup Relations,* 2006. 9(4): 533–546.

11. Ibid.

12. Ibid.

13. Charles H. Cooley, *Human Nature and the Social Order* (New York: Schocken Books, 1902/1964).

14. Ron Adams, "Hikikomori/Otaku Japan's Latest Out-Group," eclip5e.visualassault.org/assets/Hikikomori_Japans_Latest_Outcasts.pdf (accessed June 11, 2008).

15. Ibid.

16. Ibid.

17. Ibid.

18. Richard T. Schaefer and William W. Zellner, *Extraordinary Groups: An Examination of Unconventional Lifestyles, 8th ed.* (New York: Worth Publishers, 2007).

19. Georg Simmel, *The Sociology of Georg Simmel.* Kurt Wolfe ed. (New York: Free Press, 1902/1950).

20. Ibid.

21. James Tucker and S. Thomas Friedman, "Population Density and Group Size," *American Journal of Sociology*, 1972. 77(4): 742–749.

22. Henry Hamburger, Melvin Guyer, and John Fox, "Group Size and Composition," *The Journal of Conflict Resolution*, 1975. 19(3): 503–531.

23. Kurt Lewin, Ronald Lippit, and Ralph K. White, "Patterns of Aggressive Behavior in Experimentally Created Social Climates," *Journal of Social Psychology*, 1939. 10: 271–299.

24. Ibid.

25. Ibid.

26. Ibid.

27. Litsa Nicolaou-Smokovita, "Business Leaders, Work Environment, and Leadership Styles. *Current Sociology*, 2004. 52(3): 404–427.

28. Solomon Asch, *Social Psychology* (Englewood Cliffs, NJ: Prentice-Hall, 1952).

29. Irving L. Janis, *Victims of Groupthink: A Psychological Study of Foreign-Policy Decisions and Fiascoes* (Boston: Houghton Mifflin, 1972); Irving L. Janis, *Groupthink: Psychological Studies of Policy Decisions and Fiascoes* (Boston: Houghton Mifflin, 1983).

30. Irving L. Janis, *Groupthink: Psychological Studies of Policy Decisions and Fiascoes* (Boston: Houghton Mifflin, 1983).

31. Irving L. Janis, *Victims of Groupthink: A Psychological Study of Foreign-Policy Decisions and Fiascoes* (Boston: Houghton Mifflin, 1972).

32. Ibid.

33. "Shock and Awe Campaign Launched in Iraq," *CNN.com*, March 22, 2003, http://www.cnn.com/2003/fyi/news/03/22/iraq.war/ (accessed November 12, 2008).

34. Dan Glasiter, "Bush Voices Regret for Macho Rhetoric in Run-up to Iraq War," *Guardian.co.uk*, June 11, 2008, http://www.guardian.co.uk/world/2008/jun/11/georgebush.usforeignpolicy.

35. George W. Bush, "Address to a Joint Session of Congress and the American People," September 20, 2001, http://www.whitehouse.gov/news/releases/2001/09/20010920-8.html (accessed November 12, 2008).

36. Bob Woodward, *Plan of Attack* (London: Simon and Schuster, 2004).

37. Mike Celizic, "Network Anchors Differ on Iraq War Coverage," *msnbc.com*, May 28, 2008, http://www.msnbc.msn.com/id/24855902/ (accessed November 12, 2008).

38. "Colin Powell on Iraq, Race, and Hurricane Relief," *ABC News*, September 8, 2005, http://abcnews.go.com/2020/Politics/story?id=1105979&page=1 (accessed November 12, 2008).

39. James S. Coleman, "Social Capital in the Creation of Human Capital," *American Journal of Sociology*, 1988. 94(S): 95–120.

40. James S. Coleman, "Social Capital in the Creation of Human Capital," *American Journal of Sociology*, 1988. 94(S): 95–120; Pierre Bourdieu, "The Forms of Capital," *Handbook of Theory and Research for the Sociology of Education,* John G. Richardson ed., (New York: Greenwood, 1986), pp. 241–258.

41. Carlos Garcia, "Buscando Trabajo: Social Networking Among Immigrants from Mexico to the United States," *Hispanic Journal of Behavioral Sciences*, 2005. 27(1): 3–22.

42. Ibid.

43. Ibid.

44. Ibid.

45. Ibid.

46. Mark S. Granovetter, "The Strength of Weak Ties," *American Journal of Sociology*, 1973, 78(6): 1360–1380.

47. Robert D. Putnam, "Bowling Alone: America's Declining Social Capital," *Journal of Democracy*, 1995. 6(1): 65–78.

48. Jennifer Barber, Lisa D. Pearce, Indra Chaudhury, and Susan Gurung, "Voluntary Associations and Fertility Limitation," *Social Forces*, 2002. 80(4): 1369–1401.

49. Amitai Etzioni, *A Comparative Analysis of Complex Organizations: On Power, Involvement, and Their Correlates* (New York: Free Press, 1975).

50. Ibid.

51. Ibid.

52. Ibid.

53. Amitai Etzioni and Edward W. Lehman, *A Sociological Reader on Complex Organizations. 3rd ed.* (New York: Holt, Rinehart and Winston, 1980).

54. Max Weber, "Max Weber Bureaucracy," in *Readings in Social Theory: The Classical Tradition to Post-modernism, 4th edition*, James Farganis ed. (New York: McGraw-Hill, 1978/2004), pp. 99–108; Max Weber, *Max Weber: Essays in Sociology.* Translated and edited by Hans H. Gerth and C. Wright Mills. (New York: Oxford University Press, 1946).

55. Ibid.

56. George Ritzer, *The McDonaldization of Society: Revised New Century Edition* (Thousand Oaks, CA: Pine Forge Press, 2004).

57. Martin Kenney and Richard Florida, "The Transfer of Japanese Management Styles in Two US Transplant Industries: Autos and Electronics," *Journal of Management Studies*, 1995. 32(6): 789–802.

58. John C. Maxwell, *Leadership 101: What Every Leader Needs to Know* (Nashville, TN: Thomas Nelson Publishers, 2002).

59. Ibid.

60. George Wallingford Noyes, *Free Love in Utopia: John Humphrey Noyes and the Origin of the Oneida Community,* (Chicago, The University of Illinois, 2001), p. xvii.

61. Critique of Hegel's Philosophy of Right Karl Marx, 1843, http://www.marxists.org/archive/marx/works/1843/critique-hpr/ch03.htm#027 (accessed August 28, 2008).

62. Richard D. Rosenberg and Eliezer Rosenstein, "Participation and Productivity: An Empirical Study," *Industrial and Labor Relations Review*, 1980, 33(3): 355–367; Henry Levin, "Worker Democracy and Worker Productivity," *Social Justice Research*, 2006. 19(1): 109–121.

63. Tove H. Hammer, Steven C. Curral, and Robert N. Stern, "Worker Representation on Boards of Directors: A Study of Competing Roles," *Industrial and Labor Relations Review*, 1991. 44(4): 661–680.

64. "Most U.S. Workers Not Living the Dream," *msnbc.com*, January 25, 2007. http://www.msnbc.msn.com/id/16795881/ (accessed November 12, 2008).

65. Randy Hodson, *Working With Dignity* (Cambridge: Cambridge University Press, 2000).

66. Joyce Rothschild-Whitt and J. Allen Whitt, *Cooperative Workplace: Potentials and Dilemmas of Organizational Democracy and Participation* (New York: Cambridge University Press, 1986).

67. Ibid.

68. Ibid.

69. Joyce Rothschild, "Utopian Visions: Engaged Sociologies for the 21st Century: Creating a Just and Democratic Workplace: More Engagement and Less Hierarchy," *Contemporary Sociology*, 2000. 29(1): 195–213.

70. Oprah Fansite, http://www.oprah-fansite.com/ (accessed August 29, 2008).

71. "Oneida Community," Encyclopedia Britannica Online, 2008, http://search.eb.com/eb/article-9057124 (accessed August 29, 2008).

72. Ibid.

73. Robert D. Putnam, "Bowling Alone: America's Declining Social Capital," *Journal of Democracy*, 1995. 6(1): 65–78.

74. Daniel A. McFarland and Reuben J. Thomas, "Bowling Young: How Youth Voluntary Associations Influence Adult Political Participation," *American Sociological Review*, 2006. 71: 401–425.

75. Ibid.

76. Ibid.

CRIME AND THE LEGAL SYSTEM

CRIME AND THE LEGAL SYSTEM

A criminal

justice system is a mirror in which a whole society can see the darker outlines of its face. Our ideas of justice and evil take on visible form in it, and thus we see ourselves in deep relief. Step through this looking glass to view the American criminal justice system—and ultimately the whole society it reflects—from a radically different angle of vision.

In particular, entertain the idea that the goal of our criminal justice system is not to eliminate crime or to achieve justice, but to project to the American public a visible image of the threat of crime as a threat from the poor.

In the last 40 years, crime rates have gone up and down, although mostly up until the 1990s. When crime rates increase, politicians never take responsibility for it. They play to voters' fears by advocating "law and order" or the many varieties of "getting tough on crime." The plain fact is that virtually no student of the crime problem believes we can arrest and imprison our way out of the crime problem.

So while politicians claim credit for the recent declines in crime, the real story appears to be this: The enormous growth in our prison population over the last decade, coupled with questionable police tactics, may have contributed in some measure to the decline, but most of the decline can be attributed to factors beyond the criminal justice system: the reduction in unemployment, the stabilization of the drug trade, and the decline in the popularity of crack cocaine.

In my view, it also comes as no surprise that our prisons and jails predominantly confine the poor. This is not because these are the individuals who most threaten us. It is because the criminal justice system effectively weeds out the well-to-do, so that at the end of the road in prison, the vast majority of those we find there come from the lower classes. This means that the criminal justice system functions from start to finish in a way that makes certain that the offender at the end of the road in prison is likely to be member of the lowest social and economic groups in the country.

For the same criminal behavior, the poor are more likely to be arrested; if arrested, they are more likely to be charged; if charged, more likely to be convicted; if convicted, more likely to be sentenced to prison; and if sentenced, more likely to be given longer prison terms than members of the middle and upper classes.[1]

How Do Societies Respond *to* Crime and Deviance?

At an earlier time in my career, I had an extended practicum in a prison and noticed many of the same things Jeffrey Reiman mentions in *The Rich Get Richer and the Poor Get Prison: Ideology, Class, and Criminal Justice.* Most of the offenders in our overcrowded prisons were poor and did not receive enough help to change their circumstances. Where I worked, we always had three times more applicants than spaces available for treatment programs. To make matters worse, the sheer number of inmates sapped program resources. I worked in a prison designed to house one inmate per cell, yet, within five years, three or more inmates were packed into one cell.

What is the reality of crime in the United States? What are the consequences of crime? What can be done about it? In this chapter, we will investigate these and other questions so we can adequately address these issues.

get the topic: WHAT IS CRIME?

Deviance vs. Crime

Most prisoners are incarcerated because they've broken a law. But how do we determine which behaviors are criminal? **Deviance** is the violation of norms that a society agrees upon. For example, teens who dye their hair in neon colors would be considered deviant in some parts of society. However, some acts that may be considered socially deviant, like refusing to bathe, for instance, aren't necessarily illegal, no matter how much you might wish they were. For something to be considered a **crime**, it has to be a violation of norms that have been written into law. Going above the speed limit is an example of a crime. Sociologists who specialize in **criminology** scientifically study crime, deviance, and the social policies that the criminal justice system applies.

Everyday Crime and Deviance

©River-NorthPhotography/istockphoto;
©Jack Star/Getty Images; ©stester/Shutterstock;
©Bettmann/Corbis; ©Bettmann/Corbis; ©Bettmann/Corbis

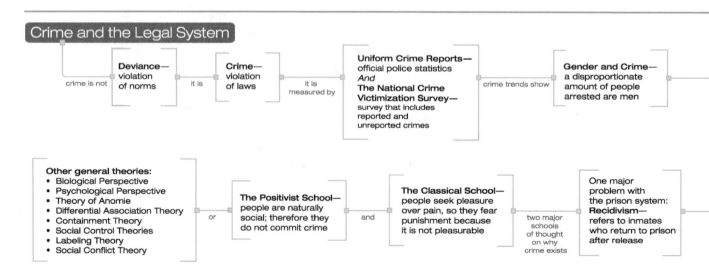

Crime and the Legal System

crime is not — **Deviance—** violation of norms — it is — **Crime—** violation of laws — it is measured by — **Uniform Crime Reports—** official police statistics *And* **The National Crime Victimization Survey—** survey that includes reported and unreported crimes — crime trends show — **Gender and Crime—** a disproportionate amount of people arrested are men

Other general theories:
- Biological Perspective
- Psychological Perspective
- Theory of Anomie
- Differential Association Theory
- Containment Theory
- Social Control Theories
- Labeling Theory
- Social Conflict Theory

or — **The Positivist School—** people are naturally social; therefore they do not commit crime — and — **The Classical School—** people seek pleasure over pain, so they fear punishment because it is not pleasurable — two major schools of thought on why crime exists — One major problem with the prison system: **Recidivism—** refers to inmates who return to prison after release

WHAT IS DEVIANCE?

If deviance refers to violating socially agreed upon norms, then how do we determine what is and what isn't considered deviant? There are four specific characteristics that sociologists use to define deviance:

1 **Deviance is linked to time.** History changes the definition of deviance, so what is considered deviant today may not be deviant tomorrow. One hundred years ago, it was considered deviant for women to wear trousers. Today, it's normal for women to dress in pants.

2 **Deviance is linked to cultural values.** How we label an issue determines our moral point of view. Cultural values come from religious, political, economic, or philosophical principles. For example, in the Netherlands, assisted suicide for the terminally ill, or "mercy killing," is legal within some circumstances. In the United States, euthanasia is considered murder and is punished accordingly. Each culture defines euthanasia differently.

> **DEVIANCE** is the violation of norms that a society agrees upon.
> **CRIME** is the violation of norms that have been written into law.
> **CRIMINOLOGY** is the scientific study of crime, deviance, and social policies that the criminal justice system applies.
> **STREET CRIME** refers to many different types of criminal acts, such as burglary, rape, and assault.

3 **Deviance is a cultural universal.** You can find deviants in every culture on the planet. Regardless of what norms a society establishes, you can always find a small number of nonconformists who will break those rules.

4 **Deviance is a social construct.** Each society views actions differently. If society tolerates a behavior, it is no longer deviant. For example, Prohibition in the 1920s and early '30s made drinking alcohol illegal in the United States, but today it's normal.

MAKE CONNECTIONS

Crime and Media

Real-world police work is nothing like what you see on television shows. Most real-world crime involves public disturbances or missing property, but most news reports are about gang shootings or drug busts. The prime-time shows don't exactly help either. Marcus Felson uses the phrase "the dramatic fallacy of crime" to describe how the media, both in news coverage and entertainment shows, paint an unreal picture of the reality of crime.[2]

Most officers never shoot their guns. They spend the majority of their time doing tedious tasks such as "driving around a lot, asking people to quiet down, hearing complaints about barking dogs, filling out paperwork, meeting with other police officers, and waiting to be called up in court."[3]

Most crime is boring and petty, like a teenager getting drunk and stealing money to buy more alcohol. Since that's not much

of a story to broadcast, the media producers prefer something more sensational.

>>> ACTIVITY Spend two or three nights watching different police shows and local newscasts. Record the different types of crimes being described. Then check out the police blotter in your local paper to see what type of crimes are actually being committed. What differences do you see?

Street Crime

Although there are many different types of crime, when most people talk about "crime," they're likely talking about **street crime**, which refers to many different types of criminal acts, such as burglary, rape, and assault. Street crime has been the focus of most criminological research, but you may wonder how much street crime actually exists. The next section will discuss street crime and how it is measured.

CRIME STATISTICS

After spending an hour watching a show like *CSI*, you'd think the police are able to solve crimes like they do on TV. Unfortunately, real life isn't as convenient as television. For example, when someone stole the tires off my car, I asked the police officer when I might get my wheels back. He said, "Probably never. These kinds of crimes are difficult to solve."

Race and Crime—a disproportionate amount of people arrested are minorities

and

Social Class and Crime—a disproportionate amount of people arrested are poor

and

Age and Crime—the majority of crimes committed are by people 15-25

laws are created from

Consensus Model—laws arise because people see a behavior they do not like
Or
Conflict Model—law creation proposed by the powerful in order to protect their own interests

types of punishment include

The Correctional System:
• Prison
• Parole
• Probation

however

and

Deterrence:
General deterrence—individuals will not commit a crime because they fear the consequences
Or
Specific deterrence—occurs to a person who violates the law and has already suffered punishment

and

Shaming:
Stigmatized shaming—permanent label given to an offender
Or
Reintegrative shaming—serves to bring the offender back into the community after punishment

> **UNIFORM CRIME REPORTS (UCRs)** are official police statistics of reported crimes gathered from police reports and paperwork.
>
> **NATIONAL CRIME VICTIMIZATION SURVEY (NCVS)** is the measurement of crime victimization based on contact with a representative sample of over 70,000 households in the United States.
>
> **CRIME INDEX** is made up of eight offenses used to measure crime: homicide, rape, robbery, aggravated assault, burglary, larceny-theft, motor vehicle theft, and arson.

Uniform Crime Reports and the National Crime Victimization Survey

Another aspect of detective work often omitted from television is the paperwork that officers must file. The information in those files is vital to understand crime statistics. Criminologists use two primary sources of data to measure the amount of street crime: the UCRs and the NCVS. The Federal Bureau of Investigation (FBI) collects **Uniform Crime Reports (UCRs)**, the official police statistics of reported crimes. The **National Crime Victimization Survey (NCVS)** measures crime victimization by contacting a representative sample of over 70,000 households in the United States.

UCRs only contain data on reported crimes, so when a car is reported as stolen, it becomes a UCR statistic. This report also lists the **crime index**, which consists of eight offenses used to measure crime. These include four violent offenses: homicide, rape, robbery, and aggravated assault, as well as four property crimes: burglary, larceny-theft, motor vehicle theft, and arson.

Criminologists understand that many crimes go unreported, so they also refer to the NCVS statistics. NCVS data always account for more crime than UCR data. For example, in 2008 the UCR showed there were 4.54 violent crimes committed per every 1,000 people.[4] The NCVS showed a rate of violent offenses of 19 per 1,000 people. Property crimes came in at 135 per 1,000 for NCVS, while UCR data suggest a rate of 32.1 per 1,000 people. You can see in these data that a great deal of victimization goes unreported to the police.[5]

CRIME TRENDS

UCR and NCVS data are also used to determine crime trends, and the trend that seems most constant is that crime rates change over time. The vast majority of crime in the United States is property crime. In 2008, these crimes made up almost 88 percent of all reported crimes, whereas violent crimes constituted less than 12 percent of reported crimes.[6] These trends are in stark contrast to the media's portrayal of crime.

Gender and Crime

Throughout history, men have traditionally committed more crime than women. The demographic characteristics of street criminals in the United States have not changed much over time. In fact, 77 percent of people arrested are men.[7] This is a significant statistic because men make up less than 50 percent of the population.[8] However, several other factors also figure in crime trends.

Race and Crime

Although the gender differences in crime statistics are fairly easy to distinguish, discussing a link between race and crime is controversial. The major problem is the long history of racism in the United States. African Americans make up about 12 percent of the population, but they represent about 27 percent of those arrested in the United States.[9] Does this disproportionate representation suggest African Americans commit more crimes, or does the criminal justice system unfairly pursue them?

Some argue that the different enforcement practices of police are responsible for these data. Racial profiling is a controversial police practice of targeting criminals based on their race. Cole shows that traffic police disproportionately stop people of color.[10] Reiman suggests that the police seek out the poor for arrest because the poor are easier to catch and easier to convict of crimes. Wealthy people can hire expensive lawyers; poor people must use the public defender system. This increases the odds that official statistics have an inherent racial bias because racial minorities disproportionately represent the poor in the United States.

Social Class and Crime

Although crime rates are higher in poorer neighborhoods, that doesn't necessarily mean people in lower classes actually commit more crime. This makes data on the link between social class and crime difficult to interpret. A number of studies have shown that poorer people are arrested at higher rates,[11] but that doesn't mean everyone who lives in poor neighborhoods breaks the law or is more likely to break the law.[12]

On the other side of the spectrum, Reiman shows that the upper classes' crimes are not prosecuted at the same rates. For example, for more than twenty years, getting caught with five grams of crack cocaine gave you the same sentence as someone caught with 500 grams of powder cocaine.[13] In August of 2010, President Obama signed a bill to amend this 100-1 ratio difference. Why did it exist at all? Conflict theorists might ask what social class used crack cocaine versus powder cocaine.

Reiman believes that social class makes a huge difference in who gets caught and who goes to prison. He argues that laws are applied differently and that dangerous activities performed by the "elite" are not even considered crimes.

For example, doctors who accidentally kill a patient during an unnecessary surgery are not accused of manslaughter. Similarly, Reiman suggests that white-collar crimes are not reported because people want to avoid a scandal. Furthermore, we do not keep official records of white-collar crimes, so there is no way of knowing exactly how much of this occurs.

Age and Crime

Essentially, crime is a young person's game. This idea is supported by the relationship between age and crime. It indicates that the majority of arrests peak between the ages of 15 to 25. After that point, they follow a slow but steady decrease throughout life. Arrest data from other cultures and times in history also support this claim.[14]

The link between age and crime is very clear in criminology. According to Steffensmeier and Harer, a 60 percent decrease in crime rates in the 1980s is attributable to a decrease in the total number of 15- to 24-year-olds.[15] Clearly, age matters when discussing crime.

International Comparisons of Street Crime

In order to gain a better perspective on crime in the United States, sociologists often make international comparisons. However, making international comparisons of crime data creates certain problems for the researcher. Therefore, for this text, I selected countries that are similar to the United States in a number of ways: They are all generally wealthy, and all keep good crime data. Here is a list of potentially complicating factors:

1. Crime numbers may or may not be accurate. Some countries deliberately skew their data to show lower crime rates in order to keep tourism high.
2. Legal definitions of crimes differ among nations. Some nations do not recognize marital rape as a crime; others have legalized drugs that are illegal in the United States.
3. Different methods of collecting data can result in differences in reported crimes. Some nations have extraordinarily reliable data collection systems, while others do not.
4. Cultures vary, as do programs to prevent, punish, and curb crime.

▶▶▶ GO GL🌐BAL

United States: Number One in Murder, Number One in Prison

Why does the United States have the highest murder rate in the industrialized world? Some blame easy access to guns, and others claim it's our violent history as a nation. Still others argue that it is the level of inequality in our country. Whatever the reasons, one thing is clear: U.S. citizens are three times more likely to be murdered compared to people in other developed nations.[16]

However, the tables below present a somewhat different picture of violence with regard to international rates of rape and robbery. The countries selected are similar to the United States and give you a quick way to compare crime in the United States to that of other countries. As you can see from these data, England leads these nations in robbery, and the United States leads in sexual assault. The United States also has high rates of violent crimes but is not the leader in all crimes.

Property crimes present a different picture. The following data give information on car theft, and burglary. Generally speaking, Americans are less likely to experience property crimes than are residents of other industrialized nations.

These data leave a mixed picture for the international comparison of crime. Living in the United States increases the odds that one might be murdered, but it also decreases the chance of being a victim of most property crimes.[17] However, prison population statistics show that the United States leads these nations in incarceration rates.

Comparing international crime rates shows that crime is common to all industrial societies. Some suggest this occurs because industrial societies have more high-value, lightweight items, such as iPods or laptops, that are easily stolen and sold.[18]

Criminal Victimization, 2003–2004: An International Perspective
(Percentage of those responding who say that they were victimized)

Crime	United States	Canada	England	France	Germany	Japan
Sexual assault of women	1.4	0.8	0.9	0.3	0.4	0.8
Assault	4.3	3.0	5.8	2.1	2.7	0.8
Robbery	0.6	0.8	1.4	0.6	0.4	0.2
Burglary	2.5	2.0	3.5	1.6	0.9	0.9
Car theft	1.1	0.8	1.8	0.6	0.2	0.1
Percentage of population feeling unsafe on the street after dark.	19	17	32	21	30	35

Source: Jan van Dijk, John van Kesteren, and Paul Smit, "Criminal Victimisation: An International Perspective, Key findings from the 2004–2005 ICVS and EU ICS," Accessed May 9, 2010, http://www.unicri.it/wwd/analysis/icvs/pdf_files/ICVS2004_05report.pdf.

International Homicide Rates, 2004
(Per 100,000 people)

Crime	United States	Canada	England	France	Germany	Japan
Homicide	5.9	2.0	1.6	0.8	0.7	0.5

Source: United Nations Office on Drugs and Crime, "International homicide rate per 100,000 population 2004," http://www.unodc.org/documents/data-and-analysis/IHS-rates-05012009.pdf.

Prison Populations

Rank	Country	Number of incarcerations per 100,000 people
1	United States of America	753
86	United Kingdom: England & Wales	154
119	Canada	116
138	France	96
148	Germany	88
178	Japan	63

Source: King's College of London, "Prison Brief—Highest to Lowest," Accessed May 9, 2010, http://www.kcl.ac.uk/depsta/law/research/icps/worldbrief/wpb_stats.php?area=all&category=wb_poprate.

CONSENSUS MODEL OF LAW suggests that laws arise because people see a behavior they do not like, and they agree to make it illegal.

CONFLICT MODEL OF LAW proposes that powerful people write laws to protect their own interests while punishing the actions of those they wish to control.

SHAMING is a deliberate effort to attach a negative meaning to a behavior.

SOCIETAL RESPONSES TO CRIME AND DEVIANCE

Why are certain things illegal and not others? There are two primary models as to how laws are created: the consensus and conflict models. The **consensus model of law** suggests that laws arise because people see a behavior they do not like, and they agree to make it illegal. For example, virtually everyone thinks child abuse is wrong. Laws against it arise out of a general agreement about the treatment of children.

The **conflict model of law** proposes that powerful people write laws to protect their own interests while punishing the actions of those they wish to control. Jerald Sanders, a small-time felon from Alabama, stole a $60 bicycle. Alabama has a three-strikes law, and because this was Sanders' third minor felony, he received a life sentence.[19] However, when Martha Stewart committed perjury, she received a sentence of less than two years, despite the fact that her perjury related to an amount worth several thousand dollars.[20]

Punishment

All societies must deal with rule breakers. Historically, punishments were often harsh and included physical torture, exile, forced slavery, or death. Alternative punishments included shaming an offender by placing him in the pillory and stocks in the town square.

Shaming is a deliberate effort to attach a negative meaning to a behavior. John Braithwaite suggests shame can either stigmatize or

©AP Images/Bebeto Matthews

∧
∧ **Martha Stewart spent five months in prison.**[21] **With the help of an attorney, Jerald**
∧ **Sanders, a small-time felon from Alabama, was finally released after spending**
12 years behind bars.[22] Why is there a difference?

reintegrate.[23] **Stigmatized shame** is a permanent label given to an offender, which could actually increase the chances of reoffending because the guilty person is forever labeled. In the United States, we stigmatize former inmates when we require them to admit their prior convictions on job applications and housing forms. **Reintegrative shaming** serves to bring the offender back into the community after punishment. Justice occurs through punishments such as restitution, community service, and prison time. However, after the punishment, no further stigma is placed on the offender.

The U.S. legal system relies on **deterrence**, which prevents a person from doing something because of fear of the consequences. **General deterrence** ensures individuals will not commit a crime because they see the negative consequences applied to others, and they fear experiencing these consequences. Prison is a general deterrent for many people. **Specific deterrence** occurs to individuals who have violated the law and have already been punished. When we send a criminal to prison, we hope he or she will be specifically deterred from committing future offenses because of lessons learned in prison.

> **STIGMATIZED SHAME** is a permanent label given to an offender, which could actually increase the chances of reoffending because the guilty person is forever labeled.
>
> **REINTEGRATIVE SHAMING** is an effort to bring an offender back into the community after punishment.
>
> **DETERRENCE** is a measure that prevents a person from doing something because of fear of the consequences.
>
> **GENERAL DETERRENCE** is a measure that ensures individuals will not commit a crime because they see the negative consequences applied to others, and they fear experiencing these consequences.
>
> **SPECIFIC DETERRENCE** is a measure that changes the attitude of individuals, who have already violated the law and have been punished, by causing them never to commit crime again.
>
> **RECIDIVISM** is the tendency for inmates released from prison to return to prison.

THINK SOCIOLOGICALLY

Reintegrative Justice in New Zealand

Criminal justice programs throughout the world are experimenting with the ideas of reintegrative shaming. In New Zealand, police officers use family conferencing with young offenders and their parents instead of juvenile detention. The goal is to heal the problems in the family and avoid labeling the teen. Teens return to the community as teens who have made a mistake, and not young offenders.

Although the effectiveness of this program is still being measured, a preliminary sample of police officers involved shows they strongly support the program. Using reintegrative justice philosophies in their work provides them with a sense that they are making a difference in the lives of families and youth. Furthermore, they report that this method discourages repeat offending.[24]

Corrections

The correctional system is the last leg of the criminal justice system. It supervises those who are convicted of crimes. In the last two decades, there has been a steady increase in the total number of inmates in the United States.

PRISON AND THE CHARACTERISTICS OF PRISON INMATES

Prison is a last resort in the criminal justice system. The guilty party is locked in a facility for a period of time depending on the crime. Of today's prison inmates, 64 percent belong to racial or ethnic minorities, an estimated 57 percent of inmates are under age 35, and about 21 percent are serving time for a drug offense.[25] According to the Bureau of Justice Statistics Correctional Surveys, one of every 15 people in the United States (6.6 percent) will be incarcerated in his or her lifetime. However, the chances of going to prison are higher for certain populations.[26] As discussed earlier, 11.3 percent of men will go to prison, whereas only 1.8 percent of women will serve time, and 32 percent of black males will enter state or federal prison during their lifetime.

State and Region Incarcerations

Ever wonder why your favorite crime dramas are rarely set in Maine? Other than the Academy Award-winning film *Fargo*, the Northern United States is poorly represented in the crime genre. Meanwhile, television shows like *CSI: Miami*, and *The Wire* find Southern states a useful backdrop for their stories.

The map on the next page shows the incarceration rates for each state. Notice that the highest rates are in the South, while the lowest rates are in the North. For example, the rate of incarceration in Minnesota is six times lower than the rate for Louisiana. Does that mean Louisiana has six times the rate of crime as Minnesota?

According to 2008 UCR data, the violent crime and property crime rates for Louisiana were 656 and 3,823 per 100,000 people, respectively. Meanwhile, in Minnesota, violent crime rates were 263 and property crime rates were 2,850.6 per 100,000 people.[27] As you can see, the Minnesota rates are lower, particularly in relation to violent crimes, but not six times lower. So, why is there a discrepancy?

Some evidence shows that Southern states have higher incarceration rates because they are "tougher" on crime and assign longer sentences for offenders, whereas Northern states are somewhat more lenient in sentencing. There is almost no evidence that these tougher policies actually have the desired effect.[28] Reiman suggests that as crime rates go up, politicians often use a "tough on crime" strategy to entice voters. However, this ignores the higher rates of poverty and lower educational attainment more common in the South.

Prisons in America

Departments of corrections directs most states' prison systems. The title infers that prisons are supposed to correct the offender and assist in successful reintegration into society. Since most inmates are eventually released from prison, what will happen to them? Unfortunately, the most likely outcome for inmates released from prison is to return to prison. This is called **recidivism**. If a return to prison is a failure of the prison system,

Rate of Incarceration (per 100,000 persons)

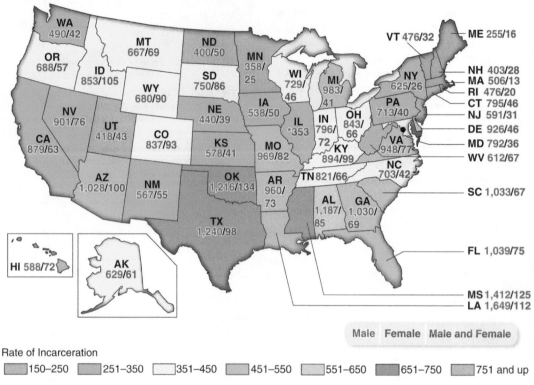

WA 490/42		
OR 688/57	MT 667/69	ND 400/50
ID 853/105		MN 358/25
WY 680/90	SD 750/86	WI 729/46
NV 901/76		MI 983/41
UT 418/43	NE 440/39	
CA 879/63	CO 837/93	IA 538/50
	KS 578/41	IL *353
AZ 1,028/100		IN 796/72
NM 567/55	MO 969/82	OH 843/66
OK 1,216/134		KY 894/99
TX 1,240/98	AR 960/73	TN 821/66
	AL 1,187/85	GA 1,030/69
HI 588/72	AK 629/61	

VT 476/32 — ME 255/16
NY 625/26
PA 713/40
VA 948/77
NC 703/42

NH 403/28
MA 506/13
RI 476/20
CT 795/46
NJ 591/31
DE 926/46
MD 792/36
WV 612/67

SC 1,033/67

FL 1,039/75

MS 1,412/125
LA 1,649/112

Male | Female | Male and Female

Rate of Incarceration

☐ 150–250 ☐ 251–350 ☐ 351–450 ☐ 451–550 ☐ 551–650 ☐ 651–750 ☐ 751 and up

Source: Data from The U.S. Department of Justice, Office of Justice Programs, Bureau of Justice Statistics, Prisoners and Jail Inmates at Midyear 2008.

then clearly the system is failing. More than 50 percent of all inmates return to prison within three years of release. Over time, the recidivism rates are getting worse.[29]

What Is Prison Like?

Many of my students suggest that recidivism rates would drop if prisons were harsher. Few of these students have ever visited or been to a prison. Prisons in the United States are increasingly overcrowded and dangerous places where violence is a normal part of life. Although the

©A. Ramey/PhotoEdit

homicide rate in prison is about the same as it is in free society, the frequency of rape and assault are much more common. If that weren't harsh enough, inmates have highly restricted freedoms, no privacy, and limited access to friends and family. To make matters worse, prisons in the United States continue to cut back on medical treatment and educational programs, even though the incarceration numbers continue to rise. In short, prisons are increasingly turning into human storehouses.[30]

Costs of Incarceration

The actual costs to incarcerate an individual are difficult to determine. Although all states report a dollar amount, there are "hidden" costs associated with the incarcerated—the children left behind in the foster care system or families who must use the welfare system to survive. These social costs can't be factored in the prison budget, so the reported cost of incarceration never includes them. Nevertheless, taxpayers are left to pay for the whole broken system. Criminologists James Austin and John Irwin[31] calculated these hidden costs and determined that it actually costs $30,000 a year to incarcerate a single inmate, a number that is significantly higher than what states report. Using this estimate, Alabama taxpayers paid roughly $360,000 for the 12-year incarceration of Jerald Sanders. Remember, he had no prior violent convictions, but the $60 bicycle he stole counted as his

<<< **Prisoners are crammed into makeshift dormitories** when overcrowding becomes an issue.

third strike.[32] Had his life sentence been enforced to the full, this amount would have been well over $1 million.

United States Incarceration Rates vs. International Incarceration Rates

Policies like the three-strikes law have contributed to the United States' much higher incarceration rate in comparison to similar countries' rates.

In fact, the United States incarcerates at a rate six times higher than Canada and 13 times higher than Japan. It's important to remember that, just as with crime rates, you should use caution when interpreting international data regarding prison populations. Think about what you already know about international crime and murder rates. What factors do you think contribute to the United States' role as the world's leader in crime and incarceration?

think sociologically: WHY DOES CRIME EXIST?

Historical Roots of Deviance and Crime Theories

Most crime theories arise from two philosophical schools of thought: Positivists ask why people commit crimes, and classicists ask what keeps people from committing them.

THE POSITIVIST SCHOOL

Positivists assume that people are naturally social beings and are not prone to act criminally unless some biological, psychological, or social factor is involved. To a positivist, the world is orderly and follows natural laws. And since natural law dictates that everything must have a cause, positivists are interested in what factors cause people to commit crime.

BIOLOGICAL PERSPECTIVES ON CRIME AND DEVIANCE

Physician Cesare Lombroso (1835–1905) believed that criminals could be distinguished by physical characteristics: big ears, protruding jaws, and deep-set eyes.[33] While this idea is clearly preposterous, scientists believe there might be a biological element to crime. The search for biological causes for criminality continues to this day in recent investigations, including the study of hormonal differences between men and women and how they impact criminal behavior. For example, higher testosterone levels make men more aggressive than women. Could this account for some of the differences between men's and women's delinquent behaviors?[34]

Many modern-day positivists continue to seek the biological causes of crime. Some test chemical imbalances in the brain caused by genetic predisposition,[35] low blood sugar,[36] and levels of serotonin.[37] All of these factors are shown to have connections to criminal behavior, but the statistical links are often weak. The search for a biological cause for crime is far from complete and often fails to isolate social factors from genetic ones.

THE CLASSICAL SCHOOL

While positivists look for the underlying causes of criminal behavior, the classical school assumes all people are self-interested by nature. Classical thinkers also suggest that people are rational and make free will choices of how to behave. Their primary question asks what keeps us from being criminal.

The classical school emphasizes that individuals make rational choices based on pleasure/pain calculations. To a classicist, the reason most people do not commit crime is because they fear being punished. So, if the goal of the criminal justice system is to deter crime, classicists believe that the punishments must be, swift, certain, and severe enough to deter people's actions.

Cesare Beccaria's 1764 essay "On Crimes and Punishments" had a great impact on the way the western world looks at justice and crime. Beccaria argued that a legal system must treat everyone equally to protect him or her against excessive government power. In fact, many ideas contained in our Bill of Rights come from Beccaria. He believed that in order to truly deter crime, we needed a fair legal system.[38]

Another classicist, Jeremy Bentham (1748–1832), believed people were inherently *hedonistic*, seeking pleasure over pain. Being a strong supporter of the idea of deterrence, Bentham felt that people would only avoid the pleasure of crime if they feared the pain of punishment. However, the punishment must be severe enough to deter them, but not so severe as to alienate them from society. In other words, the punishment should fit the crime.[39]

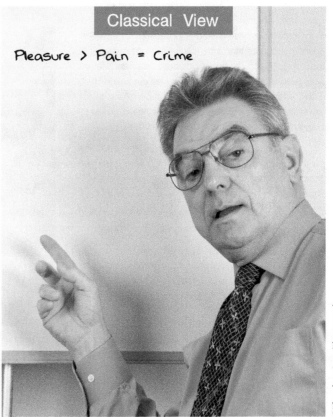

Classical View

Pleasure > Pain = Crime

©Theodore Scott/Shutterstock

PSYCHOLOGICAL PERSPECTIVES ON CRIME AND DEVIANCE

The American Psychiatric Association (APA) claims that criminals suffer from an "antisocial" personality disorder that causes them to "fail to conform to social norms with respect to lawful behaviors as indicated by repeatedly performing acts that are grounds for arrest."[40] According to the APA, criminals are impulsive, aggressive, and irritable, and they tend to lie about their behaviors and feel no remorse for their actions.

Hirschi and Hindelang support the idea that criminals have low IQs because the relationship between IQ and crime to official delinquency is strong.[41] Stanton Samenow proposes that criminals actually have thinking errors, including chronic lying, viewing others' property as their own, unfounded optimism, fear of injury or insult, and inflated self-image.[42]

Psychological theories of criminality tend to be positivistic, placing the blame on something abnormal in the individual, such as a low IQ, or a thinking error. Sociological theories tend to view criminality as a social construct. Let's look at some of these theories of criminality.

Functional Explanations of Crime and Deviance

Functional theories describe crime as a response to some social factor, and theorists look for what causes crime to grow. Emile Durkheim noted that crime and deviance are necessary social realities because they meet one of these three needs:

1. Crime marks the boundaries of morality. Frequently, we do not know what we like until we see something we don't like.
2. Crime promotes social solidarity because it unites people against it. People unify against a common enemy, and criminals are often a common enemy.
3. Deviance can bring about needed change in a social system.[43] Acts of civil disobedience are performed to change laws for the betterment of society.

THEORY OF ANOMIE

Robert Merton's theory of anomie—social instability caused by a wearing away of standards and ethics—questions whether social structures cause deviance. Poor individuals have limited opportunities for success. Merton suggests that Americans have common goals, including wealth, a home, career, cars, and family. Achieving these goals usually involves education, hard work, entrepreneurship, and some luck. Many in the lower classes have blocked access to these goals, so they adapt to their plight in one of five ways:

1. **Conformists** accept society's goals and use socially acceptable means to try to achieve them. They obey rules and work at low-paying jobs with little chance of advancement. One example is a janitor who works three jobs, but can't get ahead because of low pay.

2. **Innovators** accept common goals but not the means to getting them, using illegal means to achieve those goals instead. For example, a criminal might steal goods and sell them at a pawnshop instead of getting a job.

3. **Ritualists** accept the traditional means of achieving the goals, but are not as interested in the material goals. Social workers use their advanced degrees to pursue humanitarian efforts rather than monetary benefits.

4. **Retreatists** reject both the means and the goals of society. These people often live in isolation or deal with issues of drug and alcohol abuse, mental illness, or homelessness.

5. **Rebels** use their own means to create new goals, often seeking major societal changes.[44] Gandhi was a rebel who sought to change society through nonviolent methods.

Few sociologists accept Merton's theory today as it stands; however, it clearly draws a connection between social structures and crime, and it provokes more thinking about the relationships between poverty and crime. The theory is criticized for the assumption of universal goals and its inability to explain violent or white-collar crimes.

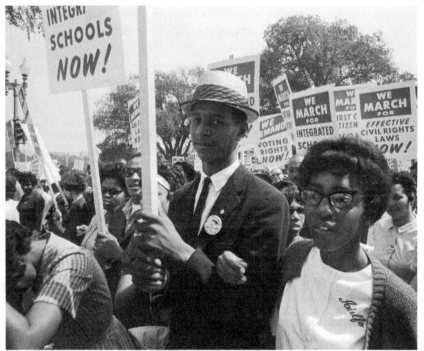

©Wally McNamee/Corbis

^ ^ ^ Though the acts in which Martin Luther King, Jr., and his followers engaged were considered illegal at the time, **these "deviant" acts helped bring about much-needed change to the racist laws of the United States.**

Social Interaction Theories

Is it how we interact with people that influences our criminality? Criminals engage in social interactions that influence the likelihood of their violation of the law. Criminologists often divide such theories into social process theories and social reaction theories. Social process theories review how criminal behaviors develop, while social reaction theories examine how societal reactions affect criminal behavior.

DIFFERENTIAL ASSOCIATION THEORY

Edwin Sutherland (1883–1950) proposed the **differential association theory**, which emphasizes that criminal and deviant behavior is learned. For instance, a teen might sneak out at night to go hang out with friends. If that teen has a younger sibling, the sibling might learn that it is acceptable to sneak out and how to do so. Similarly, criminals pass on their attitudes, values, mechanisms, and beliefs about crime to others. People commit crimes because they learn that criminal activity is acceptable and/or normal. Sutherland makes this theory clear with nine propositions listed below. Clearly he is a positivist, asserting that crime must be learned from others.

Sutherland's Nine Propositions

1. Criminal behavior is learned, not inherited.
2. Criminal behavior is learned through communication.

> **DIFFERENTIAL ASSOCIATION THEORY** emphasizes that criminal and deviant behavior is learned.
>
> **CONTAINMENT THEORY** argues that criminals cannot resist the temptations that surround them.

3. The principal part of learning behavior occurs within intimate personal groups.
4. The learning includes the techniques of committing the crime and the special direction/motives, drives, rationalizations, and attitudes necessary to carry it out.
5. The specific direction of motives and drives is learned from definitions of the legal codes as favorable and unfavorable.
6. A person becomes delinquent because of an excess of definitions favorable to the violation of the law.
7. Differential associations may vary in frequency, duration, priority, and intensity.
8. The process of learning criminal behavior by association with criminal and noncriminal patterns involves all the same mechanisms that are involved in any other learning.
9. Although criminal behavior is an expression of general needs and values, it is not explained by those general needs and values.[45]

SOCIAL CONTROL THEORIES

Social control theories suggest that people are hedonistic and self-interested. Walter Reckless argued that internal and external factors control behavior.[46] His **containment theory** argues that criminals cannot resist the temptations that surround them. Everyone has different levels of internal controls, including the ability to withstand temptations, morality, integrity, self-esteem, fear of punishment, and the desire to be and do good. External forces such as the police, our family, and/or our friends also control us. However, it is the internal control that influences criminality; for example, few people speed in front of a police car.

Travis Hirschi agrees that internal controls predict criminality and suggests that four social bonds—attachment, commitment, involvement, and belief—affect our inner controls.[47] Strong bonds indicate less likelihood toward criminality.

<<< **According to Sutherland, crime must be taught.** Only then will criminal behaviors develop.

©John Francis Bourke/Corbis

ATTACHMENT is the social bond that refers to our relationship to others.

COMMITMENT is the social bond that refers to our dedication to live a socially acceptable life.

INVOLVEMENT is the social bond that refers to the level of activity in conventional things.

BELIEF is the social bond that refers to a person's conviction of truth.

PRIMARY DEVIANCE is the initial deviant act itself.

SECONDARY DEVIANCE refers to the psychological reorientation that occurs when the system catches a person and labels him or her as a deviant.

The first bond, **attachment**, refers to our relationship to others. If a teen hangs out with conformists, friends who do not drink, smoke, or use illegal drugs, they are less likely to engage in these behaviors themselves. **Commitment** refers to our dedication to live a socially acceptable life. By attending school, you are committed to a socially acceptable behavior. Thus, as we age, we are often more committed to responsible behavior. Could this explain the age–crime connection? **Involvement** refers to the level of activities in conventional things. Teens who are involved in their schools or have extracurricular activities are less likely to be delinquent. This is in part because they have less time for deviance. The final bond, **belief**, refers to a person's conviction of truth. If we believe that living a conventional life is good, then we are unlikely to deviate from that path.

Each of these bonds can act together or independently to influence a person's inner control. For example, the theory would say that cross-dressing occurs because people attach themselves to nonconformists (other cross-dressers). They involve themselves in nonnormative behaviors by cross-dressing, and believe this is normal and okay. Involvement in conforming activities may raise the level of attachment to conventional that could increase a person's belief. Likewise, low levels on these bonds might increase the likelihood that a person will engage in nonconventional activity.

Symbolic Interactionist Theory

LABELING THEORY

Some theorists believe that certain punishments can actually contribute to future deviance or crime. Edwin Lemert[48] proposes two types of deviance: primary and secondary. **Primary deviance** refers to the initial deviant act itself, such as when a group of teenagers decides to buy beer illegally. Many people can be primarily deviant, but not get caught in the act. When they get caught, they are secondarily deviant. **Secondary deviance** refers to the psychological reorientation that occurs when the system catches a person and labels him or her. The beer-buying teens become "delinquents" when they are sent to juvenile hall. Their friends' and family's perceptions of them have changed, making them secondarily deviant. According to Lemert, secondary deviance often encourages future misdeeds.

Social Conflict Theory

Reiman states that "the rich get richer and the poor get prison," meaning if you are part of the upper class, you can get away with criminal acts.[49] Social conflict theories usually focus on issues of social class, power, capitalism, and their relation to crime. For instance, Willem Bonger argues that capitalism causes crime by emphasizing selfishness in individuals.[50] Capitalism pits people against each other in a struggle for possessions. It also doesn't help that wealthy criminals often face more lenient punishment than poor criminals. Income and wealth inequality lead to abuses of the system, and this structural inequality leads to crime.

Modern conflict criminologists agree with Bonger's stance, that power and wealth inequality leads to crime. Reiman suggests that the inequalities of the justice system are rooted in social class.[51] Although conflict theories focus on the structural reasons for crime, they don't explain why certain individuals commit them.

General Theories of Crime Causation

Figuring out the motivation behind criminal behavior is the job of causation theorists. General theories of crime causation attempt to explain a broad range of criminal behaviors. Some integrate concepts from various theories such as Robert Agnew's general strain theory[52] or Gottfredson and Hirschi's general theory of crime.[53]

The General Strain Theory takes the basic concepts of Merton's anomie and adds a more psychological bent. According to Agnew, a person experiences strain from three sources. First, a person can suffer from a failure to achieve positively valued goals, such as proposed by Merton. Second, individuals experience strain from unpleasant life events such as losing a job or loved one. The third source of strain results from negative events such as abuse, punishment, and pain. All or any of these strains can lead a person to behave criminally. Agnew believes that everyone experiences strain, but criminality is linked to the individual's coping skills. By learning to cope with stress, people are less likely to turn to crime.[54]

Michael Gottfredson and Travis Hirschi[55] propose a general theory of crime, which states that **self-control, the ability to delay gratification, affects all criminality.** Those who trade short-term rewards for long-term consequences have low self-control. **Most crimes and other criminal-like behaviors involve spur-of-the-moment decisions; this demonstrates their lack of self-control.**

These people often engage in excessive drinking, speeding, drug use, crime, accidents, marital infidelity, and a host of other risky behaviors.[56] Thus, the solution to crime is to teach children self-control.

WRAP YOUR MIND AROUND THE THEORY

Functionalists like Merton suggest most people with blocked access to success conform. **Have these students chosen society's traditional means to reach their goals of success?**

©Patrick White/Merrill Education

FUNCTIONALISM

For functionalists, crime is a part of society. Durkheim notes that crime always exists in society, and therefore must serve some function. For Merton, crime results because the pursuit of the American dream is blocked for some people. Therefore, people must adapt. Only one of these modes of adaptation leads to crime, but all occur because the system blocks some people from the goals to which they aspire.

CONFLICT THEORY

Bonger argues that capitalism causes crime in society because it teaches people to be selfish and to do what is best for themselves instead of thinking of others. The inherent competition of capitalism results in inequality of wealth and power. This leads some to lash out in criminal ways. Reiman's statement "the rich get richer, the poor get prison" points out that laws are written in the best interest of the wealthy. The wealthy can easily "make bail" when arrested, while the poor may languish in jail awaiting trial, even if they are innocent. Meanwhile, illegal acts of the wealthy are often not considered crimes, and their punishments are often little more than a slap on the wrist.

WHAT CAUSES CRIME IN OUR SOCIETY?

SYMBOLIC INTERACTIONISM

Edwin Lemert's labeling theory clearly shows the power of symbols in people's lives. Although he has no explanation for primary deviance, secondary deviance occurs as a result of the way society reacts to the first act. Thus, people learn that others see them only as criminals and so they behave in that way. Such a self-fulfilling prophecy can be enhanced by differential association theory. Sutherland suggests that we learn criminality from others, through social interactions. If for example, your friends are "gangbangers," you may believe behaving that way is acceptable. Why? Because your friends teach you that committing crimes is no big deal.

©AP Images/Kathy Willens

Conflict theorists point out that laws are often written in favor of those with wealth and privilege. **How might the bail system benefit the wealthy and exploit the poor?**

By defining what is legal and illegal, society creates crime. **How might the label of "lawbreaker" become a self-fulfilling prophecy?**

©Ken Lax/Photo Researchers, Inc.

discover sociology in action: HOW DO WE DEAL WITH CRIME?

DISCRETION is the ability to make decisions.

PLEA BARGAIN is an out-of-court agreement between the prosecutor and the defense attorney to some concession, usually a reduced sentence.

MANDATORY MINIMUMS are fixed sentences for specific crimes.

Crime Control: The Criminal Justice System

The U.S. criminal justice system has three parts: *police*, *courts*, and *corrections*. Each of these parts of the system responds to violations of the law and each reflects the social policies of our country toward crime.

POLICE

Today, there are more than 18,000 law enforcement agencies in the United States.[57] Police are on the front line against crime. This requires police officers to have the initial **discretion**, or ability to make decisions, which often involves whether or not they will enforce the law. If you've ever received a warning instead of a speeding ticket for speeding through a school zone, you've reaped the benefit of a police officer's discretion.

COURTS

The courts are the second part of the criminal justice system. Judges and district attorneys use discretion in their work as well. District attorneys decide whether they will prosecute a crime, and under what charge they will take the case to court. For example, about 89 percent of cases in this country end with a guilty plea, often called a **plea bargain**.[58] This is an out-of-court agreement between the prosecutor and the defense attorney to some concession, usually a reduced sentence.

Judicial discretion exists, but state and federal governments have limited use of judicial discretion by passing laws that mandate sentences. **Mandatory minimums** make judges give individuals fixed sentences for specific crimes. These rules eliminate discretion from judges that might impact the sentence. Mandatory sentencing laws vary by state, but they have some things in common. These rules increase the length of time people serve in prison, which creates new problems for the prison system. Since prisons have an increasingly

older population, some states build nursing homes inside prison walls to care for inmates who are too weak and old to care for themselves, but cannot be released due to these laws.[59]

Studying the cost-benefit of mandatory minimum sentencing, the Rand Corporation found mandatory minimum sentences for drug offenders are not an efficient use of tax dollars when compared to drug treatment. Drug treatment actually has a stronger effect than prison, reducing drug consumption and drug-related crime while costing the taxpayers less money.[60] We have already discussed how prisons in the United States work to house criminals, but let's turn our attention to the most serious punishment meted out: the death penalty.

DEATH PENALTY

In the United States, we reserve the death penalty for offenders who commit the most serious crimes, like murder or treason. The United States is the only modern and industrialized democracy on earth that still uses the death penalty.

Supporters of the death penalty argue that it is the ultimate deterrence to crime because potential murderers would fear receiving the death penalty. However, opponents point out that states without the death penalty actually have lower rates of murder. Likewise, the costs of prosecuting and executing offenders are actually higher than lifetime incarceration. Proponents claim that these costs could be cut if appeals were shortened. However, new DNA evidence releases many from prison, and the costs of the death penalty are primarily due to the cost of trials, not the system of mandatory appeals.[61]

Finally, opponents of the death penalty point out that it is applied in a biased manner. Levine and Montgomery studied 6,000 murder cases in Maryland from 1978 through 1999. They found that **when the victim was white, blacks were twice as likely to receive a death sentence as whites.** Furthermore, blacks convicted of killing whites are four times as likely to get a death sentence than blacks whose victims were also black.[62]

ACTIVITIES

1. Read stories about prison inmates. Do you see any commonalities in their stories?
2. Research prisons in your state. What are the demographics of the inmates? How many are serving mandatory minimums?
3. What type of community service programs are available in your state for inmates to participate in?
4. Research three states that have the death penalty. How frequently are inmates executed? Do you think it acts as a deterrent for criminals?

From Classroom to Community ⟩ Inmate Community Service

Bill was an inmate in a local prison who took a class for college credit via a videoconferencing setup. He could listen to the class and even participate in class discussions from the prison where he was incarcerated. At about the midpoint of the semester, students were offered the chance to earn extra credit by doing community learning. Bill wanted to participate, too. The program had never had an inmate do community service, so the teacher spoke with his educational officer, who agreed that community learning could occur anywhere.

Bill wrote in his paper,

"My prison is a community of inmates, most of whom committed no violent offenses like me. I spent my time volunteering to help with the drug and alcohol group, meaning that each day I would set up the chapel for the meetings, and after the meetings I would put it back in order. Initially, I didn't stay for the meetings because it didn't seem to be important: I have no drug addiction, I haven't used since I was incarcerated. But one time the group leader invited me to stay. I was stunned to hear the stories of how alcohol and drugs caused so much damage in these men's lives. Almost all of them were under the influence when they committed their crimes."

"It made me decide that I wanted to be a drug and alcohol counselor when I got out of prison. It also made me see that a lot of inmates are just like me: normal guys trying to do their time without getting hurt, and hoping for a better life on the outside when they get released."

∧
∧ **How do you think community service programs, like a support group for**
∧ **alcoholics, could be beneficial to inmates** trying to turn their lives around?

WHAT IS CRIME?

a violation of norms that have been written into law

WHY DOES CRIME EXIST?

positivists: people are social and are not prone to act criminally unless some biological, psychological, or social factor is involved

classicalists: people make rational choices to commit crimes based on pleasure/pain calculations

HOW DO WE DEAL WITH CRIME?

through a three-part criminal justice system: police, courts, and corrections

get the topic: WHAT IS A CRIME?

Deviance vs. Crime
Historical Roots of Deviance and Crime Theories

Functional Explanations of Crime and Deviance
Social Interaction Theories
Symbolic Interactionist Theory

Social Conflict Theory
General Theories of Crime Causation
Crime Control: The Criminal Justice System

Theory

FUNCTIONALISM

- crime is a response to some social factor
- Durkheim's three functions of crime and deviance: they mark the boundaries of morality, promote social solidarity, and bring about needed change
- theory of anomie: social instability caused by a wearing away of standards and ethics
- Merton: crime results because the pursuit of the American dream is blocked for some people

CONFLICT THEORY

- capitalism teaches people to be selfish and competitive, resulting in inequality
- the wealthy create the laws that punish the poor, while many illegal acts committed by the wealthy are often not considered crimes
- "the rich get rich, the poor get prison"

SYMBOLIC INTERACTIONISM

- labeling theory
- people react to how others view them
- people learn criminality through social interactions

Key Terms

deviance	crime index	specific deterrence	belief
crime	consensus model of law	recidivism	primary deviance
criminology	conflict model of law	differential association theory	secondary deviance
street crime	shaming		discretion
Uniform Crime Reports (UCRs)	stigmatized shame	containment theory	plea bargain
National Crime Victimization Survey (NCVS)	reintegrative shaming	attachment	mandatory minimums
	deterrence	commitment	
	general deterrence	involvement	

MY SEARCH LAB

1. ***The Rich Get Richer and the Poor Get Prison*** by Reiman, Jeffrey, *The Rich Get Richer and The Poor Get Prison: Ideology, Class and Criminal Justice*, 5th Edition, © 1998, pp. 101–148. Adapted by permission of Pearson Education, Inc., Upper Saddle River, NJ.

INTRODUCTION

In this excerpt from his 1998 book, Reiman provides compelling evidence that demonstrates the inequities in the criminal justice system.

DISCUSSION QUESTIONS

1. In general, how are white-collar criminals treated by the justice system? How does this compare to blue-collar criminals?
2. What steps would you recommend to make the criminal justice system more equitable?

2. *Race and Class in the American Criminal Justice System* by David Cole. Reprinted by permission of The New Press.

INTRODUCTION

In this selection from his 1999 book *No Equal Justice*, David Cole summarizes his findings on inequality within the American criminal justice system.

DISCUSSION QUESTIONS

1. The author claims that the U.S. criminal justice system "affirmatively depends on inequality." What does he mean by this? Do you agree?
2. Explain how inequality is built into every stage of the criminal justice process. How can this be fixed?

THE THINKSPOT

City Journal is an urban-policy magazine, called the "Bible of New Urbanism" by London's *Daily Telegraph*. Go to the ThinkSpot to read Heather MacDonald's take on crime and race, in which she asks, "Is the criminal justice system racist?" You might be surprised to find out what she thinks. While you're reading the essay, think about MacDonald's argument and whether she has included enough facts to support her position. After reading the essay, do

you still feel the same way about crime, race, and the justice system?

Change.org's article, titled "Rehabilitation, not Incarceration," ties in with what we discussed in the section "Societal Responses to Crime and Deviance." Read this article on the Youth PROMISE Act and take some time to read the comments that come after it. Do you think the Youth PROMISE Act is the answer to address the root causes of crime and delinquency? What is one specific thing that can be done, in your opinion, to cut down on crime and delinquency in communities?

Sample Test Questions

These multiple-choice questions are similar to those found in the test bank that accompanies this textbook.

1. Deviance is *not* linked to
   a. time.
   b. society.
   c. legal norms.
   d. cultural values.

2. Which type of crime is most common?
   a. Violent crime
   b. Property crime
   c. White-collar crime
   d. Drug-related crime

3. Which of the following is an alternative punishment?
   a. Prison
   b. Death
   c. Torture
   d. Shaming

4. What is the last resort in the criminal justice system?
   a. Counseling
   b. Probation
   c. Parole
   d. Prison

5. According to Robert Merton, which type of lower-class person obeys social rules and works with little chance of advancement?
   a. Conformist
   b. Innovator
   c. Retreatist
   d. Ritualist

ESSAY

1. How are police shows different than real-life police work?

2. Do the poor commit more crimes than other members of society?

3. Why is it difficult to make international comparisons about crime statistics?

4. Why are only certain things illegal?

5. What is wrong with the U.S. prison system?

WHERE TO START YOUR RESEARCH PAPER

To learn more about crime in the United States, go to
http://www.fbi.gov/
http://www.usdoj.gov/

To learn more about positive deviance, go to
http://www.positivedeviance.org/

To see Uniform Crime Reports, go to
http://www.fbi.gov/ucr/ucr.htm

To see National Crime Victimization Survey information, go to
http://www.icpsr.umich.edu/NACJD/NCVS/

To learn more about international police organizations, go to
http://www.interpol.int/Default.asp

To learn more about the prison system, go to
http://www.bop.gov/

ANSWERS: 1 c; 2. b; 3. d; 4. d; 5. a

Endnotes

1. Reiman, Jeffrey, *The Rich Get Richer and the Poor Get Prison* © 2007. Reproduced by permission of Pearson Education, Inc.

2. Marcus Felson, *Crime & Everyday Life* (Thousand Oaks, CA: Pine Forge Press, 1998).

3. Ibid.

4. US Department of Justice, Federal Bureau of Investigation, "2008 Crime in the United States," http://www.fbi.gov/ucr/cius2008/.

5. Ibid; U.S. Department of Justice, Office of Justice Programs, Bureau of Justice Statistics, "National Crime Victimization Survey," http://bjs.ojp.usdoj.gov/content/pub/ascii/cv08.txt.

6. "2008 Crime in the United States," *Federal Bureau of Investigation*, http://www.fbi.gov/ucr/cius2008/.

7. "*Crime in the United States: Uniform Crime Reports," Federal Bureau of Investigation, Department of Justice* (Washington, D.C.: Government Printing Office, 2002).

8. "U.S. Summary 2000," *U.S. Census Bureau*, April 2000, http://www.census.gov/prod/2002pubs/c2kprof00-us.pdf.

9. Ibid.

10. David Cole, *No Equal Justice: Race and Class in the American Criminal Justice System* (New York: New Press, 1999).

11. John Braithwaite, "The Myth of Social Class and Criminality Reconsidered," *American Sociological Review*, 1981. 46: 36–57; Margaret Farnsworth, *Social Background and the Early Onset of Delinquency: Exploring the Utility of Various Indicators of Social Class Background* (Albany: Hindelang Criminal Justice Research Center, 1990).

12. Elijah Anderson, "Ideologically Driven Critique," *American Journal of Sociology*, 2002. 197(6):1533–1550.

13. Alexandra Marks, "More Equity in Cocaine Sentencing," *The Christian Science Monitor*, November 2, 2007, http://www.csmonitor.com/2007/1102/p01s02-usju.html.

14. Michael Gottfredson and Travis Hirschi, *A General Theory of Crime* (Stanford, CA: Stanford University Press, 1990).

15. Darrell Steffensmeier and Miles Harer, "Did Crime Rise or Fall During the Reagan Presidency?" *Journal of Research in Crime and Delinquency*, 1991. 28: 330–359.

16. J. N. van Kesteren, P. Mayhew, and P. Nieuwbeerta, *Criminal Victimization in Seventeen Industrialized Countries: Key-findings from the 2000 International Crime Victimization Survey* (The Hague, Ministry of Justice, WODC, 2000).

17. Ibid.

18. Marcus Felson, *Crime & Everyday Life* (Thousand Oaks, CA: Pine Forge Press, 1998).

19. Adam Liptake, "Sentences are Too Long or Too Short. Rarely, Just Right," *The New York Times*, August 24, 2003, http://www.nytimes.com/2003/08/24/weekinreview/24LIPT.html.

20. Susan Saulny, "Martha Stewart is Denied New Trial by U.S. Judge," *The New York Times*, May 6, 2004, http://www.nytimes.com/2004/03/06/business/06martha.html.

21. Kate DuBose Tomassi, "Martha Stewart Closes the Book," *Forbes*, August, 7, 2006, http://www.forbes.com/business/2006/08/07/martha-stewart-settle-cx_ kt_0807martha.html.

22. "EJI Wins Relief for Persons Sentences to Die In Prison for Nonviolent Crimes." *Equal Justice Initiative*, September 13, 2007, http://eji.org/eji/node/48.

23. John Braithwaite, *Crime, Shame, and Reintegration* (New York: Cambridge University Press, 1989).

24. L. Thomas Winfree, Jr., "New Zealand Police and Restorative Justice Philosophy," *Crime and Delinquency*, 2004. 50: 189–213.

25. "Criminal Victimization in the United States," *Bureau of Justice Statistics* (Washington, D.C.: Government Printing Office, 2002).

26. Ibid.

27. Federal Bureau of Investigation, Criminal Justice Information Services Division, "2008 Crime in the United States," http://www.fbi.gov/ucr/cius2008/data/table_05.html.

28. James Austin and John Irwin, *It's About Time: America's Imprisonment Binge*, 3rd ed. (Belmont, CA: Wadsworth Publishing Company, 2001).

29. "Criminal Victimization in the United States," *Bureau of Justice Statistics* (Washington, D.C.: Government Printing Office, 2002).

30. James Austin and John Irwin, *It's About Time: America's Imprisonment Binge*, 3rd ed. (Belmont, CA: Wadsworth Publishing Company, 2001).

31. Ibid.

32. Adam Liptake, "Sentences Are Too Long or Too Short. Rarely, Just Right," *The New York Times*, August 24, 2003, http://www.nytimes.com/2003/08/24/weekinreview/24LIPT.html.

33. Cesare Lombroso, "Introduction," in Gena Lombroso-Ferrero, *Criminal Man According to the Classification of Cesare Lombroso* (Montclair NJ: Patterson Smith, [1911] 1972).

34. Alan Booth and D. Wayne Osgood, "The Influence of Testosterone on Deviance in Adulthood: Assessing and Explaining the Relationship," *Criminology*, 1993. 31: 93–117; J.R. Sanchez-Martin, E. Fano, L. Ahedo, J. Cardas, P.F. Brain, and A. Azpiroz, "Relating Testosterone Levels and Free Play Social Behavior in Male and Female Preschool Children," *Psychoneuroendocrinology*, November 25, 2000, 773–783.

35. James J. Hudziak and Lawrence P. Rudiger, "A Twin Study of In-attentive Aggressive and Anxious/Depressed Behaviors," *Journal of American Academy of Child and Adolescent Psychiatry*, 2000. 39: 469–476.

36. William Duffy, *Sugar Blues* (Pandor, PA: Childton Book Co., 1975).

37. Abdulla Badawy, "Alcohol and Violence and the other Possible Role of Serotonin," *Criminal Behaviour and Mental Health*, 2003. 12: 31–45.

38. Cessare Beccaria, *Essays on Crimes and Punishments*, translated by Henry Paolucci (Indianapolis: Bobbs-Merrill, [1764] 1963).

39. Jeremy Bentham, *An Introduction to the Principles of Morals and Legislation*, edited by J.H. Burns and H.L.A. Hart (London: Athlone Publishing, [1789] 1970).

40. DSM, *Diagnostic and Statistical Manual of Mental Disorders, 4th edition*. (Washington, D.C.: American Psychiatric Association, 1994).

41. Travis Hirschi and Michael J Hindelang, "Intelligence and Delinquency: A Revisionist Review," *American Sociological Review*, 1977. 42: 57–87.

42. Stanton E. Samenow, *Inside the Criminal Mind: Revised and Updated Edition* (New York: Crown Publishers, 2004).

43. Emile Durkheim, *The Rules of Sociological Method*, 8th ed, Translated by Sarah A. Solovay and John H. Mueller, and edited by George E. G. Catlin (New York: Free Press, [1895] 1964).

44. Robert K. Merton, "Social Structure and Anomie," *American Sociological Review*, 1938. 3: 672–682.

45. Edwin Sutherland and Donald Cressey, *Principles of Criminology*, 10th edition. (Philadelphia: Lippincott, 1978).

46. Walter C. Reckless, *The Crime Problem* (New York: Appleton-Century-Crofts, 1955).

47. Travis Hirschi, *Causes of Delinquency* (Berkeley, CA: University of California Press, 1969).

48. Edwin M. Lemert, *Social Pathology* (New York: McGraw-Hill, 1951); Edwin M. Lemert, *Human Deviance, Social Problems and Social Control* (Englewood Cliffs, NJ: Prentice-Hall, 1967).

49. Jeffrey Reiman, *The Rich Get Richer and the Poor Get Prison: Ideology, Class and Criminal Justice* (Needham Heights, MA: Pearson Education, 1998).

50. Willem A. Bonger, *Criminality and Economic Conditions* (Bloomington, IN: Indiana University Press, 1969).

51. Jeffrey Reiman, *The Rich Get Richer and the Poor Get Prison: Ideology, Class and Criminal Justice* (Needham Heights, MA: Pearson Education, 1998).

52. Robert Agnew, "Foundation for a General Strain Theory of Crime and Delinquency," *Criminology*, 1992. 30: 47–66.

53. Michael Gottfredson and Travis Hirschi, *A General Theory of Crime* (Stanford, CA: Stanford University Press, 1990).

54. Robert Agnew, "Foundation for a General Strain Theory of Crime and Delinquency," *Criminology*, 1992. 30: 47–66.

55. Michael Gottfredson and Travis Hirschi, *A General Theory of Crime* (Stanford, CA: Stanford University Press, 1990).

56. H. Grasmick, C. R. Tittle, R. Bursik, and B. Arnkelev, "Testing the Core Empirical Implications of Gottfredson and Hirschi's General Theory of Crime," *Journal of Research in Crime and Delinquency*, 1993. 30: 5–29; Marianne Junger and Richard E. Tremblay, "Self-Control, Accidents, and Crime," *Criminal Justice and Behavior*, 1999. 26: 485–502; Carter Hay, "Parenting Self-Control, and Delinquency: A Test of Self-Control Theory," *Criminology*, 2001. 39: 707–736; Richard Tremblay, Frank Vitaro, Lucie Bertrand, Marc Leblanc, Helene Beauchesne, Helene Boileau, and Lucille David, "Parent and Child Training to Prevent Early Onset Delinquency: The Montreal Longitudinal Experimental Study," *Life-Course Criminology: Contemporary and Classic Readings*, edited by Alex Piquero and Paul Mazerolle (Belmont, CA: Wadsworth Publishing Co., 2001); Charles R. Tittle, David Ward, and Harold Grasmick, "Gender, Age, and Crime/Deviance: A Challenge to Self Control Theory," *Journal of Research in Crime and Delinquency*, 2003. 40: 426–454.

57. Joseph J. Senna and Larry J. Siegel, *Introduction to Criminal Justice*, 8th ed. (Belmont, CA: West/Wadsworth Publishing Co., 1999).

58. Jodi M. Brown and Patrick A. Langan, *State Court Sentencing of Convicted Felons, 1994* (Washington, D.C.: Government Printing Office, 1998).

59. Ronald H. Aday, *Aging Prisoners: Crisis in American Corrections* (Westport, CN: Praeger Press, 2003).

60. "Are Mandatory Minimum Drug Sentences Cost-Effective?" *Rand Corporation: Drug Policy Research Center*, RB-6003, 1997, http://www.rand.org/publications/RB/RB6003/.

61. Richard Dieter, "Costs of the Death Penalty," March 27, 2003, Testimony before Joint Committee on Criminal Justice of the Legislature of Massachusetts, http://www.deathpenaltyinfo.org/MassCostTestimony.pdf.

62. Susan Levine and Lori Montgomery, "Large Racial Disparity Found in Study of Maryland Death Penalty," *Washington Post*, January 8, 2003.

SOCIAL CLASS IN THE UNITED STATES

SOCIAL CLASS IN THE UNITED STATES

It is no

surprise that many Americans believe a whole host of social ills can be traced to the lapse in judgment that a poor, unmarried woman shows when she bears a child she can't afford. The solution to these problems seems obvious to most Americans: These young women should wait to have children until they are older and more economically stable, and they should get married first. It is indeed true that if more of these mothers married their children's fathers, fewer would be poor.

What is striking about the body of social science evidence is how little of it is based on the perspectives and life experiences of the women who are its subjects. We provide new ideas about the forces that may be driving the trend by looking at the problems of family formation through the eyes of 162 low-income single mothers living in eight economically marginal neighborhoods. Their stories offer a unique point of view on the troubling questions of why low-income, poorly educated young women have children they can't afford and why they don't marry.

To most middle-class observers, a poor woman with children but no husband, diploma, or job is either a victim of her circumstances or undeniable proof that American society is coming apart at the seams. But in the social world inhabited by poor women, a baby born into such conditions represents an opportunity to prove one's worth.

For the poor and affluent alike, marriage is now much less about sex, co-residence, and raising children than it used to be. Whereas most couples used to view marriage as a starting point in their quest to achieve a series of life goals, today the poor insist on meeting these goals before marriage.

If the poor shared both the middle class's marriage standards and their childbearing behaviors, few Americans would question their behavior. What troubles most middle-class citizens is why women don't wait until they are married to have children. The poor view childlessness as one of the greatest tragedies in life.

The public often assumes that early childbearing is the main reason why so many girls from poor inner city areas fail to complete high school, go on to college, gain valuable work skills, or earn decent wages, but there is virtually no evidence to support this idea. Disadvantaged girls who bear children have about the same long-term earnings trajectories as similarly disadvantaged youth who wait until their mid or late twenties to have a child. In other words, early childbearing is highly selective of girls whose other characteristics—family background, cognitive ability, school performance, mental health status, and so on—have already diminished their life chances so much that an early birth does little to reduce them much further.[1]

Stratification *in a* Modern Society

On the hit TV show *Ugly Betty*, Betty's thirty-something sister Hilda became pregnant as a teenager and has been raising her son as a single mother ever since. Sure, Hilda's fashion-loving, chic son Justin is a fictional character, but he represents an important demographic in the United States today: children who are born out of wedlock. In 2006, 32.7 percent of all children born in the United States were born to women who had never been married, divorced, or widowed.[2] Why are so many women having children out of wedlock?

Kathryn Edin and Maria Kefalas found that most of these women thought that being a mother would be their most important life accomplishment. In a world where circumstances leave these women little hope for their futures, children make their lives meaningful. Marriage, however, does not hold the same promise. To these women, the cost of marrying a man who could be unreliable, unfaithful, and abusive far outweighs the financial benefits that marriage might bring.

Statistics show that single mothers are often impoverished and lack the resources they need to raise their children. Many have difficulty finding work, and the jobs they do get pay little. They are also most likely to be living in the South.[3] These women make up only one part of the poor in the United States. How does social position affect a person's life? As sociologists, we want to find out.

get the topic: WHAT IS SOCIAL STRATIFICATION?

SOCIAL STRATIFICATION is the ranking of people and the rewards they receive based on an objective criteria, often including wealth, power, and/or prestige.

INCOME is the money received for work or through investments.

WEALTH is all of your material possessions, including income.

It seems that it's in our nature to rank things. Pick up any magazine at the end of a given year, and you're sure to find "top ten" lists ranking the best movies, albums, or books of that year. Sociologists also like to

rank individuals based on objective criteria, such as wealth, power, or prestige. This is known as **social stratification**.

All forms of society have ways to rank, or stratify, the members of their populations, but the level of stratification can vary a great deal between societies.[4] Some societies may use political power to separate people by giving party members special privileges unavailable to others. For example, in the United States' "closed" presidential primary elections, party members are the only ones who are allowed to vote. Societies also tend to use wealth to stratify people into social classes; the more money you have, the higher your status. Still others use birth status and family

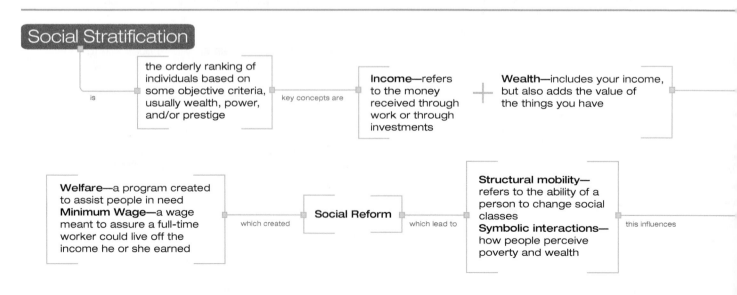

Social Stratification

is → the orderly ranking of individuals based on some objective criteria, usually wealth, power, and/or prestige

key concepts are → **Income**—refers to the money received through work or through investments

+ **Wealth**—includes your income, but also adds the value of the things you have

Welfare—a program created to assist people in need
Minimum Wage—a wage meant to assure a full-time worker could live off the income he or she earned

which created → **Social Reform**

which lead to → **Structural mobility**—refers to the ability of a person to change social classes
Symbolic interactions—how people perceive poverty and wealth

this influences →

Income Distribution in the United States

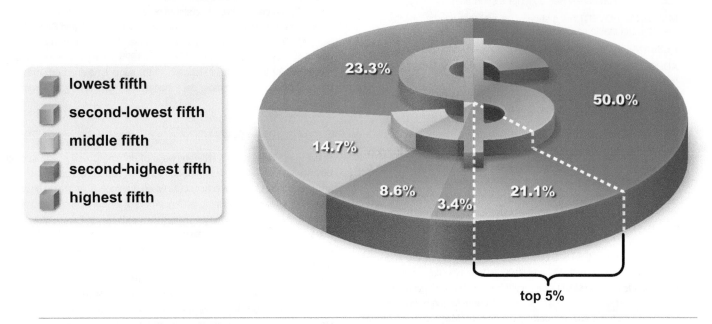

- lowest fifth
- second-lowest fifth
- middle fifth
- second-highest fifth
- highest fifth

23.3%

50.0%

14.7%

8.6%

3.4%

21.1%

top 5%

∧
∧
∧

The **poorest 20 percent of the country receives only 3.4 percent of the money,** while the **richest 5 percent has more than six times that much.** What will this pie chart look like in 10 years?

of origin as a means to divide people; certain families regarded as "nobility" hold privileged positions.

In the United States, we tend to divide groups by their access to wealth and/or income. **Income** refers to the money received for work or through investments. Whether it's the paycheck you get every two weeks or the dividends you receive from your stock investments, the money you receive regularly is considered income. **Wealth**, on the other hand, refers to all your material possessions, including income. If you were to take everything you owned—your car, your computer, clothes, etc.—and sell it all at a fair market value, you could probably raise a considerable sum that would be more than your monthly income. It's important to know the

difference between the two and to understand how each of these factors can affect your social standing.

INCOME DISTRIBUTION

When I was a college student, I could put everything I owned in the back of my Honda Civic. I worked for 25 cents above the minimum wage, and I had few expenses. I earn much more now than I did in college, but my expenses have also increased significantly as I got married, bought a house, and started a family. In the United States, there is a diverse group of income earners. The entire income of the country can be divided into five groups,

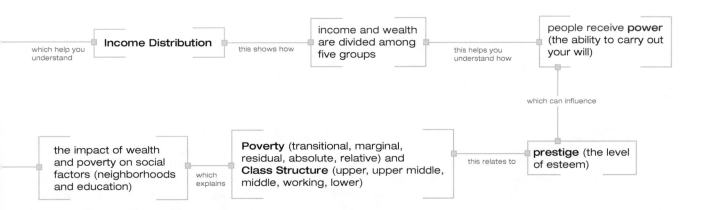

which help you understand — **Income Distribution** — this shows how — income and wealth are divided among five groups — this helps you understand how — people receive **power** (the ability to carry out your will)

which can influence

the impact of wealth and poverty on social factors (neighborhoods and education) — which explains — **Poverty** (transitional, marginal, residual, absolute, relative) and **Class Structure** (upper, upper middle, middle, working, lower) — this relates to — **prestige** (the level of esteem)

TRANSITIONAL POVERTY is a temporary state of poverty that occurs when someone loses a job for a short time.

MARGINAL POVERTY is a state of poverty that occurs when a person lacks stable employment.

RESIDUAL POVERTY is chronic and multigenerational poverty.

ABSOLUTE POVERTY is poverty so severe that one lacks resources to survive.

RELATIVE POVERTY is a state of poverty that occurs when we compare ourselves to those around us.

each with the same number of households. Among these groups, the poorest 20 percent of the country's earners received only 3.4 percent of the total income, whereas the top 20 percent received 50 percent. The median, or midpoint, household income is $50,303, a decline of 3.6 percent from the year before. However, one of every five households in the United States has an income of $20,712 or lower. Those in the second quintile had incomes between $20,713 and $39,000. The third quintile contains the median income, with a range from $39,001 to $62,725. Those in the fourth quintile had incomes between $62,726 and $100,240, and the richest 20 percent of households earn $100,241 or more.[5] If income trends continue, the rich are going to get richer; from 1970 to 2000, income for the bottom 90 percent of taxpayers actually dropped by 0.1 percent. Meanwhile, the top 10 percent of households saw income increases ranging from 89.5–558 percent.[6] Consider the pay of corporate executives. The ratio of a CEO's pay to a worker's pay was $24 to $1 in 1965, meaning that for every dollar a worker earned, the CEO made $24. By 2000, the ratio increased to $300 to $1.[7] Now, it is reported to be $319 to $1.[8]

WEALTH DISTRIBUTION

This change in income only worsens the wealth disparity in the United States. When stocks, bonds, and many other items are included, it turns out that the top one percent of wealthy Americans control more total wealth than the bottom 90 percent.[9] This means that a relatively small group of people control most of the country's money and assets.

The wealth distribution of the United States shows other trends as well. Generally, men have more wealth than women do. Stocks and personal residences make up the two largest categories of wealth. Top wealth holders in the United States are predominantly married (49 percent) or widowed (26 percent).[10] Wealth distribution also shows geographic trends. What does the map below tell you about wealth in the United States?

In 2000, Keister and Moller found that wealth inequality had worsened over a 34-year period between 1962 and 1995.[11] They show that wealth has grown for the top wealth holders. At the same time, the percentage of the U.S. population with more debt than assets increased eight percent.

How Does the United States Define Poverty?

Sociologists have several different ways of defining poverty. **Transitional poverty** is a temporary state that occurs when someone loses a job for a short time. **Marginal poverty** occurs when a person lacks stable employment. For example, if your job is lifeguarding at a pool during the summer season, you might experience marginal poverty when the season ends. The next, more serious level, **residual poverty**, is chronic and multigenerational. People who live in a seemingly never-ending cycle of poverty that passes on to their children and grandchildren experience this type of poverty. A person who experiences **absolute poverty** is so poor that he or she doesn't have resources to survive. The people who are starving to death in the Darfur region of the Sudan are living in absolute poverty. **Relative poverty** is a state that occurs when we compare ourselves to those around us. You might experience relative poverty if you feel like your cell phone is old and insufficient compared with your friend's phone.

The U.S. government defines poverty much differently. The government establishes a poverty line to determine who is eligible to receive specific services, If a family's income is below that line, assistive services such as food, health care, and job placement programs are available.[12] If your income is above the line, you receive little or no government assistance. Of course, using a national standard for poverty may be misleading. Consider the cost of living where you live—are the costs the same elsewhere in the country? A one-room apartment in Manhattan might go for as much or more than a much bigger house in Arkansas. Costs for many things vary depending upon the location in the country, and yet the poverty line is the same in 48 states.[13]

The depth of poverty is sometimes hidden by official poverty numbers. For example, in the United States in 2008, 5.7 percent of all people over age 17 had incomes below one-half of their poverty threshold. Of all those who are poor, this accounts for approximately 43 percent of that total number in poverty. Children make up 36.8 percent of this group.

Sociologists sometimes talk about a group known as the **near poor**. Definitions may differ, but the term generally refers to people who live above the poverty line, but close to it. The Census Bureau provides numbers for those who live between the poverty line and 25 percent above that line. Seventeen percent of the population live in his category. Add the 13.2 percent of the population who live below poverty, and you find that slightly more than 39 percent of the population are poor, or near poor.[14] In addition to region, gender also comes into play; women are more likely to be poor than are men. The women

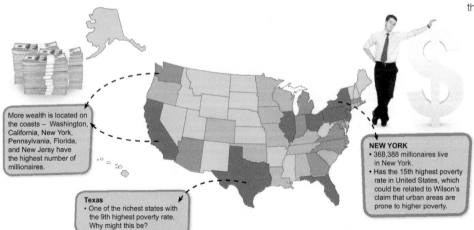

Millionaires in the United States in 2006

More wealth is located on the coasts – Washington, California, New York, Pennsylvania, Florida, and New Jersy have the highest number of millionaires.

NEW YORK
- 368,388 millionaires live in New York.
- Has the 15th highest poverty rate in United States, which could be related to Wilson's claim that urban areas are prone to higher poverty.

Texas
- One of the richest states with the 9th highest poverty rate. Why might this be?

Number of millionaires in the United States, by State

| 0 – 49,999 | 50,000 – 99,999 | 100,000 – 199,999 | 200,000 – 700,000 |

Source: *The Geography of American Poverty*, U.S. Census Bureau, www.Census.gov, February 7, 2008.

Edin and Kefalas interviewed were affected by this gender bias known as the feminization of poverty. For example, median annual earnings for men are $43,367, whereas the median for women is $35,745. Women earn 77 cents for every dollar that men earn.[15] Poverty is particularly concentrated in female-headed households: 28.7 percent of female households without a male present are below poverty, while only 13.8 percent of male households without a female present are below poverty.

POWER

Another measure of stratification is **power**—the ability to carry out your will and impose it on others. In college classrooms, professors rule. Why are things this way? Because the power to educate in college is delegated, meaning given or assigned, to faculty by the college or university. Members of Congress have **delegated** power when they represent the people who elected them. They can use this power to authorize the deployment of troops into a military conflict or steward the economy into or out of a recession.[16]

C. Wright Mills suggested that within the United States a small group called the **power elite** holds immense power.[17] The power elite come from three distinct but related groups: high-ranking political officials, corporate leaders, and military leaders. They decide what information and knowledge to share with the rest of us, and they use their social position and influence to direct the country's decisions. For example, there are five media giants: Time Warner, Disney, News Corporation, Bertelsmann of Germany, and Viacom.[18] As one of the five largest media corporations, the Disney Corporation listed $35.5 billion in revenue for the year 2007. The people in charge of this company, such as former Disney CEO Michael Eisner and current CEO Robert Iger, are counted as members of society's power elite.[19]

Most politicians must be voted into power, but who exercises their right to vote? People with high incomes and people who've achieved high levels of education are more likely to vote than their less wealthy, less-educated neighbors.[20] So what does this mean? Older, wealthier, educated people are making key decisions for the entire country. How does this affect the kinds of

> **POWER** is the ability to carry out your will and impose it on others.
> **DELEGATED** means given or assigned.
> **POWER ELITE** is a small group of people who hold immense power.
> **PRESTIGE** is the level of esteem associated with one's status and social standing.

politicians we elect, the social measures we pass, and the economic packages we approve?

PRESTIGE

Prestige refers to the level of esteem associated with our status and social standing. Most of us want others to hold us in high regard, but various types of jobs hold differing levels of prestige. Generally, low-paying jobs have less prestige because of the stigma attached to such jobs. Not only do low-wage workers struggle to pay the bills, they also struggle to earn respect in a society that stigmatizes their work.

Prestigious jobs are generally ranked on a scale from 0 to 100, with 0 being the lowest. As you might suspect, physicians and lawyers top the list with ratings of 86 and 75; and street corner drug dealers bring up the rear with a 13.[21]

A prestigious job may carry its benefits into other areas of life. For example, you might take a stock tip from a successful start-up CEO, but I doubt you'd take the advice of a minimum-wage-earning grocery bagger. You don't expect someone who works as a bagger to be able to give you a great stock tip. Otherwise, why would he or she be working in such a low-status job? Occupational prestige varies a great deal between jobs and shows the general respect we have for certain work. Few people look at their newborn baby and hope she'll grow up to become a fry cook rather than a doctor.

Wealth, power, and prestige are the basis for the stratification system used to characterize the population, so these three components can also be used to analyze the class system of the United States.

▶▶▶ GO GL◉BAL

From One Extreme to Another

Out of all wealthy nations, except for Mexico, the United States has the greatest percentage of children living in poverty.[22] In our country, 17.4 percent of children under the age of 18 live in poverty,[23] and 17 percent of these children live in households classified as "food insecure," which are households that change the quantity or quality of their food or frequently skip meals because of limited incomes.[24]

Ironically, the United States leads the world in the total number of millionaires as well as the highest percentage of new millionaires.[25] Many of these millionaires run for

©Visions, LLC/photolibrary.com

positions in government or contribute large donations to political causes. In fact, of the 100 members in the 1995 Senate, 40 were millionaires.[26]

<<< Although there are government programs designed to help the poor, many **impoverished children may suffer from lack of nutritious food, dirty living conditions, and poor health.**

UPPER or ELITE CLASS is a social class that is very small in number and holds significant wealth.

CLASS STRUCTURE IN THE UNITED STATES

If someone asked you what your social class is, what would you say? I often ask students to identify their social class. More often than not, they claim to be part of the "middle class." In fact, most people in the United States claim to belong to the middle class.[27] But are their claims accurate? If you had to divide the United States into classes, how would you make class distinctions?

Sociologists have varying opinions on how many classes there should be and what constitutes each class. For our discussion, however, let's look at five different social classes in the United States: upper class, upper middle class, middle class, working class, and lower class. Ask yourself how your membership to one class or the other might influence your perspective, opportunities, and long-term outcomes.

Upper/Elite Class

The **upper** or **elite class** is very small in number and holds significant wealth. We've already learned that only about 1 percent of the population belongs to this group.[28] Since there are about 300 million people in the country, approximately three million people are considered "upper class." The upper class possesses much of the country's "old money," which affords them great access to the three components of class: wealth, power, and prestige.[29] Many entertainers and professional athletes are part of this class.

Sociologist G. William Domhoff[30] has done extensive work studying the upper class. According to his findings, membership to this class comes from attending an exclusive prep school, belonging to exclusive social clubs, and being born into a wealthy or powerful family.

When the workday is done, many in the upper class relax in private clubs. One such club is the all-male Bohemian club. Located in northern California, the club offers luxurious retreats to its exclusive members. Members are a who's who of U.S. business tycoons and political figures, including officers or directors from 40 of the 50 largest corporations in the United States. Members come from every part of the country, and membership is highly restricted.

Domhoff suggests that such a club allows the upper class to unify.[31] At these retreats, politicians and national speakers provide information and ideas about the future. The relaxing nature of a social club such as the Bohemian also increases social integration of members because of its climate; social cohesion increases in relaxed atmospheres. The upper class's money affords them opportunities that most people only dream of having. However, members of the upper middle class come pretty close to matching the elite's status.

©Kurt Krieger/Corbis

<<< **Paris Hilton is a celebrity primarily because she was born into extraordinary wealth,** but she has used the wealth, power, and prestige of her family name to pursue television, modeling, and musical careers.

THINK SOCIOLOGICALLY

Net Jets is one of the largest private jet corporations in the world. It is a leader in what is known as the fractional jet ownership market. Owners can purchase a part of a private jet for less money than it would cost to own their own, but reap the benefit of flying in a private jet. Net Jets is a Berkshire-Hathaway company, which is an investment of one of the richest men on the planet, Warren Buffett. If you're tired of flying commercial, you can simply buy into one of their jets. How much would you pay for this convenience? Prices for fractional ownership start at around $400,000, but that is only the initial buy-in and for the smallest plane.[32] Larger planes can go for much more than that. However, once you've bought into your plane, there are other fees. These include a monthly management fee that covers pilot salaries, training, hangaring of your plane, and insurance and other services. Of course, owning your own private jet is something few of us will experience, and yet a company like Net Jets has more than 600 jets in service, all owned by businesses and individuals with the money to rule the skies.

Upper Middle Class

As with all distinctions of class, the definition of the upper middle class is fairly subjective. For the purposes of our discussion, the **upper middle class** consists of high-income members of society who are well educated but do not belong to the elite membership of the super wealthy. These people occupy professional positions and have achieved a level of income that makes their lives comfortable. They own property, have high occupational prestige, and often hold positions of authority within their jobs.[33]

This group makes up about 15 percent of the population. Their pay tends to exceed $100,000 a year. The two primary components of this group are occupational prestige and education. Owning a small business, having a professional career, or holding a high-status job often propels a person into this group. Your dentist, your lawyer, or the owner of your local grocery store chain may belong in this group.[34]

Middle Class

Almost half of Americans claim that they are members of the middle class. This isn't exactly a new phenomenon: Studies conducted in 1957, 1979, and 1996 all show that more than 40 percent of Americans believe they are part of the middle class.[35] If you're trying to decide where you fall along the country's economic spectrum, you might think, "Well, I'm not poor, and I'm not rich, so I must be somewhere in the middle. That's middle class, right?" However, the sociological definition for middle class is a bit more complex.

In general, **middle class** people have moderate incomes. They may be lower paid white-collar workers, such as schoolteachers, or well-paid

> **UPPER MIDDLE CLASS** is a social class that consists of high-income members of society who are well educated but do not belong to the elite membership of the super wealthy.
>
> **MIDDLE CLASS** is a social class that consists of those who have moderate incomes.
>
> **WORKING CLASS** is a social class generally made up of people with high school diplomas and lower levels of education.

blue-collar workers, like factory foremen. Middle class workers generally aren't involved in manual labor, but they may be skilled laborers (such as electricians). The middle class makes up about 34 percent of the U.S. population, meaning that the majority of the 40 percent of people who claim to be in the middle class actually are in this class.[36]

The middle class members have at least a high school diploma and many have technical training or college credits. Such attainment affords them a moderate level of occupational prestige. When you graduate from college and get your first job, you are likely to start out in the middle class. Members own property but generally hold much less wealth than the previously discussed groups. Incomes for the middle class range a great deal, approximately anywhere from $40,000 to $80,000 a year.

Working Class

The **working class** is generally made up of people with high school diplomas and lower levels of education. This group makes up around 30 percent of the U.S. workforce,[37] and its members hold jobs that usually require manual labor or clerical skills. Blue-collar factory workers or white-collar clerical workers make up most of the working class. Unlike those in the middle- and upper middle-class, members of the working class earn an hourly wage instead of a salary. Because they work by the hour and lack formal education, the working class has very limited opportunities for job improvement. Many nontraditional college students come from the working class. They understand that "good jobs" are increasingly rare and that education opens doors. However, their ability to raise their social class is hindered by the increasing number of blue-collar and even white-collar jobs that are moving overseas. There is an increasing amount of competition for work, which is a further motivation for workers to boost their marketable skills.[38]

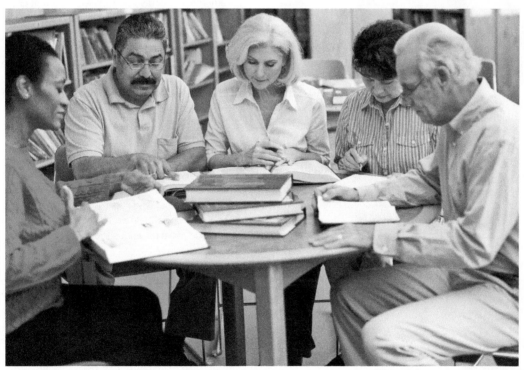

©Monkey Business Images/Shutterstock

∧∧∧ **Many nontraditional students are working-class adults who want to gain more skills through education.** More and more adults are going back to school for additional training and new careers.

Poverty in 2008 by Race and Age

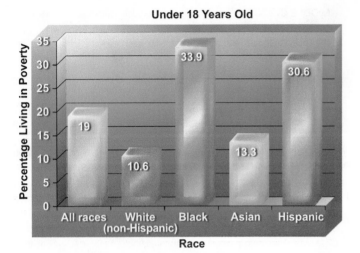

Under 18 Years Old

18–64 Years Old

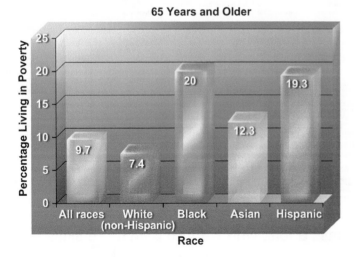

65 Years and Older

Source: Carmen DeNavas-Walt, Bernadette D. Proctor, and Cheryle Hill Lee, "Income, Poverty and Health Insurance Coverage in the United States: 2008," Current Population Reports, U.S. Census Bureau.

Lower Class

Finally, a notch below the working class are the members of society who truly feel the effects of poverty: the **lower class**. Thanks to the skyrocketing costs of tuition, food, and rent, many college students might think they understand what it means to be poor. In most cases, though, the relative poverty of their situation pales in comparison to the experiences of the working poor. After all, the privileges of attending a university and receiving a higher education are designed to lead students to employment that will land them in the middle class. When I was in college, I worked at a landscape nursery doing physical labor. Our pay was low and the hours were long. For me, a college student living at home, it was a good job. For my colleagues at the nursery who were trying to feed their families, it was not.

In the United States, a whopping 37 million people live in poverty.[39] Members of the lower class often live paycheck to paycheck, if they even have a job at all. Those people who do work are often one hospital bill or layoff away from financial ruin.

Notice, in the graphs to the left, how at all age levels **blacks have the highest rates of poverty, and the rate of poverty for whites is always lower than the national average.**

More than two-thirds of African Americans in the United States live near or below the poverty line. Hispanics follow closely behind at about 60 percent.[40] About 10 percent of senior citizens live at the poverty line, while almost half of the children in the United States are poor or near poor.[41] Why are so many children living in poverty? In *Promises I Can Keep*, Edin and Kefalas find that a poor woman is three times more likely to have a child before marriage than affluent women are. This is one reason why we have so many impoverished children in the United States, however the complete answer is more complex than this one fact.

The Urban Underclass

The homeless and chronically unemployed are also usually impoverished. Members of this group often live in substandard housing and may be receiving government assistance. They rarely have health care coverage and often lack a high school diploma. When they find a job, it's usually a minimum-wage position that propels them no higher than the working poor class. Many in this group make up what sociologists call the urban underclass.

The **urban underclass** lives in disadvantaged neighborhoods that are characterized by four components: poverty, family disruption, male unemployment, and lack of individuals in high-status occupations.[42] Many workers in disadvantaged neighborhoods are forced to take low-paying positions that go nowhere, leaving them with little hope of escaping the neighborhoods that are holding them down.

Sociologist William J. Wilson stated that these components could trigger a cycle of undermining social organization. Wilson discusses the urban underclass further in the book *The Truly Disadvantaged*, in which he notes that the U.S. urban poor are increasingly living in neighborhoods with few opportunities, poor schools, weak social structures, large amounts of crime, and rampant drug use.[43] However, what makes them truly disadvantaged is that they lack any vision and/or role models for any other way of life. These issues make life significantly more difficult for the residents and children who live in these ghettos.

NEIGHBORHOODS AND SOCIAL CLASS

Recently, sociologists have observed how neighborhoods influence behavior. Their findings have determined an increase in the geographic concentration of poverty and affluence in the United States. Over time, poor people are living in neighborhoods densely populated by other poor people. Simultaneously, the well-off members of society, particularly those who live in cities, tend to cluster in economically affluent neighborhoods such as the Gold Coast in Chicago or Manhattan's Upper East Side.[44] Looking at each end of the spectrum gives us a clear vision of the dynamics between poverty and affluence in the United States.

The concentration of poverty in a single geographic area is correlated to various issues such as high crime rates, increased drug use, and increasing numbers of single-parent homes. In *Promises I Can Keep*, Edin and Kefalas study women from the poorest areas of Philadelphia and its poorest suburb, Camden, New Jersey. The percentage of non-marital births in Philadelphia increased from 20 percent in 1950 to 30 percent in 1960 to 62 percent in 2000, which is twice the national rate. The bulk of these births were in the poor neighborhoods that they studied. Often, people who achieve any sort of economic advantage move out of these poor neighborhoods. This sort of residential segregation increases the disadvantages for those left behind.[45] Children who grow up in such neighborhoods are at increased risk for lower birth weights, poorer health, lower levels of educational attainment, and higher dropout levels.[46]

Conversely, children growing up in affluent neighborhoods do better in school, have lower rates of teen pregnancy, and have higher test scores. Interestingly, when a poor child is raised in a more affluent neighborhood, due to foster care or some type of rent control supplement, the child tends to do better than his or her peers who remain living in poor neighborhoods. In short, living in a more affluent neighborhood seems to decrease the power of the negative effect that poverty has on children. Why do you think this is the case? Apparently being "the poor kid on the block" is better for a child than being another poor kid on the block.[47] Why?

EDUCATION AND SOCIAL CLASS

We've all heard it said that the United States is the land of opportunity, and in many ways, it lives up to its name. It grants free education to every child, regardless of socioeconomic status. Unfortunately, all educational opportunities aren't exactly the same. For example, public schools frequently offer different educational opportunities. But what difference do these opportunities really make?

In a two-year study of more than 25 different communities, Jonathan Kozol observed public schools in the United States and noted that not all schools are created equal.[48] Kozol saw that urban schools frequently lacked basic supplies necessary to teach: Playgrounds often had little or no equipment, chemistry labs were missing beakers and test tubes, and students had to share textbooks. Meanwhile, suburban schools often had a surplus of supplies and staff. Kozol pointed out that while these two systems often turned out different qualities of education, the major cause for this disparity rested in the structures that supported the educational systems. Property values and taxes are higher in the suburbs, so their schools receive more funding than urban schools. This extra financial support allows suburban schools to purchase up-to-date materials and hire ample staff for the students. Unfortunately, because most urban schools are underfunded, the students who need the most help actually get the least, which adds to the endless cycle of educational inequality. Is this really "equal opportunity"?

The studies of Roscigno et al. show similar findings to Kozol's. They note that both urban and rural students frequently attend schools with fewer resources than suburban students.[49] These inequalities are directly linked to parents' socioeconomic status. Students lacking resources in school and at home are more likely to attain a lower level of educational achievement. On average, both inner-city and rural students score lower on achievement tests when compared with suburban students. These findings support the notion that college attendance is not linked to academic outcomes, but to the social class of a student's family.[50] For those in the lower classes, access to financial aid is key for students who wish to attend college.[51] Unfortunately, the availability of aid remains a serious issue for less affluent students.[52] Clearly, complete educational equality does not exist in United States. Because poor neighborhoods lack the resources necessary to succeed, many residents of these communities are denied the opportunity to overcome poverty.

> **LOWER CLASS** is a social class living in poverty.
>
> **URBAN UNDERCLASS** is a social class living in disadvantaged neighborhoods that are characterized by four components: poverty, family disruption, male unemployment, and lack of individuals in high-status occupations.

MAKE CONNECTIONS

Nickel and Dimed into Poverty

Before writing the book *Nickel and Dimed*, Barbara Ehrenreich spent a year living among the working class. Going from state to state, she worked as a waitress, a maid, a nursing home aid, and a Wal-Mart salesperson. Ehrenreich's experiences led her to dispute the idea that these jobs require low-level skills. Instead, she believes that such low-wage jobs are physically demanding and actually require a great deal of interpersonal and technical skills. These jobs don't normally provide health care or sick leave, so workers who fall ill have to choose between their health and their pay. Yet despite the hurdles society has placed in their way, these workers are actually more motivated to succeed and are not depressed by a system of low wages and long hours.

>>> **ACTIVITY** Recent college graduate Adam Shepard wrote *Scratch Beginnings: Me, $25, and the Search for the American Dream* in rebuttal to Ehrenreich's book. Read Shepard's book or search the Internet to learn his findings. Which author paints a more accurate picture of life for the working poor? Why?

SOCIAL MOBILITY is the ability to change social classes.

HORIZONTAL MOBILITY refers to moving within the same status category.

VERTICAL MOBILITY refers to moving from one social status to another.

INTRAGENERATIONAL MOBILITY occurs when an individual changes social standing, especially in the workforce.

INTERGENERATIONAL MOBILITY refers to the change that family members make from one social class to the next through generations.

STRUCTURAL MOBILITY occurs when social changes affect large numbers of people.

EXCHANGE MOBILITY is a concept suggesting that, within the United States, each social class contains a relatively fixed number of people.

MERITOCRACY ARGUMENT states that those who get ahead do so based on their own merit.

Social Mobility

Wherever we are in life, there's always the chance that something could happen to us that would change our status. Whether it's winning the lottery or investing in the right stocks, our social class could change in an instant. Likewise, the mortgage crisis and corporate downsizing have sent many middle-class families plummeting into poverty. **Social mobility** is a term that describes this ability to change social classes. If social class is a ladder, social mobility occurs when we climb either up or down it. Several patterns of social mobility are possible.

Horizontal mobility, as the name suggests, refers to moving within the same status category. For example, when a teacher leaves one school to take a position at another school, horizontal mobility has occurred. The teacher is earning the same amount of money and performs the same tasks; she just happens to be doing these things at a different location. Her movement is lateral, not vertical. **Vertical mobility** involves moving from one social status to another. This type of mobility can either be upward, in the form of a promotion at work, or downward, in the form of a demotion at work. For example, if the same teacher from our previous example got a master's degree and became a principal, then vertical mobility has occurred.

In the United States, the labor market has changed immensely. Many companies are outsourcing manual labor overseas to developing countries. **U.S. citizens who previously performed this type of work find themselves out of a job, which, in turn, slows upward mobility.**

Intragenerational mobility occurs when an individual changes social standing, especially in the workforce. Climbing the corporate ladder is a prime example of this type of mobility. For instance, if you begin your working career as an unskilled laborer doing construction work and then ten years later own a construction company, you are experiencing intragenerational mobility.

Intergenerational mobility refers to the change that family members make from one social class to the next through generations. If you hope to live a better life than your parents did, then you hope for upward intergenerational mobility. However, if you expect to do much better than your parents, the odds are probably stacked against you. A number of researchers have found that while intergenerational mobility does occur, children tend to climb only a little higher on the social class ladder when compared with their parents, if they climb at all.[53]

The effects of this kind of mobility on the poor are even greater. Edin and Kefalas describe how the young, unwed, poor men and women having children rarely have jobs and find it hard to find employment because new jobs and opportunities often require high levels of education and experience, leaving many poor struggling to survive. One key variable in mobility is connected to education and particularly the occupations that it can make available to a person. Studying mobility in Japan, the United States, Germany, and Sweden, researchers note that families tend to pass on occupational opportunities, which play a key role in maintaining social position and/or allowing for social mobility.[54]

Because many living in poverty are not getting the same level of education that other students receive, how can they be expected to keep up with technological advancements? Children raised in poor homes are more likely to experience poverty in adulthood. Poor black children are 2.5 times more likely to remain poor in adulthood compared with other black children who are not raised in poverty. For white children, the rates are even worse. Poor white children are 7.5 times more likely to continue being poor as adults when compared with their wealthier counterparts.[55]

Structural mobility occurs when social changes affect large numbers of people. During economic booms, some climb the ladder and benefit from changes in the economy. Think of the success that the Chrysler Company experienced during the economic prosperity of the mid-1990s.

When the economy heads into a recession, workers who have lost their jobs to outsourcing experience downward structural mobility. For example, the same Chrysler Company that flourished in the 1990s was forced to close many plants and lay off more than 13,000 workers a little more than a decade later.

The concept of **exchange mobility** suggests that, within the United States, each social class contains a relatively fixed number of people. If you move upward into a class above you, someone else must move down. When you consider the changes in income over time that we talked about earlier, you can see that such data generally support the idea that social stratification levels do not change much, though the people who make up each layer may be different.

think sociologically: WHAT ARE THE THEORIES BEHIND SOCIAL STRATIFICATION?

Functionalism

Functionalists believe that systems find equilibrium, or balance, so stratification must be the result of some kind of functional balance. Theorists Kingsley Davis and Wilbert Moore summarize the common argument that the U.S. stratification system is inevitable and aids in the smooth functioning of society.[56] This **meritocracy argument** states that those who get ahead do so based on their own merit.

Davis and Moore believe each society has important positions that must be filled. The more important the position, the more we reward those who choose to pursue it. Doctors in the United States generally get hefty paychecks because everyone needs a doctor to tend to their health care needs. In order to get someone to fill an important position, society offers a reward to anyone who's willing to fill it. The rarer the skill or the longer the training period, the greater the rewards can be. If you faint at the sight of blood or if you can't stand the thought of spending a good portion of your life in school, you probably shouldn't become a doctor.

On the other hand, the reason KFC is able to pay its employees minimum wage is because you can learn to fry chicken in about two hours. I should know; I once cooked chicken for the Colonel. But why would anyone become a medical doctor considering the stress and training involved? Davis and Moore say that society has to offer greater rewards to entice people to take particularly tough or stressful jobs. To sum up the functionalist view, stratification inevitably happens because people have different abilities, and those abilities are more or less important to society.

Therefore, if you get ahead, it is based on some ability or drive that you have that pushes you to get there. Delayed gratification, or the ability to wait in order to get something you want, can also determine your success. If you're willing to put in the time to go to school and work hard, you're likely to be successful.

In this sense, it means that **stratification is inevitable, since we do not all have the same intelligence, drive, and desire.** Those who get ahead in this country tend to be those who use these individual forces to reap society's rewards.

After teaching sociology for many years, I believe that most of my students are functionalists. They support the idea that people succeed or fail in the United States based on their own merit.

The graphic on the right provides information from student surveys that I have used in my classes. This nonscientific study yields the same results virtually every year. I ask students if they "agree with the following statements," and the percentages show those who agreed with the statement. What do you think? Do people in the United States determine their own success?

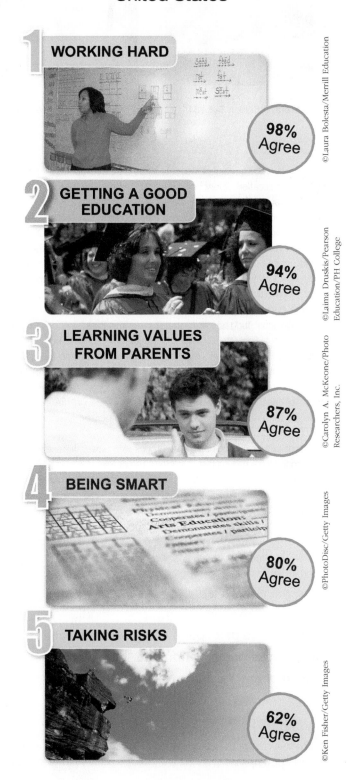

Top 5 Reasons My Students Think People Get Ahead in the United States

1 **WORKING HARD** — 98% Agree

2 **GETTING A GOOD EDUCATION** — 94% Agree

3 **LEARNING VALUES FROM PARENTS** — 87% Agree

4 **BEING SMART** — 80% Agree

5 **TAKING RISKS** — 62% Agree

©Laura Bolesta/Merrill Education

©Laima Druskis/Pearson Education/PH College

©Carolyn A. McKeone/Photo Researchers, Inc.

©PhotoDisc/Getty Images

©Ken Fisher/Getty Images

©Michal Heron

Average Salary: $48,254[57]

©Marc Serota/Getty Images

2008 Earnings: $40 million[58]

<<< Police officers are essential for society, but professional athletes, like Lebron James, are not. **Why do you think there is such a discrepancy between their salaries?**

Conflict Theory

Unlike functionalists, conflict theorists focus on the role of conflict as the basis of stratification. Every society has limited resources to go around, so groups struggle with one another for those resources. Melvin Tumin offers a critique of Davis and Moore that supports the conflict point of view. For Tumin, social inequality is rooted in a system that is more likely to reward you based on where you start—not solely based on the abilities you have.[59] There is nothing inevitable about inequality, it is merely those with wealth doing the best they can to keep that wealth and pass it on to their children. In this way, social inequality is rooted in the unjust capitalist system and not the people who live under it.

Tumin also suggests that stratification is not as simple as some might suggest. First, the societal importance of a job does not seem to be the only basis for financial rewards. Think about it: Who is arguably more important to society, a police officer or a professional athlete? Now ask yourself who makes more money? Being a soldier, firefighter, police officer, or teacher requires dedication, training, and unique skills. But these groups are actually paid very little in comparison to entertainers, corporate CEOs, and professional athletes.

Conflict theorists point out that groups with power will extract what they can from the groups beneath them. The dominant group takes control of social institutions in order to preserve the best resources for itself. By extension, conflict theorists argue, the wealthy try to maintain the status quo so that access to training will remain limited to their group, thus helping them gain even more wealth and power. Why do doctors make so much money? People need them and have very little choice about it.

Students from working-class backgrounds are far more likely to talk about social class as an issue on college campuses than upper middle-class students. **The perception of social stratification then, comes primarily from the "have-nots" instead of the "haves."**

Symbolic Interactionism

Symbolic interactionists are interested in how people perceive poverty and wealth. They seek to understand if people actually have a sense of social class. According to research by Stuber, our particular social class impacts how we talk about class in general.[60] The higher our socioeconomic status (SES), the less we believe that social class matters. For example, upper middle-class college students tend to disregard issues of class and often don't notice that others cannot do what they can do financially. They may be socialized not to care about social class, or they might not have thought much about it.

This could be because working-class students must make financial choices that upper middle-class students don't even have to consider. In addition, students from the working class have lower expectations about future earnings and successes. Basically, the disparity in these college students' social status demonstrates how ascribed positions affect expectations.

The perception of class differences is most pronounced in the dichotomous way that people look at welfare recipients. Generally, the recipient of food stamps, Section Eight housing, or cash payments incurs a serious social stigma.[61] Students in my classes frequently become angry when discussing the welfare system. As one young woman put it, "I have to work, and they get to drive around in Hummers and live off the government." Putting aside the obvious problems with this statement, this woman's words certainly illustrate the difference between what the general public perceives and the reality of welfare.

In *So You Think I Drive a Cadillac?*, Karen Seccombe investigates how female welfare recipients view the welfare system and deal with the associated stigma. Some of their coping strategies include distancing and denial: Women who avoid any discussion about their situations are distancing themselves from the fact that they receive assistance at all. Others who come up with plausible excuses—such as losing a job or fleeing an abusive marriage—are denying they are similar to other welfare recipients. But, when they viewed other women on welfare, they restated common stereotypes that echoed my student's anti-welfare tirade.

Seccombe points out that upper- and middle-class women actually have more in common with poor women than they might think. They all tend to worry about how to care for their children and homes, and they all tend to view public assistance negatively. Poor women realize society views them negatively, so they see accepting welfare as a last resort. Seccombe specifically shows that low wages and a lack of financial support from men are the driving factors behind female poverty. The reason that many of these individuals are poor is because they cannot earn enough to make ends meet or because they're not receiving court-ordered child support from their ex-husbands.

WRAP YOUR MIND AROUND THE THEORY

The average salary for a physician is over $140,000.[62] On the other hand, **the average salary for a fast food cook is approximately $17,400.[63] What factors might have influenced such different outcomes** for these two people?

FUNCTIONALISM

Functionalists suggest that social class is connected to a person's ability to negotiate the social world. Therefore, intelligence, drive, and personal choice influence a person's social class. All people are different, so it makes sense that differences in social class exist in the United States. Some people simply have more skills and abilities than others, and these skills naturally help them reap economic rewards. Have you ever heard the phrase "The cream rises to the top"? In many ways, this statement explains why stratification continues to occur.

WHAT FACTORS INFLUENCE SOCIAL CLASS IN THE UNITED STATES?

CONFLICT THEORY

Conflict theorists believe that social mobility rarely occurs in a dramatic way, largely because the U.S. system doesn't allow it. Generally, one's parents and the opportunities they can provide determine social class. Parents in positions of wealth wish to make sure their children keep that advantage, so they pass wealth to their children in the form of an inheritance, they make sure their children attend the "best schools," and they use their social prestige to help their children succeed. Children who lack such things generally remain poor.

SYMBOLIC INTERACTIONISM

Social class and our understanding of it are relative to our personal belief system. In *Promises I Can Keep*, Edin and Kefalas argue that middle-class citizens would not question poor people's behavior if they held similar beliefs about marriage and childbearing. According to Edin and Kefalas, "[T]he poor view childlessness as one of the greatest tragedies in life. Surveys show that the differences between the social classes are striking; female high school dropouts are more than five times as likely and male high school dropouts more than four times as likely as their college-educated counterparts to say they think childless people lead empty lives."

Conflict theorists point out that affluent parents often give their children opportunities, such as music lessons and access to organized sports. How might such things **influence a child's popularity at school or position among his or her peers?**

Interactionists suggest that how we define our position in society affects us. **What future might lie in store for the children of unwed young mothers?**

discover sociology in action: WHAT SOCIAL POLICIES HAVE BEEN CREATED TO EASE POVERTY?

ENTITLEMENT PROGRAM is a program offering assistance to which a person is entitled, requiring no qualification.

Social Policy: Welfare for the Poor

When you call the fire department for help, you probably have no doubt that they will immediately respond to your call. Even if this is the tenth time your house has caught fire, firefighters will come because you are entitled to fire protection. For many years, the U.S. welfare program was a lot like the fire department because anti-poverty assistance was treated as an **entitlement program**, a program offering assistance to which a person is entitled, requiring no qualification. This all changed in 1996 when President Bill Clinton changed welfare in the United States by signing the Personal Responsibility and Work Opportunity Reconciliation Act, which created the Temporary Assistance to Needy Families (TANF) program. TANF is an ongoing government program that targets a particular section of the population to receive benefits such as cash assistance and child-care. Under the new welfare law, children in poor families are no longer entitled to poverty protection because the program is temporary.

Before the introduction of TANF, people generally believed that welfare recipients lived on the system for years. However, Edin and Kefalas found no sign that the poor women they interviewed desired to "milk the system." These women expected to have to work to make ends meet. Nevertheless, the government imposed time limits to curb abuses. The program officially allows a person to receive TANF funds for five years in their lifetime, and for only two years at a time. Thus, children cannot receive benefits throughout their childhood. But when you look at the families that participated in Aid to Families with Dependent Children (AFDC), statistics show that two-thirds of all recipients were never on the program for longer than two years. Furthermore, less than 15 percent of AFDC recipients were continuous users of the system.[64] In other words, most people were never on the system longer than the established time limits.

TANF supports the cutting of welfare benefits and argues that a job should pay more than welfare payments. Crudely put, the act established that people should not be able to stay home and live on the taxpayers' dime. However, numerous studies show that even taking food stamps and other benefits of the welfare program into account, mothers receiving TANF payments still live well below the poverty line.[65]

One of the central ideas behind welfare reform focused on job training for the poor. Conventional wisdom dictates that people need proper

∨
∨ The Temporary Assistance to Needy Families **(TANF) program left many**
∨ **needy people still living in poverty.**

A New Beginning

training in the requisite skills to get a good job. Unfortunately, the relatively short duration of TANF assistance prevents people from engaging in any kind of long-term training like college. Additionally, many of these programs don't accept the pursuit of higher education as an acceptable way for welfare recipients to spend their time. The system is designed in a way that effectively prevents people from improving their economic situation and ensuring they will continue to work low-wage jobs for a lifetime. Welfare reformers might argue that low-paying jobs are supposed to be a gateway to better opportunities. But do low-wage jobs really grow into more financially rewarding ones? Like many other welfare reform ideas, data do not support the answer. The transition from welfare to work usually results in a job that does not pay a living wage.[66] These low-skilled, minimum-wage jobs usually have no opportunity for growth or advancement. Although recipients technically have jobs, these jobs can't support them and their families. When jobs are not available, both individuals and communities suffer. Without sufficient jobs and training, how are people supposed to survive?

While you might categorize a minimum wage job as something limited to teenagers venturing into the workforce for the first time, **only 21.8 percent of these workers are 16–24** years old. **The greatest percentages of minimum wage workers (78.2 percent) are over 25 years old.**[67]

ACTIVITIES

1. Get to know some of the homeless and poor in your community. Visit or take a tour of a shelter in your community.
2. Check with your state to find out the monthly welfare payments for a mother and two children. Do you think you'd be able to live on that?
3. Create a household budget for two parents who are both working minimum-wage jobs. Budget for rent, utilities, food, child care, and transportation for a family of four living in your local area. Don't make up expenses. Research the minimum wage and prices in your area, and provide your sources. How difficult is it to survive even with two incomes?

Social Policy: Taxes and Social Insurance

In the United States, we have two types of taxes that guide our tax system: progressive and regressive taxes. Progressive taxes increase as incomes rise. The income tax structure of the United States follows a progressive philosophy. The tax structure has people at the lowest levels paying 10 percent, while those who earn the most pay 35 percent of their incomes in taxes.[68]

Regressive taxes are those that fall more heavily on the poor. If you consider sales taxes, particularly for necessities such as gasoline or food, you can see the effect of a regressive tax. The federal government adds 18 cents to every gallon of gas.[69] Let's perform a simple calculation. A person who earns 10 dollars an hour buys a gallon of gas and pays the tax. This is 1.8 percent of his income. If a different person earns 100 dollars and buys that same gallon of gas, the tax burden becomes 0.18 percent. You can see that the more you earn, the less the tax actually affects you.

The government also takes money from your check for social insurance programs such as Medicare and Social Security. Currently, it is 15.3 percent of your income.[70] That percentage comes out of the first $106,000 you earn. If you're self-employed, you pay it all; if not, your employer pays half. Notice however, that the richer you are, the lower the percentage of your income actually goes into FICA. Someone earning $100,000 pays $15,300, or approximately 15 percent of his income, while a person who earns $10,000,000 still pays the same $15,300, which is only 0.15 percent of her income. The reason is Social Security is supposed to be a social insurance program. You pay in, you get out. But for most working people it amounts to another 15 percent tax on their incomes. So, is it even more of a regressive tax?

Maybe reading about wealth and poverty has made you think about how you might use these ideas in your everyday life. One major way in which you can take action is working at a community homeless shelter. Students who lend a hand at shelters and soup kitchens get firsthand knowledge about the complexities of poverty in America.

From Classroom to Community } Helping Homeless Children

Kirk decided to seek some extra credit by volunteering to help homeless children at a school designed only for them. The program gives kids without homes a place to go to school.

"These kids are rarely anywhere for very long, and so the people at the school try really hard to make them enjoy learning and discovery while they're there," he said.

"I can remember meeting this seven-year-old girl whose only real toy was a stuffed rabbit. She told me that she'd kept it with her no matter where she went. Her mom would get jobs for a short time, and then they'd move somewhere else in search of work."

"When I met the girl's mother, she was really nice, but I could tell that she didn't have much education. She was working as a cleaning person in a hotel, but the hours were long and the work was hard. She told me that the pay barely covered the costs of her uniforms and transportation to work, so she and her daughter would be staying at the shelter for as long as they could."

"Coming from a middle-class background, I never thought about all the things I had growing up and how lucky I was to have a house with a backyard and toys. We weren't rich, but compared to this girl, I had everything. Until I volunteered at the school, I guess I really didn't understand poverty."

WHAT **IS SOCIAL STRATIFICATION?**

the ranking of people and the rewards they receive based on objective criteria, often including wealth, power, and/or prestige

WHAT **ARE THE THEORIES BEHIND SOCIAL STRATIFICATION?**

functionalism: stratification is the result of some kind of functional balance, is inevitable, and aids in the smooth functioning of society

conflict theory: social inequality is rooted in a system that is more likely to reward you based on where you start than based on your abilities

symbolic interactionism: a person's particular social class affects how he or she discusses class in general

WHAT **SOCIAL POLICIES HAVE BEEN CREATED TO EASE POVERTY?**

U.S. welfare program; Temporary Assistance to Needy Families (TANF); Aid to Families with Dependent Children (AFDC); minimum wage

get the topic: WHAT IS SOCIAL STRATIFICATION?

How Does the United States Define Poverty?
Social Mobility

Functionalism
Conflict Theory
Symbolic Interactionism

Social Policy: Welfare for the Poor
Social Policy: Taxes and Social Insurance

Theory

FUNCTIONALISM

- social class is connected to a person's ability to negotiate the social world
- intelligence, drive, and personal choice influence a person's social class
- all people are different, so it makes sense that differences in social class exist

CONFLICT THEORY

- social mobility rarely occurs in a dramatic way
- generally, one's parents and the opportunities they can provide determine social class

- the higher our socioeconomic status, the less we believe social class matters

SYMBOLIC INTERACTIONISM

- social class and our understanding of it are relative to our personal belief system
- for example, middle-class citizens would not question poor people's behavior if they held similar beliefs about marriage and childbearing
- many poor women think childless people lead empty lives, so they place more emphasis on the maternal relationship than on marriage

Key Terms

social stratification	relative poverty	middle class	intragenerational mobility
income	power	working class	intergenerational mobility
wealth	delegated	lower class	structural mobility
transitional poverty	power elite	urban underclass	exchange mobility
marginal poverty	prestige	social mobility	meritocracy argument
residual poverty	upper or elite class	horizontal mobility	entitlement program
absolute poverty	upper middle class	vertical mobility	

MY SEARCH LAB

1. *The Credit Card: Private Troubles and Public Issues* by George Ritzer, reprinted from *Expressing America: A Critique of the Global Credit Card Society*, 1995. Copyright by Pine Forge Press. pp. 1–30. Reprinted with permission.

In this selection, George Ritzer uses the sociological imagination to examine credit cards.

1. Why do we as a society tend to blame the individual for social problems such as indebtedness?

2. Explain how the credit card industry generates both personal troubles and public issues. How might the credit card industry be regulated or changed?

2. *When Work Disappears: The World of the New Urban Poor* by William Julius Wilson, 1996, Knopf. pp. 25–50, 283–307. Copyright © 1996 by William Julius Wilson, published by Knopf. Reprinted with permission of the Carol Mann Agency.

INTRODUCTION

William Julius Wilson, a professor at Harvard University, argues that inequality is increasing faster within the black community than in other racial or ethnic groups. In this 1996 selection from *When Work Disappears: The World of the New Urban Poor*, Wilson demonstrates the plight of the inner-city working poor.

DISCUSSION QUESTIONS

1. What are some probable consequences/concerns for neighborhoods when the population drops and the proportion of non-working adults rises?
2. According to Wilson, how did post–World War II government policies contribute to the decline of inner-city neighborhoods?

3. *Some Principles of Stratification* by Kingsley Davis and Wilbert E. Moore, reprinted from *American Sociological Review*, pp. 242–249.

INTRODUCTION

Written in 1945, Davis and Moore use a structural functionalist perspective to examine the principles and functions of stratification in society.

DISCUSSION QUESTIONS

1. Is stratification inevitable? Is it possible to have a classless society?
2. Do you agree that stratification is necessary for a fully functioning society? Why or why not?

THE THINKSPOT

www.thethinkspot.com

Are you part of the middle class? How would you know? The standards for being in the middle class may have changed since you first heard the term. Check out the ThinkSpot and read a *U.S. News and World Report* article called "How to Gauge Your Middle-Class Status." I bet you'll learn some interesting statistics about middle-class Americans as you find out what the characteristics are.

Are we "circling the drain," as the late comic George Carlin seemed to think? Is America headed for economic disaster? Do the people who lead our country not care about poor people? Go to the ThinkSpot and watch several of George Carlin's interview and television appearances in which he discusses his feelings about poverty, wealth, and social stratification.

Sample Test Questions

These multiple-choice questions are similar to those found in the test bank that accompanies this textbook.

1. People with seasonal jobs most likely experience
   a. residual poverty.
   b. absolute poverty.
   c. marginal poverty.
   d. transitional poverty.

2. Which of the following is *not* a member of the power elite?
   a. The Secretary of State
   b. A military general
   c. A corporate CEO
   d. A town mayor

3. Which of the following is true of the upper, or elite, class?
   a. Most members are newly wealthy.
   b. They have higher rates of teen pregnancy.
   c. They make up one percent of the country's population.
   d. They are generally regarded highly for their specialized skills.

4. A doctor transferring from one hospital to another is an example of
   a. intergenerational mobility.
   b. horizontal mobility.
   c. vertical mobility.
   d. exchange mobility.

5. A high school graduate who works on an assembly line in a manufacturing plant is most likely a member of which social class?
   a. Urban underclass
   b. Working class
   c. Middle class
   d. Lower class

ESSAY

1. How does prestige affect one's social standing?
2. How is the mobility of the urban underclass restricted?
3. What is the relationship between social class and education?
4. In terms of marriage and family, how do the values of the low-income single mothers interviewed by Kathryn Edin and Maria Kefalas differ from the values held by most middle-class women? Why do you think this difference exists?
5. How does the concept of exchange mobility conflict with the beliefs of conflict theorists?

WHERE TO START YOUR RESEARCH PAPER

For more information on working in homeless shelters, including a complete list of shelters, go to
http://www.artistshelpingchildren.org/shelters.html
http://www.hud.gov/

For more information about hunger and poverty in the world, go to
http://www.poverty.com/

For more information about minimum wage laws in the United States, go to http://www.dol.gov/esa/minwage/america.htm

To view information collected from a *New York Times* study of social class, go to http://www.nytimes.com/pages/national/class/

ANSWERS: 1. c; 2. d; 3. c; 4. b; 5. b

Endnotes

1. From Kathryn Edin and Maria Kefalas, *Promises I Can Keep: Why Poor Women Put Motherhood Before Marriage.* Copyright © 2007 by the Regents of the University of California. Reprinted by permission of the University of California Press.

2. Jane Lawler Dye, "Fertility of American Women: June 2006," U.S. Census Bureau, http://www.census.gov/prod/2008pubs/p20-558.pdf (accessed May 4, 2010).

3. Ibid.

4. Philip Carl Salzman, "Is Inequality Universal?" *Current Anthropology,* 1999. 40: 31–61.

5. Carmen DeNavas-Walt, Bernadette D. Proctor, and Jessica C. Smith, "Income, Poverty and Heath Insurance Coverage in the United States: 2008," *Current Population Reports,* U.S. Census Bureau, http://www.census.gov/prod/2009pubs/p60-236.pdf (accessed May 4, 2010).

6. David Cay Johnson, *Perfectly Legal: The Covert Campaign to Rig our Tax System to Benefit the Super Rich and Cheat Everybody Else* (New York: Penguin Group Inc., 2003).

7. Lawrence Mishel, Jared Bernstein, and Sylvia Allegretto, *State of Working America 2006/2007* (Ithaca, New York: Cornell University Press, 2007).

8. American Federation of Labor – Congress of Industrial Organizations, "Trends in CEO Pay," http://www.aflcio.org/corporatewatch/paywatch/pay/index.cfm.

9. Barry W. Johnson and Brian G. Raub, "Personal Wealth, 2001," *Statistics of Income Bulletin, 2005,* Internal Revenue Service, http://www.irs.ustreas.gov/pub/irs-soi/98perwel.pdf (accessed August 29, 2008).

10. Ibid.

11. Lisa A. Keister and Stephanie Moller, "Wealth Inequality in the United States," *Annual Review of Sociology,* 2000. 26: 63–81.

12. U.S. Department of Health & Human Services, "Frequently Asked Questions Related to the Poverty Guidelines and Poverty," http://aspe.hhs.gov/poverty/faq.shtml (accessed July 15, 2008).

13. Ibid.

14. Carmen DeNavas-Walt, Bernadette D. Proctor, and Jessica C. Smith, "Income, Poverty and Heath Insurance Coverage in the United States: 2008," *Current Population Reports,* U.S. Census Bureau, http://www.census.gov/prod/2009pubs/p60-236.pdf (accessed May 4, 2010).

15. Ibid.

16. Mark Haugaard, "Reflections on Seven Ways of Creating Power," *European Journal of Social Theory,* 2003. 6: 87–113.

17. C. Wright Mills, *The Power Elite* (New York: Oxford University Press, 1956).

18. Ben Bagdikian, *The New Media Monopoly* (Boston: Beacon Press, 2004).

19. Disney, "The Walt Disney Company and Affiliated Companies—Investor Relations," http://corporate.disney.go.com/investors/index.html (accessed July 16, 2008).

20. Kelly Holder, "Voting and Registration in the Election of November 2004," *Population Characteristics,* 2006, U.S. Census Bureau, http://www.census.gov/prod/2006pubs/p20-556.pdf (accessed August 29, 2008).

21. Keiko Nakao, and Judith Treas, "Updating Occupational Prestige and Socioeconomic Scales: How the New Measures Measure Up." *Sociological Methodology,* 1994. 24: 1–72.

22. Child poverty in rich nations. United Nations Children's Fund. Innocenti Report Card. Issue #1, June 2000, http://www.unicefirc.org/publications/pdf/repcard1e.pdf (accessed August 12, 2010).

23. U.S. Census Bureau, "U.S. Census Bureau Press Releases," http://www.census.gov/Press-Release/www/releases/archives/income_wealth/010583.html (accessed June 18, 2008).

24. U.S. Census Bureau, *Federal Interagency Forum on Child and Family Statistics,* http://www.childstats.gov/americaschildren/tables/econ3a.asp (accessed August 29, 2008).

25. Robert Frank, "US Led a Resurgence Last Year Among Millionaires Worldwide," *Wall Street Journal,* June 15, 2004, A1–A8.

26. Ralph Dannheisser, "Rich Candidates Abound as Presidential Campaign Costs Rise," *America.gov,* http://www.america.gov/st/washfile-english/2007/October/20071016174359ndyblehs0.8567926.html (accessed July 21, 2008).

27. Elia Kacapyr, "Are You Middle Class? Definitions and Trends of the U.S. Middle-class Households," *American Demographics,* 1996. 18: 30–36.

28. Harold R. Kerbo, *Social Stratification and Inequality: Class Conflict in Historical, Comparative and Global Perspective, 6th edition* (New York: McGraw-Hill, 2006).

29. Austin Scaggs, "Paris Hilton," *Rolling Stone,* 2004. 964: 92–94.

30. G. William Domhoff, *Who Rules America?: Power and Politics* (New York: McGraw-Hill, 2002); G. William Domhoff, *The Higher Circles* (New York: Random House, 1970).

31. Ibid.

32. Barney Gimbel, "Private jets for non-gazillionaires," *Fortune 500,* May 22, 2006, http://money.cnn.com/2006/05/09/pf/goodlife_fortune_travel/index.htm.

33. Harold R. Kerbo, *Social Stratification and Inequality: Class Conflict in Historical, Comparative and Global Perspective, 6th edition* (New York: McGraw-Hill, 2006).

34. Dennis Gilbert, *The American Class Structure in an Age of Growing Inequality, 6th edition* (Belmont CA: Wadsworth, 2003).

35. Elia Kacapyr, "Are You Middle Class? Definitions and Trends of the U.S. Middle-class Households," *American Demographics,* 1996. 18: 30–36.

36. Dennis Gilbert, *The American Class Structure in an Age of Growing Inequality, 6th edition* (Belmont CA: Wadsworth, 2003).

37. Ibid.

38. Bettina Lankard Brown, "Effects of Globalization on Careers: Myths and Realities No. 29," http://eric.ed.gov/ERICDocs/data/ericdocs2sql/content_storage_01/0000019b/80/1b/8b/1c.pdf (accessed July 15, 2008).

39. Paul Harris, "37 Million Poor Hidden in the Land of Plenty," *The Observer,* February 19, 2006, http://www.guardian.co.uk/world/2006/feb/19/usa.paulharris (accessed August 29, 2008).

40. Carmen DeNavas-Walt, Bernadette D. Proctor, and Cheryle Hill Lee, "Income, Poverty and Heath Insurance Coverage in the United States: 2005," *Current Population Reports,* U.S. Census Bureau, www.census.gov/prod/2004pubs/p60–226.pdf (accessed February 9, 2007).

41. Ibid.

42. Lauren J. Krivo and Ruth D. Peterson, "Extremely Disadvantaged Neighborhoods and Urban Crime," *Social Forces,* 1996. 75: 619–648.

43. William J. Wilson, *The Truly Disadvantaged: The Inner City, The Underclass, and Public Policy* (Chicago: University of Chicago Press, 1987).

44. Paul A. Jargowsky, "Take the Money and Run: Economic Segregation in U.S. Metropolitan Areas," *American Sociological Review,* 1996. 61: 984–998; Martha A. Gephart, "Neighborhoods and Communities as Contexts for Development," in *Neighborhood Poverty: Context and Consequences for Children. Vol. 1,* ed. Martha A. Gephart and Jeanne Brooks-Gunn, (New York: Russell Sage Foundation, 1997); Craig St. John, "Interclass Segregation, Poverty, and Poverty Concentration: Comment on Massey and Eggers," *The American Journal of Sociology,* 1995. 100 (1995):1325–1333; Craig St. John, "The Concentration of Affluence in the United States," *Urban Affairs Review,* 2002. 37: 500–520.

45. Catherine E. Ross, John Reynolds, and Karlyn Geis, "The Contingent Meaning of Neighborhood Stability for Residents Psychological Well-being," *American Sociological Review,* 2000. 65: 581–597.

46. Jeanne Brooks-Gunn, Greg Duncan, Pamela Klebanove, and Naomi Sealand, "Do Neighborhoods Influence Child and Adolescent Development?" *American Journal of Sociology,* 1993. 99; 353–395; Catherine L. Garner and Stephen W. Raudenbush, "Neighborhood Effects on Educational Attainment: A Multilevel Analysis," *Sociology of Education,* 1991. 64: 251–262; Gary Solon, Marianne Page, and Greg J. Duncan, "Correlations Between Neighboring Children and Their Subsequent Educational Attainment," *Review of Economics and Statistics,* 2000. 82: 383–393.

47. Jeanne Brooks-Gunn, Greg Duncan, Pamela Klebanove, and Naomi Sealand, "Do Neighborhoods Influence Child and Adolescent Development?" *American Journal of Sociology,* 1993. 99: 353–395.

48. Jonathan Kozol, *Savage Inequalities: Children in America's Schools* (New York: Crown Publishers Inc., 1991).

49. Vincent Roscigno, Donald Tomaskovic-Devey, and Martha Crowley, "Education and the Inequalities of Place," *Social Forces,* 2006. 84: 2121–2145.

50. Karl L. Alexander, Scott Holupka, and Aaron M. Pallas, "Social Background and Academic Determinates of Two-year Versus Four-year College Attendance: Evidence from Two Cohorts a Decade Apart," *American Journal of Education,* 1987. 96: 56–80; Robert Haveman and Timothy Smeeding, "The Role of Higher Education in Social Mobility," *Opportunity in America,* 16 (2):125–150, http://www.futureofchildren.org (accessed February 9, 2007).

51. Susan M. Dynarski, "Does Aid Matter? Measuring the Effect of Student Aid on College Attendance and Completion," *The American Economic Review,* 2003. 93: 279–288.

52. Ilana Fried, "Governor Preys on Weak Student Clout," *The Daily Bruin,* February 6, 2004, www.dailybruin.ucla.edu; "Editorial: Accountability, Reason Needed in Funding Debate," *Kansas State Collegian,* October 28, 2004, http://collegian.ksu.edu (accessed November 12, 2008).

53. Gary Solon, "Intergenerational Income Mobility in the United States," *The American Economic Review,* 1992. 82: 393–408; David J. Zimmerman, "Regression Toward Mediocrity in Economic Stature," *American Economic Review,* 1992. 82: 409–429.

54. Jan O. Jonsson, David B. Grusky, Matthew Di Carlo, Reinhard Pollak, and Mary C. Brinton, "Microclass Mobility: Social Reproduction in Four Countries," *The American Journal of Sociology,* 2009. 114(4): 977–1036.

55. Mary Corcoran, "Rags to Rags: Poverty and Mobility in the United States," *Annual Review of Sociology,* 1995. 1995. 21: 237–267.

56. Kingsley Davis and Wilbert E. Moore, "Some Principles of Stratification," *American Sociological Review,* 1944. 10: 242–249.

57. Salary.com, "Salary Wizard," http://swz.salary.com/salarywizard/layouthtmls/swzl_compresult_national_LG12000003.html (accessed June 18, 2008).

58. *Forbes.com,* "The Celebrity 100," http://www.forbes.com/lists/2009/53/celebrity-09_LeBron-James_IIOW.html.

59. Melvin Tumin, "On Inequality," *American Sociological Review,* 1963. 28: 19–26.

60. Jenny M. Stuber, "Talk Of Class: The Discursive Repertoires of White Working and Upper Middle Class College Students," *Journal of Contemporary Ethnography,* 2006. 35: 285–318.

61. Kathryn Edin and Laura Lein, "Stratification Processes: Women, Work, and Wages: Work, Welfare, and Single Mothers' Economic Survival Strategies," *American Sociological Review,* 1997. 62: 253–266.

62. Salary.com, "Salary Wizard," http://swz.salary.com/salarywizard/layouthtmls/swzl_compresult_national_HC07000025.html (accessed June 17, 2008).

63. Salary.com, "Salary Wizard," http://www.cbsalary.com/national-salary-chart.aspx?specialty5Food1Fast1Food1Cook&cty5&sid5&kw5Food&jn5jn035&edu5&tid563803 (accessed June 17, 2008).

64. Harvard Law Review, "Dethroning the Welfare Queen: The Rhetoric of Reform," *Harvard Law Review,* 1994. 107: 2013–2030.

65. Ibid.

66. Kathryn Edin and Laura Lein, "Stratification Processes: Women, Work, and Wages: Work, Welfare, and Single Mothers' Economic Survival Strategies," *American Sociological Review,* 1997. 62: 253–266.

67. U.S. Department of Labor, Bureau of Labor Statistics 2006, "Current Population Survey (CPS)," http://www.bls.gov/cps/minwage2006.htm (accessed March 25, 2007).

68. International Revenue Service, "2009 Tax Table," http://www.irs.gov/pub/irs-pdf/i1040tt.pdf.

69. GasPriceWatch.com, "Gasoline Tax Rates by State," http://www.gaspricewatch.com/usgastaxes.asp.

70. SocialSecurityOnline, "Social Security & Medicare Tax Rates," http://www.ssa.gov/OACT/ProgData/taxRates.html.

GLOBAL STRATIFICATION

From Chapter 8 of *THINK Sociology 2011*. John D. Carl. Copyright © by Pearson Education. Published by Prentice Hall. All rights reserved.

GLOBAL STRATIFICATION

The

real challenge of development is that there is a group of countries at the bottom that are falling behind, and often falling apart.

The countries at the bottom coexist with the 21st-century, but their reality is the 14th-century: civil war, plague, ignorance. They are concentrated in Africa and Central Asia, with a scattering elsewhere. Even during the 1990s, in retrospect, the golden decade between the end of the Cold War and 9/11, incomes in this group declined by 5 percent. We must learn to turn the familiar numbers upside down: a total of five billion people who are already prosperous, or at least on the track to be so, and one billion who are stuck at the bottom.

This problem matters, and not just to the billion people who are living and dying in the 14th-century conditions. It matters to us. The 21st-century world of material comfort, global travel, and economic interdependence will become increasingly vulnerable to these large islands of chaos. And it matters now. As the bottom billion diverges from an increasingly sophisticated world economy, integration will become harder, not easier. . . .

All societies used to be poor. Most are now lifting out of it; why are others stuck? The answer is traps. Poverty is not intrinsically a trap, otherwise we would all still be poor. Think, for a moment, of development as chutes and ladders. In the modern world of globalization, there are some fabulous ladders; most societies are using them. But there are also some chutes, and some societies have hit them. The countries at the bottom are an unlucky minority, but they are stuck.[1]

Wealth and Poverty *in the* World

In *The Bottom Billion: Why the Poorest Countries Are Failing and What Can Be Done about It,* economist Paul Collier investigates global stratification, particularly as it applies to the poorest people on the planet.

With approximately 6 billion people on the planet, the "bottom billion" people live in conditions that are intensely difficult and unbelievable. Many in these countries live without access to clean water and/or sewage. Most find themselves living in the midst of civil war and armed conflict. Still others become victims to the very governments that are supposed to be protecting them. Today in the world, the top 5 billion seem to be improving, so it is fair to say that most of the world, while still poor, is getting richer. However, it is the bottom billion that remain behind, failing to benefit from the global marketplace and technologies that seem to be lifting so many others from their poverty. This leads to extremes on both ends of the spectrum. In this chapter, we investigate these issues.

get the topic: WHAT IS GLOBAL STRATIFICATION?

> **GLOBAL STRATIFICATION** is the categorization of countries based on objective criteria, such as wealth, power, and prestige, which highlight social patterns and inequality throughout the world.

Global Stratification

Nearly 3 billion people, or half of the world's population, live on less than two dollars a day.[2] In the United States, that salary wouldn't be enough for someone to afford a gallon of gas. Although poverty exists in the United States and countries all around the world, the widest gap in social inequality is not within nations, but between them. Thus, when you look at the standard of living in a wealthy country, such as the United States, and compare it to a poorer nation, such as Chad, you see great disparity in the way people live. **Global stratification** categorizes countries based on objective criteria, such as wealth, power, and prestige, which highlight social patterns and inequality throughout the world.

POPULATION AND GEOGRAPHIC AREA

When comparing nations and regions, size matters. In particular, factors such as population and geographic size can determine a country's use of and access to natural resources and talented people. However, large populations and large land area do not always go hand in hand. Consider the staggering population differences between Russia and Bangladesh. Russia is the world's largest country in geographic area, but ranks 10th in population size. Bangladesh, on the other hand, is the seventh largest country in terms of population and ranks 94th in geographic area. Why the disparity? Population is not always distributed evenly. For example, Russia

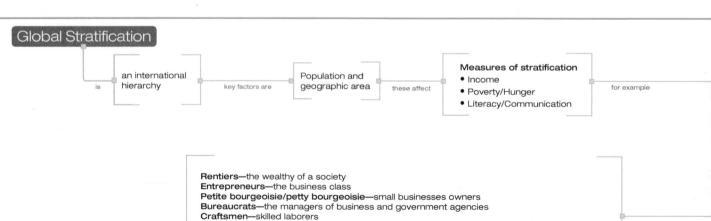

Global Stratification **is** an international hierarchy — **key factors are** — Population and geographic area — **these affect** — Measures of stratification
• Income
• Poverty/Hunger
• Literacy/Communication — **for example**

Rentiers—the wealthy of a society
Entrepreneurs—the business class
Petite bourgeoisie/petty bourgeoisie—small businesses owners
Bureaucrats—the managers of business and government agencies
Craftsmen—skilled laborers
Semiskilled manual workers—workers with limited training that may work in factories
Unskilled workers—the lowest class; unorganized group who often perform manual labor jobs that are often unpleasant and sometimes dangerous

The average annual income of Norway is 624 times higher than that of the average annual income of Burundi. This clearly illustrates one component of global stratification: The gulf between the richest countries and the poorest countries is extremely wide.

Gross National Income Per Capita in 2008

Top 10 Countries

1.	Norway	$87,340
2.	Luxembourg	$69,390
3.	Denmark	$58,800
4.	Switzerland	$55,510
5.	Sweden	$50,910
6.	Ireland	$49,770
7.	The Netherlands	$49,340
8.	United States	$47,930
9.	Finland	$47,600
10.	United Kingdom	$46,040

Bottom 10 Countries

199.	Guinea	$350
200.	Niger	$330
201.	Sierra Leone	$320
202.	Eritrea	$300
203.	Ethiopia	$280
204.	Malawi	$280
205.	Guinea-Bissau	$250
206.	Liberia	$170
207.	Congo, D. R.	$150
208.	Burundi	$140

©Tim Wilkes Studio/Corbis; Tim Ridley ©Dorling Kindersley

Source: The World Bank, "GNI per capita, Atlas method (current US$)," *http://data.worldbank.org/indicator/NY.GNP.PCAP.CD*

includes Siberia, which is a vast, desolate region with very few people. In Bangladesh, the measure of population density provides insight into life there. The cities are overcrowded with small housing units that lack the infrastructure to provide regular electricity and acceptable sanitation standards or access to clean water.[3]

Geography also plays a role in who remains in the bottom billion. According to Collier, the majority of the bottom billion are landlocked and surrounded by neighboring countries that are also poor and experience frequent intervals of armed conflict, which makes climbing out of poverty difficult.[4]

INCOME

To determine a country's per-capita income, you must divide the country's total gross income by the number of people in that country and assume it is equally distributed, which, of course, it is not. However, the per-capita income can provide interesting comparisons. Look at the top and bottom income-producing countries in this graphic. Most of the top 10 income-producing countries are located in Europe, while most of the bottom income-producing countries are located in Africa. Most of the bottom billion live in Africa and central Asia.[5]

Generally speaking, the wealthiest citizens in the United States enjoy a greater share of the total income of the country than do their affluent counterparts in other rich nations. Furthermore, taxation policies allow these people to keep more of their wealth than might be the case in other places in the world. Generally, tax burdens are lowest in the United States in comparison with other developed countries.[6]

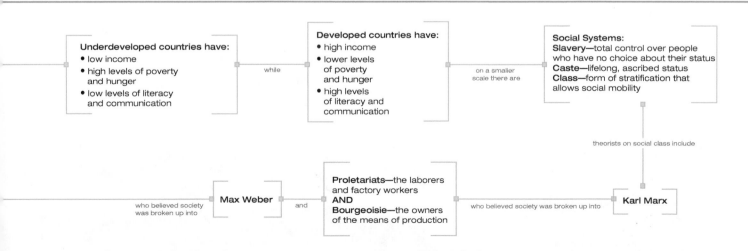

Underdeveloped countries have:
- low income
- high levels of poverty and hunger
- low levels of literacy and communication

while

Developed countries have:
- high income
- lower levels of poverty and hunger
- high levels of literacy and communication

on a smaller scale there are

Social Systems:
Slavery—total control over people who have no choice about their status
Caste—lifelong, ascribed status
Class—form of stratification that allows social mobility

theorists on social class include

who believed society was broken up into

Max Weber

and

Proletariats—the laborers and factory workers
AND
Bourgeoisie—the owners of the means of production

who believed society was broken up into

Karl Marx

MEASURES OF STRATIFICATION IN UNDERDEVELOPED NATIONS

Underdeveloped nations are countries that are relatively poor and may or may not be in the process of becoming industrialized. The United Nations aids the least developed countries on a basis of three criteria: a country must have a low gross national income; its population must meet health and education criteria; and factors like population size and remoteness determine need.

Developing countries are those in the process of becoming industrialized. However, issues like poverty and hunger still affect these countries as they grow.

Poverty and Hunger

According to international stratification measures, sub-Saharan Africa is the most disadvantaged region of the world. This region has the highest rates of childhood death, hunger, and people living on less than one dollar a day. Sub-Saharan Africa also has the lowest rates of sanitation, which leads to higher rates of illness and death.[7]

Disadvantaged regions illustrate disparity between wealthy countries and poor ones. For example, 1 in every 16 women in these poor countries dies during childbirth, whereas only 1 in 2,800 women dies during childbirth in rich countries.[8]

But if poverty were a trap from which people could not arise, then all countries would be poor, because at one time, each country was poor. Collier suggests that four "traps" keep some countries poor while allowing other countries to climb out of the bottom billion. The traps include:

- Conflict: The presence of frequent civil wars and coups keeps a country from being able to climb out of poverty.
- Natural resource trap: The presence of natural resources can actually lead a country to more poverty, especially if their resources are exported and the profits are not used to improve the country.
- Landlocked with non-beneficial neighbors: Even countries like Uganda, which has copious natural resources and relative stability, can still have problems with entering the global market if they do not have ports and they're surrounded by other impoverished countries.
- Bad governance: Many of those who live in the bottom billion live in countries with a long history of bad governance. Leaders often protect the interests of the few, without reinvestment of wealth to help the many. Such bad policy results in continued poverty.[9]

MAKE CONNECTIONS

Access to Communication and Literacy

Think about different media and electronic communication forms that you use every day, such as e-mail, texting, and cell phones. You may be surprised to learn that much of the world doesn't have the same access to these communication devices as you do. These figures show selected countries' access to cell phones, personal computers, and the Internet, as well as their literacy rates.

People living in underdeveloped countries without the ability to read or write are often forced to take unskilled, labor-intensive jobs and work long hours to help support their families. As a college student in the United States, you probably can't imagine living under these conditions. But for many around the world, other options aren't available.

>>> ACTIVITY Spend a day without using any type of communication device. This means no cell phones, computers, books, magazines, televisions, radios, journals, etc. After spending a day without using a communication device, think about your experience. What did you spend your day doing? How did you feel? Bored? Appreciative? Peaceful? How do you think your life would be different without these items?

Source: Data from World Factbook.

Cellular Phones per 1000 People

Japan	871
France	774
United States	728
Pakistan	320
Haiti	45
Malawi	32
Burundi	18
Ethiopia	5

©Christopher Jones/Shutterstock

Personal Computers and Internet Users per 1000 People

United States	633
Japan	502
France	413
Haiti	61
Pakistan	13.1
Malawi	3.77
Burundi	3.5
Ethiopia	1.6

©Jossnat Shutterstock

Residents Over 15 Who Can Read and Write per 1000 People

United States	990
France	990
Japan	990
Malawi	627
Burundi	593
Haiti	529
Pakistan	499
Ethiopia	427

©Dimitry Shironosov/Shutterstock; ©C Squared Studios/PhotoDisc/Getty Images

MEASURES OF STRATIFICATION IN DEVELOPED NATIONS

Developed countries, like the United States, have a well-educated population, regular elections, abundant industry, and free enterprise. Germany, Japan, and Great Britain are all developed nations and share many of the same characteristics, both socially and politically, with the United States.

Poverty

When studying global stratification, it's important to consider international comparisons of poverty among developed countries. Before you look at the numbers, you'll need to understand that U.S. dollars are the standard measure of income and that poverty definitions vary depending on the country. As a result, our data use half of the median income of the country as the definition for poverty, which allows for a more standardized comparison between nations. The table below shows how the poverty rates of 10 developed countries stack up against one another.

Not only are you likely to find relatively high percentages of poverty in the United States, these percentages are still the highest even after welfare programs are taken into account. In part, this is because the United States has the greatest gap between the rich and poor of all high-income countries. What does that mean? Of the top 21 nations in the world by income, the distance between the top 10 percent of incomes and the bottom 10 percent is greatest in the United States. In the 1990s, for example, after taxes and other benefits, the incomes of the top 10 percent were 5.64 times higher than incomes in the bottom 10 percent in the United States. This means that if the bottom 10 percent in the United States made an average salary of $20,000, then the average salary for the top 10 percent would be 5.64 times more, which would be $112,800. This ratio represents the greatest distance between rich and poor in the industrialized world. The country with the lowest ratio was Sweden, where the wealthy earn 2.59 times more than their poor counterparts.[10] Therefore, if the bottom 10 percent of incomes in Sweden averaged $20,000, then the average for the top 10 percent would be $51,800.

Poverty Rates of 10 Developed Countries				
Country	Percentage of Total Population in Poverty (Rank)	Percentage of Children in Poverty	Percentage of Children in Poverty After Taxes and Welfare Transfers	Percentage of Elderly in Poverty
United States	17 (1)	26.6	21.9	24.7
Ireland	16.5 (2)	24.9	15.7	35.8
United Kingdom	12.4 (3)	25.4	15.4	20.5
Canada	11.4 (4)	22.8	14.9	5.9
Denmark	9.2 (5)	11.8	2.4	6.6
Germany	8.3 (6)	18.2	10.2	10.1
France	8 (7)	27.7	7.5	9.8
Belgium	8 (8)	16.7	7.7	16.4
Austria	7.7 (9)	17.7	10.2	13.7
Switzerland	7.6 (10)	7.8	6.8	18.4

Source: Data from Lawrence Mishel, Jared Bernstein, and Heidi Shierholz, *State of Working America 2008/2009* (Ithaca, New York: Cornell University Press, 2009).

QUALITY OF LIFE

Which world city offers the best quality of life? A 2009 study shows that Vienna, Austria, is the best city in which to live, replacing Zurich, Switzerland. Baghdad, Iraq, remains at the bottom of the list. You might be surprised to note that the top 20 does not include a U.S. city. Honolulu, Hawaii, ranks highest among American cities, coming in at 29th.[11]

This year's ranking uses a set of common criteria to compare cities. These include electricity and water supply, telephone and mail services, public transport, automobile traffic, and the variety of flights from local airports. So, how might one measure the quality of life in one country or another? Many use measures of health and longevity to determine a location's quality of life. Common sense follows that the quality of life must be highest in the countries in which fewer babies die and people live longer.

The small Asian nation of Macau boasts the highest life expectancy (84.33 years), while Singapore has the lowest infant mortality rate at 2.3 deaths per 1,000 babies born. Meanwhile, Angola has 80 times the infant mortality rate of Singapore with 184.4 deaths per 1,000 births.[12] These numbers tell only part of the story about a country's quality of life.

Sociologists and economists look for variables to make international comparisons.[13] The United Nations creates the Human Development Index as a way to rank and compare nations. The index takes into account three basic features that create the breeding ground for healthy and happy human development. Those components include a long and healthy life, education, and a decent standard of living. The 2010 report ranks 182 different nations. Norway comes in first, followed closely by Australia, Iceland, and Canada. Six of the top 10 countries are in Europe, while the United States ranks 13th. Niger, where some of the bottom billion live, ranks last.[14]

These rankings are similar to other international rankings. Kai Müller created a list ranking world economic and social development using a variety of measures.[15] Although income is important, it is only one of many factors to be considered. Other measures include access to telephones, televisions, and newspapers. Structural measures such as the country's debt ratio and the gross national product are also included. Finally, infant mortality, life expectancy, and literacy round out a series of items. By this method, Müller proposes that Norway is the best country in the world to live and the Congo is the worst. The United States does not rank in the top 20.

Ong and Mitchell provide a slightly different list.[16] By ranking 21 different countries on four criteria—economic, social, cultural, and political—they provide another view of how to compare countries. These rankings showed that some countries might rank very high in one area, but lower in others. For example, the United States ranks first in cultural components, but 14th in social aspects and eighth over all. Ong and Mitchell combined all the tested areas to compile their quality of life list.

Efforts to compare and contrast different countries and measure quality of life often involve subjectivity. If you were to develop a schema, what variables would you use? Although the amount of air pollution is easy to measure, determining that one country has more beauty than another is very much open to debate.

Social Systems

All societies have systems by which they stratify, or rank, their members and by which those people receive the rewards of that society. Sociologists often characterize populations using wealth, power, and prestige as the basis of stratification systems. The three most common **social stratification systems** are slavery, caste, and class systems.

SLAVERY

Slavery refers to the total control over people who have no choice about their status. You may believe that slavery is a thing of the past; however, estimates suggest that there are as many as 27 million slaves worldwide.[17] That number equals the total populations of Iowa, Missouri, Illinois, and Indiana combined.[18] This staggering figure is probably difficult to believe, but the important thing to remember is that today's slavery hardly resembles the slavery of the past.

In *Disposable People*, Kevin Bales points out that there is more slavery in the world now than ever before.[19] **Under old systems, slavery was legal and slaves were never paid. Today, slavery is illegal,** but today's slaves may be bound by debts, rarely earning enough to repay them.

Slaves were once expensive; in 1850, a field slave sold for approximately $1,000 to $1,800, or about $50,000 to $100,000 today. Because of their expense, slave owners viewed slaves as long-term investments. The high price and required care of slaves meant annual profits might have been only 5 percent of the initial investment. Today, slaves are much cheaper and virtually disposable. Once "used up," they are sent away, which increases profits. Bales estimates annual profits from modern slaves are about 50 percent of the initial investment. Owners of modern slaves are in a win-win situation; they have a continuous supply of labor and stand to make a huge profit.

Bales suggests that several new factors drive slavery today. Apart from rapid population growth and extreme poverty, weak governments, worldwide desire for cheap labor, and capital investment can support slavery. Weak governments may tolerate bribery or cannot control the behavior of local warlords and wealthy landowners. With rapid population growth, potential slaves abound. Many countries use their abundant labor supply to attract foreign investment, which can easily lead to the potential consequence of slavery.

Contrary to popular belief, slavery is not a thing of the past. Modern-day slaves exist in countries all around the world. How do you think the slaves in these pictures differ?

Source: "Returning from the Cotton Fields in South Carolina," ca. 1860, stereograph by Barbard, negative number 47843. © Collection of The New-York Historical Society.

"Returning from the Cotton Fields in South Carolina," ca. 1860, stereograph by Barbard, negative number 47843. ©Collection of The New-York Historical Society; ©Shou Sheng/epa/Corbis

Forms of Slavery

Modern slavery takes three forms: chattel, debt bondage, and contract slavery. **Chattel slavery** is the closest to the old form of slavery because a slave is considered property. A chattel slave may work a lifetime for one family. Future generations will also become servants of the "owner."

Debt bondage occurs when a debtor is housed and fed by his or her lender. Debtors' wages are never enough to cover their expenses or debt. This form of slavery usually begins when someone borrows money in order to repay a different debt. The borrower then promises to work for the lender. Of course, the pay for the work is never high enough to decrease the debt while covering expenses for food and shelter. Thus, the person remains enslaved by his or her debt.

Contract slavery occurs when a person signs a work contract, receiving food and shelter by an employer. This is different from debt bondage because it is conducted under the façade of a legal contract. Workers sign contracts to work, often in another country, and the employer transports them to a job site. The employer also feeds and houses them. Employers deduct these costs, which often exceed the pay, and use fear and intimidation to keep workers from running away.[20]

CASTE SYSTEMS

Caste systems are similar to slave systems in that people have an ascribed status. However, unlike most slave systems, people are born into a caste system and the status is lifelong. Within **caste systems**, a person's position may be a position of power and privilege or of disadvantage, but in either case, his or her place is permanently fixed. Caste systems do not allow people to move up and down the ranks, as the U.S. class system does. A person who is born to the lower class in a caste system will never have an opportunity to move vertically and join a higher class.

SOCIAL STRATIFICATION SYSTEMS are slavery, caste, and class systems.

SLAVERY is the total control over people who have no choice about their status.

CHATTEL SLAVERY is a form of slavery in which a slave is considered property.

DEBT BONDAGE is a form of slavery in which someone borrows money in order to repay a different debt, and works off the new debt.

CONTRACT SLAVERY is a form of slavery in which a person signs a work contract, receiving food and shelter from an employer, but is threatened when he or she tries to leave the contract.

CASTE SYSTEMS are systems in which a person's position may be a position of power and privilege or of disadvantage, but in either case, his or her place is permanently fixed.

Perhaps the most widely known caste system is in India. Although now illegal, the caste system remains a powerful force in India today, especially in rural areas where the system decides whom you marry, what job you have, and where you live.[21] The *Go Global* box on the next page provides a brief overview of the Indian caste system.

CLASS SYSTEMS

Unlike caste systems, class systems represent a form of stratification that allows social mobility. Sociologically speaking, there is no "official" agreement on the number and kind of social classes within the United States. In fact, the United States prides itself on being a class-less society. In 2000, 20 percent of Americans thought they would make it into the top one percent of income earners during their lifetime. Another 19 percent thought they were already there, which means that a whopping 39 percent of people thought they could become rich or were already rich.[22] However, it's unlikely for a person from the lower class to climb too high on the social class ladder. If a person does manage to climb vertically, he or she goes up only a few rungs.

THINK SOCIOLOGICALLY

Slaves in Tulsa

Could slavery still exist in the United States? According to Kevin Bales, the United States imports about 50,000 slaves every year.[23] In February 2002, the midwestern city of Tulsa, Oklahoma, was shocked to learn that they had slaves working in their midst. Workers recruited by a Mumbai (formerly Bombay), India, company signed contracts for labor overseas. Many paid the company a fee of more than $2,000 to gain employment in the United States. Workers flew to Tulsa where they worked as welders for an industrial equipment manufacturer.

These workers left their country with a promise of long-term residency, good jobs, and high pay. What they found was signifi-

cantly different. The group lived in barracks on the factory grounds, sometimes working 12-hour days and earning as little as $2.31 an hour. The company's food was substandard, and many workers had to share beds because of a shortage of space. In the dormitory, a sign stated that workers who left the grounds could be sent back to India and that armed guards patrolled the grounds. Many also reported verbal threats and deliberate intimidation to keep the workers on the property.

After the workers were found, the U.S. firm claimed they were not involved in slavery and any fault was that of the Mumbai labor company. The corporation claimed that the workers were merely temporary trainees, so they did not deserve the mini-

mum wage or other employment benefits. The courts saw the matter differently and found the company guilty of exploiting the workers through human trafficking. A fine of $1.2 million provided about $20,000 for each worker.

After the case broke, many local community members helped the Indian workers find legitimate jobs, and immigration hearings allowed them to legally stay in the country. With new jobs, the workers now seek to make their American dream come true. This case has a happy ending, largely because it occurred in a country with a free press and a strong government. Unfortunately, most contract labor occurs in countries without either of these two important components.[24]

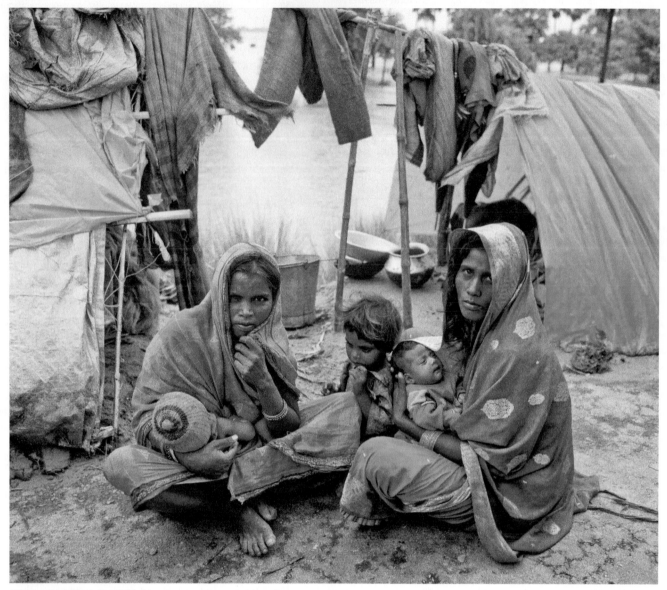

©Gideon Mendel for Action Aid/Corbis

The Indian Caste System

India is often referred to as a land of castes. India's caste system has five different levels: *Brahmin, Kshatriya, Vaishya, Shudra,* and the *Harijans (Dalit)*. Citizens are born, live, work, marry, and die within their caste. There is no room for movement up (or down) in the hierarchy of the system, and social order dictates that castes remain separate.

In India, *Brahmins* make up the priestly and scholar caste. *Kshatriyas* represent the warrior caste. These were the political leaders who protected the people and fought wars. Merchants, artists, and traders come from the *Vaishya* caste. Mohandas Gandhi,

∧
∧ *Dalits*, sometimes called "Untouchables," are at
∧ the bottom of the Indian caste system. **Although there are laws to protect *Dalits*' rights, much of Indian society still treats them poorly.**

the "father" of the Indian nation, was part of this caste. The Shudra caste represents the country's workers, such as laborers from the fields and cities. The lowest caste is "the untouchables." Gandhi referred to them as the *Harijans*, or the people of God. Today,

they are known as the *Dalit*. They were seen as unsanitary people who performed the lowest form of labor in the society. In such a system, Harijans were socially unacceptable. They lived outside the mainstream, remaining separate from the rest of society.[25]

Karl Marx on Class Systems

Remember that Karl Marx suggested that the class structure of western Europe consisted of two groups: the proletariat and the bourgeoisie.[26] The *proletariat* were the poor factory workers, while the *bourgeoisie* were the owners of the factories. They hired the workers and paid them as little as possible to help increase their own personal wealth.

Marx pointed out that **workers willingly participate in their own exploitation because they have a false consciousness,** or a false sense of their place in society.

Marx suggested that the owners foster this ideology in order to maintain their powerful position in society. Remember the 39 percent of U.S. citizens who were certain they could reach the top 1 percent? These citizens illustrate what Marx would call an ideology of false consciousness.[27] It's statistically impossible for all these people to fit into the top 1 percent.

Only through class consciousness, or an understanding of your position in the social system, will workers unite and eventually benefit from their labor. The bourgeoisie promote false consciousness to further exploit workers for their own benefits. The only way to break through this façade is for the exploited to unite and take power from the dominant class.[28]

According to Marx, class consciousness begins the revolution, whereby the proletariats usher in a perfect society and everyone shares resources equally.[29]

Max Weber's Class System

Max Weber expanded Marx's idea that property is the sole determinant of social class. Weber's class system included class, status, and party. When Weber discusses class, he refers to wealth, much as did Marx. However, a person's position in society is not only determined by one factor for Weber. Status or prestige includes people with fame or important positions.[30] Status matters in society. Party refers to the political dimension of power. Power elevates a person's importance, which in turn causes his or her rank to rise.

Weber's class system is more detailed than that of Marx. For Weber, **rentiers** are the wealthy of a society. They come from a privileged class who own businesses and land; they are the people with "old money." **Entrepreneurs** are the business class. They, too, may have a great deal of money, but they must work to maintain their place. They are "new money." These two groups make up social classes similar to what Marx called the bourgeoisie.

The **petite bourgeoisie** own small businesses. The people who own your local convenience store might be considered members of this group. Although they own a business and have power similar to the entrepreneurs, they do not have the same wealth, prestige, or power.

Bureaucrats make up a separate class. They are the managers of business and government agencies. They own nothing, but they have great power in the corporate structure. Corporations hire accountants and middle managers to oversee their business, often with high salaries. Weber felt this class would grow along with society's tendency to become more bureaucratic.

Next, Weber turns to laborers, which he divides into three groups. **Craftsmen** are skilled laborers such as plumbers or carpenters. They hold a special position in society because they have a needed skill that is unusual. **Semiskilled manual workers** have some training and may work in factories. I was a semiskilled worker when I was a bicycle mechanic. Without

RENTIERS are the wealthy members of a society, as identified by Weber.

ENTREPRENEURS are the business class, as identified by Weber.

PETITE BOURGEOISIE are small business owners in Weber's class system.

BUREAUCRATS are managers of business and government agencies.

CRAFTSMEN are the skilled laborers such as plumbers or carpenters.

SEMISKILLED MANUAL WORKERS are the workers who have some training and may work in factories.

UNSKILLED WORKERS are the lowest class, consisting of people who frequently perform manual labor jobs that are often unpleasant and sometimes dangerous.

©Stephen Coburn/Shutterstock

∧∧∧ **Weber divides the laborer group into three classes: craftsmen, semiskilled manual workers, and unskilled workers.** Craftsmen, like the carpenter shown here, have unique skills that make them valuable members of society.

at least a little training, I would not have been able to perform well at my job. **Unskilled workers** make up the lowest class. They are an unorganized group who frequently perform manual labor jobs that are often unpleasant and sometimes dangerous. When I fried chicken at a fast-food restaurant, I was doing unskilled labor. The work was hot, dirty, and dangerous because the hot grease often burned me. However, it didn't take any specialized skills for me to fry chicken for the Colonel. Unskilled labor pays the least and frequently places the heaviest physical demands on the worker.

For Weber, people have differing levels of wealth, power, and prestige. Those with the most of all three components make up the upper class or the rentier. While Weber links social class to job type, class is also related to these other factors. Marx, on the other hand, primarily links social class to business ownership. **You are either a worker or an owner. Only through class consciousness will the poor rise up and create an egalitarian society.**[31]

Now you have a solid framework for discussing global stratification and its effect on citizens around the world. Why do you think global stratification occurs?

think sociologically: WHAT ARE THE THEORIES BEHIND GLOBAL STRATIFICATION?

Global Stratification—No Longer a Third World

When I was in college, I was told the world was divided into three parts: the first, second, and third world. The first was the United States and our allies; the second consisted of the Soviet Union and their allies; and the third world was made up of everyone else. Of course, this system bases its divisions on political and economic ideologies. Sociologists rarely use this system today. First, it's ethnocentric, inferring that the West should be first. Second, the "second world" no longer exists; the Soviet bloc has largely dissolved. Finally, lumping more than 60 percent of the world into one category hardly provides an accurate description of the included countries.

IMMANUEL WALLERSTEIN'S WORLD SYSTEMS THEORY

Immanuel Wallerstein's world systems theory presents an alternative view to the old system.[32] Wallerstein suggests that the world is divided by its connection to economic power. At the center of the system are core nations who are constantly trying to expand their capitalist markets, decrease costs, and increase profits. The economies of these nations influence the actions of others.

All core nations eventually run out of natural resources and they constantly seek expansion, so they find ways to enter *periphery* countries. Historically, core nations made colonies of periphery nations in order to expand their influence. For example, Great Britain used its Indian colony to expand its market and gain access to resources. Indians had to buy salt from British companies because it was illegal to make and use sea salt. Today, core nations do not have colonies. Instead, they use multinational corporations, trade treaties, and other techniques in order to access the periphery's resources and send the wealth home. Periphery nations hope to generate wealth through the sale of their human and natural resources. Countries like Nigeria and Iraq are periphery nations because of rich natural resources such as natural gas and petroleum.[33]

If a periphery nation can use some of its wealth to build its own economy, a small group of elites will arise who build industries of their own. In that way, the country becomes *semi-periphery*. Semi-periphery nations are developing nations who use their raw materials to manufacture goods that can be sold to the core nations while keeping more wealth in the country. Investments in future services and industries mean that the country has the chance to move closer to the core. Countries like Brazil and South Korea are semi-periphery nations.

External nations are underdeveloped nations that have little interaction with the rest of the system. These countries would generally be included in Collier's bottom billion. These countries often have few national resources and little ability to attract investment or interest from core nations. Burundi, Chad, and many of the nations of sub-Saharan Africa fit this category. From the perspective of the world system, they exercise little or no impact on other countries.

World Systems Theory

Semi-Periphery   **Core**   **External**

Periphery

<<< Wallerstein's theory suggests that **core nations are at the center of the "universe, and affect all surrounding nations.** External nations, however, are unaffected because they are seen as having little to offer to the rest of the system."

Source: Adapted from Wallerstein's The Modern World Systems, 1974.

NEOCOLONIALISM

Most of North and South America was once under colonial rule of a European power. Over time, however, it became difficult to stop rebellions, so many countries gave up their colonies.[34]

Michael Harrington says countries now use **neocolonialism**, a process in which powerful nations use loans and economic power to maintain control over poor nations.[35] Through loans for food, weapons, and development, poor nations become dependent upon rich ones. Once in debt, poor countries often cannot repay the loans and so agree to alliances, sale of natural resources, and trade agreements that primarily benefit the wealthy nation.[36]

Extending the ideas of neocolonialism, some propose that wealthy nations now use multinational corporations to control poorer nations.[37] Multinational corporations offer jobs, income, and potential riches to poor nations. The corporations benefit because they may gain tax-free status, weak environmental oversight, or some other concession that may not be in the best interest of the country. These corporations may create working conditions that lead to the enslavement of the native people. Bales points out that although company executives might not want to be involved in slave labor, they probably want to maximize their profits. Think back to the Tulsa slave case. After the slave workers were discovered, the company left Tulsa and moved to the Middle East.[38]

> **NEOCOLONIALISM** is a process in which powerful nations use loans and economic power to maintain control over poor nations.
>
> **GLOBALIZATION** is a complex process by which the world and its international economy are becoming more and more intertwined.
>
> **BRAIN DRAIN** occurs when the best talent leaves poor countries and thereby provides an even greater advantage to wealthy countries.

Through multinational corporations, wealthy countries continue to control weaker ones with corporate investment. This may, in effect, lead countries to engage in a "race to the bottom." To win the prize of foreign investment, they cut local regulations and salaries. This "race" can lead to wage and gender discrimination and less worker safety.[39] Of course, there is another side of this: they provide jobs and incomes to workers with few other opportunities.

GLOBALIZATION

Globalization involves a complex process by which the world and its international economy are becoming more and more intertwined. Globalization connects the world through business, travel, immigration, education, health issues, and production of goods.[40] Workers in China put together shoes made from leather tanned in Brazil, with rubber soles from Indonesia. Frequently, rich countries recruit the best and brightest from poor countries to become doctors, scientists, and other vital occupations. This is **brain drain**—the best talent leaves poor countries and thereby provides an even greater advantage to wealthy countries.[41]

©Michael S. Yamashita/Corbis

∧
∧
∧ **Multinational corporations** often set up factories in countries where they can **pay lower wages to the workers in order to make a heftier profit.** The Chinese women in this image are workers in the Reebok shoe factory.

Some argue that an aspect of globalization is exploitation. Others suggest that it is the only hope for poor nations. As the world becomes more interconnected, are the various cultures around the world becoming more similar or less so? Those who believe cultures are becoming more similar suggest that the world's cultures are adopting more Western values. On the other hand, some suggest that globalization will have the opposite effect on culture as local groups work hard to maintain their own religions, customs, and languages.[41] With this theory, globalization polarizes the world and creates gaps between groups. These theorists predict more war, terrorism, and unrest as Western countries continue to expand. Do you share these views on globalization?

Functionalism

In 1997, Jared Diamond published *Guns, Germs, and Steel*, a book explaining how the Western world advanced so quickly while other regions of the world were left behind. Diamond points out that there was a time in history when all people on the Earth were poor and lived in underdeveloped conditions. So why did some regions advance while other locations did not?[42]

Simply put, the fastest developing regions of the world had the climate, geography, and available natural resources that allowed them to advance. Other areas did not possess such advantages. The dawn of agrarian civilization occurred in the Fertile Crescent, an area that is present-day Iraq. The land in this region is fertile and easy to traverse. Most mountain ranges are passable, allowing for travel and trade amongst peoples. Goods and knowledge were shared throughout the region. With knowledge, civilizations became more organized, complex, and powerful because they used information to improve the quality of life. This led to greater power and wealth, which allowed for more trade.[43]

Tribal groups in Europe competed for many centuries, which built up the region's military know-how. Internal struggles led to alliances between groups, increasing trade and the transmission of information.[44]

Tribes in Europe and Asia were able to domesticate a number of animals and plants. Herders raised sheep and goats while farmers grew grains. Domesticated animals and plants allowed groups to amass more wealth and knowledge, which left people available to specialize as teachers, craftsmen, artists, and warriors.[45]

Unlike Europe and Asia, native animals that live in sub-Saharan Africa defy domestication. Although native plants can be eaten, the Africans did not have the long grains that grew in the Fertile Crescent. Additionally, because the diverse African landscape ranges from desert to mountainous, regions could not share the same technologies used to grow food.[46] Jacques Diouf explains that countries cannot develop as their people starve and live in poverty.

These countries must produce high food quantities to sustain the increasing demands of development. **Only when a country resolves its hunger issues can it begin to prosper from the benefits of global markets.**[47]

An abundance of food allowed Europeans to thrive. They created cities where they faced another hardship, which actually helped them more than hurt them. Open sewers spread disease and created high death rates for city dwellers. Consequently, their descendents developed a strong immune system and were genetically hardier than their ancestors.[48]

Those areas with great natural resources were able to acquire the power needed to function as the wealthy power brokers in the world. Remember that functionalism studies how social structures affect society. Diamond believes that Europeans and Asians advanced because they had abundant resources, strong military skills, set trade routes, and strengthened immune systems. Geographic areas with fewer advantages developed at a much slower place.[49]

With this theory, globalization polarizes the world and creates gaps between groups. These theorists predict more war, terrorism, and unrest as Western countries continue to expand. Do you share these views on globalization?

Conflict Theory

Vilfredo Pareto provides a theory of how elite members of society reach positions of power and strive to maintain it.[50] Society seeks equilibrium, and changes in one part of society cause changes in another. This creates a circulation of the elite as the old elite members are replaced by the new.

Gaetano Mosca suggests that elites seek greater power for themselves and are unlikely to give it up.[51] Leaders use position to garnish benefits for themselves and their supporters. Consider Latin America. Cardosa and Faletto acknowledge that Latin American nations follow this pattern of leadership circulation.[52] They also discuss dependency on foreign investment and exploitation by more powerful countries. Aristocrats seek short-term rewards over long-term benefits to all. These landowners control natural resources, and they influence the government to gain more wealth. This is called the dependency theory.

It's interesting that Cardosa, one of the founding thinkers of dependency theory, led his country toward free market capitalism when he was elected President of Brazil in 1995. Cardosa, originally a financial minister, said he was an "accidental president," becoming president because he was working to quell Brazilian economic woes.[53] His two presidential terms stabilized and expanded the country's economy by increasing social programs to help the poor while opening the Brazilian economy to become a free market.[54]

Nations are dependent because they have no other choice but to borrow from wealthy places, but this often leaves them with nothing. However, the next elected president was a man who ran against Cardosa in the previous presidential elections. President Lula stood in opposition to many of Cardosa's reforms, illustrating Pareto's circulation of elites.

Pareto suggests two primary elites: lions and foxes. Lions are leaders who are patriotic, unified, and support the status quo. People choose lion leaders because they use force to create order in times of chaos. An example of this was the military dictatorship that overran Brazil prior to Cardosa's election. Cardosa was a new type of leader. Pareto refers to this type as a fox. Foxes are clever and rational with new ideas that try to change the status quo. Societies ebb and flow between leadership run by foxes or lions, balancing the desire for change with the need for stability.

Symbolic Interactionism

After World War II, European nations sought ways to prevent future wars and work together. Representatives created treaties that led to what is now called the European Union. This union grew from simple trade agreements between six countries to a group of more than 20 nations.[55]

Taken as a whole, the countries that make up the European Union have a weak central government to handle trade disputes, a common currency (the euro), and an increasingly common language (English). Although it does not have military forces, there are NATO (North Atlantic Treaty Organization) troops, which often come from a variety of European Union countries and the United States.

As a single nation, the European Union would be the richest country in the world. Business flourishes in the European Union, and many of the world's largest banks and corporations are centered here. The European Union also produces more scientific discoveries than any other country. Its inhabitants enjoy the highest standards of living, and Europeans work fewer hours, receiving more paid vacation time than U.S. workers.[56] The European Union shows how unity and cooperation can drastically benefit a region and its people. In fact, T.R. Reid suggests that the European Union residents see themselves as "Europeans," not members of a single nation. Reid suggests this collaboration could lead to a United States of Europe, becoming the world's greatest superpower.[57]

Working Hours Around the World

	Annual hours	Average per week
Mexico	1848	35.5
United States	1824	35.1
Australia	1816	34.9
Japan	1789	34.4
Canada	1751	33.7
United Kingdom	1669	32.1
Italy	1585	30.5
Sweden	1585	30.5
Germany	1443	27.8
France	1441	27.7
Norway	1363	26.2

<<< **On average, Europeans work fewer hours and have more paid vacation time than Americans.** Why do you think U.S. workers spend more hours at the office?

©Jose Elias da Silva Neto/Shutterstock; ©vgstudio/Shutterstock

Source: Data from the Organisation for Economic Co-operation and Development (OECD) 2005.

WRAP YOUR MIND AROUND THE THEORY

Dorling Kindersley ©Jamie Marshall

Life exists where there are reliable water sources and vegetation. **How does geography influence stratification?**

FUNCTIONALISM

From a functionalist point of view, global stratification is a result of geographic conditions. Diamond states that the European countries thrived because they had natural resources that helped those societies function more efficiently. Domesticated plants and animals, trade with others, warfare, and disease all played a role in increasing the advantages for western Europe. These were the result of how societies used their resources to function more efficiently.

CONFLICT THEORY

Conflict theorists believe that an imbalance of power between the elites and the poor in a country causes stratification. Pareto argues that even among elites, power changes occur. He also believes that in times of struggle, lions will rule the day, but eventually foxes will take charge. Mosca states that leaders will do what they can to remain in power because it's in their best interests to do so. How do these power struggles between the elites affect those who are not in power?

WHAT CAUSES GLOBAL STRATIFICATION BETWEEN COUNTRIES AROUND THE WORLD?

SYMBOLIC INTERACTIONISM

Symbolic interactionists look at how language and symbolic events influence society. When the European Union was created, an entirely new notion entered the lives of Europeans. T.R. Reid suggests that Europeans increasingly identify themselves as members of Europe, not the specific country in which they were born. What impact might this have on the long-term influence of that region of the world over others?

Eric Lansner/Black Star

©Jon Hicks/Corbis

Richer, more powerful countries exploit poor countries and their workers. Can development come through exploitation?

Core nations have markets with local goods, but many of the cheaper items are made by slave labor in foreign countries. **How do people in developed nations justify their high standards of living at the expense of others?**

discover sociology in action: WHAT IS BEING DONE TO ASSIST UNDERDEVELOPED COUNTRIES?

Social Policy: Foreign Aid

Some students in my classes are angered by the issue of foreign aid. They oppose paying huge amounts of tax dollars to help other nations when there are people in our own country in need.

"Helping the world's poor is a strategic priority and a moral imperative. Economic development, responsible governance, and individual liberty are intimately connected. **The United States must promote development programs that achieve measurable results—rewarding reforms, encouraging transparency, and improving people's lives."**[58]

The stated purpose of foreign aid by the United States is that it aids the strategic interests and safety of the nation while also promoting development and freedom in the underdeveloped parts of the world. This makes aid good for both parties involved. Collier studies the impact of foreign aid on the poorest nations. Certainly, there are well-documented examples of foreign aid falling into the hands of armed bandits and corrupt politicians. Without denying these events, Collier shows that despite these problems, foreign aid has historically been a net gain for the bottom billion.[59] This is why many of the richest countries agree to provide 0.7 percent of their gross national product in foreign aid. Only the top five countries meet their agreed goal. The United States ranks last on this list, giving the smallest percentage of its wealth. However, in total dollars, the United States ranks first.[60]

An example may help you understand the difference. If you and I both donate $100 to charity but you only have $100 and I have $1,000, who has actually given more? We both gave the same amount, but you gave 100 percent of your wealth, while I gave only 10 percent. The United States, while giving the most money, gives the least as a percentage of the total wealth of the nation. In order for the United States to donate its proper percentage, it would need to increase its contribution about six times the amount of money currently applied to foreign aid.

ACTIVITIES

1. Check the tags of your clothes. Where were your shoes made? Do you have any assurances that slaves were not used to make your apparel?
2. Discuss with a partner what can be done to help the bottom billion. Search the term "bottom billion" and read the articles you find. Discuss possible solutions.
3. Visit www.antislavery.org. Surf the Web site. Write a paragraph explaining what you learned about modern slavery, how to stop human trafficking, and the lengths people are going to stop slavery.

From Classroom to Community } Becoming a Peace Corps Volunteer

After Caroline graduated from college, she didn't know what to do. She knew she could get a job, but somehow she wanted to see the world and use her college education to improve the lives of others. She felt her double major of sociology and Spanish could be a great asset. After joining the Peace Corps, she took a 27-month appointment in Ecuador.

"I never really thought I could live in another country, but I fell in love with Ecuador and the people there."

Caroline learned just how hospitable and welcoming the Ecuadorian people could be. "The families I encountered were so close and loving. At night, it was normal to see families crowded around a television watching soap operas with one another."

"I also learned firsthand that rules about privacy are very different in Ecuador."

"As a teenager growing up in my house, it was customary for me to hole myself up in my room surfing the Web or talking on the phone, but it's considered very rude in Ecuador! The wildlife and scenery was amazing, but my favorite experience was spending time with the kids at school."

While there, Caroline taught English in a local school and provided education to women regarding health issues. In her free time, she traveled throughout the country and taught the local children how to play soccer. "The children were so eager to learn from me. Once they got over their initial shyness, we became good friends." Once back in the United States she found a job working with abused children.

"I love my life, but a part of me will always be in Ecuador."

WHAT IS GLOBAL STRATIFICATION?

the categorization of countries based on objective criteria, such as wealth, power, and prestige, which highlight social patterns and inequality throughout the world

WHAT ARE THE THEORIES BEHIND GLOBAL STRATIFICATION?

world systems theory: the world is divided by its connection to economic power

neocolonialism: powerful nations use loans and economic power to maintain control over poor nations

globalization: a complex process by which the world and its international economy are becoming more and more intertwined; some argue that an aspect of globalization is exploitation. Others suggest that it is the only hope for poor nations.

WHAT IS BEING DONE TO ASSIST UNDERDEVELOPED COUNTRIES?

foreign aid, Peace Corps

©Joseph Project—Malawi/Alamy ©Michael S. Yamashita/Corbis Dorling Kindersley ©Jamie Marshall

get the topic: WHAT IS GLOBAL STRATIFICATION?

Global Stratification
Social Systems

Global Stratification—
    No Longer a Third World
Functionalism

Conflict Theory
Symbolic Interactionism
Social Policy: Foreign Aid

Theory

FUNCTIONALISM

- global stratification is a result of geographic conditions
- Diamond: European countries thrived because they had natural resources that helped those societies function more efficiently

CONFLICT THEORY

- an imbalance of power between the elites and the poor in a country causes stratification

- Pareto: even among elites, power changes occur; in times of struggle, lions will rule the day, but eventually foxes will take charge
- Mosca: leaders will do what they can to remain in power because it's in their best interests to do so

SYMBOLIC INTERACTIONISM

- looks at how language and symbolic events influence society
- Reid: Europeans increasingly identify themselves as members of Europe, not the specific country in which they were born

Key Terms

global stratification	debt bondage	petite bourgeoisie	unskilled workers
social stratification	contract slavery	bureaucrats	neocolonialism
systems	caste systems	craftsmen	globalization
slavery	rentiers	semiskilled manual	brain drain
chattel slavery	entrepreneurs	workers	

MY SEARCH LAB

1. *The Uses of Global Poverty: How Economic Inequality Benefits the West.* Reprinted by permission of Daina Stukuls Eglitis.

INTRODUCTION

In this essay, Eglitis uses the functionalist perspective to analyze global stratification, listing 11 functions of global poverty to explain why global poverty exists and persists.

DISCUSSION QUESTIONS

1. Explain the 11 functions of global poverty. Do you agree that global poverty benefits the West?

2. According to the author, as long as global poverty remains useful to the West, steps will not be taken to eradicate poverty. Do you agree or disagree with this statement?

2. *The Global Economy and the Privileged Class* by Robert Perrucci and Earl Wysong. Reprinted from The New Class Society: Goodbye American Dream?, (2003), by permission of Rowman and Littlefield Publishers, Inc.

INTRODUCTION

This article examines how the global economy has affected millions of workers in the United States and functioned to increase the distance between the "haves" and "have-nots" in society.

DISCUSSION QUESTIONS

1. How did business leaders in the 1970s and 1980s justify the massive plant closings and site flight to developing countries?
2. Explain how corporate downsizing has created a protected privileged class and an insecure working class.

THE THINKSPOT

The ascribed status, of the Badi people in Nepal is that of "untouchables." As a result, many of the women in this minority group have been doomed to a life of prostitution and work in the sex trade for generations. Go to the ThinkSpot to learn about one 14-year-old girl and her family and how her contribution of just a few dollars a day from her work as a prostitute is helping feed this impoverished family and why her situation is not likely to change.

Many people think that slavery is a thing of the past, but that is not the case. Go to the ThinkSpot to find out what delegates at the United Nations are discussing with relation to the modern-day slave trade in Africa.

Sample Test Questions

These multiple-choice questions are similar to those found in the test bank that accompanies this textbook.

1. Which of the following is characterized by the worker becoming property of an owner?
   a. False consciousness
   b. Contract slavery
   c. Chattel slavery
   d. Debt bondage

2. Which citizens illustrate what Marx would call an ideology of false consciousness?
   a. Petite bourgeoisie
   b. Bourgeoisie
   c. Proletariat
   d. Rentiers

3. Which of the following is *not* one of the three labor groups described by Weber?
   a. Craftsmen
   b. Bureaucrats
   c. Unskilled workers
   d. Semiskilled manual workers

4. Immanuel Wallerstein's theory suggests that the world is divided by its connection to
   a. military power.
   b. economic power.
   c. political stability.
   d. technological innovation.

5. Nations that have wealth, technology, and strong military power, which they use to influence the entire global system, are called
   a. core nations.
   b. external nations.
   c. periphery nations.
   d. semi-periphery nations.

ESSAY

1. What are the positive and negative effects that globalization can have on underdeveloped nations?
2. What are the differences between a caste system and a slave system?
3. According to Marx, how does the bourgeoisie successfully promote false consciousness?

4. What characteristics does Weber use to determine social class?
5. How could wealthy nations be using multinational corporations to control poorer nations?

WHERE TO START YOUR RESEARCH PAPER

For more information on the Asian Development Bank, go to http://www.adb.org/

For more information about how people are ending child prostitution, child pornography, and trafficking of children for sexual purposes, go to http://www.ecpat.net

To learn more about international anti-slavery movements, go to http://www.freetheslaves.net/NETCOMMUNITY/Page.aspx?pid=183&srcid=-2

For interactive maps and data to visualize world issues, go to http://www.gapminder.org/

For more information on *Guns, Germs, and Steel* and a view of the ideas contained there, go to http://www.pbs.org/gunsgermssteel/

To learn more about human trafficking, go to http://www.humantrafficking.org/

To learn more about the International Monetary Fund, go to http://www.imf.org/

For information regarding health, crime, and standards of living, go to http://www.nationmaster.com/

To learn more about the OECD and read its reports on economic development throughout the world, go to http://www.oecd.org/

For information on population problems, refugees, and reports on world poverty, go to http://www.worldbank.com/

For more information regarding the use of cheap and child labor in the garment industry, go to http://www.sweatshopwatch.org/

To learn more about international aid funded by the U.S. government, go to http://www.usaid.gov/

For U.S. statistics and reports, go to the U.S. Census Bureau Web site http://www.census.gov/

For more information about the World Food program, go to http://www.wfp.org/

For more information about World Health Organization and data, including issues of hunger, HIV, and other statistics from a variety of countries throughout the world, go to http://www.who.int/en/

ANSWERS: 1. c; 2. c; 3. b; 4. b; 5. a

Endnotes

1. Paul Collier, The Bottom Billion: Why the poorest countries are failing and what can be done about it (New York: Oxford University Press, 2007).

2. "The Millennium Development Goals Report: Statistical Annex 2006," *United Nations*, http://unstats.un.org/unsd/mdg/Default.aspx (accessed April 23, 2007).

3. "UNFPA Annual Report 2007," United Nations Population Fund, at http://www.unfpa.org/ (accessed July 8, 2007).

4. Paul Collier, The Bottom Billion: Why the poorest countries are failing and what can be done about it. (New York: Oxford University Press, 2007).

5. Ibid.

6. "OECD Country Taxes as Share of GDP 2000," *Tax Policy Center*, Washington D.C., 2003, http://www.taxpolicycenter.org/TaxFacts/tfdb/TFTemplate.cfm?topic2id5 95 (accessed April 21, 2006).

7. "The Millennium Development Goals Report: Statistical Annex 2006," *United Nations*, at http://unstats.un.org/unsd/mdg/Default.aspx (accessed April 23, 2007).

8. "Mortality," World Health Organization, http://www.who.int/en/ (accessed May 10, 2007).

9. Paul Collier, The Bottom Billion: Why the poorest countries are failing and what can be done about it (New York: Oxford University Press, 2007).

10. Timothy M. Smeeding and Lee Rainwater, *Comparing Living Standards Across Nations: Real Incomes at the Top, the Bottom, and the Middle*, Social Policy Research Centre, December 2002, http://www.sprc.unsw.edu.au/dp/DP120.pdf.

11. City Mayors, "German-speaking cities occupy top places in best-cities survey," http://www.citymayors.com/features/quality_survey.html (accessed April 30, 2010).

12. Eric Neumayer, "HIV/AIDS and Cross-National Convergence in Life Expectancy," *Population and Development Review*, 2004. 30(4): 727–742.

13. Daniel J. Slottje, "Measuring the Quality of Life Across Countries," *Review of Economics and Statistics*, 1991. 73(4): 684–693.

14. Human Development Reports, "Composite indices — HDI and beyond," http://hdr.undp.org/en/statistics/indices/ (accessed April 30, 2010).

15. Kai Müller, "The World Economic and Social Development Ranking List," *Global Policy Forum*, March 18, 2000, http://www.glosbalpolicy.org/nations/kaiswork.htm.

16. Li Lian Ong and Jason D. Mitchell, "Professors and Hamburgers: An International Comparison of Real Academic Salaries," *Applied Economics*, 2000. 32: 869–876.

17. Kevin Bales, *Disposable People: New Slavery in the Global Economy* (Berkeley, CA: University of California Press, 1999).

18. "American Fact Finder: Population," *Census.gov*, http://www.census.gov (accessed April 15, 2007).

19. Kevin Bales, *Disposable People: New Slavery in the Global Economy* (Berkeley, CA: University of California Press, 1999).

20. Ibid.

21. John Henry Hutton, *Caste in India, its Nature, Function and Origin,* 4th ed (Oxford: Oxford University Press, 1963).

22. David K. Shipler, *The Working Poor: Invisible in America* (New York: Vintage Books, 2005).

23. Kevin Bales, *Disposable People: New Slavery in the Global Economy* (Berkeley, CA: University of California Press, 1999).

24. Michael Overall, "Workers Allege Abuses," *Tulsa World,* February 1, 2002, p. 1; Michael Overall, "Workers Free to Leave, Pickle Testifies," *Tulsa World,* September 11, 2003, p. A1; Michael Overall, "Verdict: Guilty: Judgment Exceeds $1 Million," *Tulsa World,* May 25, 2006, p. A1.

25. John Henry Hutton, *Caste in India: Its Nature, Function, and Origins* (Bombay: Oxford University Press, 1963); Narendra Jadhav, *Untouchables: My Family's Triumphant Journey Out of the Caste System in Modern India* (New York: Scribner, 2007).

26. Karl Marx, "Economic and Philosophic Manuscripts of 1844," *Readings in Social Theory: The Classical Tradition to Post-Modernism*, 4th edition, edited by James Farganis (New York: McGraw-Hill, 1844/2004), 37–42; Karl Marx, *Capital: A Critique of Political Economy*, Vol. 1. (New York: International Publishers, 1867/1967); Karl Marx and Friedrich Engels, "Manifesto of this Communist Party," *Readings in Social Theory: The Classical Tradition to Post-Modernism*, 4th edition, edited by James Farganis (New York: McGraw-Hill, 1845/2004), 26–36.

27. David K. Shipler, *The Working Poor: Invisible in America* (New York: Vintage Books, 2005).

28. Karl Marx, "Economic and Philosophic Manuscripts of 1844," *Readings in Social Theory: The Classical Tradition to Post-Modernism*, 4th edition, edited by James Farganis (New York: McGraw-Hill, 1844/2004), 37–42; Karl Marx, *Capital: A Critique of Political Economy*, Vol. 1. (New York: International Publishers, 1867/1967); Karl Marx and Friedrich Engels, "Manifesto of this Communist Party," *Readings in Social Theory: The Classical Tradition to Post-Modernism*, 4th edition, edited by James Farganis (New York: McGraw-Hill, 1845/2004), 26–36.

29. Ibid.

30. Max Weber, *Economy and Society: An Outline of Interpretive Sociology, 2 Volumes,* edited by Guether Rothe and Claus Wittich (Berkeley: University of California Press, 1978); Max Weber, "Class, Status, Party," *Readings in Social Theory: The Classical Tradition to Post-Modernism,* 4th edition, edited by James Farganis (New York: McGraw-Hill, 1978/2004), 116–126.

31. Karl Marx, "Economic and Philosophic Manuscripts of 1844," *Readings in Social Theory: The Classical Tradition to Post-Modernism*, 4th edition, edited by James Farganis (New York: McGraw-Hill, 1844/2004), 37–42; Karl Marx, *Capital: A Critique of Political Economy*, Vol. 1. (New York: International Publishers, 1867/1967); Karl Marx and Friedrich Engels, "Manifesto of this Communist Party," *Readings in Social Theory: The Classical Tradition to Post-Modernism*, 4th edition, edited by James Farganis (New York: McGraw-Hill, 1845/2004), 26–36.

32. Immanuel Wallerstein, *The Modern World System: Capitalist Agriculture and the Origins of the European World-Economy in the Sixteenth Century* (New York: Academic Press, 1974); Immanuel Wallerstein, *The Capitalist World-Economy* (New York: Cambridge University Press, 1979).

33. "Nigeria," The World Factbook, https://www.cia.gov/library/publications/the-world-factbook/print/ni.html (accessed July 24, 2008); "Iraq," The World Factbook, at https://www.cia.gov/library/publications/the-world-factbook/print/iz.html (accessed July 24, 2008).

34. Richard H. Robbins, *Talking Points on Global Issues: A Reader* (Boston: Allyn and Bacon, 2004); Richard H. Robbins, *Global Problems and the Culture of Capitalism* (Boston: Allyn and Bacon, 1999).

35. Michael Harrington, *The Vast Majority: The Journey to the World's Poor* (New York: Simon and Schuster, 1977).

36. Margaret Hanson and James J. Hentz, "Neocolonialism and Neoliberalism in South Africa and Zambia," *Political Science Quarterly*, 1999. 114(3): 479–502.

37. Leslie Sklair, "The Transnational Capitalist Class and Global Politics: Deconstructing the Corporate State Connection," *International Political Science Review*, 2002. 23(2): 159–174.

38. Michael Overall, "Workers Allege Abuses," *Tulsa World,* February 1, 2002, p. 1; Michael Overall, "Workers Free to Leave, Pickle Testifies," *Tulsa World,* September 11, 2003, p. A1; Michael Overall, "Verdict: Guilty: Judgment Exceeds $1 Million," *Tulsa World,* May 25, 2006, p. A1.

39. Günseli Berik, Yan van der Meulen Rodgers, and Joseph E. Zveglich, "International Trade and Gender Wage Discrimination, Evidence from East Asia," *Review of Development Economics,* 2004. 8(2): 237–254.

40. A. Aboubakr Badawi, "The Social Dimension of Globalization and Health," *Perspectives on Global Development and Technology,* 2004. 3(1–2): 73–90.

41. Jonathan Crush, "The Global Raiders: Nationalism, Globalization and the South African Brain Drain," *Journal of International Affairs,* 2002. 56(1): 147–173.

42. Jared Diamond, *Guns, Germs, and Steel: The Fates of Human Societies* (New York, NY: W.W. Norton & Company, 1997).

43. Ibid.

44. Ibid.

45. Ibid.

46. Ibid.

47. Jacques Diouf, "Food Security and the Challenge of the MDGs," *UN Chronicle,* No. 4, 2007.

48. Ibid.

49. Jared Diamond, *Guns, Germs, and Steel: The Fates of Human Societies* (New York, NY: W. W. Norton & Company, 1997).

50. Vilfredo Pareto, *The Rise and Fall of Elites: An Application of Social Theory.* (New Brunswick, NJ: Transaction Publishers, 1901/2000).

51. Gaetano Mosca, *The Ruling Class.* (New York: McGraw-Hill, 1895/1965).

52. Fernando Cardosa and Enzo Faletto, *Dependency and Development in Latin America,* Translated by Marjory Mattingly Urquidi (Berkeley, CA: University of California Press, 1979).

53. Fernando Enrique Cardosa, *The Accidental President of Brazil: A Memoir* (New York: Public Affairs, 2006).

54. Caspar W. Weinberger, "Brazil in 1997," *Forbes,* July 28, 1997. 160(2): 37.

55. T.R. Reid, *The United States of Europe: The New Superpower and the End of American Supremacy* (New York: Penguin, 2004).

56. Jeremy Rifkin, *The European Dream* (New York: Jeremy P. Tarcher/Penguin, 2005).

57. T.R. Reid, *The United States of Europe: The New Superpower and the End of American Supremacy* (New York: Penguin, 2004).

58. USAID, "New Frontiers in U.S. Foreign Aid," http://www.usaid.gov/policy/ (accessed July 9, 2007).

59. Paul Collier, The Bottom Billion: Why the poorest countries are failing and what can be done about it. (New York: Oxford University Press, 2007).

60. Organization for Economic Co-operation and Development, "Official Development Assistance," OECD, http://www.oecd.org/ (accessed April 30, 2010).

RACE AND ETHNIC STRATIFICATION

RACE AND ETHNIC
STRATIFICATION

The

traditional concept of race as a biological fact is a myth. I am going to show you that nearly everything you think you know about race is a social construct. You don't have to be a racist to be wrong about what race is. That doesn't make the effects of a belief in race any less damaging, or the situation any less perilous. Most Americans still believe in the concept of race the way they believe in the law of gravity—they believe in it without even knowing what it is they believe in.

If you ask the average American college student if biological races exist, most will say yes. In my classes, when I asked students to identify their own race, most couldn't be any more specific than a vague catchall like "white." They couldn't say what the criteria are for membership in a racial group, and most believed that black, white, Asian, Hispanic, and American Indian are biological races. Some of them thought that every country has produced its own biological race.

A few students responded that races had existed since the beginning of time. I asked them if they meant 1980, when the universe began for them, or 19 billion years ago, in the big bang? Several had to think about it for a while. Some thought races had existed since the break up of Pangaea, around 300 million years ago—which would have been tough, since humans didn't evolve until 299,999,999 years later! Some thought that races were formed in antiquity at about the time of the fall of the Tower of Babel, as described in the biblical book of Genesis. (Surprisingly, none related the curse of Ham as a source of modern human races.)

Many also believed that race determined intelligence quotient (IQ) and other personality traits, as well as sexual characteristics, athletic ability, and disease predisposition, following commonly held social stereotypes. When asked about intellect, most cited the superior performance of their Asian classmates in their science courses. When asked about sex, most stated that blacks had higher sexual appetites and larger genitals. When asked about athletic ability they again cited the superior performance of black basketball and football players. Finally, almost all agreed that sickle cell anemia, Tay-Sachs, and cystic fibrosis were all proof positive of the existence of racially defined disease.

These examples clearly show the prevailing ignorance that our society exhibits about the definitions and significance of human biological diversity, and its confusion with socially constructed races. In this book, I'm going to show you in detail how to tell the difference and why it's so important.[1]

Is It a Question *of* Color?

For three ground-breaking seasons, comedian Dave Chappelle used sketch comedy to satirize and lampoon the complex issue of race on *Chappelle's Show*. One skit called "Racial Draft" was set up like a mock NFL draft featuring various racial groups drafting multiracial celebrities—for instance, African Americans selected Tiger Woods while the Asian Americans drafted the Wu-Tang Clan. Through humor, this skit perfectly illustrates the arbitrary categories society uses—like skin color—to define race.

According to recent science, race is purely a social construct, not a biological one. And yet, people, especially in the United States, often seek to define race solely on biological terms. Often, this mentality is instilled at an early age because we often teach children, who don't even have a concept of race, about racial differences that do not really exist. In fact, I remember when my daughter came home from preschool and said, "Ho is different than me."

Ho was a Chinese boy whose father worked with me at the university. "What makes you say that?" I asked. "The kids in the class say he's different because his skin looks different than mine," she said. "Does that make him different?" I asked. "I don't know, but I still like to play with him at recess." What is telling about this story is that it took two years of schooling and outside influence to teach a 5-year-old about racial differences. This is how we learn about race: from our social experiences.

RACE

is defined as → socially-constructed divisions of people based on certain physical characteristics

differs from → **Ethnicity**—a shared cultural heritage

can be broken down into groups →

Majority Groups—groups that have greater representation in a society and hold significant power and privilege

OR

Minority Groups—groups that hold less power than the dominant group

OR

Dominant Groups—groups who discriminate because they have greater power

Education
- schools continue to be unofficially segregated
- poorly funded schools are in poor neighborhoods where the majority of black and Hispanic students live

and

Income—minorities are the most likely to live in poverty

get the topic: WHAT IS THE DIFFERENCE BETWEEN RACE AND ETHNICITY?

If you walk down any street, you'll find people with different hair-styles, fashion sense, age, body type, and, yes, skin color. Because society feels it's necessary to separate groups of people, **race**, then, refers to the divisions of people based on certain physical characteristics. The most prominent of these characteristics is skin color. Examples of racial categories include white, black, and Asian. **Ethnicity** is a little more complex than race because it usually involves grouping people who share a common cultural, linguistic, or ancestral heritage. Thus, there are many more ethnic than racial categories. Examples of several ethnic groups in the United States include those from Arab, German, Italian, Jewish, Hispanic, Cuban, or Puerto Rican backgrounds.

As the population grows and intermarriage becomes more common, though, traits like skin

RACE is the division of people based on certain physical characteristics.

ETHNICITY is the classification of people who share a common cultural, linguistic, or ancestral heritage.

color may no longer be such a simple signifier of identity. However, sociological questions regarding race are not fixated on the differences in looks. Instead, these questions focus on how society interprets those differences in appearance and how those interpretations affect an individual's opportunities.

CENSUS DEFINITIONS

The reality show *Survivor* has been known to engage in some interesting social experiments. One of the more controversial—and compelling—seasons of the program involved splitting each tribe by race. The tribal divisions implied that there are only four racial categories: white, black, Asian, and Latino. To highlight the fact that race is a social construct rather than

©Chad Ehlers/Alamy

<<< Although these women differ in physical appearance, they are the same biologically. **Why does society see fit to place them in separate racial categories?**

---

differences can sometimes lead to

Racism—discrimination based on a person's race

Genocide—the attempt to destroy or exterminate a people based on their race and/or ethnicity

Hate Groups—groups motivated by the hatred of other racial groups

Ethnic Cleansing—refers to persecution through imprisonment, expulsion, or murder of members of an ethnic minority to achieve ethnic homogeneity in a majority controlled territory.

conflicts are rooted in a number of factors, such as

Conquest—when one group uses its superior military to dominate another

Annexation—the incorporation of one territory into another

Voluntary Immigration—the willing movement of people from one society to another

Involuntary Immigration—the forced movement of people from one society to another

Migrant Superordination—occurs when a more powerful group enters an area and conquers the natives

Indigenous Superordination—occurs when immigrant groups become subordinate to the dominant group

relations are best understood by studying differences between

stratifies our society by

• our need for a scapegoat, or another group on which to blame our problems
• segregation—the separation of people on the basis of their race, gender, or ethnicity

which are caused by

Prejudice—negative attitudes about an entire category of people

AND

Discrimination—the unfair treatment of people based on a prejudice

Race by Percentage in the United States in 2006

| Native Hawaiian/
Pacific Islander
0.2% | Black/African
American
12.8% | White
(non–Hispanic)
65.6% |

Persons reporting
two or more races
1.7%

| American Indian/
Alaskan Native
1.0% | Asian
4.4% | Hispanic or Latino
(of any race)
15.4% |

©Comstock/Getty Images

Source: Data from U.S. Census Bureau, "State and Country Quickfacts," 2008.

a biological one, we can point to the U.S. Census Bureau's six definitions of race.[2] The survey choices are white, black or African American, American Indian or Alaska Native, Asian, Native Hawaiian or other Pacific Islander, or some other race. The format of this survey allows individuals to declare their own race and even provides one option for people who feel they do fit into any of the previous categories. The graphic above provides data that the U.S. Census Bureau collected in 2008 regarding race in the United States. You may be surprised to see that the Census Bureau does not classify Hispanic or Latino as a race. While Hispanics are in the photograph, they represent an ethnic group and not a race.

MAJORITY AND MINORITY GROUPS

The graphic above also provides a snapshot of race in the United States. For example, non-Hispanic whites make up about two out of every three Americans. This makes them a **majority group** that not only has a greater numerical representation in society but also holds significant power and privilege. A **minority group** refers to any group that holds less power than the majority group. Louis Wirth assigns minority group status to people who are singled out for unequal treatment. Minorities also have a collective sense of being discriminated against.[3]

In some societies, having a numeric majority isn't necessarily required to wield power or practice discrimination. Sociologists refer to those who are more powerful as the **dominant group** because even if

they may not have greater numbers, they have greater power. Apartheid, the five-decade–long system of oppression in South Africa, showed how a group's numbers don't necessarily reflect a group's political and economic power. In the era of apartheid, whites, who were the numeric minority of South Africa, passed laws that forced blacks, the native majority, into segregated housing, took away their right to vote, and generally treated them like second-class citizens.[4] The idea of a minority group ruling over a majority population, especially in periphery nations is almost always the direct result of **colonialism**, in which more powerful countries impose their will on weaker nations. More often than not, though, dominant groups tend to also be a country's numeric majority as well.

In the United States, minority populations are on the rise. By 2050, the percentage of the population that is Hispanic or Asian is expected to nearly double. Meanwhile, the percentage of whites will decline by approximately 19 percent. Migration patterns certainly influence these projections. In the future, minority group members will have greater representation in the population.[5]

RACISM

The simplest definition of **racism** is that it refers to discrimination based on a person's race. However, there is more to racism than just discrimination. To truly understand racism, you must recognize that it involves a complex calculus of intergroup privilege, power, and oppression. According to Graves, racism in the United States has relied on three assumptions that often go unchallenged: (1) Races exist; (2) Each race has distinct genetic differences; (3) Racial inequality is due to those differences. Graves provides five pillars of racist thought that run rampant in the United States.

1. Biological races exist in the human species.
2. Races have genetic differences that determine their intelligence.
3. Races have genetically determined differences that produce unique diseases and cause them to die at different rates.
4. Races have genetically determined sexual appetites and reproductive capacities.
5. Races have genetically determined differences in athletic and musical ability.

An extreme example of racism is the use of **genocide**, the attempt to destroy or exterminate a people based on their race or ethnicity. The most well-known example is the Holocaust during World War II. The Nazis slaughtered millions of Jews, Gypsies, and mentally and physically handicapped people in an attempt to cleanse Europe of people they felt were inferior. Extreme racism is not a thing of the past either. The 2004 film *Hotel Rwanda* depicted the events of 1994, when members of two Rwandan political parties began killing opposition leaders and journalists. Quickly, the violence spread to the rural areas where members of the majority Hutu tribe slaughtered members of the Tutsi tribe. Don Cheadle received an Oscar nomination for his portrayal of Paul Rusesabagina, a hotel manager who heroically saved the lives of nearly 1,300 Rwandans. Demographic data show that gender made little difference in predicting who might survive. Men, women, children, and the elderly were all killed.[6] The idea of racial purity was not just the dominion of Nazi Germany or tribal Rwanda. The history of the United States is stained by similarly horrible acts, including the Trail of Tears,

MAJORITY GROUP is the group that has the largest population in society and holds significant power and privilege.

MINORITY GROUP is a group that has a smaller population and less power than the majority group.

DOMINANT GROUP is the group that has the greatest power, but not necessarily the greatest numbers.

COLONIALISM is the imposition of control over a weak nation by a more powerful country.

RACISM is discrimination based on a person's race.

GENOCIDE is the attempt to destroy or exterminate a people based on their race and/or ethnicity.

HATE GROUPS are organizations that promote hostility or violence toward others based on race and other factors.

Japanese internment camps during World War II, slavery, lynchings, segregation, and Jim Crow laws.

Such behavior has a long history and still continues today. The Southern Poverty Law Center tracks **hate groups** in the United States. These groups are organizations that promote hostility or violence toward others based on race and other factors. They include white supremacists, neo-Nazis, and other groups that advocate hate against immigrants, gays, and other minorities. The center notes that within the United States, there were 888 organized hate groups in 2008, a 48 percent increase since the year 2000.[7]

Hate and racist groups do not always seek to exterminate those they do not like. Sometimes, they purge their society of these people by forcing the minority group to move, while abusing them in the process. Anyone who has studied the Trail of Tears knows that the U.S. government did the same thing to the Cherokee, Chickasaw, Choctaw, Creek, and Seminole tribes before the Civil War. Forcing these people to leave their homelands in the

©Jacques Langevin/Sygma/Corbis

∧
∧ **In 1994, the Hutu tribe discarded the bodies of slaughtered Tutsi tribe**
∧ **members** in mass graves.

CONQUEST is the domination over a group of people by a superior force.

ANNEXATION is the incorporation of one territory into another.

VOLUNTARY IMMIGRATION is the willing movement of people from one society to another.

INVOLUNTARY IMMIGRATION is the forced movement of people from one society to another.

ETHNIC CLEANSING refers to persecution through imprisonment, expulsion, or murder of members of an ethnic minority by a majority to achieve ethnic homogeneity in majority-controlled territory.

MIGRANT SUPERORDINATION is the conquest of a native population by a more powerful group.

INDIGENOUS SUPERORDINATION is the subordination of an immigrant group to a dominant group.

PLURALISTIC MINORITIES are groups that enter into an area voluntarily but seek to maintain their own culture while also integrating into the dominant group.

ASSIMILATIONIST MINORITIES are groups that seek to shed their old ways and integrate themselves into mainstream society.

southeastern United States, the government moved these people to modern-day Oklahoma. This forced relocation resulted in thousands of Native Americans dying on the trail.[8] Such practices are still going on around the world, from Kenya to Iraq, as armed conflicts continue to force the relocation of minority people.[9]

PATTERNS OF INTERACTION

As we've already discussed in reference to genocide and ethnic cleansing, interracial conflict is as old as history itself. But how did all this get started? To better think like sociologists, we need to understand the origins of racial and ethnic stratification.

Conquest and Annexation

Racial and ethnic tension is rooted in a number of factors. The first is **conquest**. When one group uses its superior military to dominate another, it comes in contact with people who have a different culture and often a different physical appearance. During the 16th and 17th centuries, European powers used their superior technology and military strength to colonize Africa and the Americas.[10]

Annexation is the incorporation of one territory into another. Under this system, members of ethnic and racial groups are forced to become members of a new society. For example, when James Gadsden negotiated the purchase of parts of modern-day New Mexico and Arizona from Mexico in 1853, all the people who were already living in those areas became residents of a new country in one day.[11] This annexation brought ethnic tensions as whites moved into the territories and sought ways to control land that Native American and Mexican groups had largely owned. Annexation often leads to tension between groups, as those who are annexed resist the new occupiers.

Immigration

Another pattern that can create racial and ethnic tension is immigration, whether it is voluntary or involuntary. **Voluntary immigration** refers to the willing movement of people from one society to another. Remember, people may choose to migrate for a variety of reasons. However, the countries receiving these people may not always welcome the new immigrants with open arms. The current political weather that hovers over immigration—many of whom are Mexican or Asian—is just as stormy. Some anti-immigrant activists claim "foreigners" who water down U.S. culture with bilingualism and multiculturalism are invading the country. Sometimes, politicians equate immigration with "invasion"—as the conservative pundit Pat Buchanan famously did in 2006. Does such an idea sound like it has racial overtones to you? Why or why not?[12]

Involuntary immigration refers to the forced movement of people from one society to another. Bringing millions of Africans as enslaved people against their will, forcing Native Americans onto reservations, and imprisoning hundreds of thousands of Japanese Americans in detention camps are all examples of involuntary immigration in U.S. history.[13]

Superordination

Regardless of whether the migration is voluntary or involuntary, some predictable patterns of interaction can occur when people come into

▶▶ GO GLOBAL

Ethnic Cleansing
Bosnia

Following the breakup of the former country of Yugoslavia in 1990, the Serbian majority seized control and forced large numbers of minority group members, particularly Bosnian Muslims, or Bosniaks, to leave their lands or face extermination. In 1992, the Serbian army launched an ethnic cleansing campaign against Bosniaks in eastern Bosnia. **Ethnic cleansing** refers to persecution through imprisonment, expulsion, or murder of members of an ethnic minority by a majority to achieve ethnic homogeneity in majority-controlled

territory. Bosniak civilians were rounded up and detained in camps, Bosnian civilians, men and women, were rounded up and detained in separate camps. Many were beaten or killed during capture. The surviving men were sent to concentration camps and the women were sent to detention centers known as rape camps. In July 1995, near the end of the war, the Serbs rounded up and killed an estimated 8,000 Bosniaks in the region of Srebrenica. This act of genocide, known as the Srebrenica Massacre, is the largest mass murder in Europe since World War II.[14] The Serbian and Croatian forces carried out these tactics of torture and murder in the hope of creating ethnically pure states. During this war, armies

used ethnic differences as a justification for thousands of deaths and the forced removal of millions of people from their homes.[15]

These crimes, however, have not gone unnoticed by the rest of the world. In 1995, the International Criminal Tribunal for the former Yugoslavia in the Hague indicted former Bosnian Serb leader Radovan Karadzic. Charged with multiple counts of genocide, war crimes, and crimes against humanity, Karadzic went into hiding for more than 12 years before he was eventually captured in 2008. If convicted, Karadzic could face a possible life sentence for crimes committed during the Bosnian War.[16]

contact with unfamiliar groups. Often people become involved in **migrant superordination**, which occurs when a more powerful group enters an area and conquers the native population. In the 16th century, Spain used military strength to dominate Central and South America and to elevate their own culture above the native culture. In this case, the migrants' status was elevated, or superordinated. The opposite of this is **indigenous superordination**. When arriving immigrants enter the United States today, they are expected to learn English and subordinate their old ways to their new country. In other words, they must become subordinate to the dominant group. For example, in recent years, several states have passed "English Only" laws. These laws run the gamut from nominal statutes that merely declare English to be the "official" state language to laws that limit bilingual education programs in state schools and that curb other non-English government services. The American Civil Liberties Union argues that such laws restrict or cut funding for multilingual programs that some U.S. residents can't do without such as health services, voting assistance, and driver's licensing tests.[17]

These two patterns of interaction are often justified through ethnocentric thinking. Remember, *ethnocentrism* is thinking about or defining another culture on the basis of your own. Generally, the greater the differences, the more negatively groups tend to view each other. At the same time, there is often competition between groups, which becomes more intense when resources are scarce. Consider the migrant pattern to New York City in the early 1900s. Racial and ethnic immigrants divided up the low-income jobs that were available to them. Chinese immigrants might have worked in laundries, while Jewish immigrants sewed clothing, and Italian immigrants

controlled the docks. If you were a member of one of these groups, you could find a job in those industries. But if you were a Chinese immigrant who wanted to make clothing, you were unlikely to be hired. This is because ethnic groups often had differences in power. Once a group has power, it is unlikely to let it go, unless it can somehow expand its market and wealth.[18]

Minorities

When minority groups face superordination, there are a number of ways they can choose to react. **Pluralistic minorities** are generally groups that enter into an area voluntarily. They seek to maintain their own culture, but want to integrate with the dominant group as well. Thus they hope to keep their cultural ties while participating in the political and economic system of the new society. **Assimilationist minorities**, on the other hand, seek to shed their old ways and integrate themselves into society. Groups that most closely resemble the dominant group—either racially or ethnically—are able to do this more easily.

For example, when German immigrants first came to the United States, their culture and language were generally accepted. In the original colonies, German newspapers were printed and German colonists served in the Revolutionary War. However, with the beginning of World War I in 1914 came outright hostility toward almost anything German. My grandfather was born in the United States, but is of German descent. He told me that when World War I began, his father told him to speak only English from that point on. Throughout the United States, laws were passed to forbid teaching subjects in German, and German Americans rapidly gave up their language and culture to show their loyalty to the United States.[19]

Sometimes, groups voluntarily decide to separate themselves from

©Bettmann/Corbis

∧∧∧ **During WWII, nearly 120,000 Japanese Americans,** many of them U.S. citizens, **were forced to relocate to internment camps.**

the dominant group and become **secessionist minorities**. Such a group does not seek assimilation or cultural unification. Instead, it views the dominant group with disdain, believing that it will corrupt its belief system. The Amish of Pennsylvania can be considered an extreme example of a secessionist minority. This group has carved out a lifestyle and culture in which a Swiss German language is common and modern conveniences are rare. They emphasize the importance of family, religion, and a simple lifestyle. Their children are educated at Amish schools and a great deal of their life is exactly as it was 100 years ago. Although some Amish people are increasingly opening themselves up to other businesses besides farming, as well as allowing in a few modern technologies, their community remains secessionist.[20]

Sometimes, minorities react to their subordination through militancy. **Militant minorities** seek to overthrow the existing system that they see as unjust. Often the militant minority is actually a numeric majority and may take the path of violence and war to fight perceived injustice, as was the case in Cuba in 1958 when Fidel Castro overthrew a government that he believed was corrupt.[21] Militants can also be peaceful, as when Mohandas Gandhi led a peaceful revolution that ended in 1947 and ultimately brought about the end of British occupation of India.[22]

Types of Minority Groups

Secessionist Minority

Assimilationist Minority

Strives to remain separate from the majority group

Seeks to integrate into the majority group

Dominant Group

Attempts to change the existing system

Militant Minority

Pluralistic Minority

Maintains individual culture while integrating with the majority group

©Bob Krist/Corbis; ©Morgan Lane Photography/Shutterstock; ©Jozcef Szasz-Fabian/Shutterstock; ©Michael Newman/PhotoEdit; ©Munshi Ahmed/Munshi Ahmed Photography; ©Eduardo Miller/Shutterstock; ©DreamPictures/Blend Images/Corbis

Source: U.S. Census Bureau, Current Population Survey, *2007 Annual Social and Economic Supplement and Statistical Abstract 2000.*

Acceptance—Multiculturalism and Assimilation

Research suggests that racial and ethnic identity is related to four key factors: relative size, power, appearance, and discrimination.[23] These factors also tend to encourage a sense of solidarity among members of a single racial or ethnic group. In a sense, being different from the dominant group holds people together. The reason many minority groups tend to cluster together in neighborhoods is because their differences from the dominant group often lead to discrimination. Furthermore, the shared values of similar people make adjustment easier. Finally, their social capital increases their chances of success. On the other hand, belonging to a group that looks like the dominant group rarely leads to discrimination. Such people often let go of their ethnic heritage because their appearance makes it easier to assimilate into the dominant culture.

This lack of privilege to belong to the dominant group is the reason many minority groups often bond together. This is especially true for new immigrants of color. it is quite common for immigrants to live in neighborhoods where people from similar cultures live together and assert cultural distinction, which are called **ethnic enclaves**, like a Chinatown or Spanish Harlem. Such enclaves assist the new immigrant in making an easier transition into the new culture. An important factor in this assimilation is educational attainment. Recent arguments suggest that second-generation immigrants' educational attainment is a means to move up, but it often requires moving out of the enclave and into mainstream culture.[24]

PREJUDICE VS. DISCRIMINATION

To truly understand the complexity of race relations, it is vital to understand the differences between prejudice and discrimination. **Prejudice** usually refers to negative attitudes about an entire category of people. These prejudices are often reinforced by **stereotypes**: simplified perceptions people have of an entire group, usually based on a false assumption. Although negative stereotypes, such as believing all black people are prone to violence or that all Latinos are illegal immigrants, are absolutely wrongheaded, so-called positive stereotypes can be just as damaging. While you may think you're offering a compliment when you assume your Asian American classmate is a mathematical genius, the problem is that doing so confines that individual to a box that you have constructed in your mind. That is the danger of stereotypes. If we aren't careful, we might allow our prejudices to overtake our common sense.

These attitudes, if left unchecked, may lead to **discrimination**, or the unfair treatment of people based on a prejudice. Essentially, prejudice is an attitude, while discrimination is an action that stems from that attitude. The Jim Crow laws of the past were perpetuated by whites' attitudes toward black people. However, discrimination doesn't always have to be as blatant as the segregated water fountains of the pre–Civil Rights 1950s and 1960s to be insidious. A teacher with a prejudice against African Americans may treat black students with contempt in the classroom. Similarly, a teacher who assumes the Asian American student in class is a naturally studious person could overlook the fact that the student might actually need help.

> Essentially, prejudice is an attitude, while discrimination is an action that stems from that attitude.

Many of these prejudices and stereotypes are so prevalent, it's difficult to trace exactly where they come from. Generally, sociologists agree that while we aren't born with prejudiced attitudes, we often learn prejudice

SECESSIONIST MINORITIES are groups that voluntarily separate themselves from the dominant group and view the dominant group with disdain, believing that it will corrupt the group's belief system.

MILITANT MINORITIES are groups that seek to overthrow the existing system because they see it as unjust.

ETHNIC ENCLAVES are neighborhoods where people from similar cultures live together and assert cultural distinction from the dominant group.

PREJUDICE refers to negative attitudes about an entire category of people.

STEREOTYPES are simplified perceptions people have of an entire group that are usually based on false assumptions.

DISCRIMINATION is the unfair treatment of people based on a prejudice.

INSTITUTIONAL DISCRIMINATION maintains the advantage for the dominant group, while providing the appearance of fairness to all.

from those around us.[25] We can even learn a prejudice against a group to which we belong. This self-loathing occurs when we internalize the values of the dominant group.[26] In my classes, I often have my students take an online test designed to measure biases. Generally, minorities hold similar beliefs to their non-minority counterparts. Recently an African American student took the "Know Your Bias" test and was shocked to find that she held negative attitudes toward African Americans. This illustrates how we are all socialized to hold biases that are in accordance with the dominant society, even if we belong to a minority group.

INSTITUTIONAL DISCRIMINATION IN THE UNITED STATES

While personal biases often cause individuals to view others negatively, those attitudes can carry over into the structures of society and often go unnoticed by others who don't even hold those views. When this happens, social institutions end up supporting racial and ethnic inequality. This **institutional discrimination** maintains the advantage for the dominant

THINK SOCIOLOGICALLY

They're Coming to America

For centuries, immigrants have come to the United States. This trend continues to this day, constantly changing the face of the country.

Researchers are interested in what helps these immigrants not only survive but thrive in a new country. Sociologists Alejandro Portes and Alex Stepick conducted a study of Cuban immigrants in Miami, and Min Zhou studied Chinese immigration in New York City. They note that one key component of immigrant success is a successful neighborhood, or enclave, in which they can live.

A number of factors are required for a successful enclave. Location and a sense

of permanence are both very important. When Cuban immigrants first fled the regime of Fidel Castro, many of them chose to settle in Miami. After the failure of the Bay of Pigs invasion on Cuba in 1961, they decided to put down permanent roots.[27] Some suggest this will result in the Balkanization of the United States, meaning that we will have a more divided nation, much like that of the former Yugoslavia.[28] Others suggest that this is unlikely because immigrants, even in enclaves, eventually move out and assimilate into their new culture.[29]

Once the roots are in place, a stable market that small firms can control is necessary. Small businesses require very little start-up costs, and businesses related to ethnic food or culture also help. In

New York City's Chinatown, these two factors helped Chinese immigrants successfully create an economic market.[30] Once these businesses are established, the enclave provides a steady stream of cheap labor, another characteristic of a successful enclave. As immigrants continue to enter the United States, they provide a constant source of people willing to work at heavy-labor, low-wage jobs. As their children assimilate, they are less likely to take these jobs, and so a continual flow of new immigrants helps the enclave, and all who live in it, thrive.[31]

>>> ACTIVITY Locate the nearest ethnic enclave in your city or state. To what ethnicity does it cater? Does it appear to cater to tourists?

group, while providing the appearance of fairness to others. Such institutionalized racism is best illustrated by the Jim Crow era of U.S. history. Many of the laws that separated blacks and whites during the first half of the 20th century were based on the premise of things being "separate but equal." Unfortunately, while institutions like education and housing were separate, they were hardly equal. Jim Crow may be a relic of the past, but that doesn't mean institutional discrimination has also been erased. In fact, racism and discrimination are still institutionalized today. The U.S. education system is one area in which "separate but equal" is essentially still the norm. Jonathan Kozol's award-winning book *Savage Inequalities* supports the notion that not all education in the United States is the same. Minority children tend to be overrepresented in inner-city schools that are usually underfunded and less equipped than schools that cater to upper-middle class, and predominantly white, children. This is largely due to the way schools are funded through property taxes. If a child lives in a poor neighborhood, his or her school is likely to struggle financially because lower property taxes mean less revenue to pay for books or teachers. Meanwhile, children from more affluent neighborhoods attend schools with state-of-the-art supplies and highly qualified educators that poorer schools can't afford. In this way, institutional discrimination works to decrease the chances of poor children using education as a vehicle to climb out of the poverty cycle and amounts to the society reinforcing the roadblocks to their success.

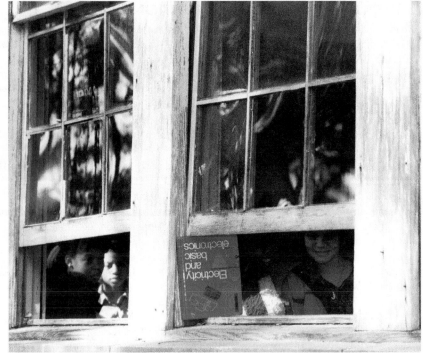

©AP Images/David Martin

∧
∧ **Schools in poor neighborhoods are more likely to be**
∧ **underfunded** and unequally funded than schools in affluent neighborhoods.

CAUSES FOR PREJUDICE AND DISCRIMINATION

So why does any kind of discrimination happen at all? John Dollard suggests that frustration leads to prejudice.[32] Often we don't have the ability to attack the real source of our irritation, and so we **scapegoat**, or unfairly accuse, another group as the cause of our problem. Usually a racial or ethnic minority becomes the target for a common societal problem like widespread poverty. If you are poor, you may not be able to increase your salary, but you can blame others for your problems. This happened in 1982 when two white unemployed autoworkers, Ronald Ebens and Michael Nitz, beat Vincent Chin, a young Chinese American man, to death. What started as a barroom brawl—Ebens and Nitz reportedly used a racial slur to refer to Chin, after which a fistfight broke out—ended in murder. The two men blamed Japanese auto companies—and by extension, all Japanese people—for the economic downturn and violently attacked Chin simply because they thought he was Japanese. To make matters worse, neither man ever spent a day in jail for Chin's murder. After they pled guilty to manslaughter, the judge sentenced Ebens and Nitz to three years' probation and fines totaling less than $4,000. The judge later defended the light sentence by claiming, "These weren't the kind of men you send to jail. We're talking here about a man [Ebens] who's held down a responsible job with the same company for seventeen or eighteen years and his son [Nitz] who is employed and is a part-time student . . . You don't make the punishment fit the crime; you make the punishment fit the criminal." In a civil trial later that year, Ebens was convicted of violating Chin's civil rights and sentenced to 25 years in jail. However, Ebens appealed the decision on the basis of a technicality and was later acquitted in a retrial, which was held in a different state.[33]

How could two men get away with committing such a hateful and racist act? Researchers often suggest the importance of education and intelligence in predicting a discriminatory type of personality. Generally, studies support the notion that people who are less educated and of lower intelligence are more likely to be prejudiced. This lends support to the idea that prejudice is learned, and can be unlearned.[34] Furthermore, structural issues such as the mix of racial and ethnic groups, as well as income inequality and differences in economic opportunities, may assist in the perpetuation of extreme forms of racism. White supremacist groups often cite these issues as evidence of minority group dominance and use these issues as a rallying cry for a white backlash against these groups.[35]

SEGREGATION

People who are discriminated against are often separated from the dominant group in terms of housing, workplace, and social settings. This enforced separation is called **segregation** when factors such as race, gender, or ethnicity are involved. Earlier, we discussed the so-called separate but equal schools, neighborhoods, restaurants, and public restrooms of the 1960s and earlier. Although these and other forms of segregation are no longer legal, issues such as unofficial segregation continue to this day.

In a study of housing segregation, Massey and Denton show that blacks of all incomes experience similar levels of segregation from whites. They note that racial segregation is linked to a number of factors, including personal choice. Sometimes, minorities prefer to live in areas that are populated by their own groups.[36] The phenomenon "white flight" refers to the housing pattern that occurs when many white people move out of a neighborhood in response to blacks or other people of color moving in. This reinforces the idea that when the government closes one opportunity for discrimination, others will emerge. Even to this day, issues of fair lending practices influence who can and cannot get a loan for a home. So-called predatory loans set minority groups up to fail, thus keeping them in segregated neighborhoods.[37]

Of course, income potentially influences housing segregation. An emerging trend in housing in the United States is the construction of larger, more expensive homes, which tend to be sold only to the affluent, leaving behind less expensive, smaller, older homes. This segregates individuals based on their incomes, which also tends to segregate people by race.[38]

Racial Stratification in the United States

Now that you have a context in which to look at race and ethnicity, let's turn our attention to how race stratifies our society. Although we live in a free society that claims to be equal, there are still injustices that occur because of race. How does the well-being of different racial and ethnic groups compare? Take a look at the chart below to find out. You've seen the numbers, so now let's take a closer look at racial stratification.

INCOME

In the United States, minorities tend to be overrepresented in poverty statistics, particularly African Americans and Hispanics. This is

SCAPEGOAT means making an unfair accusation against a person or group as the cause of a problem.

SEGREGATION is forced separation because of factors such as race, gender, or ethnicity.

CYCLE OF POVERTY is a generational barrier that prevents poor people from breaking into the middle and upper classes.

caused in part by the **cycle of poverty**, which makes it difficult for people to break into the middle class if their parents were poor. Given that black people have been forced into poverty ever since slavery, it's easy to see how future generations could remain trapped in that cycle. Hispanic immigrants have the disadvantage of the language barrier, which makes it nearly impossible to get a high-paying job in this country. Their children will likely be born into the cycle of poverty and will have to struggle to break out of it.[39]

In 2008, the median income for Asians was $65,637 and $55,530 for whites. For people of Hispanic origin, it was $37,913, and the median income for blacks was $34,218. That same year, 8.6 percent of whites and 11.8 percent of Asians lived in poverty, whereas 23.2 percent of Hispanics and 24.7 percent of blacks did. To see how disproportionately these groups are represented, the official poverty rate for the entire U.S. population was only 12.5 percent.[40]

Racial–Ethnic Groups Compared

Racial–Ethnic Group	Median Household Income (2008)	Percentage Living at or Below Poverty Line (2008)	Percentage Without Health Insurance (2007–2008)	Home Ownership (2007)	Percentage of Children With a Computer at Home (2006)	Life Expectancy at Birth (2010 Estimate)
White	$55,530	8.6%	14.4%	74.9%	76.9%	Male: 76.5
						Female: 81.3
Hispanic or Latino	$37,913	23.2%	31.4%	48.5%	40.6%	Male: 78.4
						Female: 83.7
Black/ African American	$34,218	24.7%	19.3%	47.7%	41.0%	Male: 70.2
						Female: 77.2
Asian	$65,637	11.8%	17.2%	58.6%*	75.7%	Male: 76.3
						Female: 81.1
American Indian and/or Alaskan Native	$35,343	25.3%	30.7%	**	54.1%	Male: 76.6
						Female: 81.5

*Number represents a combination number of all other racial categories.
**Data included in percentage for Asian Americans.

Source: Based on Carmen DeNavas-Walt, Bernadette D. Proctor, and Jessica Smith, U.S. Census Bureau, *Current Population Reports, P60-236, Income, Poverty, and Health Insurance Coverage in the United States: 2008; Statistical Abstract 2008:* Table 609; National Projections Program, U.S. Census Bureau.

Educational Attainment by Race/Ethnic Group

Source: U.S. Census Bureau, Current Population Survey, *2007 Annual Social and Economic Supplement and Statistical Abstract 2000.*

COLOR-BLIND RACISM is the idea that racism still exists in society in more subtle ways.

EDUCATION

One of the most important factors in determining income is education. Without access to quality education, it's difficult to get a well-paying job and advance in the workplace. There is a strong correlation between level of education and income, with people who have advanced degrees earning the most money. But who exactly is earning these advanced degrees? The graphs on the left shows the educational attainment of the population by race. With the exception of the Asian group, minorities tend to have low educational attainment.

For example, only about half of the Hispanic population over the age of 25 has graduated from college. These data help explain why such a wide gap exists between the median income of African Americans and the median income of Asian Americans. In 1999, full-time employees with high school diplomas earned an average of $30,400 a year, while those with bachelor's degrees earned $52,200 on average. Income for those with master's degrees was $62,300 and $109,600 for those with a professional degree.[41]

As discussed earlier, schools continue to be unofficially segregated. Poorly funded schools tend to be those in which the majority of the children are black or Latino. This imbalance further adds to the income disparity between whites and other races. The lack of a proper education forces people into low-paying jobs, or worse, and the cycle of poverty continues.

MAKE CONNECTIONS

In July of 2009, Fox News commentator and talk show host Glenn Beck made news for suggesting that President Barack Obama was a racist. Beck stated that the President's behavior suggested a "deep-seated hatred for white people or the white culture." The clamor to have Beck taken off Fox News for such a suggestion was met with indifference by the media giant. Instead, commentators on the airways began to discuss whether a person who is part of a minority group could

actually be a racist, and then whether the president fit this description.[42]

That fall, my classes began to discuss the issue of whether Obama was or was not the first "black president." After all, his mother was a white woman from Kansas, and his father was an African. So, I asked them, is he really "black"? What does it mean to be "black"?

Students struggled to find language to answer this question. We had read Graves's

The Race Myth, and they understood that biologically there is almost no difference between races, and that race is, in fact, a social construct, not a biological one.

Why would a conservative white talk show host accuse a black president of racism? Ratings? Air time? One thing is certain—after the comment, more Americans had heard of Glenn Beck than had before. So, why did he say this? Was it really about race or ratings?

think sociologically: WHAT CAUSES RACIST ATTITUDES, AND HOW DO THESE ATTITUDES AFFECT PEOPLE?

Symbolic Interactionism: Color-Blind Racism

Symbolic interactionists stress the importance of symbolism and language in the creation of society. In the United States, overtly racist language is socially unacceptable in most circles; however, sociologists don't believe that this means we have become a "color-blind" society. In fact, **color-blind racism**, the idea that racism still exists in more subtle ways remains a part of U.S. society to this day. For example, there is no doubt that many people of color in the United States remain in disadvantaged positions—they are poorer, achieve lower educational outcomes, live shorter lives, attend underfunded schools, experience problems with assimilation, and generally believe that the police and other social institutions work to increase their disadvantage.[43] Despite these facts, though, most whites in the United States claim these outcomes have nothing to do with racism. How can that be? Furthermore, most whites claim they are not racist.

Eduardo Bonilla-Silva suggests that this is because whites have developed a series of excuses for the status quo through four key factors: First, whites tend to hold onto ideals such as equality, individualism, and choice in an effort to explain why racial groups are disadvantaged.[44] In other words, people are only poor because they made bad choices, not because of some historical or cultural connection that supports racism. Second, white people often use cultural stereotypes to explain racial inequality. Rather than understand the source of the problem, too many people simply latch onto stereotypes to explain the issue. When radio shock jock Don Imus got into trouble for using a racially insensitive term to refer to the Rutgers University women's basketball team in 2007, the media frenzy focused more on the ills of hip-hop music rather than the racial power dynamic of Imus's words. The third factor is the false belief that segregation is a personal choice. The suggestion is that it's natural for racial groups to prefer "their own kind." Often, this attitude prevents white people from understanding the complex role institutionalized racism has on "segregated" communities. Finally, many whites in the United States simply believe that racism is a thing of the past and deny that it has any impact on minorities' lives today. Such thinking serves to defend the way things are, and excuses the dominant group from any responsibility to make things better.

Although racism is not as overt as it once was, that doesn't mean the problem has been eradicated. Racial prejudice still exists; it's just hidden behind a series of clever language constructions. For example, white college students rarely use racist terms such as "the n-word," but they might tell racist jokes. They usually first explain that the joke doesn't really reflect their beliefs, and conclude the joke with an apologetic comment—all to eliminate the perception of racism.[45] Also, consider the recent trend of white college students attending parties in blackface, the act of whites applying makeup to mock the appearance of African Americans. The students who participate in these parties claim they're merely being "ironic," even though the act is highly offensive to most people of color.[46]

Whites may try to prove they're not racist by claiming some of their "best friends are black." This is supposed to give the speaker an air of credibility for not being racist. Unfortunately, such disclaimers are usually followed by a negative stereotype. They might try to excuse a long history of structural racism or try to take all sides when it comes to matters of race. Whites may also excuse the long history of racism and a lack of equal opportunities by denying any personal responsibility for it. Comments like "I didn't own slaves; it's not my fault" lead the conversation away from structural problems that continue to exist regarding race, while excusing the speaker from any possible advantage based on his or her race.

W.E.B. Du Bois suggested that African Americans have a sort of **double consciousness**, meaning black people have to keep a foot in two worlds, one white and one black.[47] Minority group members must learn to integrate into the dominant group in order to successfully live in the society. They must also learn to live within their own culture. Many people of color are forced to "code switch;" that is, to speak and act one way among their own group and another in white society. Du Bois considered blacks to be in a unique position because they were accountable to white culture as well as their own. This influences their sense of self and affects how they live in the world. Only through understanding this position can blacks hope to navigate the world successfully.

Du Bois's classical ideas also apply to the study of other minority groups, including Hispanics and women.[48] Generally, sociologists find that members of the dominant group do not think much about race, but as one student put it, "When you're a minority, race is always a factor."

> **DOUBLE CONSCIOUSNESS** is the sense that a person must keep a foot in two worlds, one in the majority group's world and one in the minority group's world.

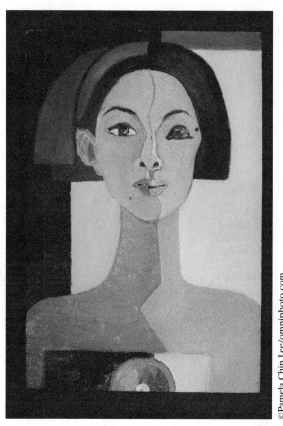

©Pamela Chin Lee/omniphoto.com

∧ **African Americans,** and
∧ other minorities, **often have to live in two worlds—one black and the other white.**

WRAP YOUR MIND AROUND THE THEORY

Functionalists might ask how racism works in society. **Is that what drives these protestors to fight against the biases that the dominant group holds toward them?**

©A. Ramey/PhotoEdit

FUNCTIONALISM

Functionalists might view racism as having both intended and unintended consequences. For example, consider slavery in the United States. It was extremely functional to building wealth and a successful agricultural economy in the southern United States. Of course, the unintended function was to enslave fellow human beings and treat them like animals. The underlying horrors of slavery eventually became well known enough to push whites to make slavery illegal; however, it took more than 100 years for this to occur. Consider the institutional racism that occurs within the U.S. educational system today. What are the consequences of it? Are the tax savings that some receive really worth the costs of an undereducated future generation?

CONFLICT THEORY

From a conflict theorist's lens, racism is the result of one group wanting to keep its advantage over another. For example, in 1838, the U.S. government forced the relocation of Native Americans from eastern areas of the United States to western lands in a tragic episode known as the Trail of Tears. Why did this occur? It certainly was not for the good of the Native Americans; it was intended to benefit whites who wanted to expand their lands for farming. The forced relocation of native peoples resulted in more than 20 million acres of land becoming available for white settlement. This cost the government approximately $3 million. Thus, the pursuit of even more wealth drove those with power to drive native peoples from their ancestral lands and "give" them lands that had little or no worth.[50]

HOW DO THE THREE PARADIGMS VIEW RACISM?

SYMBOLIC INTERACTIONISM

Symbolic interactionists point to the micro interactions of our daily life and how they either support or attack an issue. Had I been teaching in a college classroom 100 years ago, I may have been willing and able to utter racial slurs in class. If I were to do that today, I would be reprimanded and could even lose my job. What has changed? Certainly tolerance for negative terms of racial groups has decreased dramatically in 100 years. Interactionists would suggest that by changing the acceptable terms, we can change the reality. Perhaps we should eliminate racial slurs altogether.

Following the Indian Removal Act of 1830, **thousands of Cherokee were forced to travel from their ancestral lands** to "Indian Territory" via the **Trail of Tears**. Was this because they held lands that the dominant group wanted?

©Bettmann/Corbis

In 1957, when schools were integrated, the government tried to force an end to segregation. **Have we found other, less obvious ways to continue segregation?**

The Granger Collection, New York

discover sociology in action: HOW DOES AFFIRMATIVE ACTION HELP MINORITY GROUPS IN THE UNITED STATES?

Affirmative Action

Affirmative action is a social policy designed to help minority groups gain opportunities through employment and education. Legal affirmative action in the United States means that if all candidates are equal, an employer or college may use minority status as a deciding factor. However, it is not acceptable to simply hire the minority member if that person is unqualified for the job. The logic behind this preference is based on hundreds of years of discrimination, as well as the obvious disadvantages that still exist for women and minorities.

A great deal of controversy surrounds affirmative action because some believe that the policy would require universities and companies to establish quotas for minority groups. The truth is that quotas are not part of acceptable affirmative action policies since that could encourage employers to hire minority members who are not qualified. While acknowledging the continuation of discrimination, sociologist William J. Wilson suggested that class-based policies should replace race-based ones.[49] He argued that financial needs and not race should determine advantage. This would allow poor whites, blacks, Hispanics, etc., to receive benefits and, since minority groups are disproportionately poor, they would still reap the lion's share of these benefits. Basing the policies on class rather than on race would eliminate the perception of racial bias. Whereas color-blind policies like this are attractive to the dominant group, they do not necessarily yield the desired results. Color-blind college entrance policies in Texas, for example, may actually lead to less qualified students entering college. Research shows that students from lower socioeconomic brackets who are admitted based on such color-blind policies have a higher likelihood of dropping out and, in the long run, may actually hurt minority educational attainment.[51]

ACTIVITIES

1. Engage someone not in this class in a conversation about race. See what you learn about his or her beliefs. Ask the following questions:
   - What are the races in the United States?
   - Are there any biological differences in races?
   - Does race play a role in opportunities?
2. Research 10 ways to stop hate on a college campus. Follow this link to the list: http://www.tolerance.org/campus/index.jsp. Does your college do these things? If not, can you organize a group to address these problems?
3. Talk to your classmates about your own experiences of racial tension. Then, test your hidden biases at this Web site (http://www.tolerance.org/hidden_bias/index.html) to see what they might be.

From Classroom to Community | Teaching in a Migrant Community

A student named Maryann confronted her own notions of white privilege when she assisted at a school that was located in a poor, urban neighborhood. She was stunned to find a school filled with children who did not speak English. The experience allowed Maryann to reflect on her own upbringing.

"I never really thought that I was well-off when I was in school," she said. "What I found at this school shocked me."

Some of her observations included seeing kids not allowed on the playground because of drive-by shootings in the neighborhood. She also noticed facilities that were falling apart and an environment that was not good for the students. Maryann's response to these conditions was the desire to

"get out of there as soon as possible."

She spent most of her time trying to help the students learn to read English. Though the children were smart, outside factors were affecting their schoolwork. They often lived with parents who spoke only Spanish and in enclaves where little English was spoken. Because English was not reinforced at home, these students had difficulty succeeding in class.

"One child missed school one day because he had to translate for his father at a doctor's appointment," remembered Maryann.

"I couldn't imagine being 8 years old and talking to a doctor for my dad."

The statistics show that many of these kids will never finish high school. The teachers hope to teach them enough so that they will be able to read and speak English, yet very few of them make it to college. After spending time among these students, Maryann concluded that society is not structured to help students in these situations.

"I kept wondering how this was equal education. I decided that it wasn't."

(Image credits, vertical text) ©Bettmann/Corbis; ©Bettmann/Corbis; ©Bettmann/Corbis

WHAT IS THE DIFFERENCE BETWEEN RACE AND ETHNICITY?

race is the division of people based on certain physical characteristics, but *ethnicity* is the classification of people who share a common cultural, linguistic, or ancestral heritage

WHAT CAUSES RACIST ATTITUDES, AND HOW DO THESE ATTITUDES AFFECT PEOPLE?

color-blind racism, racial stereotypes, belief that segregation is a personal choice, belief that racism is a thing of the past, which denies its impact on minorities; these lead to a feeling of double consciousness for minorities

HOW DOES AFFIRMATIVE ACTION HELP MINORITY GROUPS IN THE UNITED STATES?

by allowing employers and educators to use minority status as a deciding factor if candidates are equal

get the topic: WHAT IS THE DIFFERENCE BETWEEN RACE AND ETHNICITY?

Racial Stratification in the United States   Symbolic Interactionism: Color-Blind Racism   Affirmative Action

Theory

FUNCTIONALISM

- racism has both intended and unintended consequences
- slavery in the South functioned to build wealth and agriculture, but it came at the expense of people being treated like animals

CONFLICT THEORY

- racism is a result of power conflicts among different groups
- the group with more power oppresses the weaker groups, a result of which can cause racism to occur

- 1838 relocation of Native Americans for the farmer's own personal gain

SYMBOLIC INTERACTIONISM

- by changing what is acceptable in society, we change reality
- racial slurs that were acceptable 100 years ago are highly discouraged today
- acceptable terms leads to what is said and thought in society

Key Terms

race	hate groups	pluralistic minorities	institutional discrimination
ethnicity	conquest	assimilationist minorities	scapegoat
majority group	annexation	secessionist minorities	segregation
minority group	voluntary immigration	militant minorities	cycle of poverty
dominant group	involuntary immigration	ethnic enclaves	color-blind racism
colonialism	ethnic cleansing	prejudice	double consciousness
racism	migrant superordination	stereotypes	
genocide	indigenous superordination	discrimination	

MY SEARCH LAB

1. *Color-Blind Privilege: The Social and Political Functions of Erasing the Color Line in Post Race America.* Reprinted by permission of Charles A. Gallagher, Professor and Chair, Department of Sociology, Social Work and Criminal Justice, La Salle University.

INTRODUCTION

In this selection, Charles Gallagher uses interviews and focus groups with whites across the country to argue that many believe that race no longer matters in the United States.

DISCUSSION QUESTIONS

1. Explain the "color-blind" or race-neutral perspective. Do you agree that America is becoming a color-blind nation?
2. According to the author, what are the effects of the color-blind perspective?

2. *Race-Specific Policies and the Truly Disadvantaged* by William Julius Wilson, reprinted from *The Truly Disadvantaged: The Inner City, the Underclass, and Public Policy*, 1987, pp. 109–124. Copyright by The University of Chicago.

INTRODUCTION

In this excerpt, Wilson presents his argument that social class and economic factors are more damaging to the urban poor than racial inequality.

DISCUSSION QUESTIONS

1. Compare/contrast the three philosophies and political approaches to equality: equality of individual opportunity, equality of group opportunity, and equality of life chances. Which do you believe is the best approach and why?
2. The author argues that race-specific policies do not benefit the truly disadvantaged, while others have argued that the benefits of race-specific policies will eventually "trickle down" and help those at the bottom. Which side do you believe and why?

3. *Thoughts on Class, Race, and Prison* by Alan Berkman and Tim Blunk, reprinted from Cages of Steel: The Politics of Imprisonment in the United States, edited by Ward Churchill, and J.J. Vanderwell, 1992, Maisonneuve Press. pp. 190–193. Reprinted by permission.

INTRODUCTION

In this article, Dr. Alan Berkman, founder of Health GAP (Global Access Project), and Tim Blunk discuss what they have learned about poverty, race, oppression, and the prison system.

DISCUSSION QUESTIONS

1. What did they learn from their prison experience?
2. The authors take a sympathetic view of prison riots. Why? Do you agree or disagree with this stance?

THE THINKSPOT

How tolerant are you really? I suspect you think you are very tolerant and extremely rational when it comes to race and segregation. Let's test your thoughts by sending you to the ThinkSpot where you'll find a video called "The Logic of Life: Racial Segregation" in which Tim Harford, the Undercover Economist, discusses the idea of racial segregation using a carton of brown and white eggs. What he uncovers might surprise you and make you question your own belief system about race.

It is hard to believe that internment camps were once a fact of American life, but it is true. As you saw in this chapter, during World War II, more than 100,000 Japanese men, women, and children were taken from their homes and forced to live at internment camps. Go to the ThinkSpot and learn more about why this happened and other details about this forced internment of American citizens.

Sample Test Questions

These multiple-choice questions are similar to those found in the test bank that accompanies this textbook.

1. Which of the following is *not* a racial category for the U.S. Census Bureau?
   a. White
   b. Black
   c. Latino
   d. Asian

2. Immigrants who learn their new home's language and culture while maintaining their own customs and beliefs are
   a. assimilationist minorities.
   b. secessionist minorities.
   c. pluralistic minorities.
   d. militant minorities.

3. What are the Jim Crow laws an example of?
   a. Ethnocentrism
   b. Ethnic segregation
   c. Color-blind racism
   d. Institutional discrimination

4. A dominant group
   a. always has the most in number and in power.
   b. always has the least in number and in power.
   c. usually has the most in number and in power.
   d. usually has the least in number and in power.

5. Joseph Graves states that race is a social construct, not a biological feature.
   a. True
   b. False

ANSWERS: 1. c; 2. c; 3. d; 4. c; 5. a

ESSAY

1. What are Joseph Graves' five pillars of racism?
2. Why does Wilson believe that class-based affirmative action should replace our current race-based system?
3. Why do some people have a sort of "double consciousness"?
4. What is the difference between prejudice and discrimination?
5. What are some ways that the United States is trying to break the cycle of poverty for minority groups?

WHERE TO START YOUR RESEARCH PAPER

To learn about stopping hate on campus, go to
http://www.tolerance.org/campus/index.jsp

To find more information about race and ethnicity by government standards, go to http://www.whitehouse.gov/omb/inforeg/race.pdf

To take the "Know Your Biases" test, go to
http://www.tolerance.org/hidden_bias/index.html

To learn more about multiculturalism in the United States, go to
http://www.nmci.org/

To read more about what people are doing to stop genocide in the world today, go to http://www.genocidewatch.org/

For more information about the ways the United States helps immigrants entering the country, go to
http://www.usimmigrationsupport.org/

Find out ways people are trying to stop discrimination, go to
http://www.discrimination.com/

To see what people are doing to break the cycle of poverty, go to
http://www.brakethecycle.org/

To find more information on minority groups, go to
http://www.minorityrights.org/

To read about the World Conference against Racism, go to
http://www.un.org/WCAR/

Endnotes

1. "Introduction: The Problem Simply Stated," from *The Race Myth* by Joseph L. Graves, Jr., copyright © 2004 by Joseph L. Graves, Jr. Used by permission of Dutton, a division of Penguin Group (USA) Inc.

2. U.S. Census Bureau, "Race," American FactFinder, http://factfinder.census.gov/home/en/epss/glossary_r.html (accessed August 14, 2008).

3. Louis Wirth, 1945, "The Problem of Minority Groups," In *The Science of Man in the World Crisis,* Ralph Linton, ed. (New York: Columbia University Press, 1945).

4. Apartheid, *Africana: The Encyclopedia of the African and African American Experience*, ed. Kwame Anthony Appiah and Henry Louis Gates, Jr., in Featured Selections, http://www.africanaencyclopedia.com/apartheid/apartheid.html (accessed August 12, 2008).

5. U.S. Census Bureau, "Population Projections," www.census.gov/ipc/www/usinterimproj (accessed August 12, 2008).

6. "Children Targeted in the Genocide," Human Rights Watch, http://hrw.org/reports/2003/rwanda0403/rwanda0403-03.htm (accessed September 10, 2008).

7. SPLC, "Stand Strong Against Hate," Southern Poverty Law Center, Montgomery, Alabama. http://www.splcenter.org/center/petitions/stand-strong/ (accessed August 14, 2008).

8. Gloria Jahoda, *Trail of Tears: The Story of American Indian Removals 1813–1855* (New York: Wings Books, 1995).

9. Jeffrey Gettleman and Kennedy Abwao, "U.S. Envoy Calls Some Kenya Violence Ethnic Cleansing," *New York Times,* January 31, 2008;—James Hider, "Ethnic Cleansing Claim as Iraqi Hostages Found Dead," *The Times,* April 21, 2005.

10. Jared Diamond, *Guns, Germs, and Steel: The Fates of Human Societies* (New York: W.W. Norton and Company, 1999).

11. Benjamin Banneker Center for Economic Justice and Progress, "The Gadsden Purchase: Odd Land Deal," The Progress Report, http://www.progress.org/gads.htm (accessed August 12, 2008).

12. Media Matters for America, "Buchanan said immigration will Cause the 'Complete Balkanization of America' Create 'a Giant Kosovo in the Southwest," June 6, 2006, http://mediamatters.org/items/200606060011 (accessed August 12, 2008).

13. Martin N. Marger, *Race and Ethnic Relations: American and Global Perspectives,* 4th edition (Belmont, CA: Wadsworth Publishing, 1997).

14. Public Broadcasting Service, "Srebrenica: A Cry from the Grave," http://www.pbs.org/wnet/cryfromthegrave/massacre/massacre.html (accessed August 12, 2008).

15. Marcus Cox, "The Right to Return Home: International Intervention and Ethnic Cleansing in Bosnia and Herzegovina," *The International and Comparative Law Quarterly,* 1998. 47(3): 599–631.

16. Chris Stephen, "Court Wants Exemplary Karadzic Trial," *BBC News,* July 24, 2008, http://news.bbc.co.uk/2/hi/europe/7522908.stm (accessed August 12, 2008).

17. The 'Lectric Law Library, "ACLU Briefing Paper Number 6: 'English Only,'" http://www.lectlaw.com/files/con09.htm (accessed August 12, 2008).

18. Roger Waldinger, *Still the Promised City?: African-Americans and New Immigrants in Postindustrial New York* (Cambridge, Mass: Harvard University Press, 1996).

19. William L. Reinshagen, "German Immigrants" in *Immigration in U.S. History,* ed. Carl L. Bankston III, Danielle Hidalgo, and R. Kent Rasmussen (Pasadena, CA: Salem Press Inc., 2006).

20. Donald Kraybill, *The Riddle of Anabaptist Culture*, 2nd edition (Baltimore: Johns Hopkins University Press, 2001).

21. "Castro, Fidel," Encyclopædia Britannica, 2008, Encyclopædia Britannica Online, http://search.eb.com/eb/article-9020736 (accessed September 30, 2008).

22. "Gandhi, Mohandas Karamchand," Encyclopædia Britannica, 2008, Encyclopædia Britannica Online, http://search.eb.com/eb/article-22639, September 30, 2008.

23. Ashley W. Doane, Jr., "Dominant Group Ethnic Identity in the United States: The Role of 'Hidden' Ethnicity in Intergroup Relations," *The Sociological Quarterly,* 1997. 38(3): 375–397.

24. Philip Kasinitz, John H. Mollenkopf, Mary C. Waters, and Jennifer Holdaway, *Inheriting the city: The children of immigrants come of age* (New York and Cambridge: Russell Sage Foundation and Harvard University Press, 2008).

25. Kathryn Blee, *Inside Organized Racism: Women in the Hate Movement* (Berkley, CA: University of California Press, 2002).

26. Mark E. Hill, "Skin Color and Perception of Attractiveness Among African Americans: Does Gender Make a Difference?" *Social Science Quarterly,* 2002. 65(1): 77–91.

27. Alejandro Portes and Alex Stepick, *City on the Edge: The Transformation of Miami* (Berkeley, CA: University of California Press, 1993).

28. William Frey, "Immigration, Domestic Migration and Demographic Balkanization in America: New Evidence for the 1990's," *Population and Development Review,* 1996. 22: 741–763.

29. Mark Ellis and Richard Wright, "The Balanization Metaphor in the Analysis of U.S. Immigration," *The Annals of the Association of American Geographers,* 1998. 88: 686–708.

30. Min Zhou, *Chinatown: The Socioeconomic Potential of an Urban Enclave* (Philadelphia: Temple University Press, 1992).

31. Alejandro Portes and Rueben G. Rumbaut, *Immigrant America* (Berkeley, CA: University of California Press, 1996).

32. John Dollard, *Frustration and Aggression,* (New Haven, Connecticut: Yale University Press, 1939).

33. "Vincent Chin," Vincent Who?, posted June 14, 2007, http://vincentchin.net/vincent/ (accessed August 12, 2008).

34. M. Brewster Smith, "The Authoritarian Personality: A Re-review 46 Years Later," *Political Psychology* 1997. 18(1): 159–163; John Levi Martin, "The Authoritarian Personality, 50 Years Later: What Lessons Are There for Political Psychology?" *Political Psychology* 2001. 22(1) : 1–26.

35. Rory McVeigh, "Structured Ignorance and Organized Racism in the United States," *Social Forces,* 2004. 82(3): 895–936.

36. Douglas Massey and Nancy Denton, *American Apartheid: Segregation and the Making of the Underclass,* (Cambridge MA: Harvard University Press, 1993).

37. Douglas S. Massey, "Racial Discrimination in Housing: A Moving Target," *Social Problems,* 2005. 52(2): 148–151.

38. Rachel E. Dwyer, "Expanding Homes and Increasing Inequalities: U.S. Housing Development and the Residential Segregation," *Social Problems,* 2007. 54(1): 23–46.

39. Mary Corcoran, "Rags to Rags: Poverty and Mobility in the United States," *Annual Review of Sociology,* 1995. 21: 237–267.

40. Carmen DeNavas-Walt, Bernadette D. Proctor, and Jessica Smith, "Income, Poverty, and Health Insurance Coverage in the United States: 2006; Statistical Abstract 2008: Table 609," Current Populations Report, P6—233, National Projections Program, U.S. Census Bureau; "Number in Poverty and Poverty Rate: 1959 to 2007," Current Population Survey, U.S Census Bureau, http://www.census.gov/hhes/www/poverty/povertyrate.html (accessed October 17, 2008).

41. "The Big Payoff: Educational Attainment and Synthetic Estimates of Work-Life Earnings," U.S. Census Bureau, http://www.census.gov/prod/2002pubs/p23-210.pdf (accessed September 9, 2008).

42. Richard Huff, "Pundit Glenn Beck calls President Barack Obama a 'racist', Fox News Channel execs downplay comments," *Daily News,* July 29, 2009, http://www.nydailynews.com/news/politics/2009/07/29/2009-07-29_fox_news_glenn_beck_president_barack_obama_is_racist_with_deepseated_hatred_of_w.html.

43. Jonathan Kozol, *Savage Inequalities: Children in America's Schools* (New York: Crown Publishers 1991); Mary C. Waters and Karl Eschbach, "Immigration and Ethnic and Racial Inequality in the United States," *Annual Review of Sociology,* 1995. 21: 419–446; Grace Kao and Jennifer S. Thompson, "Racial and Ethnic Stratification in Educational Achievement and Attainment," *Annual Review of Sociology,* 2003. 29: 417–443; Rory McVeigh, "Structured Ignorance and Organized Racism in the United States," *Social Forces* 2004. 82(3): 895–936.

44. Eduardo Bonilla-Silva, "The Linguistics of Color Blind Racism: How to Talk Nasty about Blacks Without Sounding 'Racist,'" *Critical Sociology,* 2002. 28(1–2): 41–64.

45. Ibid.

46. Adam Peck, "Blackface: Racism Across College Campuses," *The Statesman,* February 22, 2007, http://media.www.sbstatesman.com/media/storage/paper955/news/2007/02/22/News/Blackface.Racism.Across.College.Campuses-2734300.shtml (accessed August 12, 2008).

47. W.E.B. Du Bois, *The Souls of Black Folk* (New York: Penguin, 1903/1996).

48. Patricia Hill Collins, *Black Feminist Thought* (New York: Routledge, 1990); Darlene Clark Hine, "In the Kingdom of Culture: Black Women and the Intersection of Race, Gender, and Class," in *Lure and Loathing: Essays on Race, Identity and the Ambivalence of Assimilation,* ed. Gerald Early (New York: Penguin Press, 1993).

49. William J. Wilson, *The Declining Significance of Race: Blacks and Changing American Institutions, 2nd ed.* (Chicago: University of Chicago Press, 1980).

50. Gloria Jahoda, *Trail of Tears: The Story of American Indian Removals 1813–1855* (New York: Wings Books, 1995).

51. Roland G. Fryer and Glenn C. Loury, "Affirmative Action and Its Mythology," *The Journal of Economic Perspectives,* 2005. 19(3): 147–162.

GENDER STRATIFICATION

GENDER STRATIFICATION

Guyland

is not some esoteric planet inhabited only by alien creatures—despite how alien our teenage and 20-something sons might seem at times. It's the world of everyday "guys." Nor is it a state of arrested development, a case of prolonged adolescence among a cadre of slackers. It has become a state of life, a "demographic," that is now pretty much the norm. Without fixed age boundaries, young men typically enter Guyland before they turn 16, and they begin to leave in their mid- to late-20s. This period now has a definable shape and texture, a topography that can be mapped and explored. A kind of suspended animation between boyhood and manhood, Guyland lies between the dependency and lack of autonomy of boyhood and the sacrifice and responsibility of manhood. Wherever they are living, whatever they are doing, and whomever they are hooking up with, Guyland is a dramatically new stage of development with its own rules and limitations. It is a period of life that demands examination—and not just because of the appalling headlines that greet us on such a regular basis. As urgent as it may seem to explore and expose Guyland because of the egregious behaviors of a few, it may be more urgent to examine the ubiquity of Guyland in the lives of almost everyone else.[1]

The Social Side *of* Sex

In *Guyland*, Michael Kimmel investigates young men coming of age. He shows that adulthood and maturity are often put off in favor of extending the "fun" of college. The traditional paths to manhood—moving out, going to college, finding a job and a partner, and becoming a parent—are increasingly getting delayed for today's "guys." In interviews with 400 young men, mostly white from the East Coast and college-educated, Kimmel suggests that "Guyland" is more than a lifestyle of extended adolescence, but also a social space where guys live by a "guy code."

This includes emphasis on pornography and sexual conquests, drinking, and locker room-like behaviors. They remain tied to video games, sports, and frequent but disconnected sexual relationships and have difficulty developing meaningful and resilient relationships. Such behaviors affect women's responses to these young men.

Women are an essential component in Guyland, and they must drink, be willing to hook up, and be slender. Women who enter Guyland often find themselves in demeaning positions that offer few choices—put up or get out. In Guyland, guys still call the shots and women will either be a "bitch" or a "babe," depending upon how they choose to respond to the demands of the guys. Babes play along, and bitches play by their own rules and agendas. College-aged women often struggle with such expectations, which leads to frustration for many of them. Kimmel suggests that most young women enter Guyland with the hope that its resident guys will eventually change. That remains to be seen.

GENDER *is defined as* the personal traits and position in society connected with being a male or female *differs from* **Sex** —which refers strictly to the biological makeup of a male or female *can be constructed through* **Socialization**
- which programs children to understand what behaviors are gender appropriate
- helps children create their gender identity, which is their conception of themselves as male or female

differences can lead to

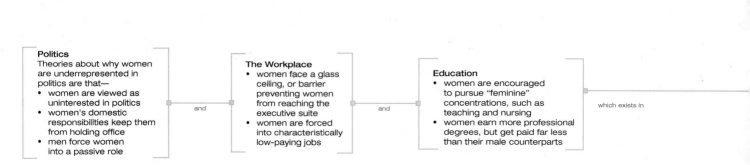

Politics
Theories about why women are underrepresented in politics are that—
- women are viewed as uninterested in politics
- women's domestic responsibilities keep them from holding office
- men force women into a passive role

and

The Workplace
- women face a glass ceiling, or barrier preventing women from reaching the executive suite
- women are forced into characteristically low-paying jobs

and

Education
- women are encouraged to pursue "feminine" concentrations, such as teaching and nursing
- women earn more professional degrees, but get paid far less than their male counterparts

which exists in

get the topic: WHAT IS THE DIFFERENCE BETWEEN SEX AND GENDER?

Gender vs. Sex

"Gender—it's bigger than sex."[2] With this phrase, many viewers were hooked to the *20/20* special called "It's More Than Just Sex: The Difference Between Men and Women" in 2006.[3] During this broadcast, anchors John Stossel and Elizabeth Vargas attempted to find out why women flock to the bathroom in groups and why men just don't listen.[4] The name of this program brings up an interesting and often overlooked point: although related, one's gender and one's sex are not necessarily the same thing.

Gender is defined as the personal traits and position in society connected with being a male or female. For instance, in traditional U.S. society, wearing a fancy dress is associated with the female gender, while wearing a tuxedo is associated with the male gender. **Sex** refers strictly to the biological makeup of a male or female. The biological differences between men and women do correlate with some behavioral differences. For example, boys may be more aggressive, and girls more verbal. Such simple correlations support the notion that ideas about gender are based on sex.[5] However, sociologists suggest that socialization, rather than biology, determines gender.

GENDER CONSTRUCTION

I am not a househusband, but I frequently cook, shop, and do a myriad of chores around the house that some might see as "not manly." In their book, *The Second Shift*, Arlie Hochschild and Anne Machung contend that the women's liberation movement has actually created additional burdens for many women, not taken them away. These women have entered the working world, but then return home to a second shift of work, requiring them to continue doing all the tasks their mothers did.[6] Researchers Scott South and Glenna Spitze find that men generally work

SEX is the biological makeup of a male or female.
GENDER IDENTITY is our perception of ourselves as male or female.

Gender is not a set of traits or roles; "it **is the product of social doings of some sort.**"

outside the home more hours than their wives, and perform only 18 hours of household labor per week, while women clock over 32 hours.[7] Interestingly, Hochschild finds that most of the women think this distribution of labor is fair. But why?

Probably because we've been socially programmed with ideas of how men and women should behave. The father as the primary caregiver contradicts our traditional cultural norm. But gender is not a set of traits or roles; "it is the product of social doings of some sort."[8] Sociologists West and Zimmerman suggest that gender is developed in two ways: Not only do we "do gender" or participate in its construction, but we also have gender done to us as members of society.[9] Childhood is the prime time for development of **gender identity**, or our perception of ourselves as male or female. During our childhood, we learn what behavior is "appropriate" for each gender and how to fit in with others like us.

To find out how children display or learn their gender, sociologist Michael Messner examined the interactions between two soccer teams—the all-boy Sea Monsters and the all-girl Barbie Girls.[10] Before a season-opening ceremony began, the Barbie Girls rallied together around a miniature Barbie float decorated with their team colors. A boom box on the float played music, and the girls gathered together

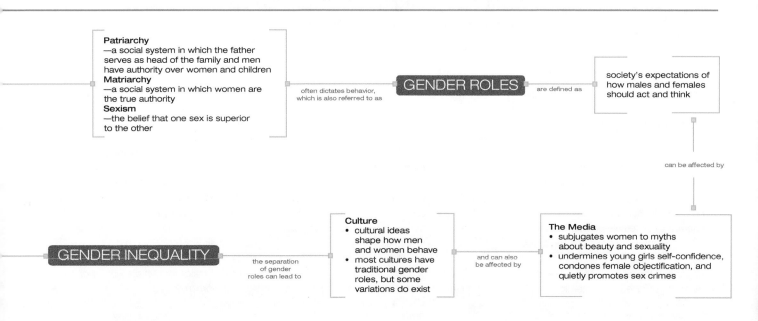

Patriarchy
—a social system in which the father serves as head of the family and men have authority over women and children
Matriarchy
—a social system in which women are the true authority
Sexism
—the belief that one sex is superior to the other

often dictates behavior, which is also referred to as

GENDER ROLES

are defined as

society's expectations of how males and females should act and think

can be affected by

GENDER INEQUALITY

the separation of gender roles can lead to

Culture
• cultural ideas shape how men and women behave
• most cultures have traditional gender roles, but some variations do exist

and can also be affected by

The Media
• subjugates women to myths about beauty and sexuality
• undermines young girls self-confidence, condones female objectification, and quietly promotes sex crimes

©Monkey Business Images/Shutterstock

to sing and dance. At first the little boys watched in confused awe, but soon took up a chant of "No Barbie!" When this chant failed to get the girls' attention, the little boys invaded their space, and a game of chase ensued. The parents observed this behavior from the sidelines and remarked that little boys and little girls are like members of two different species.

Messner argues that the parents easily recognized the differences, but failed to recognize the distinct similarities between the girls' and boys' teams during the rest of the season. Players on both teams regularly displayed many of the same behaviors—crying over skinned knees, racing to get snacks after the game, paying attention to birds or airplanes rather than to the coach—that would indicate a lack of major gender differences. Parents have no problem pointing out the differences between the boys and girls, but have difficulty identifying similarities due to "an institutional context that is characterized by informally structured sex segregation among the parent coaches and team managers, and by formally structured sex segregation among the children."[11] In other words, the adults couldn't see the similarities because they were socialized to see boys and girls as different.

Patriarchy and Sexism

William Wordsworth once said, "father—to God himself we cannot give a holier name." Wordsworth's sentiment is often reflected in the television shows we watch today. For instance, in *Desperate Housewives*, plumber Mike Delfino refuses to tell his wife Susan about his financial debt, even though she has the money to help him. He explains that he needs to be the breadwinner and protector of his family and refuses to let his wife assist him in this endeavor.

Humans have long considered the father the leader of the family unit. This role carries over into the rest of society through **patriarchy**, a social system in which men exert authority over women and children. The power position of men extends into government, business, and even religion. Few societies have been identified as a **matriarchy**, a social system in which women are the main authority and hold power over men.

The patriarchal system often results in **sexism**, or the belief that one sex is superior to the other. In many societies, attitudes often suggest women are the "weaker sex." This belief system may be adopted by women who seek jobs that fulfill these views. A few years ago, a very bright female student told me she wanted to be a medical doctor. I asked, "What's your major?" "Nursing" was the reply. She explained that her father, fiancé, and religious beliefs all dictated that women shouldn't be doctors. Clearly, these patriarchal beliefs possibly prevented a great mind from becoming a great doctor.

Gender Roles

Television's female characters have come a long way since Carol Brady and June Cleaver, for whom kissing their husbands good-bye and seeing the kids off to school started off a day of cleaning, baking, and homemaking. Today, we're used to seeing women portrayed as surgeons and attorneys and men actively participating in raising their children. What makes these arrangements acceptable to us now? The prevailing culture and the socialization that parents provide to their children shape ideas about gender-appropriate behaviors.

While women are succeeding in traditionally masculine fields like medicine and business, most of our children are still socialized to fit specific **gender roles**, or society's expectations of how males and females should act and think. Children's toys are an example of socialization at a young age.

∧∧∧ During our childhood, society shapes our gender identity. **What social cues might this young girl have picked up from the world around her?**

The Horrors of Female Circumcision

In some of the world's most patriarchal societies, it's traditional for men to control every aspect of a woman's life, including her body. Female circumcision, also referred to as female genital mutilation (FGM), is one such tradition. The procedure consists of the alteration or removal of parts of the female genital organs for no medical purpose.[12] The intention is to keep women sexually "pure" by ensuring that they will remain virgins until marriage.[13] Women who undergo FGM may suffer from a number of long-term medical consequences, including recurrent urinary tract infections, infertility, and increased risk of childbirth complications.[14]

This practice is most common in the western, eastern, and northeastern regions of Africa, some countries in Asia and the Middle East, and certain immigrant communities in Europe and North America.[15] It's estimated that between 100 and 140 million girls and women worldwide have undergone FGM.[16] Cultural tradition and ideas about proper sexual behavior perpetuate the practice, subjecting new generations of female children to a painful and dangerous operation.

Although this practice is rooted in cultural tradition, many believe it's a violation of human rights and a sign of male domination over women. The practice represents an inequality between the sexes, and it is a major form of discrimination against women.[17]

Manhattan Toy makes a line of dolls called Groovy Girls, which allows girls to "celebrate their own unique personalities," with various fashion options for the dolls.[18] The Hasbro Company's Nerf toys, geared toward more aggressive play like football and mock war situations, continue to be popular among young boys.[19]

However, gender roles in the United States are in a constant state of flux. This is not to say that we now encourage males to possess feminine characteristics, or vice versa, but the differences between the sexes are less pronounced than they once were. Young girls race down soccer fields or shoot hoops after school, and they're just as likely to wear jeans and T-shirts as skirts. The traditional roles of man as provider and woman as homemaker are shifting as well, since many households today have two breadwinners.

1

The Lolita Effect

Girls don't choose boys. Boys choose girls, but only sexy ones.

There's only one kind of sexy—slender, curvy, white beauty.

Girls should work to be that type of sexy.

The younger a girl is, the sexier she is.

Sexual violence can be attractive.

Source: Based on M. Gigi Durham, *The Lolita Effect: The Media Sexualization of Young Girls and What We Can Do About It* (Woodstock, NY: The Overlook Press, 2008).

©ZoomTeam/Shutterstock

PATRIARCHY is a social system in which the father serves as head of the family, and men have authority over women and children.

MATRIARCHY is a social system in which women are the main authority and hold power over men.

SEXISM is the belief that one sex is superior to the other.

GENDER ROLES are society's expectations of how males and females should act and think.

GENDER ROLES AND THE MEDIA

Although change is evident, we have not completely moved beyond old ideas about gender. Look no further than the reality shows like ABC's *The Bachelor*, and you'll see evidence that traditional gender roles are still in place. On these programs, women compete in challenges in order to win the affections of the man on the show. The shows **2** also continue to perpetuate myths about beauty and sexuality, as the emphasis is placed on young, "sexy" girls.

In Dr. M. Gigi Durham's *The Lolita Effect: The Media Sexualization of Young Girls and What We Can Do About It*, five myths about sex and sexuality are examined. These myths, which are listed in the graphic to the left, give many impressionable young women an "if you've got it, flaunt it" attitude.

3 Durham has labeled these myths the "Lolita Effect," which works to undermine girls' self-confidence, condones female objectification, and quietly promotes sex crimes.[20] The goal of Durham's book is to break down these myths in order to help girls recognize ideas about healthy, progressive sexuality, and to protect themselves from media degradation and sexual vulnerability.[21] Durham hopes to empower girls to make healthy decisions about their sexuality. Although the media's portrayal of sexuality is often a skewed one, people in the real world are not forced to abide by these **4** views. However, the media play a big role in our culture, so we cannot help but be affected by the things we see on TV and in magazines. What other effect might culture have on our ideas of gender?

THE FLUIDITY OF GENDER ROLES: INDONESIA'S BUGIS PEOPLE

Some cultures, like the Bugis people living on the Indonesian island of Sulawesi, have a different view of gender and gender roles. Australian anthropologist Sharyn Davies studied the Bugis people and found that gender-specific pronouns like "he" and "she" don't exist in their language.[22] Gender stratification among the Bugis is complicated with five different gender classifications: *oroané* (masculine male), *makkunrai* (feminine female), *calalai* (masculine female), *calabai* (feminine male), and *bissu* (embodying both male and female energies, revered as a shaman).[23] Each gender has specific behaviors, articles of clothing, social and religious roles, and sexual practices. The oroané and makkunrai genders are "normal" or comparable to what we know; the calalai, calabai, and bissu are what we might call "gender benders."

The **calalai** are anatomical females who assume the characteristics of men. They hold masculine jobs and dress as men, practice homosexuality, and typically live with female partners to adopt children.

The **calabai** are anatomical males who adhere to some of the responsibilities of women. Calabai males are homosexual and dress as women, yet they don't follow all cultural suggestions for women. They do, however, take on traditionally female responsibilities, like planning weddings.

The **bissu** embody the perfect mixture of male and female. A bissu that is externally male is considered to be internally female, and vice versa if the bissu is female. The Bugis people believe that bissu embody the best characteristics of both sexes, so they are able to communicate with the spirits and therefore occupy a special place in the community.

The Bugis have ideas about gender that are different from our own, but seem to be more accepting of different kinds of people. Men and women are allowed to live the gender role that suits them best in Bugis society.

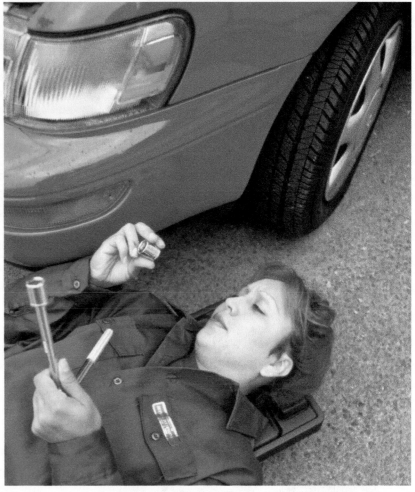

©Tony Freeman/Photo Edit

∧
∧ **In most societies, choosing an occupation typically
∧ associated with the opposite gender will make
someone stand out.** Why is it less conspicuous for calalai females to assume masculine jobs?

THINK SOCIOLOGICALLY

Culture's Effect on Gender Roles

Anthropologist Margaret Mead conducted a study of gender roles among three tribes in New Guinea: the Arapesh, the Mundgumor, and the Tchambuli.[24] She concluded that gender roles are largely dependent on culture. The men and women of the Arapesh tribe would both be considered "feminine" by our standards. The Mundgumor men and women were aggressive and violent, possessing "masculine" qualities. However,

among the Tchambuli people, men stayed home and raised the children, and women provided for the household.[25] This study drew much criticism; many accused Mead of doctoring her results to show what she had hoped to find.[26] Nevertheless, this study showed that gender is culturally constructed.

Other studies of gender roles have found that, in most societies, traditional gender roles have degrees of variation for any individual task. Anthropologist George Murdock's 1937 study of more than

200 societies found that women performed farming tasks and construction of homes in almost as many societies as men. Although not every society is uniform, Murdock's findings showed definite cross-cultural similarities in the roles of men and women.[27]

Changes in gender roles have left working women with children in a tough position. In *Guyland*, Kimmel shows that the expectations guys have of women give them the limited options of "bitch" or "babe," and neither position is the path to self-respect.

Gender and Inequality

In many societies, the idea of gender is not as fluid as the Bugis people suggest, and a hierarchy of sorts exists between the sexes. In the United States, for example, men and women are ranked differently in terms of power and wealth. In 2008, the Census Bureau reported that the median annual income for full-time working men was $46,367 compared to only $35,745 for full-time working women.[28] Because women are more likely to earn less than men, they're also more likely to live below the poverty line. Why is there such inequality between income levels and poverty statuses of men and women? We'll look into this further in the section relating to work. But first, let's look at a topic that should be relevant to everyone reading this book—gender and education.

GENDER AND EDUCATION

A few years ago, my daughter started her second grade school year very excited, but came home feeling down. When I asked why she was so upset, she said it was because she had "a boy for a teacher." I had to explain to her that "boy teachers" could be just as smart and fun as "girl teachers." Two months later, she couldn't wait to catch the bus in the morning to get to his class. Male elementary school teachers don't break any major social taboos today, but 30 years ago, when I was in school, the only men at my school were the gym teacher, the principal, and the janitor.

CALALAI are anatomical females in Bugis society who assume the characteristics of men.

CALABAI are anatomical males in Bugis society who adhere to some of the responsibilities of women.

BISSU are androgynous members of Bugis society who embody the perfect mixture of male and female.

Historically, men and women have received vastly different educations. When Oberlin College became the first college to offer coeducational enrollment in 1837, women students were encouraged to study "feminine" concentrations, such as nursing and teaching. Men, conversely, focused on fields that either involved vocational or intellectual skills. These differences are becoming less pronounced today, but there is still a clear educational divide between men and women nationally.[29]

Even though higher education used to be a primarily masculine pursuit, women now earn the majority of associate's and bachelor's degrees. Moreover, women earn slightly more than half of all master's and professional degrees and about 40 percent of doctoral degrees.[30] Although this is a major improvement for women in education, the differences in choices of majors still reflect traditional gender roles. Women receive the majority of art, music, and social

The Gender Income Gap by Level of Education in 2008

Median Earnings

| High School Diploma | Bachelor's Degree | Doctorate Degree |

Men $30,878
Women $18,293
Men $57,278
Women $36,294
Men $90,575
Women $60,619

©Orange Line Media/Shutterstock; ©Yuri Arcurs/Shutterstock; ©vgstudio/Shutterstock; ©Yuri Arcurs/Shutterstock; ©Yuri Arcurs/Shutterstock; ©Valentin Mosichev/Shutterstock

Source: "Historical Income Tables—People," U.S. Census Bureau, 2008, http://www.census.gov/hhes/www/income/histinc/incpertoc.html/p16.html.

HUMAN CAPITAL MODEL assumes that men and women bring different natural skills to the workplace.

CHOICE MODEL explains the income gap by analyzing the kinds of jobs women choose.

PATRIARCHY MODEL assumes that we have a male-dominated society that doesn't allow women to hold upper-tier jobs.

GLASS CEILING is an invisible barrier preventing women from reaching executive-level positions in the workplace.

science degrees, while men receive the majority of engineering, chemistry, and medical degrees.[31]

If women are earning degrees in greater numbers than men, shouldn't we see the income gap between men and women decrease? Census data show that the income gap between men and women actually becomes wider with higher levels of educational background. This seems curious. To investigate this further, let's turn to women in the workplace.

GENDER AND THE WORKPLACE

Today, women make up almost half of the United States' paid labor force and more than half of all married couples depend on two incomes.[32] While it's now accepted and necessary for women to work, the types of jobs as well as the compensation for these jobs remain different for men and women. Three theoretical models—the human capital model, the choice model, and the patriarchy model—attempt to explain these discrepancies.

The **human capital model** assumes that men and women bring different natural skills to the workplace. For example, society perceives men to have more mechanical skills, thus they make better engineers. Because society considers women to be more nurturing, they are assumed to be better teachers. Such an argument suggests it is not discrimination to hire men to do jobs for which they are more suited. This explains why men seem to have advantages in higher-income professions, such as medicine, engineering, and law.[33]

The **choice model** explains the income gap by analyzing the kinds of jobs women choose. Women choose to major in social work or elementary education, therefore knowingly entering fields that pay less. This argument suggests that if you choose a career that you know pays very little, you have only yourself to blame.[34]

The **patriarchy model** assumes that we have a male-dominated society that doesn't allow women to hold upper-tier jobs or steers them away from such careers early in life. For example, when discussing majors with an enrollment counselor, students may experience stereotypical gender role expectations. Male students are asked to consider business or engineering. Female students are asked about education or communication fields as possible professions.

The patriarchy model also supports the idea of a **glass ceiling**, or the invisible barrier that prevents women from reaching the executive suite. For example, few women become the CEOs of large companies. On the 2009 Fortune 500 list, women headed only 15 companies.[35]

Cornell sociology professor Shelley J. Correll studied labor distribution by sex and found that cultural beliefs about gender shape both male and female attitudes about their abilities.[36] If this is the case, our ideas about gender may need to undergo a radical change before the income gap between men and women disappears.

©Charly Franklin/Taxi/Getty Images

<<< **Women in the workplace often have to work twice as hard as men** to break through the glass ceiling above them.

Men Are a Gender, Too

It's important to remember that men are a gender, too. As noted earlier, men have many advantages in U.S. society. Christine Williams discusses how men have a "glass elevator" when it comes to getting jobs in traditionally female-dominated occupations. Men who sought jobs in the nursing, library, and elementary education fields said they felt they had an advantage over women applying for the same job because there were fewer men in those fields.[37]

However, it's important to know that with the male gender role come gender expectations. In his book, Kimmel suggests that the gender expectations of Guyland, while seemingly bringing happiness to guys, actually keep them from what will bring them long-term happiness. The data, according to Kimmel, show that marriage and commitment actually bring happiness to men, while hanging out in Guyland cannot do that.[38]

>>> ACTIVITY Write out as many household jobs as you can think of, and place an M next to roles that are for the men and a W next to those for the women. Do you see any gender bias in your life?

GENDER AND POLITICS

Women are making huge political strides. Hillary Rodham Clinton became the first widely supported female politician to bid for the 2008 Democratic presidential nomination, and Republican Presidential nominee John McCain tapped Alaska Governor Sarah Palin as his running mate. California Representative Nancy Pelosi is the Speaker of the House, and Clinton is now the Secretary of State.

Women regularly hold high political office in other parts of the world. England has had several women in power, beginning in 1553 with Queen Mary I. Margaret Thatcher was prime minister from 1979 to 1990. Golda Meir led Israel as prime minister from 1969 to 1973, and Benazir Bhutto was prime minister of Pakistan from 1988 to 1990 and from 1993 to 1996.[39] Let's examine three theories that attempt to explain why women in the United States have not held similar positions.

Theory #1: Women, by nature, are uninterested in politics. This theory has been disproved time and again by data that show that women vote more regularly than men.[40] Women have also risen to political prominence throughout the country, as shown.

Theory #2: The structure of women's lives does not lend itself to the rigors of political office. I like to call this theory the "baby bias." The idea of the "supermom" suggests that a woman in office would be too overwhelmed by her mothering duties to succeed. For this reason, some women put off political involvement, as did Pelosi and Clinton, until their children are grown.

Theory #3. Society forces women into a politically passive role. Traditionally, this has been the case. But women are more independent today and have an increased interest in holding political office. Furthermore, politicians tend to be lawyers and business people, traditionally "men's" worlds. Although this is changing, female representation in politics remains disproportionately low.

Voter Turnout by Sex in November 2008

65.7% (Women) **61%** (Men)

Proportion of Voters

Source: Data from the U.S. Census Bureau, "Reported Voting and Registration, by Marital Status, Age, and Sex: November 2008."

221

Feminism

Feminism refers to the vast collection of social movements and theories about gender differences. Feminism proposes social equality for all people. Feminist thinkers believe that women are equal to men and deserve the same opportunities as men.

The history of the feminist movement goes back to the 18th century. Mary Wollstonecraft Shelley's famous essay "A Vindication of the Rights of Woman" is one of the earliest examples of Western feminist thought. Published in 1792, it argued for a woman's right to an education. Wollstonecraft's essay predates modern feminism, which can be divided into three "waves."

FIRST-WAVE FEMINISM

What is considered the first wave began in the late 19th and early 20th centuries and revolved around the women's suffrage movement. The fight for women's right to vote began in 1848 with activists such as Susan B. Anthony and Elizabeth Cady Stanton. Gradually, women were granted to vote at the state level, but national women's suffrage was not won until 1920. The Nineteenth Amendment, which prohibited denying the vote to anyone based on sex, was ratified after years of marches and protests in support of women's suffrage.[41]

SECOND-WAVE FEMINISM

The second wave of feminism occurred during the women's liberation movement that began in the 1960s. While first-wave feminism protested legal inequality, second-wave feminism also included equality in the workplace, equality in education, and social independence from men.

In 1963, Betty Friedan published a book called *The Feminine Mystique*, bringing attention to the idea that a woman should seek personal fulfillment outside her home and family. The book attacks a social system in which women are treated as nothing more than homemakers and childbearers.[42] Friedan is said to have ignited the women's liberation movement with this book, although she has also been criticized for focusing exclusively on the plight of white middle- and upper-class women.[43]

In addition to equal rights in education and the workplace, second-wavers demanded reproductive rights and protection from domestic and sexual violence. These demands caused a great deal of controversy, as many conservatives felt that contraceptives and abortion go against traditional morals. Some feminists also tried to get the Equal Rights Amendment passed, which would ensure that "[e]quality of rights under the law shall not be denied or abridged by the United States or by any state on account of sex."[44] However, the bill has not been passed since its introduction to Congress in 1923. Some feminists are still trying to ratify the bill today.

One of the forces behind this proposed amendment is the National Organization for Women (NOW). NOW was founded in 1966 and remains the largest feminist organization in the United States.[45] Although the combined efforts of all those involved in the second wave of feminism did result in many successes, a new wave of feminism arose 30 years later to respond to the feelings of failure and disappointment the second wave had left behind.[46]

THIRD-WAVE FEMINISM

Beginning in the early 1990s, the third wave of feminism branched out to include multiple racial and socioeconomic groups. Gloria Anzaldua, bell hooks (née Gloria Jean Watkins), Maxine Hong Kingston, and Audre Lorde are feminist leaders associated with the third wave. Author and social activist bell hooks, for example, connected topics like race, capitalism, and gender within her works. She emphasized the fact that all three topics were interconnected and that they needed to be addressed at the same time.[47]

The History of Feminism

Second-Wave Feminism

1848
Activists such as Elizabeth Cady Stanton and Susan B. Anthony fought for women's right to vote

1917
Groups such as the Silent Sentinels came together to support women's suffrage

1960s
The Women's Liberation Movement began

1960s and 1970s
Women began to go to college and pursue careers

Mary Wollstonecraft Shelley's *A Vindication of the Rights of Woman* was published, which argued for a woman's right to vote
1792

Women in Wyoming were permitted to vote
1869

19th Amendment was ratified, which gave all women in the United States the right to vote
1920

Betty Friedan published *The Feminine Mystique*, which helped further ignite the Women's Lib Movement
1963

First-Wave Feminism

The underground feminist punk movement of the 1990s called "riot grrrl" also influenced the third wave. The subculture movement produced music, art, and magazines that addressed issues like rape, domestic abuse, female empowerment, and sexuality. The movement encouraged the modern woman to be empowered, outspoken, and passionate.[48]

Many activist organizations resulted from the third wave. Take Back the Night is an organization that raises awareness and offers support to victims of rape and sexual assault. The nonprofit organization Dress for Success collects business suits through donations for

> **FEMINISM** is the vast collection of social movements and theories about gender differences, proposing social equality for all people.

women receiving welfare so they can interview for jobs with confidence.[49] The Third Wave Foundation and Feminist Majority Leadership Alliance are activist groups that work for gender, racial, economic, and social justice.[50]

think sociologically: WHAT ARE THE PERSPECTIVES ON GENDER AND GENDER INEQUALITY?

Feminist Theory

Feminists study how gender affects the experiences and opportunities of men and women. Although feminists may not always agree about how to achieve gender equality, they do tend to adopt four general beliefs:

1 **Increasing equality in work and education.** Year after year, women are earning more professional degrees than men and entering the workforce in large numbers. However, feminists continue fighting for equality in both the workplace and schools against the gender wage gap and the glass ceiling that women commonly face in the workplace.

2 **Expanding human choice for outcomes.** In the book *Woman Hating*, feminist Andrea Dworkin comments that "Being female in this world is having been robbed of the potential for human choice by men who love to hate us."[51] Not all feminists agree with Dworkin's suggestion, but virtually all feminists work to create a society in which men

and women have equal opportunities. For example, by expanding enrollment in professional and graduate schools, women have greater opportunities to choose careers they enjoy.

3 **Eliminating gender stratification.** Feminism commits itself to assure equal rights, equal opportunity, and equal pay for women. For example, women are now successful Marines, a job that used to be an option for men only.

4 **Ending sexual violence.** Feminist theorists believe that male violence against women perpetuates gender inequality in our society.[52] For example, the "rule of thumb" refers to the alleged British common law that allowed a man to beat his wife with a stick, as long as it was not any larger than the diameter of his thumb. It's important to note that this was never an actual law; however men were allowed to punish their wives corporally.[53]

Third-Wave Feminism

Early 1990s
The third wave of feminism begins to address the failures of the second wave

Early 1990s
Bands like Bratmobile, Bikini Kill, and Huggy Bear communicated the message of third-wave feminism

The National Organization for Women —the leading feminist organization— was founded **1966**

Feminist leaders Gloria Anzaldua, bell hooks, Maxine Hong Kingston, and Audre Lorde promote feminist cause **Early 1990s**

Groups such as Take Back the Night and Dress for Success emerged **1990s**

LIBERAL VS. RADICAL FEMINISM

Although there are many different kinds of feminism and there is not universal agreement about the titles of the different types, we will address two types—liberal feminism and radical feminism.

Liberal feminists tend to be in line with their historical roots, suggesting that women's equality is the primary motivation for the movement. If you believe that women should receive the same pay for the same work, have equal opportunities in the workplace, college, political office, and be free from domestic violence, then you are a liberal feminist. As you can see, this group is the larger group, because most people agree that women should not be discriminated against based on their gender. As a result, they support the idea that women should be free to pursue their own interests and achieve equality.

Radical feminists agree with the liberal agenda, but generally carry the ideas further. They might focus on capitalism and the ways that men use their historical advantage over money to maintain control over women. Radicals see that patriarchy is firmly rooted in society. Some suggest that only an overthrow of capitalism can result in equality for women. Others suggest that women should avoid "traditional activities" such as childbearing, since this often leads women to subordinate their own goals for their husbands and families.

©David Young-Wolff/PhotoEdit

∧
∧ Notice the difference in
∧ dress between these male and female cheerleaders.

Conflict theorists would argue that cheerleading is just one way that men exploit women in our society.

Functionalism

While feminists fight gender inequality in the United States, functionalists examine how the separation of gender roles actually functions in a society. Society places men and women in different spheres, and these differences help maintain society. Because men and women often play different roles, competition is eliminated between the sexes, and family life runs smoothly.[54] For example, if men are expected to go out and work to provide for the family, while women are expected to perform domestic tasks and care for the children, their roles are complementary to each other. Each is doing a job that must be done. As women steadily enter the workforce, the separation of gender roles becomes less distinct. Even so, women are generally expected to maintain the home.

Talcott Parsons studied the separation of gender roles in the context of the family. Parsons noted that as children, "sex discrimination is more than anything else a reflection of the differentiation of adult sex roles."[55] Girls at a young age are socialized to display expressive qualities, such as calmness and nurturing (qualities expected of many adult women), while boys are prone to be rational and competitive, which are instrumental qualities.[56]

According to Parsons, young girls are able to step into the adult feminine role early in their development.[57] These girls see their mothers performing domestic tasks and are often expected to help out. Young boys, however, have fathers who work outside the house. As a result, boys are trained to prepare for their futures in the workforce.

Conflict Theory

Conflict theorists argue that capitalism and patriarchy are deeply intertwined. In a capitalist society, women generally are at the bottom of the system, regardless of their job. Furthermore, they often engage in unpaid, domestic tasks that serve to maintain the status quo.[58] However, men often devalue the work that women do, which reinforces the power that men have over women.[59] Women who work tend to make less money than men in the workforce, so women are often subordinate to their better-paid husbands. Women are locked in a never-ending cycle that makes them submissive and subservient to men.

Symbolic Interactionism

Symbolic interactionists believe that people's definition of gender develops from everyday interactions with others from the same and opposite sex.[60] Sociologists West and Zimmerman's idea of "doing gender" best illustrates the symbolic interactionists' point of view.[61] We all "do gender" every day, which means we act in a certain way that is associated with a particular gender. The way you style your hair, the mannerisms you have, and the way you talk are all part of the way you communicate your gender to others.

Sociologist Janet Chafetz argues that "doing gender" not only "(re)produces gender difference, it (re)produces gender inequality."[62] One way this happens is through conversation. Deborah Tannen's *You Just Don't Understand: Men and Women in Conversation* argues that our lives are essentially a series of conversations, and we pass on "different, asymmetrical assumptions about men and women" in these conversations.[63]

Chafetz would argue that men and women communicate differently. Men often dominate conversations, and women struggle to follow the sometimes arbitrary rules that men impose on the dialogue. Women use "verbal and body language in ways that weaken their ability to assert themselves," which makes them appear less powerful than their male counterparts.[64] For example, while eating out one day, I noticed a

MACHISMO is overt and exaggerated displays of masculinity.

men's softball team and a few of their wives/girlfriends at a nearby table. The guys were talking and laughing, but the women were passive. Gender socialization generally teaches boys to make their voice heard, while girls are taught to be "good," meaning quiet and docile.

Men and women often follow scripted behavior, acting in ways that are associated with their gender.[65] For example, men and women use different types of languages and gestures. Men tend to be more direct in describing their wants and desires, displaying **machismo**, overt and exaggerated displays of masculinity.[66]

∨
∨
∨ What do you think about your conversations with people of the opposite sex? **According to *Guyland*, these people are not likely to be talking about important things; they're more likely to be getting ready to hook up.**

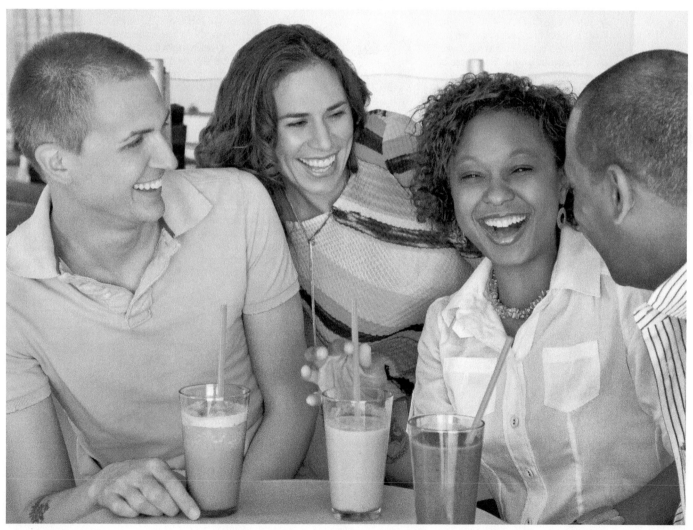

©CREATISTA/Shutterstock

WRAP YOUR MIND AROUND THE THEORY

Men and women play complementary roles in society. How might these roles fit into the modern family system?

FUNCTIONALISM

The functionalists view society as a system of many parts, working in concert with one another to form a whole. Talcott Parsons believed that gender differences were essential in maintaining a properly functioning society. Parents socialize boys and girls for their future roles of father and mother. Boys are taught to be confident, rational, and competitive because these characteristics are instrumental qualities for men to succeed. Parents socialize girls with the primary goal of preparing to raise children. They learn nurturing qualities that Parsons refers to as expressive qualities. These complementary roles assist in the smooth functioning of society.

CONFLICT THEORY

Social conflict theorists are interested in the struggle for power between groups. In the case of gender, conflict theorists see the gender roles as beneficial to men, as their role as main bread-winner gives them power and control. Friedrich Engels, a contemporary of Karl Marx, suggested that women are the first oppressed group.[67] Although he agreed with Marx that the proletariat was oppressed, Engels points out that women, too, are exploited. This may not seem to be a major idea in today's world, but in 1884, it was staggering.

WHY DOES GENDER STRATIFICATION EXIST?

SYMBOLIC INTERACTIONISM

The symbolic interactionist perspective might focus on how people self-select by gender. For example, men may choose fields associated with "maleness," whereas women select careers based on the types of work that are considered "normal" for them. Thus, women tend not to become engineers or work in other professions that require a mathematical background, in part, because it isn't expected of them. Gendered definitions influence career choices of men and women.[68] When I became a social worker, a job dominated by women, I had family members who actually said, "Isn't that a woman's job?" Such a definition might influence a career choice.

Patriarchal structures help men continue to have advantages over women. How might capitalism contribute to this?

Gender roles are taught to us early in life. **What are the pros and cons of selecting a career outside the traditional roles for your gender?**

discover sociology in action: WHAT POLICIES ARE IN PLACE TO PREVENT SEXUAL HARASSMENT AND DOMESTIC VIOLENCE?

Although more subtle forms of oppression can be damaging, physical, sexual, emotional, economic, and psychological abuse are all forms of oppression. The National Institute of Justice and the Centers for Disease Control and Prevention survey found that a large number of crimes go unreported. Generally, only one-fifth of rapes, one-fourth of physical assaults, and one-half of stalking committed against women by their intimate partners are reported.[69] The most common reasons for not reporting assault or rape were fear of the perpetrator, belief that police couldn't help, and worry that police wouldn't believe them.[70] Because victims begin to internalize their emotions, these women either believe they deserved the assault or that no one can help them.[71]

Resources are available to help the victims, but victims are often too scared or ashamed to come forward. However, in response to the rising concern about these crimes, such offenders are receiving longer sentences and are required to register as sex offenders in the public domain.[72]

Social Policy—Stopping Sexual Harassment and Gender Violence

Sexual harassment and gender violence are persistent issues, as stories of office harassment, domestic violence, and rape are commonplace items in the news. The National Violence Against Women survey found that approximately 25 percent of surveyed women and 7.6 percent of surveyed men claim that they were raped or physically assaulted by a spouse, cohabiting partner, or date in their lifetimes.[73] The good news is that more and more victims are reporting incidents to the police, even when the offenders are intimate partners.

Significant efforts have been made to curb sexual offenses. Law enforcement and community organizations have initiated campaigns against sexual assault and domestic violence. Shelters for battered women give victims a place to stay to recuperate from domestic violence, and counseling services help battered women with self-esteem issues, as well as other psychological trauma brought on by abuse. It is important to help men, women, and families suffering from abuse because damages extend far beyond a bruise. Abuse harms people on three levels: physical, financial, and emotional.[74]

ACTIVITIES

1. Research your state's sex offender laws. What is the suggested penalty for first-time rape offenders? Are sex offenders required to register and inform the neighborhood in which they reside of their status?
2. Locate a battered women's shelter in your area. How is the shelter funded? What services does the shelter provide?

From Classroom to Community ⟩ Visiting a Women's Shelter

Jane was in her late 40s when she decided to go back to school. As part of her class work, she volunteered some time in a local battered women's shelter, and she was surprised by how little things had changed since she was younger.

"When I was 22, I left an abusive man and lived with my son in a shelter for about six months. During that time, I learned a lot about the cycle of violence, and traced the roots of my willingness to tolerate this behavior with a counselor."

For Jane, volunteering at the shelter brought all of those memories back. "Why is it that so many men think it is their right to beat the women in their lives? Why do they need to be so controlling? If girls aren't taught to behave this way, why are men?"

Jane answered phones, filed documents, and served meals from time to time. She was so determined to help these women because of her own experience.

"I escaped this lifestyle and never wish to return. I sure hope that I helped some of those women avoid falling back into abuse. No one deserves this."

©Tony Freeman/ Photo Edit

©Chuck Savage/ Corbis

©Ariel Skelley/Corbis

WHAT IS THE DIFFERENCE BETWEEN SEX AND GENDER?

sex: the biological makeup of a male or female

gender: the personal traits and position in society connected with being a male or female

WHAT ARE THE PERSPECTIVES ON GENDER AND GENDER INEQUALITY?

feminist theory: feminists share the belief that equality in work and education should increase, human choice for outcomes should be expanded, gender stratification should be eliminated, and sexual violence should end

functionalism: the separation of gender roles eliminates competition between the sexes and makes family life run smoothly

conflict theory: capitalism and patriarchy are intertwined; as a result, women are locked in a never-ending cycle that makes them submissive and subservient to men

symbolic interactionism: people's definition of gender develops from everyday interactions with others from the same and opposite sex

WHAT POLICIES ARE IN PLACE TO PREVENT SEXUAL HARASSMENT AND DOMESTIC VIOLENCE?

campaigns against sexual assault and domestic violence, shelters, and counseling services

get the topic: WHAT IS THE DIFFERENCE BETWEEN SEX AND GENDER?

Gender vs. Sex
Patriarchy and Sexism
Gender Roles
Gender and Inequality

Feminism
Feminist Theory
Functionalism
Conflict Theory

Symbolic Interactionism
Social Policy—Stopping Sexual Harassment and Gender Violence

Theory

FUNCTIONALISM

- gender differences help maintain a functioning society
- parents socialize boys and girls to their future roles of fathers and mothers
- boys are taught to be competitive and confident; girls are taught to be nurturing and caring

CONFLICT THEORY

- gender roles are beneficial to men, as their role as main breadwinner gives them power and control
- capitalism emphasizes male domination, as women are encouraged to spend money on goods

- Engels: women are the first oppressed group

SYMBOLIC INTERACTIONISM

- women select careers based on the types of work that are considered "normal" for women to perform
- certain careers are perceived as "masculine," which drives many capable women away from even attempting to enter these fields
- differences in the career choices of men and women begin early in life
- people "do gender" every day, which creates gender differences and inequality

Key Terms

sex	sexism	bissu	glass ceiling
gender identity	gender roles	human capital model	feminism
patriarchy	calalai	choice model	machismo
matriarchy	calabai	patriarchy model	

MY SEARCH LAB

1. *Night to His Day: The Social Construction of Gender* by Judith Lorber, reprinted from *Paradoxes of Gender*, 1994, pp. 13–27. Used by permission of Yale University Press.

INTRODUCTION

In this excerpt, Lorber describes gender as a social institution that affects every area of life.

DISCUSSION QUESTIONS

1. How are you "doing gender" at this very moment? What about others around you?
2. Lorber claims that "As a social institution, gender is one of the major ways human beings organize their lives." Explain this statement and give examples to demonstrate.
3. Why do you think Lorber calls this excerpt "Night to His Day"?

2. *Sex and Temperament in Three Tribes* from *Sex and Temperament in Three Primitive Societies* by Margaret Mead. Copyright © 1935, 1950, 1963 by Margaret Mead. Used by permission of HarperCollins Publishers.

INTRODUCTION

In this much-cited article by anthropologist Margaret Mead, three tribes in New Guinea are used to address the nature (biology) versus nurture (society) debate.

DISCUSSION QUESTIONS

1. Compare/contrast the three tribes. How do they compare to expectations about masculinity and femininity in U.S. culture?
2. After reading this article, what do you conclude about the nature versus nurture debate?

THE THINKSPOT

How far have we gotten away from the old ideas about gender? Go to the ThinkSpot and watch this amateur video, which makes a pretty good case for the fact that we haven't moved that far away at all. Do you agree or disagree with the statements the videographer makes in her piece? For instance, do the media portray men as dominant while women are portrayed as the weaker sex? What examples can you come up with to refute each of the videographer's claims?

What effect does gender stratification have on education? Go to the ThinkSpot where you'll find a video that discusses the question of whether a same-sex classroom or a mixed-gender classroom is best. This is a topic that is being discussed worldwide, as you'll see from the video. What do you think? Same-sex or mixed-gender? And why?

Sample Test Questions

These multiple-choice questions are similar to those found in the test bank that accompanies this textbook.

1. Gender identity is mostly developed at which stage in life?
   a. Childhood
   b. Middle age
   c. Adolescence
   d. Late adulthood

2. Children are socialized to fit specific
   a. gender roles.
   b. social classes.
   c. gender inequities.
   d. occupational roles.

3. Which of the following is *not* one of Dr. M. Gigi Durham's myths about sexuality?
   a. Girls don't choose boys. Boys choose girls, but only sexy ones.
   b. There's only one kind of sexy—slender, curvy, white beauty.
   c. Girls should be satisfied with their current body type.
   d. The younger a girl is, the sexier she is.

4. Which of the following is a major cause of the increase in working mothers?
   a. More educational opportunities for women
   b. Increase in homosexuality
   c. Rising divorce rate
   d. Lack of children

5. According to functionalist analysis, children are socialized in order to
   a. keep men in a dominant position in society.
   b. maintain a society that runs properly.
   c. establish a clear career path.
   d. entertain their parents.

ESSAY

1. How have gender roles in the United States changed and stayed the same since the 1950s?
2. What are the underlying causes of sexism, and will society ever be able to overcome them?
3. How might society be different if traditional gender roles were reversed?
4. Which of the three models explaining inequality in the workplace do you think is the strongest?
5. How effective do you the think the feminist movement has been in championing women's equality?

WHERE TO START YOUR RESEARCH PAPER

For information and articles on the "riot grrrl" movement, go to http://grrrlzines.net/writingonzines.htm

For more information on the National Organization for Women (NOW), go to its Web site http://www.now.org/

To learn more about Take Back the Night, go to http://www.takebackthenight.org/

To learn more about Dress for Success, go to http://www.dressforsuccess.org/

ANSWERS: 1. a; 2. a; 3. c; 4. c; 5. b

Endnotes

1. Michael Kimmel, *Guyland: The perilous world where boys become men: Understanding the critical years between 16 and 26* (New York: Harper Collins, 2008).

2. "20/20: The Difference Between Men and Women: 9/29/06," *ABC News*, at http://abcnewsstore.go.com/webapp/wcs/stores/servlet/DSIProductDisplay?catalogId511002&storeId520051&productId52003060&langId5-1&categoryId5100032.

3. Ibid.

4. Ibid.

5. Ivy Kennelly, Sabine N. Merz, and Judith Lorber, "What is Gender?" *American Sociological Review*, 2001. 66(4): 598–605.

6. *The Second Shift* by Arlie Hochschild and Ann Machung, copyright © 1989, 2003 NY: Penguin publishing.

7. Scott J. South and Glenna Spitze, "Housework in Marital and Nonmarital Households," American Sociological Review, 1994. 59(3): 327–347

8. Candace West and Don H. Zimmerman, "Doing Gender," *Gender and Society*, 1987. 1(2): 125–151.

9. Ibid.

10. Michael A. Messner, "Barbie Girls versus Sea Monsters: Children Constructing Gender," *Gender and Society*, 2000. 14(6): 765–784.

11. Ibid.

12. "Female Genital Mutilation," World Health Organization, http://www.who.int/mediacentre/factsheets/fs241/en/ (accessed July 28, 2008).

13. Ibid.

14. Ibid.

15. Ibid.

16. Ibid.

17. Ibid.

18. Manhattan Toy Online Store, http://store.manhattantoy.com (accessed July 28, 2008).

19. Nerf, http://www.hasbro.com/nerf (accessed July 28, 2008).

20. M. Gigi Durham, *The Lolita Effect: The Media Sexualization of Young Girls and What We Can Do About It* (Woodstock, NY: The Overlook Press, 2008).

21. Ibid.

22. Sharyn Graham Davis, *Challenging Gender Norms: Five Genders Among the Bugis in Indonesia* (Belmont, CA: Thomson Wadsworth, 2007).

23. Ibid.

24. Margaret Mead, *Sex and Temperament* (New York, Harper Perennial, 1935).

25. Ibid.

26. Derek Freeman, *Margaret Mead and Samoa: The Making and Unmaking of an Anthropological Myth* (Cambridge, MA: Harvard University Press, 1983).

27. G. P. Murdock, "Comparative Data on the Division of Labor by Sex." *Social Forces*, 1937. 15: 551–553.

28. Carmen DeNavas-Walt, Bernadette D. Proctor, and Jessica Smith, *Income, Poverty, and Health Insurance Coverage in the United States: 2008*, U.S. Census Bureau, Current Population Reports, 60-236, U.S. Government Printing Office, Washington, DC, 2009.

29. "Colleges for Women," National Women's History Museum, http://www.nmwh.org/exhibits/education/1800s_6.htm (accessed August 18, 2008).

30. Jerry A. Jacobs, "Gender and the Stratification of Colleges." *The Journal of Higher Education*, 1999. 70(2): 161–187.

31. Ibid.

32. Carmen DeNavas-Walt, Bernadette D. Proctor, and Jessica Smith, *Income, Poverty, and Health Insurance Coverage in the United States: 20086*, U.S. Census Bureau, Current Population Reports, P60-236, U.S. Government Printing Office, Washington, DC, 2009.

33. Brian L. Rich, "On Inequality," *Sociological Perspectives*: Papers from the 56th Annual Meeting, Autumn, 1995. 38(3): 357–380.

34. Miriam David, "Choice, Diversity and Equity in Secondary Schooling," *Oxford Review of Education*, 1997. 23(1): 77–87.

35. David A. Cotter, Joan M. Hermsen, Seth Ovadia, and Reeve Vanneman, "The Glass Ceiling Effect," *Social Forces*, 2001. 80(2): 655–682; CNN.com, "Fortune 500 Women CEOs," http://money.cnn.com/magazines/fortune/fortune500/2009/womenceos/ (accessed June 16, 2010).

36. Shelley J. Correll, "Gender and the Career Choice Process: The Role of Biased Self-Assessments." *The American Journal of Sociology*, 2001. 106(6): 1691–1730.

37. Christine Williams, "The Glass Escalator: Hidden Advantages for Men in the "Female" Professions." *Men's Lives*, 2007, http://jan.ucc.nau.edu/hdh9/e-reserves/Williams_-_The_glass_escalator_PDF-1.pdf (accessed August 15, 2008).

38. Michael Kimmel, *Guyland: The perilous world where boys become men: Understanding the critical years between 16 and 26* (New York: Harper Collins, 2008).

39. "Prime Minister Golda Meir," The President and Prime Minister Memorial Council, http://www.pmo.gov.il/PMOEng/Government/Memorial/PrimeMinisters/

Golda.htm (accessed August 15, 2008); "Benazir Bhutto," *Benazirbhutto.org*, http://www.benazirbhutto.org/mbb-profile.html (accessed August 15, 2008); "Benazir Bhutto," Encyclopædia Britannica Online, 2008, http://search.eb.com/eb/article-9079076 (accessed August, 27, 2008).

40. Susan Carroll, "Women Voters and the Gender Gap," http://www.apsanet.org/content_5270.cfm (accessed August 18, 2008).

41. "Topics in Feminism," *Standford Encyclopedia of Philosophy*, March 15, 2004, http://plato.stanford.edu/entries/feminism-topics/#Oth.

42. Betty Friedan, *The Feminine Mystique* (New York: W.W. Norton and Company, 1963).

43. Barbara Epstein, "Feminist Consciousness After the Women's Movement," *Monthly Review*, 2002, Vol. 54, No. 4, http://www.monthlyreview.org/0902epstein.htm.

44. "The Equal Rights Amendment," *EqualRightsAmendment.org*, http://www.equalrightsamendment.org/era.htm (accessed August 15, 2008).

45. "About NOW," National Organization for Women, http://www.now.org/about.html (accessed August 15, 2008).

46. Mountain Writer, "Feminism in Waves: A Brief Overview of the First, Second and Third Wave." *Associated Content*, October 1, 2007, at http://www.associated-content.com/article/392800/feminism_in_waves_a_brief_overwiew.html?page55&cat575.

47. "Bell hooks," *Contemporary Educational Thought*, University of Miami, http://www.education.miami.edu/ep/contemporaryed/Bell_Hooks/bell_hooks.html (accessed August 15, 2008).

48. Sofia Klatzker, "Riot Grrls," 1998, http://eamusic.dartmouth.edu/;wowem/electronmedia/mish/riot-grrrl.html, http://www.riotgrrrlink.com/.

49. "Take Back the Night," http://www.takebackthenight.org/ (accessed August 26, 2008); "Dressed for Success," http://www.dressforsuccess.org/ (accessed August 26, 2008).

50. Third Wave Foundation, http://www.thirdwavefoundation.org/ (accessed August 26, 2008); Feminist Majority Leadership Alliance, http://www.feminist-campus.org/ (accessed August 26, 2008).

51. Mary F. Brewer, *Race, Sex, and Gender in Contemporary Women's Theatre: The Construction of "Woman,"* (Sussex, UK: Sussex Academic Press, 1999), p. 106.

52. Janet Saltzman Chafetz, "Feminist Theory and Sociology: Underutilized Contributions for Mainstream Theory," *Annual Review of Sociology*, 1997. 23: 97–120.

53. "Rule of Thumb," The Phrase Finder, http://www.phrases.org.uk/meanings/rule-of-thumb.html (accessed August 28, 2008).

54. Talcott Parsons, "Age and Sex in the Social Structure of the United States," *American Sociological Review*, 1942. 7(5): 604–616.

55. Ibid.

56. Ibid.

57. Ibid.

58. Janet Saltzman Chafetz, "Feminist Theory and Sociology: Underutilized Contributions for Mainstream Theory," *Annual Review of Sociology*, 1997. 23: 97–120.

59. Ibid.

60. Ibid.

61. Candace West and Don H. Zimmerman, "Doing Gender," *Gender and Society*, 1987. 1(2): 125–151.

62. Janet Saltzman Chafetz, "Feminist Theory and Sociology: Underutilized Contributions for Mainstream Theory," *Annual Review of Sociology*, 1997. 23: 97–120.

63. Deborah Tannen, *You Just Don't Understand: Women and Men in Conversation* (New York: HarperCollins Publishers, 2007).

64. Janet Saltzman Chafetz, "Feminist Theory and Sociology: Underutilized Contributions for Mainstream Theory," *Annual Review of Sociology*, 1997. 23: 97–120.

65. Ibid.

66. Gloria Gonzalez-Lopez, "Beyond Machos and Machoism: Mexican Immigrant Men, Sexuality, and Intimacy," *Men's Lives*, July 11, 2003, http://www.allacademic.com/meta/p_mla_apa_research_citation/1/0/9/1/5/pages109159/p109159-1.php.

67. Friedrich Engels, *The Origin of the Family, Private Property and the State* (Resistance Books, 1884).

68. Shelley J. Correll, "Gender and the Career Choice Process: The Role of Biased Self-Assessments." *The American Journal of Sociology*, 2001. 106(6): 1691–1730.

69. Patricia Tjaden and Nancy Thoennes, "Extent, Nature, and Consequences of Intimate Partner Violence," Findings From the National Violence Against Women Survey, Washington, DC: National Institute of Justice and Centers for Disease Control, July 2000, http://www.ncjrs.gov/pdffiles1/nij/181867.pdf

70. Patricia Tjaden and Nancy Thoennes, "Extent, Nature, and Consequences of Intimate Partner Violence," Findings From the National Violence Against Women Survey, Washington, DC: National Institute of Justice and Centers for Disease

Control, July 2000, http://www.ncjrs.gov/pdffiles1/nij/181867.pdf; "Sexual Violence Prevention," Centers for Disease Control and Prevention, http://www.cdc.gov/ncipc/dvp/SV/svp-consequences.htm (accessed August 18, 2008).

71. United States Department of Justice. "About Domestic Violence," http://www.ovw.usdoj.gov/domviolence.htm (accessed August 15, 2008).

72. Ibid.

73. Patricia Tjaden and Nancy Thoennes, "Extent, Nature, and Consequences of Intimate Partner Violence," Findings From the National Violence Against Women Survey, Washington, DC: National Institute of Justice and Centers for Disease Control, July 2000, http://www.ncjrs.gov/pdffiles1/nij/181867.pdf.

74. "Cost of Intimate Partner Violence Against Women in the United States," Centers for Disease Control and Prevention, http://www.cdc.gov/ncipc/pub-res/ipv_ cost/01_executive.htm (accessed September 17, 2008).

Index

Page references followed by "f" indicate illustrated figures or photographs; followed by "t" indicates a table.